Studies in Regional and Local History

General Editor Nigel Goose

Previous titles in this series

Volume 1: *A Hertfordshire demesne of Westminster Abbey: Profits, productivity and weather* by Derek Vincent Stern (edited and with an introduction by Christopher Thornton)
(ISBN 978-1-900458-92-7)

Volume 2: *From Hellgill to Bridge End: Aspects of economic and social change in the Upper Eden Valley, 1840–95* by Margaret Shepherd
(ISBN 978-1-902806-32-7, £18.95 pb)

Volume 3: *Cambridge and its Economic Region, 1450–1560* by John S. Lee
(ISBN 978-1-902806-47-1, £35.00 hb; ISBN 978-1-902806-52-5, £18.99 pb)

Volume 4: *Cultural Transition in the Chilterns and Essex Region, 350 AD to 650 AD* by John T. Baker
(ISBN 978-1-902806-46-4, £35.00 hb; ISBN 978-1-902806-53-2, £18.99 pb)

Volume 5: *A Pleasing Prospect: Society and culture in eighteenth-century Colchester* by Shani D'Cruze
(ISBN 978-1-902806-72-3, £35.00 hb; ISBN 978-1-902806-73-0, £18.99 pb)

Volume 6: *Agriculture and Rural Society after the Black Death: Common themes and regional variations* by Ben Dodds and Richard Britnell
(ISBN 978-1-902806-78-5, £35.00 hb; ISBN 978-1-902806-79-2, £18.99 pb)

Volume 7: *A Lost Frontier Revealed: Regional separation in the East Midlands* by Alan Fox
(ISBN 978-1-902806-96-9, £35.00 hb; ISBN 978-1-902806-97-6, £18.99 pb)

Volume 8: *Land and Family: Trends and local variations in the peasant land market on the Winchester bishopric estates, 1263-1415* by John Mullan and Richard Britnell
(ISBN 978-1-902806-94-5, £35.00 hb; ISBN 978-1-902806-95-2, £18.99 pb)

Volume 9: *Out of the Hay and into the Hops: Hop cultivation in Wealden Kent and hop marketing in Southwark, 1744–2000* by Celia Cordle
(ISBN 978-1-907396-03-8, £35.00 hb; ISBN 978-1-907396-04-5, £18.99 pb)

A Prospering Society

Wiltshire in the later Middle Ages

John Hare

University of Hertfordshire Press
Studies in Regional and Local History

Volume 10

First published in Great Britain in 2011 by
University of Hertfordshire Press
College Lane
Hatfield
Hertfordshire
AL10 9AB
UK

© John Hare 2011

The right of John Hare to be identified as the author of this work has been asserted by him in accordance with the Copyright, Designs and Patents Act 1988.

All rights reserved. No part of this book may be reproduced or utilised in any form or by any means, electronic or mechanical, including photocopying, recording or by any information storage and retrieval system, without permission in writing from the publisher.

British Library Cataloguing in Publication Data
A catalogue record for this book is available from the British Library

ISBN 978-1-902806-84-6 hardback
ISBN 978-1-902806-85-3 paperback

Design by Geoff Green Book Design, CB4 5RA
Printed in Great Britain by Henry Ling Ltd, DT1 1HD

In Memoriam
ARNOLD HARE (1921–99)
SYBIL HARE (1919–87)

Publication grant

Publication has been made possible by a generous grant from the Marc Fitch Fund

Contents

List of Illustrations	ix
List of Tables	x
Acknowledgements	xi
General Editor's preface	xiii
Abbreviations	xv

Part I: Themes and context

1 The county and beyond — 1
- The national context — 1
- Studying the county — 2
- The sources — 4
- The structure of the study — 5

2 Regions and people — 7
- The land — 7
- Settlement and fields — 12
- Colonisation and agricultural expansion — 18
- Population decline and settlement shrinkage — 26

3 Landlords and estates — 31
- The church — 32
- The crown and the nobility — 34
- The gentry — 36
- The administration of the estates — 38

Part II: Agriculture and rural change

4 Agriculture before the Black Death — 41
- Arable farming — 43
- Sheep farming — 45
- Pigs and cattle — 50
- Peasant and tenant agriculture — 53

5 Agriculture c.1380–c.1440 — 59
- Arable farming — 60
- Sheep and wool farming — 63
- Pigs, cattle and other chalkland livestock — 70
- The growth of rabbit farming — 72
- Tenant agriculture in a chalkland valley: Downton and its tithes — 74
- The pastoral economy of the clay vale — 80

6	The leasing of the demesnes	83
	The process of leasing	83
	Leasing in the fourteenth century	84
	Leasing in the fifteenth century	86
	Types of leases	90
	Why did leasing occur?	92
7	The demesne lessees	99
	The village or peasant lessees	101
	The richer lessees	105
	Conclusions	113
8	Tenant mobility and the decline of serfdom	117
	Customary tenure	117
	Peasant mobility	121
	The decline of serfdom	124
9	The land market and the village economy	131
	The family and the land market	131
	The accumulation of holdings among the peasantry	137
	The internal market of the village	140
	Conclusion	145

Part III: Industry and commerce

10	Towns and trade	147
	Salisbury	150
	The lesser towns of Wiltshire: an urban hierarchy	159
	Industry and trade	165
	The pattern of marketing	169
11	The growth of the cloth industry	176
	The chronology and distribution of the industry	177
	The impact of the cloth industry	191
12	Growth and recession: a chronology	195
	Growth	197
	Recession	202
	Recovery	208
	Conclusion	213
	Bibliography	217
	Index	236

Illustrations

Figures

2.1	Wiltshire: relief	8
2.2	Wiltshire: agricultural regions	9
2.3	Wiltshire: parishes	11
2.4	Wiltshire: main places mentioned in the text	14
7.1	Two leasing families: the Goddards and Stannfords	108
10.1	Wiltshire: towns	148
11.1	Wiltshire: the cloth industry	178

Plates

2.1	View from chalk escarpment at Morgan's Hill near Calne	10
2.2	Map by Thomas Langdon showing open-field strips in 1616	15
2.3	Map by Thomas Langdon showing enclosed fields in 1616	16
2.4	Strip lynchets in the chalklands, near Charlton	20
2.5	A planned medieval extension at Bishopstone	22
2.6	The great barn of Shaftesbury Abbey at Bradford	24
2.7	The great barn of Shaftesbury Abbey at Bradford (interior)	24
4.1	The enclosure belonging to a sheep house or *bercaria* in Bishops Cannings	49
7.1	The brass of Thomas Goddard from Ogbourne St George church	111
10.1	Salisbury in 1611, from John Speed's map of Wiltshire	151
10.2	Salisbury, St Thomas's Church	157
10.3	Marlborough in 1668	160
10.4	Malmesbury: the market cross	161
11.1	Steeple Ashton church	190
11.2	Westwood church	191

All photos by the author except Plate 2.5 (copyright Roy Canham, with thanks to Wiltshire Archaeology Service), and Plate 7.1 from E. Kite, *The monumental brasses of Wiltshire* (1860; facsimile edn Bath, 1969). Plates 2.2, 2.3, 10.1 and 10.3 are reproduced courtesy of Wiltshire and Swindon History Centre.

Tables

4.1	Liveries of grain from the Wiltshire manors of Winchester Cathedral Priory	42
4.2	Demesne crops: sown acreage	44
4.3	Sheep flocks on the Wiltshire estates of Winchester Cathedral Priory	46
4.4	Parish and demesne tithes	54
5.1	Demesne crops after 1380	61
5.2	Livestock on the Wiltshire estates of Winchester Cathedral Priory, 1390	65
5.3	Finances of sheep farming on manors of the duchy of Lancaster, 1400–1439	69
5.4	Downton: demesne and tenant production, 1407–12	75
5.5	Downton: tithe grain production, 1384–1454	77
5.6	Downton: barley tithes in 1420s	77
5.7	Downton: crop production on the bishop's demesne, 1407–28	77
5.8	Downton: crops sown on the parsonage demesne, 1369–1429	78
5.9	Downton: tithes of lambs	78
6.1	Sheep flocks on four ecclesiastical demesnes	88
6.2	Bromham: the decline of demesne agriculture, arable sown area	94
6.3	Bromham: the decline of demesne agriculture, livestock	94
6.4	Bromham: the finances of demesne agriculture	95
6.5	Bromham: grain yields	95
7.1	Leasing families on fourteen Wiltshire manors: their origins	101
8.1	The disappearance of tenant families	122
9.1	Land transactions	132
9.2	Land-holding and tenant differentiation at Durrington and Coombe Bisset	138
9.3	Village craftsmen in the 1379 poll tax records	141
10.1	Occupations in some of the main manufacturing and market centres, 1377	166
11.1	The aulnage accounts: the distribution of Wiltshire's cloth production	181
11.2	Court receipts and chevage: Castle Combe	186
12.1	Movement of rent income	196
12.2	Rents: the duchy of Lancaster	198
12.3	Court receipts: Bromham	199
12.4	Rents: Bromham, Coombe Bisset, Durrington	200
12.5	Court receipts: Stockton	201
12.6	The Wiltshire risings of 1450: occupational groups of those indicted	204
12.7	Cash liveries to the lord: Bromham, Coombe Bisset and Durrington	209

Acknowledgements

This book seeks to examine an important period of English development through a manageable, albeit artificial, unit: the county. It seeks to explore some of the differences in late medieval society between town and country, agriculture and industry, and through regional and short-term fluctuations. The research began long ago in preparation for my thesis. It was put aside in deference to other pressures and projects, and a career teaching very different types of history, before being resumed in middle age.

Over the years many people have contributed to this book in a variety of ways, answering queries, commenting on earlier articles, or on seminar papers and lectures, or just providing scholarly encouragement. I would particularly like to thank Tony Bridbury, Richard Britnell, Bruce Campbell, Barrie Dobson, Peter Fowler, Winifred Harwood, Michael Hicks, Guy Lytle, Pamela Nightingale, Mark Page, Edward Roberts, the late Simon Walker, Chris Woolgar and Margaret Yates, for a variety of help and I apologise to any whom I have inadvertently overlooked. Three scholars deserve special mention. The late Rees Davies introduced me to the academic study of Medieval History and left me with a clear sense that the study of one's homeland could be a suitable foundation from which to explore the wider world of the period. The late Robin Du Boulay supervised my thesis and enriched my study of the period. Chris Dyer came in at a later stage but greatly improved the final text, and his support was particularly appreciated at a time of difficulty for the book. Sadly the passing of time means that the dedication to my father and mother has become an 'in memoriam'.

I wish to express my thanks to the various owners and archivists upon whom studies like this depend. The Duke of Beaufort and the Earl of Pembroke, King's College Cambridge, Magdalen, Merton and New Colleges at Oxford, the Dean and Chapters of Winchester and of Salisbury, and Winchester College all provided access to their archives. I have drawn heavily on the British Library, the National Archives, Wiltshire and Swindon Archives and the Hampshire Record Offices, as well as briefer visits to many other collections. I would particularly like to acknowledge the debt that we all as scholars owe to the tireless work of the archivists who here must remain nameless. In a time of such difficulties in the public sector, it is important to emphasise how much we owe to them.

I am grateful to the Social Science Research Council who funded my thesis and thus much of the original research. During my career I have had two periods of extended study: a term as schoolteacher fellow at Liverpool, thanks to the University and to Hampshire County Council, and later a school teacher studentship at Merton College Oxford followed by a period of unpaid leave during which the bulk of the book was written. Thanks are also due to the University of Southampton (and the Hartley fellowship), King Alfred's College, now the University of Winchester, and Peter Symonds' College.

I am grateful to Nigel Goose and the University of Hertfordshire Press for finding a home for this book. At the Press, Sarah Elvins has carried this through to publication. At various earlier stages parts of the text were edited by Tracy Wallace, Christine Linehan and Eileen Power. The whole text was then edited for the Press by Sarah Harrison. The maps were drawn by Nathalie Barret. To all I offer my thanks.

Winchester, February 2011

Studies in Regional and Local History

General Editor's preface

In volume ten of *Studies in Regional and Local History* we return to late medieval England, the period that has featured so prominently among the volumes published in this series to date. In my preface to volume one of *Studies* I drew attention to the importance of the medievalist in the development of English local history, for regional and local research has been central to medieval studies since the end of the nineteenth century, with historians such as Maitland and Vinogradoff endowing it with academic respectability. From 1899 the early volumes of the Victoria County History exhibited a very heavy emphasis indeed upon the medieval period, while subsequently scholars such as Ephraim Lipson and M.M. Postan transformed medieval studies – in terms of content, depth of analysis and analytical rigour. In Postan's work we find not only a new demographic model of English economic development that served as a profound stimulus to further research, but also a clear appreciation of the great variety of manorial economies that existed, whether governed by antiquity, size and type of ownership or by geographical location, an appreciation that perhaps reached its apogee when Postan's disciple, John Hatcher, demonstrated that Cornwall's manors lacked most of the features hitherto viewed as central to manorialism, while the county's highly diversified economy gave it advantages lacking in most other counties in the face of the demographic and agricultural depression of the fifteenth century.[1] Writing in 1969, Hatcher could already claim that it was now 'fully appreciated that the multitude of differing cultural, topographical, climatic, economic, and political conditions present in England in the Middle Ages led to the formation of a multitude of manorial structures each one differing in some way from the "classical manor"...'.[2] Since then, of course, numerous regional and local studies have appeared that have shed further light upon the variety of economic and social forms that coexisted in medieval England, the very best of them incorporating a dialogue between appreciation of common themes and regional differences, as Britnell and Dodds demonstrated so powerfully in Volume 6 of the present series.[3]

The present study by John Hare of late-medieval Wiltshire thus sits within a proud tradition of local and regional research, and one that is very much alive and well. Hare takes regional variation as his starting point, emphasising the fact that medieval England showed great contrasts between areas of growth and of decline in the later middle ages, these variations underlining the need for further local and regional studies. Indeed, the very title of this volume, *A prospering society*, immediately throws down the gauntlet to those who have seen the later middle ages as uniformly

---

1. J. Hatcher, *Rural economy and society in the Duchy of Cornwall, 1300–1500* (Cambridge, 1970).
2. J. Hatcher, 'A diversified economy: later medieval Cornwall', *Economic History Review*, 22 (1969), 208.
3. B. Dodds and R. Britnell (eds), *Agriculture and rural society after the Black Death. Common themes and regional variations*, Studies in Regional and Local History vol. 6 (Hatfield, 2008).

depressed, and provides a resounding echoing to John Hatcher's conclusion about the relative buoyancy that could be achieved, in some English counties at least. Hare's choice of the county – as opposed to a wider region or an estate – as the subject of his study is partly pragmatic, for the county provides a manageable unit with which to work. But he also makes a virtue of the fact that economic and social forms do not generally conform themselves to county boundaries, for this allows appreciation of the variety that could exist both within counties and across southern England more generally.

Wiltshire is divided between the long-settled chalklands that occupy so much of its south and east, and the clay vales which provided, in this period, opportunities for colonisation of the woodlands. 'Here,' Hare writes, 'were two different agrarian worlds, or *pays*, with contrasting landscape and settlement patterns and agricultural histories…'. Not only is this a study of a neglected county, but it also takes strength from the diversity that could be found within the county's boundaries.

Another feature of the present study is its integration of a wide variety of manorial and non-manorial documentation. Although the familiar evidence produced by manorial officials is central to this study, particularly that which survives for the great ecclesiastical estates, the use of non-manorial evidence is also crucial to one of the underlying themes of this book – the need to see agriculture as part of the wider economy, to explore the interactions between countryside and town and between agriculture and the growth of the cloth industry. In late medieval Wiltshire commercial growth was a generator of prosperity, but a prosperity that could be fragile when the cloth-making industry swung from expansion into recession. Part of the story told here is familiar from other studies of later medieval economy and society: retreat from the margins of cultivation, falling land values, falling rents and falling prices. This agrarian economic depression in turn opened up new opportunities for the lower strata in village societies, with the leasing of demesnes resulting in the steady removal of various forms of restriction upon personal freedom, while at the same time allowing for growing differentiation within landed society and the development of a new village aristocracy. But Wiltshire was also part of a rapidly emerging industrial area, for by the end of the fourteenth century the West Country produced over half the nation's cloth, and Wiltshire became one of its most important areas of production. Industry and its impact on both producers and consumers in town and countryside is thus another important theme, providing a story of growth in the late fourteenth and early fifteenth centuries, economic recession in the third quarter of the fifteenth century and then recovery towards its end. *A prospering society*, therefore, examines both the traditional influences on rural society and the impact of new commercial and industrial developments that were so crucial to particular regions of late medieval England. As such, it makes an important contribution to key debates about economic progress and social change in the later Middle Ages.

Nigel Goose
University of Hertfordshire
February 2011

Abbreviations

AHR	*Agricultural History Review*
Bad.Mun.	Badminton Muniments (now in Gloucester Archives)
BL	British Library, London
Brokage book 1439–40	*The brokage book of Southampton, 1439–40*, ed. B.D.M. Bunyard, Southampton Record Society 40 (Southampton, 1941)
Brokage book 1443–4	*The brokage book of Southampton, 1443–44*, ed. O. Coleman, Southampton Record Series 4 and 6 (Southampton, 1960–61)
Brokage book 1447–8	*The Southampton brokage book 1447–8*, ed. W.A. Harwood, Southampton Record Series 42 (Winchester, 2006)
Brokage book 1448–9	*Southampton port and brokage books 1448–9*, ed. E.A. Lewis, Southampton Record Series 36 (Southampton, 1993)
Brokage book 1477–8 and 1527–8	*The brokage books of Southampton for 1477–8 and 1527–8*, ed. K.F. Stevens and T.E. Olding, Southampton Record Series 28 (Southampton, 1985)
Cal Cl Roll	*Calendar of the Close Rolls*
Cal Pat Rl	*Calendar of the Patent Rolls*
Cal Papal Letters	*Calendar of entries in the papal registers relating to Great Britain and Ireland*
DRO	Dorset Record Office
EcHR	*Economic History Review*
HMC	Historical Manuscripts Commission
HRO	Hampshire Record Office
JRL	John Ryland's Library, University of Manchester
KCM	King's College Muniments, University of Cambridge
LSE	London School of Economics
MCM	Merton College Muniments, University of Oxford
NCA	New College Archives, University of Oxford
ODNB	*Oxford Dictionary of National Biography*
PHFCAS	*Proceedings of the Hampshire Field Club and Archaeological Society*, now *Hampshire Studies*
Pipe Roll 1210–11	*The pipe roll of the bishopric of Winchester, 1210–11*, ed. N.H. Holt (Manchester, 1964)
Pipe Roll 1301–2	*The pipe roll of the bishopric of Winchester, 1301–2*, ed. M. Page, Hampshire Record Series 14 (Winchester, 1996)
Pipe Roll 1409–10	*The pipe roll of the bishopric of Winchester, 1409–10*, ed. M. Page, Hampshire Record Series 16 (Winchester, 1999)
Port books 1427–30	*The port books of Southampton,* ed. P. Struder, Southampton Records Society 15 (Southampton, 1913)

Port book 1439–40	*The local port book of Southampton, 1439–40*, ed. H.S. Cobb, Southampton Record Series 5 (Southampton, 1961)
Port books Ed. IV	*The port books or local customs account of Southampton for the reign of Edward IV*, ed. D.B. Quinn and A.A. Ruddock, Southampton Record Society 37, 38 (Southampton, 1937–8)
RCHM	Royal Commission on Historical Monuments
SCA	Southampton City Archives
SDC	Salisbury, Dean and chapter
TNA: PRO	The National Archives: Public Record Office, Kew
VCH *Hants*	H.A. Doubleday and W. Page (eds), *A history of Hampshire and the Isle of Wight*, The Victoria History of the Counties of England, vols 1–5 (London, 1900–1912)
VCH *Wilts*	R.B. Pugh (gen. ed.), *A history of Wiltshire*, The Victoria History of the Counties of England, vols 1–17 (Oxford, 1953–2002)
WAM	*Wiltshire Archaeological and Natural History Magazine*
WCL	Winchester Cathedral Library (now in HRO)
WCM	Winchester College Muniments
Wilt.House	Wilton House Muniments (now in WRO)
Wilts IPM i	*Abstracts of Wiltshire inquisitiones post mortem: returned into the Court of Chancery in the reigns of Henry III, Edward I, and Edward II A.D. 1242–1326*, ed. E.A. Fry, Wiltshire Archaeological and Natural History Society (London, 1908)
Wilts IPM ii	*Abstracts of Wiltshire inquisitiones post mortem returned into the Court of Chancery in the reign of King Edward III A.D. 1327–1377*, ed. E. Stokes, Wiltshire Archaeological and Natural History Society (London, 1914)
WRO	Wiltshire and Swindon Record Office (now Wiltshire and Swindon Archives)

Manorial accounts were usually dated from Michaelmas (29 September) to Michaelmas. I have dated them by the closing year of account. Place name spellings are those that are current, with the exception of Bradford, where I have dropped the nineteen-century addition of 'on Avon'.

Chapter 1

The county and beyond

The national context

Behind the continuities of rural life, late medieval England witnessed immense social and economic change. Much of these developments were driven by population change. Historians may disagree about the precise scale of this fourteenth-century demographic shrinkage,[1] but the general trend is clear, and witnessed by records throughout much of the country. The impact of these changes varied; and economic historians, like their political counterparts, have held contrasting pessimistic and optimistic views of the period.[2] On a national scale, this seems a period of gloom: of falling production, shrinking settlements and a retreat from arable land, a time of difficulties for the large-scale demesne agriculture that had characterised farming in the thirteenth century. But this gloomy national situation provided opportunities for the generation of greater individual prosperity. Now, the balance between lord and tenant had shifted: the bargaining position of tenant and wage-earner had greatly strengthened, and the period also saw the erosion of the unfree status of villeinage. The improved economic situation of the bulk of the population increased the demand for luxuries or more wasteful forms of agriculture: more meat and ale rather than bread and porridge. The changing circumstances offered the peasantry new opportunities for self-improvement, by acquiring a tenancy or by accumulating several holdings. As people became better off, they became increasingly dependent on manufactured goods and services produced by others. Each individual was now engaged in more commercial transactions and had a wider range of available choices.[3]

Such social improvements were both general and subject to regional variations. Analysis of the distribution of tax assessments from the early fourteenth to the early sixteenth century shows a marked regional change in the rankings of taxation per 100 acres. Some areas, such as the east midlands, Lincolnshire and Norfolk, declined in relative assessed wealth and others, such as the west country, prospered. Wiltshire rose from fourteenth to fifth in the rankings.[4] This was to be one of those periods in English history, like the nineteenth century or the interwar years of the following

---

1. J. Hatcher, *Plague, population and the English economy, 1348–1530* (Basingstoke, 1977); R. Smith, 'Human resources', in G. Astill and A. Grant (eds), The *countryside of medieval England* (Oxford, 1988), 188–212; B.M.S. Campbell, *English seigniorial agriculture, 1250–1450* (Cambridge, 2000), 399–410.
2. Compare the views of M.M. Postan, in e.g. 'The fifteenth century' in his *Essays on medieval agriculture and general problems of the medieval economy* (Cambridge, 1973), 41–8; and those of A.R. Bridbury, *Economic growth: England in the later Middle Ages* (London, 1975).
3. For a recent and positive view of the period see C. Dyer, *An age of transition? Economy and society in England in the later Middle Ages* (Oxford, 2005). Dyer's arguments are clearly of considerable importance in relation to those put forward here and provide welcome reassurance from a much wider perspective.
4. R.S. Schofield, 'The geographical distribution of wealth in England, 1334–1649', *EcHR*, 2nd series 18 (1965), 483–510.

century, when growth and decline were to be immensely regional in character. Much of this regional divergence showed the impact of commercial growth, above all in the cloth industry. This was the period when England shifted from being an exporter of wool (a raw material) to an exporter of cloth (a manufactured product) and began to benefit from the value of the labour inputs that transformed wool to cloth. This industrial growth increased the demands on agriculture for wool, grain, meat and other foodstuffs, as well as boosting the demand for labour and consumer goods. Moreover, the expansion of the cloth industry was not spread evenly throughout the country, but was concentrated in particular areas, above all in the west country, and in Essex and Suffolk, areas which consequently showed the greatest rise in wealth according to the ranking of counties by taxation. The new industries required trade and towns, to sell their manufactured products and to use their surpluses to buy food and consumer goods. Consequently, specialism grew in both town and countryside. Towns might shrink and urban land become vacant as the population contracted, but there were also signs of urban prosperity, redevelopment and new building.

Thus, behind the dramatic falls in both population and gross national product lay a very different England. For those who survived the traumas of plague there were great opportunities for self-enhancement in the countryside. The consequent improved standards of living generated increased demand for particular foods, and more land was available. The cloth industry generated new demands both for labour and for agricultural products. Towns might have shrunk, but they were needed nevertheless, and there was little sign that shrinkage was greater than that of the population as a whole. Wiltshire, like many, but not all, parts of the country, prospered during the later Middle Ages.

Studying the county

Later medieval England showed great contrasts between areas of growth and of decline, and these variations emphasise the need for further local and regional studies. Moreover, the nature of the available evidence encourages and necessitates a focus on small units which are not only manageable but also possess suitable records. R.H. Hilton commented in reference to the peasantry that 'the microscopic view is essential if generalisations about the peasantry are to have a satisfactory evidential basis.'[5] But what should be our unit of study? In the past the focus has been on the village, the manor, or the estate.[6] These have clear inner logics, as seen in the records themselves, and their study has produced works of distinction. Some historians have tackled whole regions.[7] The choice of a county as a unit of study for

---

5. R.H. Hilton, *The English peasantry in the later Middle Ages* (Oxford, 1975), 17.
6. e.g. F.G. Davenport, *The economic development of a Norfolk manor, 1086–1565* (1906), reprinted London 1967; P.D.A. Harvey, *A medieval Oxfordshire village, Cuxham 1240–1400* (Oxford, 1965); J.A. Raftis, *The estates of Ramsey Abbey* (Toronto, 1957); B. Harvey, *Westminster Abbey and its estates* (Oxford, 1977); C. Dyer, *Lords and peasants in a changing society: the estates of the bishopric of Worcester, 680–1540* (Cambridge, 1980).
7. e.g. R.H. Hilton, *A medieval society: the west midlands at the end of the thirteenth century* (London, 1966); and E. Miller (ed.), *The agrarian history of England and Wales: vol. 3, 1348–1500* (Cambridge, 1991).

the agrarian, economic and social history of a period is less familiar. Most counties lack geographical unity and their boundaries have little economic significance. But it is precisely this regional variety that makes them so appropriate for such a study. We have a unit which is both manageable and allows us to see something of the variation that existed within medieval society, and whose significance thus extends beyond the individual county itself. Wiltshire, for instance, is divided between the long-settled chalklands that occupy so much of its south and east parts, and the clay vales in which there were, in the medieval period, opportunities for colonisation of the woodlands. Here were two different agrarian worlds, or *pays*, with contrasting landscape and settlement patterns and agricultural histories, as different as chalk and cheese. By contrast, the boundaries that divided the chalklands of Wiltshire from those of Hampshire or Dorset, or that split the cloth industry of Somerset and west Wiltshire, were of no importance in the economic life of the people. Material from the neighbouring counties has been incorporated here where it can help illuminate what was happening in Wiltshire. For the historian the artificial nature of the county thus has real values, providing a microcosm of what was happening in a wider area beyond its borders: in this case, southern England. Underpinning this study is the belief that we need to examine the local and the particular, whether an individual estate or manor, and make comparisons between estates and between regions. The diversity of Wiltshire becomes a strength, not a weakness, and offers the opportunity to examine a part of England that has tended to be neglected in the recent published literature.

The county also provides a manageable body of sources that allows us to overcome some of the problems inherent in the varied nature of manorial documentation, particularly in the latter stages of demesne agriculture. Users of such records will be familiar with a situation where we can ask particular questions on individual documented manors but not on others. The manageable scale of the county also allows us to integrate a wide variety of manorial and non-manorial documentation, especially important at a time when so many lords were gradually ceasing their direct involvement in agriculture. The use of such non-manorial evidence is also crucial as one of the underlying themes of this book is the need to see agriculture as part of the wider economy, to explore the interactions between countryside and town and between agriculture and the growth of the cloth industry. This book examines the impact of commercial growth as a generator of prosperity as well as looking at the potential disadvantages of this new dependence on cloth-making when prosperity turned to short-term recession.

This study explores issues of change and continuity from c.1380 to c.1520. Its starting point is determined by the paucity of surviving documentation for the county in the generation after the Black Death, other than for the bishopric of Winchester. Its end avoids the very different conditions of the sixteenth century, with the Tudor price rise and the change of ownership that was to befall so many of the ecclesiastical lands. The study is concerned both with the changes of our period and with longer-term patterns of agriculture and social continuities. A chapter on the better-documented agriculture of the early fourteenth century allows us to provide a firm base from which to view the great changes of the main period examined. The study also seeks to establish how far this period developed the characteristics of Wiltshire's agriculture that dominated the next few centuries: above all, the contrast between large-scale capitalist farming in the chalklands, with its dependence on wage labour and heavy investment in sheep–corn husbandry, and a smaller, more family-orientated, pastoral agriculture in the clay vale.

The sources

Historians are at the mercy of their sources and this is particularly the case for this period of study. A wide variety of documents has been used and their individual difficulties have been discussed where appropriate. But the core of the documentation is supplied by manorial records and, above all, by the accounts of the manorial officials, which provide a full view of seigneurial agriculture in the thirteenth and fourteenth centuries. In our period they survive after the leasing of the demesnes, but they then contain little information about agriculture and seem frequently to have been neglected by historians. The quantity of surviving accounts increases but they become less useful to the agrarian historian. The accounts vary a great deal in what they contain, allowing particular issues to be considered on some manors but not on others: some give us, for instance, a view of late arable or of sheep farming and others a view of peasant rent payments. The manorial accounts provide a key source for the student of the period, but also a difficult one that cannot necessarily be taken at face value. In Chris Dyer's words, 'Reading fifteenth century manorial accounts is an exercise in distinguishing between theory and reality.'[8] E.M. Carus-Wilson remarked that 'Manorial rentals and accounts, it is very evident, may for the unwary be a dangerous and wholly misleading guide to the history of England's economy in the fifteenth century.'[9] Such records provide us with less information than many of their predecessors, particularly after the demesnes were leased, and they repeat redundant items, such as an uncollectable debt or payment. Such debts may thus represent a long-term and disputed financial loss, but not a short-term agricultural problem.[10] The court rolls also continue to exist, but they too are much less full than before and record a more limited range of activities. The fifteenth century thus sees one set of sources in decline, while the new sources, such as probate inventories, that provide a key base for subsequent writing on agrarian history, had not yet emerged. But, frustrating as the manorial records may be, they are an important, valuable and often neglected source for the fifteenth century; they contain the traces of underlying economic developments, even if these tracks need to be carefully teased out from the documents.

A study such as this depends on the survival of documents, most of which come from the great ecclesiastical and collegiate estates, particularly in the chalklands. Although there is a substantial amount of material belonging to lay estates, particularly from the duchy of Lancaster, most lay estates had ceased direct arable farming by the fifteenth century. Moreover, even the ecclesiastical estates are generally poorly documented for the last years of direct cultivation. The fullest and most complete set

---

8. Dyer, *Lords and peasants*, 162.
9. E.M. Carus-Wilson, 'Evidences of industrial growth on some fifteenth century manors', in Carus-Wilson (ed.), *Essays in economic history*, 158.
10. R.R. Davies, 'Baronial accounts, incomes and arrears in the later Middle Ages', *EcHR*, 2nd series xxi (1968), 227–9.

of records, whether for here or anywhere else in the country, comes from the estate of the bishopric of Winchester, including a group of south Wiltshire manors. These include material for the mid-fourteenth century, when there is a shortage from other estates. As its Wiltshire manors had already been examined, and another scholar was studying the estate as a whole, it seemed sensible to concentrate on other unused material. The bishopric records have been used to tackle specific and limited problems, with no attempt being made to produce a systematic study of this vast archive.[11] Here, the bishopric has had to take second place to other estates, such as those of the cathedral priory at Winchester, allowing us to see the bishopric more fully in the context of other estates.[12]

In some cases it has been possible to incorporate and analyse the evidence in statistical form and this has been done wherever feasible. But on other occasions the nature of the material means that the picture has had to be built up by handling a variety of available examples, whether documentary, landscape or buildings, where the examples become a crucial part of the argument.

The structure of the study

Part I of this study examines the geographical base of the county during the Middle Ages: the evolving demographic and settlement patterns of that period. The examination of the nature of landownership within the county shows the balance of ecclesiastical and secular ownership and the pre-eminence of the great Church estates. Particular attention is given in this part to the estates upon whose documentation the remainder of the study is based. This section of the study is concerned with some of the long-term influences on the agriculture and society of the county in the period of study and beyond: its inherited characteristics and those that were passed on to its successors.

Part II examines the agriculture and rural society of the county, highlighting the existing and growing regional divisions and the elements of continuity and change during the period from about 1380 to 1520. In addition, a chapter has been included on early-fourteenth-century agriculture in order to provide a baseline for later comparison. One of the most obvious changes during the main period of study was the leasing of the demesnes, but this process removed the availability of most documentation about agriculture. In order to establish a county-wide regional pattern, we therefore need to go back to the early fourteenth century. The process of leasing itself showed clear regional characteristics. In the chalklands it was delayed (particularly on the ecclesiastical estates), and did not lead to the break-up of the demesne. Here, large-scale arable cultivation continued, as did the extensive demesne flocks that had for so long dominated the agriculture of the area. The leasing of the demesnes may have

---

11. For recent work and references to earlier studies see R.H. Britnell (ed.), *The Winchester pipe rolls and medieval English society* (Woodbridge, 2003). The task of using these magnificent records has now been made easier through the recent publication of the pipe rolls for 1301–2 and 1409–10: *Pipe roll 1301–2* and *Pipe roll 1409–10*. For the bishopric's Hampshire manors see J.N. Hare, 'The bishop and the prior: demesne agriculture in medieval Hampshire', *AHR*, 54 (2006), 187–212.
12. For earlier work on the priory see Hare, 'The bishop and the prior', 187–8.

seemed very dramatic, but the change concealed essential continuities particularly in the chalklands with the demesnes continuing to be cultivated as a single block. Meanwhile the scale of farming of some of the customary tenant cultivation increased, and there was growing differentiation among the village population. The immediate effect of the Black Death had allowed the enhancement of the position of the small cottager or tenant farmer. Now the fifteenth century saw the development of a new village aristocracy, who held several virgates, or standard units of land. The particular circumstances of the later Middle Ages opened up great opportunities for villagers, both within the village and beyond. Falling rents, long-term price falls and rising wages are familiar elsewhere in the country, and are found here, although with their own particular local characteristics.

But Wiltshire was also part of a rapidly emerging major industrial area. By the end of the fourteenth century the west country produced over half the nation's cloth, at a time when England had emerged as a major cloth exporter and Wiltshire became one of its most important areas of production. Salisbury quickly became one of the greatest provincial cities in England, and a major centre of the cloth-making industry. The large scale of this industry, and the pre-eminence of the city that initially dominated it, had a major impact on the population and economy of Wiltshire as a whole. Cloth-making encouraged immigration from afar, as well as internal migration within the county. It generated demands for foodstuffs, wool and manufactures. Such changes affected the agricultural world examined in Part II. They stimulated the land market and increased the demand from a wealthier population for better foodstuffs, whether more meat or more barley ale. Industrial growth thus encouraged specialisation in agriculture. Part III thus focuses on industry and its impact on the wider society of producers and consumers in both town and country, and attempts to establish the short-term chronology of economic change: growth at the end of the fourteenth century and in the early fifteenth; economic recession in the third quarter of the fifteenth century; and then recovery in its last quarter.

This study attempts to establish regional and chronological patterns of agricultural and industrial activity. It seeks to assess both the traditional influences on rural society and the impact of new commercial and industrial developments that were now becoming so important. At its core lies the belief that medieval society needs to be seen as a changing and evolving society in which short-term influences as well as long-term ones are of relevance; commercial and industrial as well agrarian developments. The world and society of the sixteenth century were very different from those of the thirteenth, and to explain these changes we need to turn to the dynamism and change so characteristic of the century and a half after the Black Death.

Chapter 2

Regions and people

The land

Historians of rural society need to start with the land and its landscape. Wiltshire's landscape is dominated by the great band of chalkland that stretches across the county from Dorset in the west to Hampshire and Berkshire in the east. The south-east half of Wiltshire consists of a large undulating plateau of chalk, occupying over half the county's area, which slopes down from north-west to south-east and is dissected by river valleys and dry valleys (Figure 2.1). Around its western and northern edge the chalk outcrops in spectacular form where the chalk cap has been broken and the softer rocks and clays beneath have been exposed and eroded (Plate 2.1). Beyond the scarp, to its west and north, these underlying clay soils are intermixed with bands of outcropping corallian limestone and greensand. In the west erosion has exposed the lower slopes of the oolitic limestone of the Cotswolds. In the east of the county the chalkland is partly covered by a superficial layer of clay-with-flints, and in the south-east corner are the clays and gravels of the Hampshire basin. This relatively simple geological pattern, of chalkland and vale, is distorted by a series of additional east–west folds produced by geological earth movements. The main vale thus protruded into the chalklands, in the vales of Pewsey, Wardour and Warminster (Figures 2.1 and 2.2). The claylands, whether the deep clay layers of the vale or the superficial deposits of clay-with-flints on the chalk, had supported large areas of woodland which continued to be colonised in the centuries after the Norman Conquest.

The importance of this landscape division for the agricultural history of the county has been long recognised. At the end of the eighteenth century Thomas Davis, the knowledgeable steward of one of the largest landowners in the county, argued in his *General View* of Wiltshire that instead of dividing the county in two with a line running from east to west, 'in treating of the county "agriculturally" it will make a more natural division to draw an irregular line, round the foot of the chalk hills from their entrance into the north-east part of the county ... to their south-west termination ... thereby comprehending the whole of Wiltshire Downs with their intersecting vallies and surrounding verges' into one region, which he described as South Wiltshire or South-east Wiltshire as opposed to the remaining North-west Wiltshire.[1]

Davis' distinction between the chalk hills and the north-west, and his emphasis on the agricultural and social distinctiveness of the chalklands from the rest of the county, has been carried back by Eric Kerridge into the sixteenth and seventeenth centuries, contrasting the chalk country (with its dependence on arable farming and large-scale sheep flocks, and its characteristic large-scale farming units and greater use of wage labour) and the cheese country of the clay vale (with its emphasis on pastoral farming

---

1. T. Davis, *General view of the agriculture of Wiltshire* (London, 1794), 6–7.

A Prospering Society

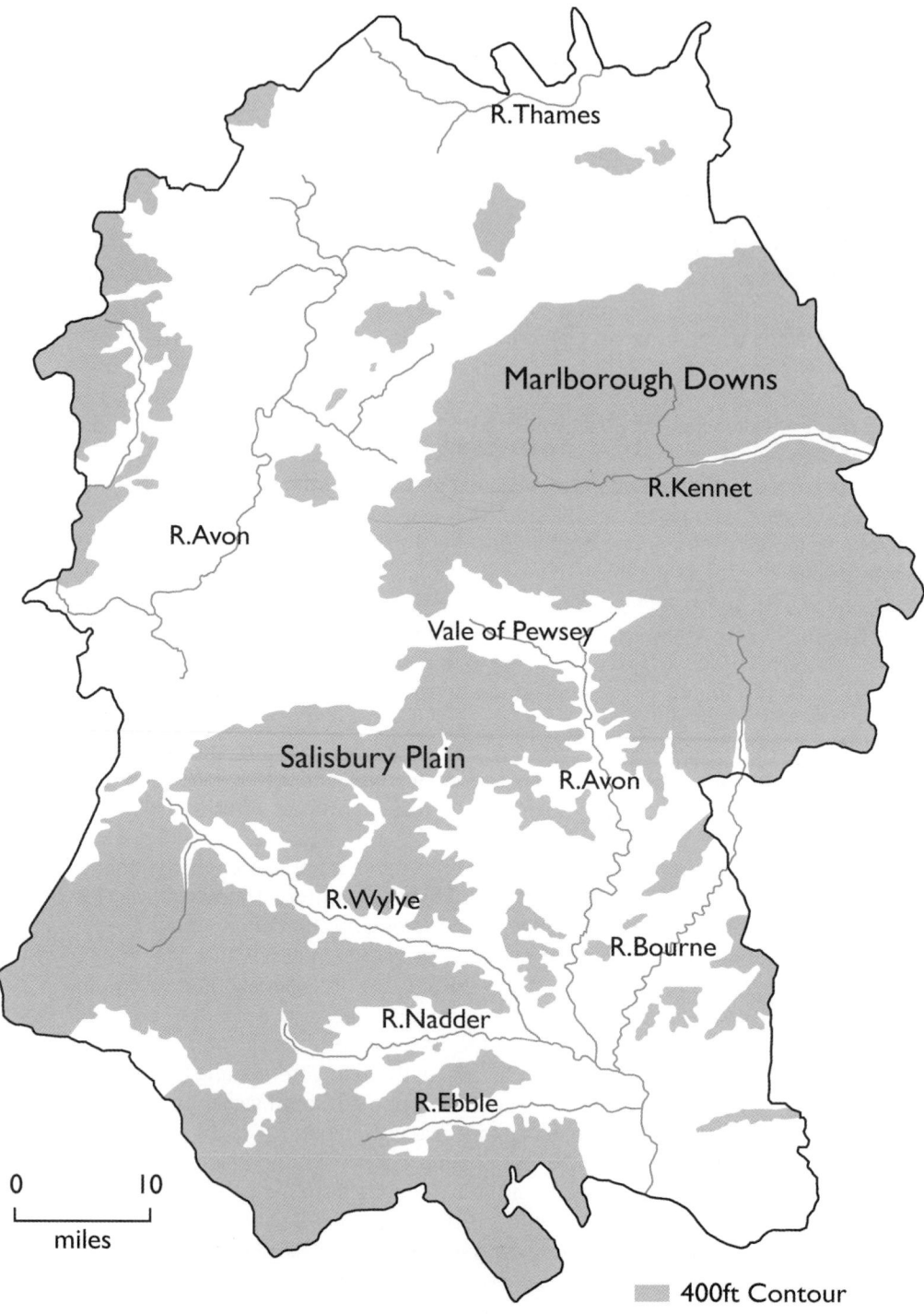

Figure 2.1 Wiltshire: relief

Regions and people

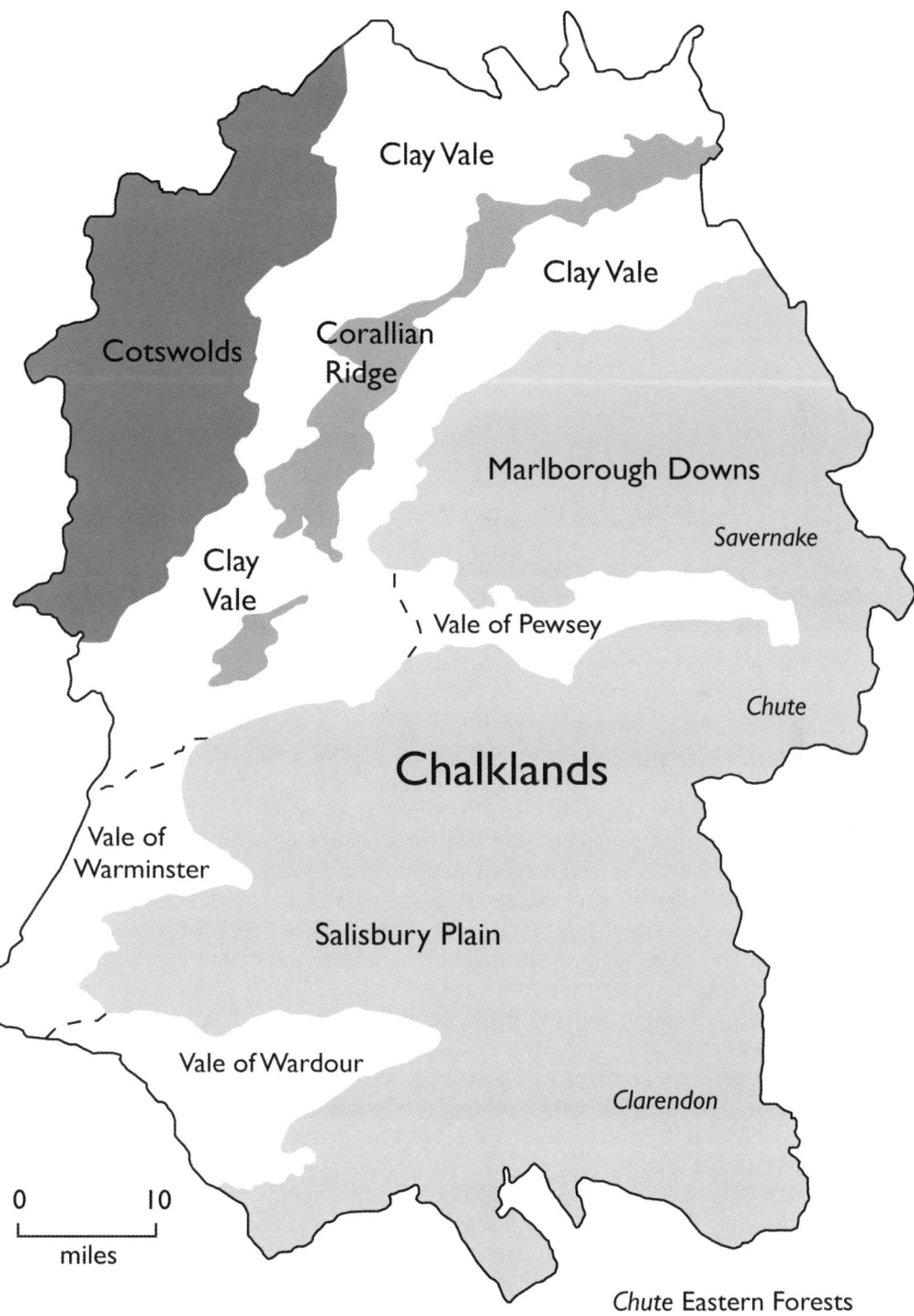

Figure 2.2 Wiltshire: agricultural regions

A Prospering Society

Plate 2.1 View from chalk escarpment at Morgan's Hill near Calne, overlooking the clay vale.

and on family units).[2] Kerridge also referred to other less far-reaching distinctions, particularly the sub-regions of the north-west region, such as the islands of lighter soils within the clay vale and the lower slopes of the Cotswolds to the west, but documentary limitations make these differences more difficult to see in the later Middle Ages. But the distinction between the chalklands themselves and the clays and other soils of the rest of the county, summarised in the later terms of 'chalk' and 'cheese', remain fundamental to our understanding of the agriculture of the period. The chalklands contrasted with those areas where a more specialist pastoral economy was present and developing. Both regions were areas of mixed husbandry, but the chalklands showed a much greater emphasis on grain production and large sheep flocks, while the economy of the claylands was based more on cattle breeding and grazing (see Figure 2.2).

The contrasts are a commonplace, and form the basis of other wider social interpretations. As early as the seventeenth century John Aubrey, the distinguished diarist, antiquary and local writer, contrasted the character of the inhabitants of the two regions of the county:

'In north Wiltshire ... (a dirty clayey country) ... hereabout is but little tillage or hard labour, they only milk the cows and make cheese; they feed chiefly on milke meats, which cooles their braines too much, and hurts their inventions. These circumstances make them melancholy, contemplative, and malicious by consequence thereof come

---

2. E. Kerridge, 'Agriculture 1500–1793', in VCH Wilts 4, 43–64. See also his *The agricultural revolution* (London, 1967), 42–51, 64–8, 123–6; J. Thirsk, 'The farming regions of England', in Thirsk (ed.), *The agrarian history of England and Wales*, 364–9.

Regions and people

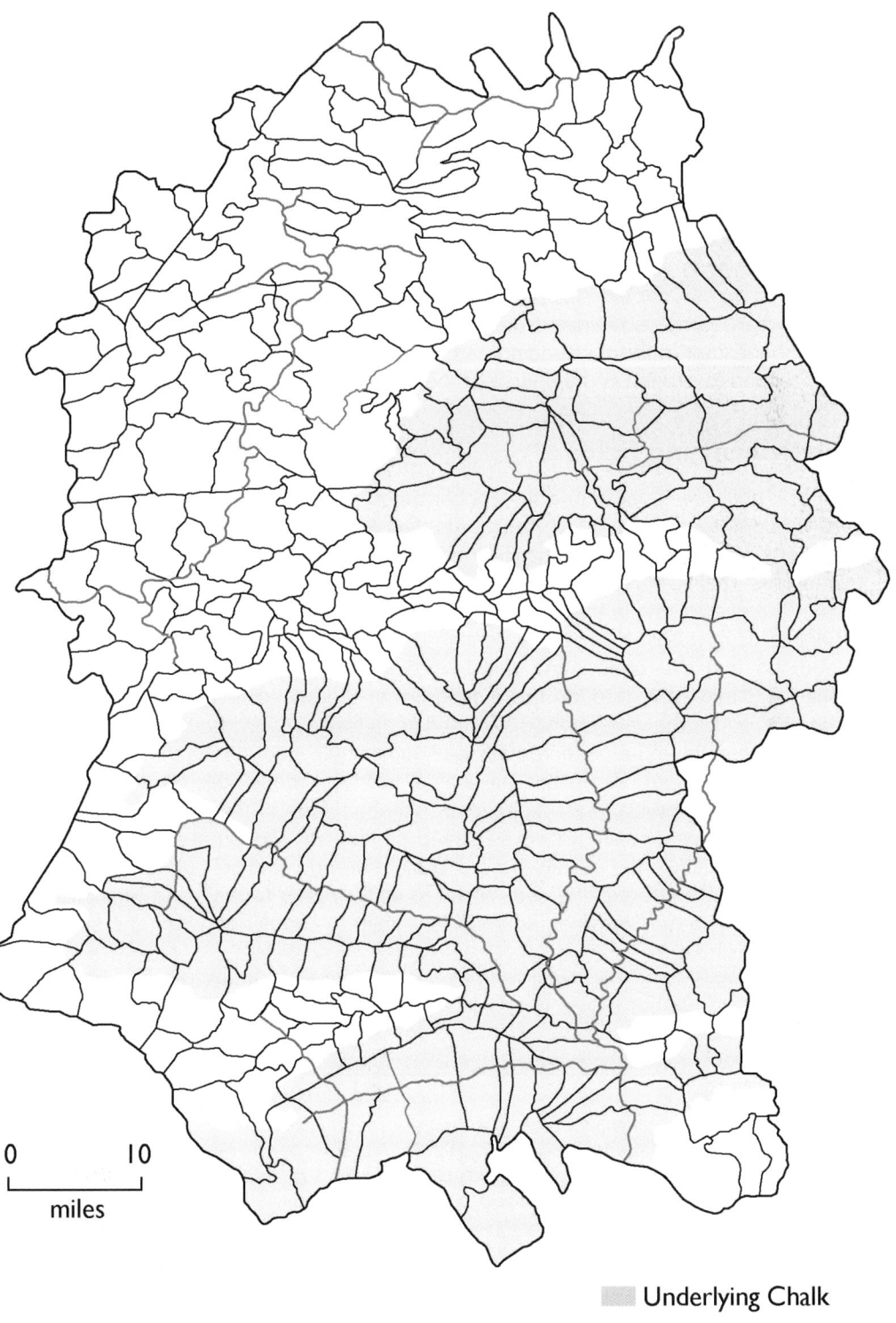

Figure 2.3 Wiltshire: parishes

more suits out of North Wilts, at least double to the southern parts. And by the same reason they are more apt to be fanatiques. On the downes, sc. the south part, where 'tis all upon tillage, and where the shepherds labour hard, their flesh is hard, their bodies strong: being weary after hard labour, they have not leisure to read and contemplate of religion, but goe to bed to their rest, to rise betime the next morning to their labour.'[3]

Whatever the quality of Aubrey's analysis of the link between agricultural variations and human thinking, he clearly saw that there were two distinct worlds here, and other historians have seen the distinction between chalk and cheese as a helpful model to explain, for example, the location of the cloth industry, or the regional nature of political activity and religious and social ideas.[4] Some of the contrasts that were so clearly apparent in the succeeding centuries were already visible in the Middle Ages, and tended to expand in the course of the later Middle Ages.[5]

Settlement and fields

In the chalklands, settlements concentrated in the river valleys, in the dry or winterbourne valleys, or at the foot of the scarp slopes of the downs. Here settlements were characteristically linear, lying along the spring lines or just above the meadow. Their parishes and estates ran back in characteristically long narrow strips from the river, taking in the rich alluvial deposits, the lowland arable and the downland heights (Figure 2.3). Each settlement thus included a variety of the local agricultural land, so that the contrasting soils were interlinked within the local agricultural economy, especially through the movement of the sheep flocks. The scarcity of the meadowland in the valley bottom (and the need for hay for winter fodder) meant that it was worth much more per acre than was good arable land. Above the meadow lay the settlement and then above this the arable, both the fertile soils on the valley slopes and the poorer downland arable beyond. Although parts of the downs were cultivated the land was essentially prized as sheep pasture. It was an area largely devoid of settlement but, like the sea elsewhere, the downland could be a unifying rather than a divisive force: it offered land over which to walk, ride or to drive and feed cattle, pigs and sheep, and thus provided an important point of contact between the settlements that lay around it.

It made sense for each soil type to be shared among the various settlements or estates, and this led to the long thin parishes so typical of the chalklands, both in

---

3. J. Aubrey, *Aubrey's natural history of Wiltshire: a reprint of 'the natural history of Wiltshire'*,(1847) ed. K.G. Ponting (Newton Abbot, 1969), 11.
4. J. Thirsk, 'Industries in the countryside', in F.J. Fisher (ed.), *Essays in the economic and social history of Tudor and Stuart England* (Cambridge, 1961); D. Underdown, *Revel, riot and rebellion: popular politics and culture in England 1603–1660* (Oxford, 1985).
5. J.N. Hare, 'Lord and tenant in Wiltshire, c.1380–1520, with particular reference to regional and seigneurial variations', PhD thesis (London, 1976) and 'Change and continuity in Wiltshire agriculture: the later Middle Ages', in W.E. Minchinton (ed.), *Agricultural improvement: medieval and modern*, Exeter Papers in Economic History 14 (Exeter, 1981), 1–18. See also C. Lewis, 'Patterns and processes in the medieval settlement of Wiltshire', in M. Aston and C. Lewis (eds), *The medieval landscape of Wessex* (Oxford, 1994), 171–82.

Wiltshire and elsewhere, from Anglo-Saxon times onwards.[6] But the pattern of parish boundaries partially conceals this development, since it sometimes lumps together a group of tithings or estates each of which possessed the characteristic long thin shape. Thus, in the early fourteenth century the parish of Enford was subdivided into seven tithings, with each of their settlements being strung along the banks of the river Avon, and each possessing arable and downland behind them.[7] The varying soil types are reflected in the value assigned to each type of land in the *Inquisitions post mortem*. Thus, at Steeple Lavington, the lord held 88 acres of sandy soil worth 3d per acre, 20 acres of deep land worth 8d per acre, and 374 poor acres upon the hill worth 2d per acre. At Mere, the value of the demesne was assessed at 8d per acre for land under the hill, 2d for land which was on the hill and 4d for lands from an old assart.[8]

Arable cultivation typically took place within the open and common fields that largely dominated chalkland agriculture until the eighteenth century (Plate 2.2).[9] Here, cultivation tended to operate within a two-course rotation in which, each year, half the land was arable and half was common pasture, as is evident on the estates of Winchester Cathedral Priory and at such places as Collingbourne Ducis, Everleigh, Newton Tony, Tinhide, Imber, Lye next Westbury and Heytesbury.[10] This two-course system was less wasteful than it might appear, given that the fallow provided valuable pasture for livestock, particularly for the sheep that were such a key feature of the local agricultural economy, and whose manure was so important to agricultural well-being. The fallow thus made an important contribution to the manorial economy and to arable productivity. Some chalkland manors used a three-course rotation, as at Durrington, Wilsford, Ashton Gifford and Aldbourne,[11] but these were unusual, and with the exception of Aldbourne may have reflected limited sheep pastures. On a very few manors, a shift from a two-course to a three-course system has been identified which occurred at some time between the early fourteenth and the sixteenth century.[12] The three-course pattern predominated, however, in the east of the county, where the chalk was covered with clay-with-flints and settlement had evolved within a much more wooded landscape with smaller demesnes and an absence of large sheep flocks, as at East Wyke, Clench, Benton and West Shalbourne.[13]

---

6. See, for example, C.C. Taylor, *Dorset* (London, 1970); O.G.S. Crawford, *The Andover region* (Oxford, 1922); D. Hooke, 'The administrative and settlement framework of early medieval Wessex', in Aston and Lewis (eds), *The medieval landscape of Wessex*, 88–9.
7. This is mapped in, for example, VCH *Wilts* 6, 116.
8. *Abstracts of Wiltshire inquisitiones post mortem: returned into the Court of Chancery in the reigns of Henry III, Edward I, and Edward II A.D. 1242–1326*, vol. 1, ed. E.A. Fry, Wiltshire Archaeological and Natural History Society (London, 1908), 192, 256.
9. Kerridge, 'Agriculture 1500–1793', 46; Davis, *General view of Wiltshire*, 13.
10. B. Harrison, 'Field systems and demesne farming on the Wiltshire estates of Saint Swithun's Priory, Winchester', *AHR*, 43 (1995), 7–9; *Abstracts of Wiltshire inquisitiones post mortem returned into the Court of Chancery in the reign of King Edward III A.D. 1327–1377*, vol. 2, ed. E. Stokes (London, 1914), 304, 312, 328; *Wilts IPM* i, 65; R. Payne, 'Agrarian conditions on the Wiltshire estates of the duchy of Lancaster, the lords Hungerford and the bishopric of Winchester', PhD thesis (London, 1940), 116.
11. *Wilts IPM* ii, 105; R. Scott, 'Medieval agriculture', in VCH *Wilts* 4, 14.
12. Scott, 'Medieval agriculture', 15.
13. *Wilts IPM* ii, 46, 55.

A Prospering Society

Figure 2.4 Wiltshire: main places mentioned in the text

Regions and people

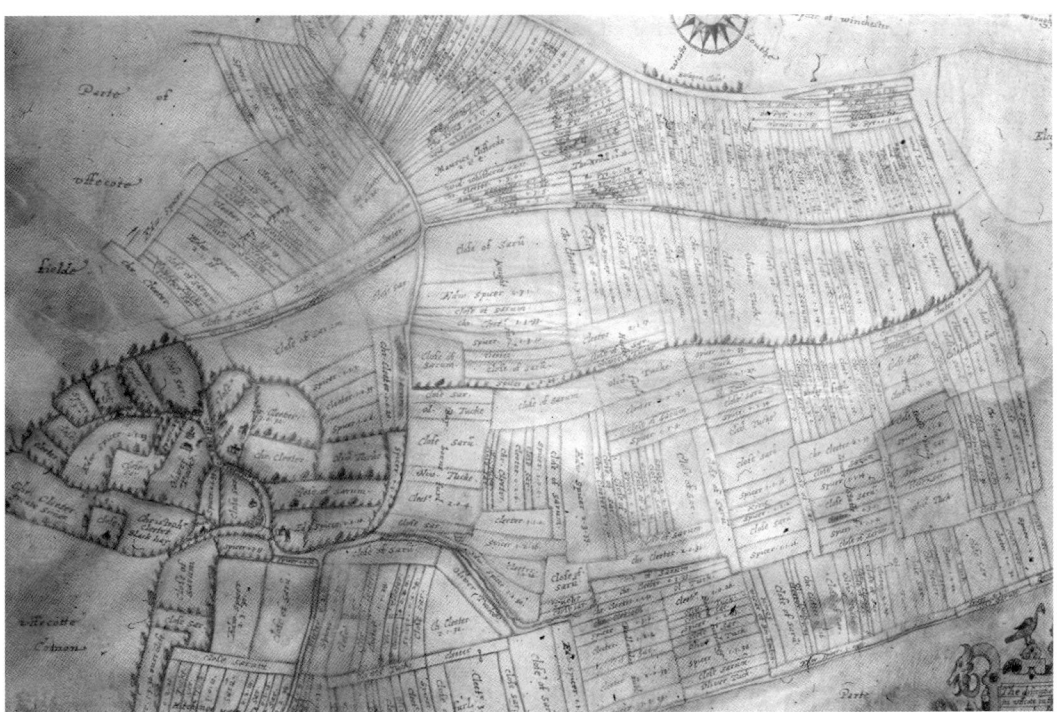

Plate 2.2 Part of a set of maps by Thomas Langdon showing the Charterhouse estate in Wroughton and the manor of Elcombe in 1616: a long thin estate straddling the chalk downs and the clay vale. This map shows part of Uffcott, with the narrow strips within the large open fields so typical of the medieval chalkland (contrast with Plate 2.3) (WRO 631/1/1).

In the north-west and away from the chalk the three-course practice was also the norm, as on most of the Malmesbury Abbey manors and at Bromham, Stanton St Quentin and Castle Eaton.[14] In the Cotswolds the two-course system which dominated the chalklands also appeared to prevail, although the medieval evidence for its field systems is ambiguous: Colerne, Atworth and Chaldfield had two fields but Castle Combe had three. Later, in the sixteenth and seventeenth centuries, however, the Cotswolds were clearly dominated by two-field rotations,[15] and it seems unlikely that the intervening period had seen a shift from three-course to the less intensive two-course rotations.

Over the centuries the wooded areas of the vale and the east had been subject to colonisation. Some settlements comprised open-field, or nucleated, villages but usually with smaller demesnes than those of the chalkland. The arable area expanded through enclosed assarts, creating a very different set of field patterns (Plate 2.3). The medieval forest records also show a gradual erosion of the woodlands, with increased numbers of settlements occurring in the thirteenth and early fourteenth centuries and

---

14. BL Add. MS 6165 (transcript); TNA PRO SC6/1045/14–1047/4; Scott, 'Medieval agriculture', 14.
15. *Wilts IPM* ii, 622, 373; E. Kerridge, 'The agrarian development of Wiltshire 1540–1640', PhD thesis (London, 1951), 76.

A Prospering Society

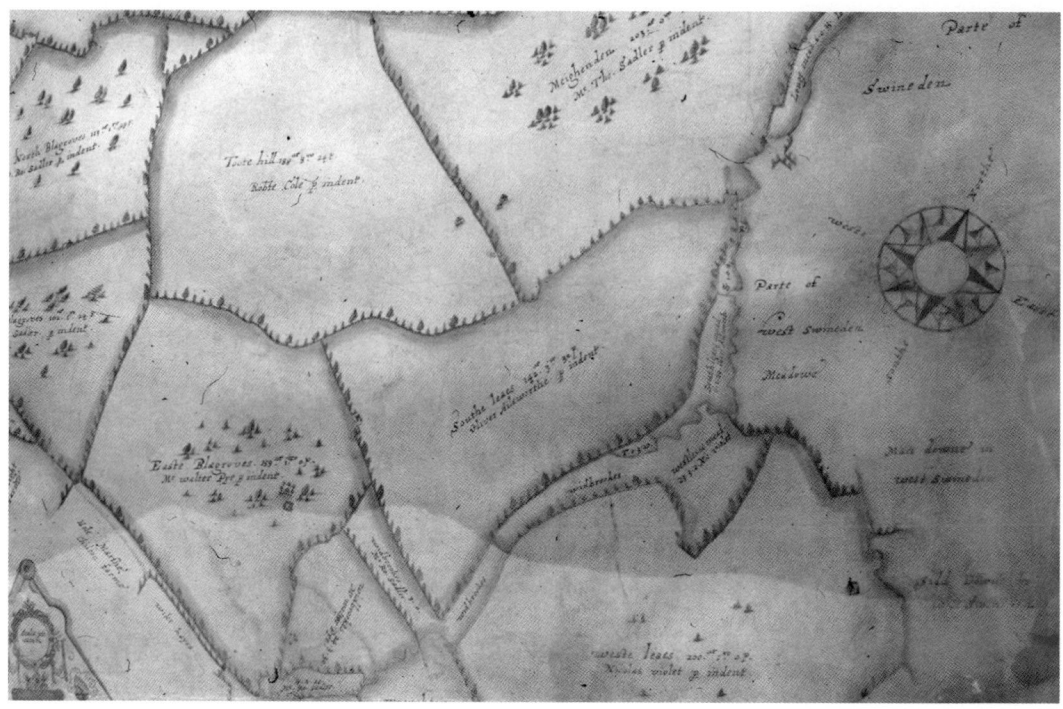

Plate 2.3 Part of Thomas Langdon's set of maps showing the Charterhouse estate. This map shows a very different landscape to Plate 2.2, the enclosed fields away from the open fields, as often found on the medieval claylands (WRO 631/1).

the substantial shrinkage of the area subject to the legal restrictions of the forest.[16] Here settlements probably consisted of smaller isolated farmsteads or groups of villagers or squatters. Something of these contrasting settlement patterns can be seen in later form in Andrews and Dury's map of 1773, where the farmsteads and small strings of houses scattered along the fringes of the woodland or common land, in the clay vale and the corallian limestone, contrasted with the nucleated settlements of the chalkland.[17] By the eighteenth century settlement in the vale was much more affected than was the chalkland by organised enclosure of its open fields – occurring in fact in the later Middle Ages as well as the post-medieval period – but the contrasts with the chalklands were already evident in the earlier period. Away from the chalk the role of the lord and the manorial structure was already weaker: manors were generally smaller and more poorly documented, and demesne agriculture finished earlier than on the chalklands.

---

16. R. Grant, 'Forests', in VCH *Wilts* iv, 391–460, as at Savernake, 451; Brayden, 445; Chippenham, 477.
17. Lewis, 'Patterns and processes'; *Andrew's and Dury's map of Wiltshire, 1773, a reduced facsimile*, ed E. Crittall, Wiltshire Archaeological and Natural History Society Records Branch 8 (Devizes, 1952).

Parts of the woods of the clay vale, and of the clay-with-flints, together with downland chases, were used for the hunt and other recreational pastimes. In particular, the area to the east was dominated by the royal residences and hunting grounds of Clarendon, Marlborough and Ludgershall. Although these settlements were documented by the reign of William the Conqueror, and had probably seen earlier royal hunting activity, they were particularly active in the later twelfth and the thirteenth centuries, when Henry III was a very regular visitor and lavished expenditure on the buildings.[18] Elsewhere, many parks were created by lords in the former woodlands.[19]

The extent of woodland colonisation is underestimated by our medieval taxation records, for these do not record the presence of new satellite settlements. The assessment for 1334[20] provides a realistic impression of the structure of settlement in the chalkland, each tithing being separately included, but this was frequently not the case away from the chalk.[21] Forest records make it clear that many settlements that were already in existence by the thirteenth century were not separately taxed; rather, they were included with the mother settlement, thus giving inflated population figures for such places as Chippenham and concealing the extent of more dispersed settlement.[22] Many of the apparently richest settlement areas are in the clay vale, but this is a reflection of the large amount of colonisation that had taken place rather than of the wealth of the core settlement. This apparent oversimplification of the pattern of settlement was to be found in much of non-chalk Wiltshire. Thus, at the manor of Bremhill, in north-west Wiltshire, on the ridge of corallian limestone, the tax assessments were made under the headings Bremhill, Foxham and Avon, but the late-thirteenth-century rental shows that there were four other settlements.[23] At Nettleton, in the Cotswolds, the taxation figures might suggest the presence of only one settlement, but the early-sixteenth-century rental of Glastonbury Abbey shows that there were four.[24] Similar examples existed at Crudwell (Malmesbury Abbey) and Grittleton (Glastonbury Abbey).[25] Something of the complexity of settlement in the former woodlands has been revealed in the detailed study of Whiteparish, in the far

---

18. Itinerary of Henry III (PRO card index). On the individual sites see R.A. Brown, H.M. Colvin and A.J. Taylor, *The history of the king's works*, vols 1 and 2 (London, 1963), 910–16, 730–31, 735–8; ed. P. Ellis, *Ludgershall Castle: excavations by Peter Addyman, 1964–72*, Wiltshire Archaeological Society 2 (Devizes, 2000), 12–15; T.B. James and A.M. Robinson, *Clarendon Palace* (London, 1988), 1–31; A. Richardson, *The forest, park and palace of Clarendon, c.1200–c.1650* (Oxford, 2005), 1–11.
19. J. Bond, 'Forests, chases, warrens and parks in medieval Wessex', in Aston and Lewis (eds), *The medieval landscape of Wessex*, 115–58; K. Watts, 'Wiltshire deer parks: an introductory survey', *WAM*, 89 (1996), 88–98 and lists at 96–8; J. Birrell, 'Deer and deer farming in medieval England', *AHR*, 40 (1992), 112–26.
20. M.W. Beresford, 'Fifteenths and tenths: quotas of 1334'; 'Poll tax payers of 1377'; 'Poor parishes of 1428', in VCH *Wilts* 4, 294–314.
21. Hare, 'Lord and tenant', 24–6.
22. Ibid., 22–4.
23. *Registrum Malmesburiense: the register of Malmesbury Abbey*, ed. J.S. Brewer and C.T. Martin, Rolls Series 72 (London, 1879/80), 162–9; Hare, 'Lord and tenant', 23.
24. BL Harl MS 3961 fo.16v.
25. *Registrum Malmesburiense*, 144–53, and BL Harleian MS 3961 fo.4.

south-east of the county. Here 'the years between 1086 and 1350 saw the appearance of seven new farmsteads or hamlets, associated with one completely new open field system, probably 800 acres of assarts in the forest and 300 acres of enclosures on the downs'. Here, again, tithings bore little relationship to current as opposed to historic settlement.[26]

Yet the tax figures, for all their imperfections, allow us to reach some broader conclusions. The 1332 Lay Subsidy Rolls show considerable variety in the distribution of taxpayers. There was a high density in the clay vale, between Devizes and Trowbridge, south of Malmesbury and around Swindon, and an above-average concentration in the immediate hinterland west of Salisbury. But the chalklands of east Wiltshire and Salisbury Plain seem to be areas of low density, reflecting the poor, less attractive soils.[27] There is a general correlation between this distribution of taxpayers in 1332 and the much wider assessment of taxpayers in the 1377 poll tax. In the latter assessment west Wiltshire, above all in the area between Warminster, Calne and Bradford, showed a relatively dense distribution of taxpayers. There was also an above-average density in Salisbury's hinterland, in the valleys of the Ebble, Nadder and Wylye. In both cases this concentration of taxpayers may have reflected the growth of the cloth industry, reinforced in one case by the immediate proximity to Salisbury. By contrast, the east of the county and Salisbury Plain continued to provide below-average figures.[28] By 1524–5 the higher concentrations of taxpayers were in the areas north and south of Salisbury, in the Marlborough area and, above all, in west Wiltshire, all areas where the expansion of the cloth industry had become an important and enduring influence.[29]

Colonisation and agricultural expansion

In Wiltshire, as in England as a whole, population grew rapidly up to the early fourteenth century, after which there was a period of dramatic demographic fall and stagnation from at least the coming of the Black Death until the start of the sixteenth century. There are debates about the precise significance of these trends. Was England, by 1300, in a demographic or Malthusian trap in which the boundaries between pasture and arable had shifted too far in the interests of grain, and in which excessive cultivation of poorer lands had led to falling yields? The Wiltshire evidence examined for this study does not, unfortunately, help to clarify the situation. But the

---

26. C.C. Taylor, 'Whiteparish: a study of the development of a forest-edge parish', *WAM*, 62 (1967), 79–102, quotation at p. 91, and his 'Three deserted medieval settlements in Whiteparish', *WAM*, 63 (1968), 39–45.
27. Lewis, 'Patterns and processes', fig. 8.8, 179.
28. Ibid., 180.
29. J. Sheail, 'The distribution of taxable population and wealth in England during the early sixteenth century', *Transactions of the Institute of British Geographers*, 55 (1972), 111–26, and 'The regional distribution of wealth in England as indicated by the 1524/5 lay subsidy returns' (PhD thesis, London, 1968) (published Richmond, 1998, ed. R. Hoyle); maps reproduced in R.M. Smith, 'Human resources', in Astill and Grant (eds), *Countryside of medieval England*, 201.

national picture of demographic growth followed by decline is clearly appropriate in Wiltshire and provides one force for change.[30]

In the chalkland valleys the increased demand for land resulted in the growth of existing centres: the open fields were extended, new cottages or groups of cottages built and other agricultural holdings created. One of the most obvious surviving signs of this pressure on land are the strip lynchets, or terraces, which still line so many of the valley sides in the downland river valleys of, for example, the Wiltshire Avon, Ebble and Wylye, as well as the chalk scarp slopes and dry valleys (Plate 2.4). People were forced to cultivate steep and unsuitable hillsides, although in later centuries, when population pressure was reduced, they were used only for pasture. The consequent lynchets, which are still so evident in the modern landscape, were both a product of man-made activity and were accentuated and reinforced by erosion and ploughing: the plough cut into the hillside on the upper side and soil accumulated on the lower side.[31] Their considerable distance from the main settlement, as at Chalke, further emphasises the acuteness of the population pressure. Although the dating of these earthworks cannot be exact, this period seems the most likely candidate for their creation, combining population pressure and the use of a heavy plough and long plough teams. Additional arable growth took place through the creation of small peasant assarts in the former woodlands and by lords' creation of large enclosed farms or fields, whether in former woodland or on the high downs. Wiltshire was never exclusively a land of open-field villages.

The growth of individual settlements can be established from the rentals and manorial accounts throughout the county from Castle Combe and Oaksey to Bishopstone, Maningford Bohun and Downton.[32] The Glastonbury surveys suggest that on the estate's ten Wiltshire manors the greatest growth in the number of tenants, although not necessarily of population, had occurred by the end of the twelfth century.[33] Physically, evidence of this growth is available in the landscape in the regular additions to existing settlements, as shown at East Overton and Lockeridge on the Marlborough Downs, which may have been provided to generate extra labour for expanding demesnes.[34] In these chalkland valleys the traditional strength of the manor and its lord meant that the latter would have been in control of the limited opportunities for new colonisation. This was particularly apparent on the estates of the bishopric of Winchester, where the Wiltshire manors of Bishopstone, Knoyle and Fonthill showed little or no thirteenth-century tenant colonisation. There was, however, considerable seigneurial expansion, as at Bishopstone (Plate 2.5). Downton, exceptionally, had both seigneurial and tenant expansion, but here the manor

---

30. e.g. Scott, 'Medieval agriculture', 9–12; J.Z. Titow, 'Land and population on the Bishop of Winchester's estates', PhD thesis (Cambridge, 1962) and for discussion of trends elsewhere: Smith,'Human resources', 191–6.
31. C.C. Taylor, 'Strip lynchets', *Antiquity*, 40 (1966), 277–83; P. Wood and G. Whittington, 'Further examination of strip lynchets north of the Vale of Pewsey in 1958', *WAM*, 28 (1960), 335–8.
32. e.g. Scott,'Medieval agriculture', 9.
33. Tabulated in ibid., 10.
34. P.J. Fowler, *Landscape plotted and pieced: landscape history and local archaeology in Fyfield and Overton, Wiltshire* (London, 2000), 151–6, 162–73.

A Prospering Society

Plate 2.4 Strip lynchets in the chalklands, near Charlton.

stretched far beyond the chalkland proper into former woodland.[35]

Lords also invested directly in agricultural expansion, and a few individual examples can show something of the variety of this colonisation. The wide expanses of poor downland soil offered opportunities for expansion, as shown by archaeological and documentary evidence at Overton, for example. At Raddon, on the Cathedral Priory's estate there, three phases of a thirteenth-century downland farmstead have been excavated far from the main village, while surrounding ridge and furrow show that the area nearby was being cultivated. The expansion of arable, and of the flocks, had clearly reached the point where the distance of the fields from the village justified the creation of a half-virgate holding on the fringe of the downland arable as a base for the lord's farming in the northern part of the manor, and the new tenant was freed from the requirement to use the lord's mill. The Priory's custumal makes it clear that one Richard of Raddon was not merely a standard holder of a half virgate, but possessed specific responsibilities away from the main part of the manor and distinct from the holders of similar tenements, as well as privileges that reflected its distant position. He looked after the sheep at Raddon and Hackpen, as well as two of the lord's ploughteams, and was responsible for the grain harvest and the ploughing of the fields that lay nearby. It seems likely, therefore, that he was the tenant of the farmstead at Raddon. But by 1248, the holding had been taken into the lord's hands and subsequent accounts make it clear that this property was maintained as a centre of

---

35. Titow, 'Land and population', 84.

the lord's sheep-farming activities. The priory's flocks reached their known peak in 1248, and it may have been this further phase of expansion that led to the lord resuming responsibility for Raddon. In the course of the thirteenth century the buildings changed from a single longhouse to a group of farm buildings, and it would be tempting to associate this change with the shift from a half-virgate holding to direct management by the lord. Such a view would not conflict with the archaeological evidence, but by its nature archaeological dating on such sites has to be inexact.[36]

At Bishopstone, the bishop of Winchester adopted a different policy, creating a new demesne farming complex in the chalkland valley of the Ebble. Its manor of Ebblesbourne, in which Bishopstone lay, had previously been part of Downton and was not accounted for separately, although there was probably already activity around the church of Bishopstone. Given its physical separation from Downton and the lack of any evidence of seigneurial agriculture it seems likely that it paid rent in cash rather than produce to the lord. The situation was transformed in the early thirteenth century when the bishop created a new demesne, with cultivation beginning there by 1212.[37] A new demesne needed more labour, and this could have been secured by the addition of a street of houses built within Bishopstone tithing. These regular, and now deserted, house-plots still survive and their form clearly suggests planning (Plate 2.5).[38] The account rolls do not provide any direct evidence of when this reorganisation and expansion occurred, but in 1211 Downton showed a dramatic increase in the sown acreage of wheat and barley and in the number of sheep kept (although not in oats or oxen). It is likely that this increase was associated with the creation of the new demesne, although the change was concealed by the traditional form of the account. The formal separation of Bishopstone from Downton in the 1212 account would have taken place once the creation of the new demesne was well underway. In 1218 a new house was built together with a grange, cowshed and additional walls. The new buildings, grange and stables were thatched.[39] By the time of the thirteenth-century custumal, however, there were eighteen half virgates in Ebblesbourne[40] and the creation of this large number would fit with the surviving

---

36. Fowler, *Landscape plotted and pieced*, 118–25; J.N. Hare, 'Agriculture and land use on the manor', in Fowler, *Landscape plotted and pieced*, 156–7; K.A. Hanna, 'An edition with introduction of Winchester Cathedral custumal', MA thesis (London, 1954), 458–68; The entry for Richard of Raddun is translated in P. Fowler and I. Bidwell, *The land of Lettice Sweetapple: an English countryside explored* (Stroud, 1998), 115–16. See also E.G.H. Kempson, 'Wroughton Copse: a note on the documentary evidence', in H.C. Bowen and P.J. Fowler, 'The archaeology of Fyfield and Overton Down', *WAM*, 58 (1962), 113–15. At Gomeldon, there was a similar shift from longhouse to farm. J. Musty and D. Algar, 'Excavations at the deserted medieval village of Gomeldon near Salisbury', *WAM*, 80 (1986), 145–6.
37. Titow, 'Land and population', tables in appendices.
38. Shown in J.N. Hare, 'Agriculture and rural settlement in the chalklands of Wiltshire and Hampshire from *c*.1200 to *c*.1500', in Aston and Lewis (eds), *The medieval landscape of Wessex*, 162.
39. Based on a study of the 1209, 1211 and 1212 accounts: J.Z. Titow, *English rural society 1200–1350* (London, 1969), 111–14; *Pipe roll 1210–11*; HRO 11M59, B1/3. On continued expenditure in 1218 and 1220 including 536 wethers sent from Downton see Payne, 'Agrarian conditions', 147 and 185.
40. VCH *Wilts* 11, 11.

Plate 2.5 A planned medieval extension at Bishopstone. The deserted street of houses and smallholdings lies between the road and the river, with the ridges of the post-medieval water meadows beyond. This extension to the village was probably the work of the bishops of Winchester. The deserted village of Throope lies in the top left hand corner.

earthworks and the need for extra labour for the new farm complex evidenced by the planned house plots. At the same time the bishop may have reorganised his other rights in the Ebble valley, as the bishopric pipe rolls now show a new manor of Ebblesbourne.

At Downton, a series of villages lay on either side of the wide valley of the Avon. By the thirteenth century a new, or greatly expanded, settlement which contained most of the demesne arable had appeared at Wyke, on the opposite side of the valley to Downton itself. This concentration of the arable here in the broad valley bottom subsequently became ever more evident as the bishop contracted his demesne from the later thirteenth century, leasing his demesnes in some of the other settlements, so that by the later fourteenth century all the cultivated demesne was at Wyke. Further east, beyond the valley, were wooded claylands, and here the bishop created two new farms at Timberhill and at Loosehanger (or Cowyk). He spent over £45 in 1252 and 1253 to create the assart at Loosehanger, and this figure does not include any of his stocking expenses. The accounts make it clear that the enclosure was at least in part on the site of former woodland.[41] Here the lord established a new farm and buildings where he was free to organise the cultivation as he wanted, without the restrictions of the communal open-field agriculture: both farms were described as closes in the thirteenth-century accounts.[42] The lord would be able to apply the manure of the sheep flock to maintain yields and, significantly, the staff of the new farm at Loosehanger included a shepherd. The bishop also created arable enclosures at Knoyle.[43]

New enclosures provided more land but also enabled lords to achieve greater independence from the open fields, with all the flexibility of cropping that this implied. Separating parts of the demesne from the open fields enabled lords to concentrate the fertilising power of the massive demesne sheep flocks on their own crops and to operate much more flexible rotations on their own land. A similar story prevailed elsewhere as lords expanded cultivation on to the chalk downlands. Thus, on the Wiltshire estates of Winchester Cathedral Priory the demesne was generally interspersed within the open fields, but on several manors large areas of demesne lay on the downland fringe of cultivation, while at Wroughton there was a distinct set of demesne fields at Hackpen, just below the Marlborough Downs.[44] The lord might have a relatively large amount of more distant or even poorer land, but he could make better use of the manure of his flocks, leaving the land nearer the village to be rented to the peasantry. But at some point he might decide to lease the land to tenants, either because the finances of cultivation were worsening and yields were falling, or because the demand for land meant that he could gain a higher revenue in rent from a desperate peasantry.

This variety of rotations and field forms also occurred away from the chalklands, as at Bromham. Here the core of settlement was represented by the three tithings of Netherstreet, Hawkstreet and Westbrook, which all fringed the upper greensand plateau. The lord may have added the present village, with its parish church, as a focus of seigneurial activity. To the north lies an area with small irregular enclosures suggesting piecemeal expansion on the part of the tenants, together with subsidiary settlements at Stockwellstreet and Slapperton. But there was also a large enclosed field, le Cley, where the manorial lord seems to have cultivated continuously. When Battle Abbey opened up the woodland for arable it had kept much of the land under its own control, divorced from the common fields. Demesne cultivation also extended to the chalklands to the east and included the cultivation of oats. Meanwhile enclosed assarts were to be found at le More.

Seigneurial expansion outside the chalklands is also seen elsewhere as at Bradford, where much of the manorial complex still survives as built to serve a large consolidated block of land outside the main village or town (Plates 2.6–2.7). In the north of the clay vale, where William of Colerne, abbot of Malmesbury (1260–96),

---

41. Titow, *English rural society*, 198–201.
42. Scott, 'Medieval agriculture', 13.
43. Scott, 'Medieval agriculture', 12.
44. Harrison, 'Field systems and demesne farming', 12; for flexibility on the Hampshire lands of the bishopric and prior see J.N. Hare, 'The bishop and the prior: demesne agriculture in medieval Hampshire', *AHR*, 54 (2006), 192–4; and B. Harrison, 'Demesne husbandry and field systems on the north Hampshire estates of Saint Swithun's Priory, Winchester, 1248–1340', forthcoming.

Plate 2.6 The great barn of Shaftesbury Abbey at Bradford. This was the major building in a large farm complex, with the surviving granary on the left.

Plate 2.7 The interior of the great barn of Shaftesbury Abbey at Bradford. This massive barn provided both storage and space for threshing, its size reflecting the large scale of many ecclesiastical estates.

showed a considerable enthusiasm for reclamation, drainage and enclosure, consolidated blocks of land were accumulated and then enclosed, whether as arable or as pasture.[45] Secular lords also showed an awareness of the value of blocks of enclosed land, as at Wootton Basset, where there were 126 acres in severalty,[46] and enclosed demesne could be assessed in the valuations of the Inquisitions at a higher rate than that which was still scattered.[47]

Away from the chalklands, the presence of woodland also opened up opportunities for a variety of lords to expand their cultivation. In Wiltshire, royal grants of land in the forest enabled lords such as Stanley Abbey and Bradenstoke Priory to convert portions of the wooded clay vale to arable or pasture. Stanley paid a substantial sum for this and for the right to have enclosed land.[48] Malmesbury Abbey carried out substantial intakes, and Battle Abbey made one at Bromham. Elsewhere, the peasantry carried out piecemeal enclosure or created and expanded new open-field settlements, as at Whiteparish[49] or in the crofts or marshes of Oaksey, Poole and Trowbridge.[50] It is not always clear whether expansion was undertaken for the lord or for the tenant, for land might first be cultivated by the lord and then subsequently let to tenants.[51] At Bromham, the blocked ditches of the peasants' enclosed fields were a source of regular complaints in court.[52]

The thirteenth century had been dominated by population growth, increasing commercialisation and consequent high food prices. The trends were general but their immediate impact varied. The period saw the growth of arable land and of settlement, but on a few well-documented manors lords reorganised their land and separated their farming activities from those of the peasantry, above all to maximise the benefits from the manure of the sheep. On a few manors this expansion gave way to dramatic contraction of the demesne by the end of the century. This is particularly seen on the estates of the bishopric of Winchester, where contraction occurred from about 1270, long before that on other estates. The demesne acreage fell at East Knoyle to 87 per cent of the earlier average total in 1271–99, to 71 per cent in both 1300–24 and 1325–49. The situation was similar at Bishopstone (where it fell to 81 per cent, 66 per cent, and then 62 per cent). But it was most dramatic at Downton, where it dropped to 75 per cent in the later thirteenth century, 61 per cent in the first quarter of the fourteenth century and then finally to 40 per cent in 1325–49.[53] This trend was also found on the Hampshire estates of the bishopric.[54]

---

45. Scott, 'Medieval agriculture', 11.
46. *Wilts IPM* ii, 103.
47. Scott, 'Medieval agriculture', 13, 23.
48. VCH *Wilts* 3, 271, 277–8.
49. Taylor, 'Whiteparish', 79–82; and 'Three deserted medieval settlements', 39–45.
50. Scott, 'Medieval agriculture', 10.
51. J.Z. Titow, 'Land and population', 72–3.
52. e.g. TNA: PRO SC2/208/22 a, b, 208/23 a–d, f.
53. Figures calculated from J.Z. Titow, *Winchester yields: a study in medieval agricultural productivity* (Cambridge, 1972), app. L, 137.
54. Hare, 'The bishop and the prior', 197–212.

Population decline and settlement shrinkage

The population fall may have begun in the early part of the fourteenth century, but the death of probably between 40 and 50 per cent of the population during the Black Death of 1348/9 inaugurated a new phase for agriculture and settlement.[55] The scale of the mortality is reflected in scattered records, and material exists on the estates of the bishopric of Winchester for a more exhaustive study, although not on most other manors. At Downton 66 per cent of the tenants died, although this figure may have been inflated by the inclusion of some tenants who took over from the plague dead only to die themselves, so that a single tenement might generate more than one dead tenant and heriot. At Stockton, on the Cathedral Priory estate, in June 1349, 13 deaths were presented out of a tenant population of 28. At West Dean and East Grimstead only 3 tenants were left out of 15.[56] But the evidence from Durrington and from the estates of the bishopric of Winchester suggests that recovery was rapid.[57] The second outbreak of plague in 1361-2 and other factors then led to a prolonged period of demographic decline, or stability at a new and lower level. These developments increased the opportunities for peasant mobility from less attractive to more attractive areas, a trend the regional impact of which was accentuated by the growth of the cloth industry in the later fourteenth century. It is not the purpose of this study to examine the immediate impact of plague. With the notable exception of the bishopric of Winchester, the documentation for the mid-fourteenth century is generally poor. Here an attempt has been made to sketch in the longer-term trends, no more.

Demographic shrinkage is generally found throughout the country and it provided one of the main influences on rural life in the fourteenth and fifteenth centuries. The balance of bargaining power between lord and tenant, and employer and employee, had been changed. The would-be tenant or labourer could increasingly choose his terms: wages rose and rents fell. Such a development was not, however, uniform within Wiltshire. In some parts of the county the demographic decline was accentuated by emigration, while in other parts the presence of economic growth, or attractive conditions for agriculture, led to an immigration that partially compensated for the mortality. Economic growth also generated the demand for food and manufactured goods required by a flourishing industry, its organisers and operatives, and those who serviced them.

Demographic decline was reflected in settlement and land use, the growing demand for labour helping to reinforce the regional contrasts between the chalklands and the area beyond. In the chalklands apparent change was relatively small. Strips were exchanged between the tenants within the open fields, some settlements went

---

55. Titow, *English rural society*, 68–72; Hare, 'Lord and tenant', 247–8; on the scale of death see J. Hatcher, *Plague, population and the English economy* (Basingstoke, 1977), 68, 21–5; and Smith, 'Human resources', 208–9; C. Dyer, *Lords and peasants in a changing society: the estates of the bishopric of Worcester, 680–1540* (Cambridge, 1980), 236–40.
56. A. Ballard, 'The manors of Witney, Brightwell and Downton', in A.E. Levett, *The Black Death on the estates of the see of Winchester* (Oxford, 1916), 213; BL Add Rl 24355; *Wilts IPM* ii, 209–10.
57. J.N. Hare, 'Durrington, a chalkland manor in the later Middle Ages', *WAM*, 74–5 (1979/80), 140–41; J.Z. Titow, 'Lost rents, vacant holdings and the contraction of peasant cultivation', *AHR*, 42 (1994), 99; see also Levett, *Black Death*, and H.E. Hallam, *The agrarian history of England and Wales, ii: 1042–1350* (Cambridge, 1988), 351–2.

out of use and were replaced by enclosed fields, and there were some shifts in land use associated with shrinkage in the arable area. Thus the farm at Cowyk (Downton), created in 1252–3, was not sown after the Black Death. On the great downland manor of Damerham the amount of arable cultivated shrank by 1518 to almost half at Boulsbury (188 to 100 acres) and to one-third at Toyd (142 to 50).[58] Essentially, however, patterns of agriculture and settlement remained traditional. Elsewhere, away from the chalk, the open fields and the traditional holdings were already being eroded. On the lands of Glastonbury Abbey enclosure was taking place at Grittleton in the Cotswolds and at Christian Malford in the clay vale, but not on its chalkland river valley manors.[59] But it was also to be a period of growing contrasts within the chalklands between those areas where the pattern of farming remained much as before, and those areas where new uses for and reorganisation of the land occurred: throughout the county, examples can be produced of vacant tofts and of former houses that were no longer rented or were leased as empty space.

In extreme cases demographic decline might lead to the desertion of a village. More than 100 deserted village sites are known in Wiltshire, of which about 30 per cent are in the chalklands. Some of these were villages that might more accurately be described as shrunken rather than deserted, and where the process continued in subsequent centuries.[60] Here, as in neighbouring Dorset, they were frequently found in the river valleys or in the dry valleys, and thus reflected the existing location of settlements. Such deserted settlements were also a common feature of the chalklands outside Wiltshire.[61] But the majority of the known deserted sites in this county lay outside the chalklands.

Mere lists of deserted sites do not, however, explain the causation of desertion or establish how far they were a product of the later Middle Ages. It is easier to locate the presence of a medieval village that is now deserted than to establish a precise chronology for the process, and the latter is a necessary first step to explaining why this development occurred. How far did they result from late medieval demographic decline, as in the west midlands?[62] How far did such desertion result from the replacement of arable by sheep in the late fifteenth or early sixteenth century, or from enclosure for parkland in the post-medieval period?[63] It is difficult to resolve such

---

58. E. Miller, *The agrarian history of England and Wales: vol. 3, 1348–1500* (Cambridge, 1991), 146.
59. For similar enclosures taking place in the Hampshire claylands, on lands of Titchfield Abbey, see V. Shillington, 'Social and economic history', in VCH *Hants* 5, 421.
60. Almost one-third of Wiltshire's deserted and shrunken villages lay in the chalklands (pers. comm. Carenza Lewis); they are mapped in Lewis, 'Patterns and processes', 181; and in M. Aston, 'A regional study of deserted villages in the west of England', in M. Aston, D. Austin and C. Dyer (eds), *The rural settlements of medieval England* (Oxford, 1989), 109.
61. Taylor, *Dorset*, 113–18; Hare, 'Agriculture and rural settlement', 166, and 'Netley Abbey: monastery, mansion and ruin', *PHFCAS*, 49 (1993), 216; M. Hughes, 'Settlement and landscape in medieval Hampshire', in S.J. Sheenan and R.T. Schadla-Hall (eds), *The archaeology of Hampshire: from the Palaeolithic to the Industrial Revolution*, Hampshire Field Club and Archaeological Society 1 (Winchester, 1981), 69 and 72.
62. C. Dyer, *Everyday life in medieval England* (London, 1994), 30–45.
63. e.g. M.W. Beresford, *The lost villages of England* (London, 1965); and 'A review of historical research (to 1968)', in M.W. Beresford and J.G. Hurst, *Deserted medieval villages* (London, 1971), 11–17; Hughes, 'Settlement and landscape', 72.

questions; we are held back by the limitations of the evidence and by the problems of determining when a village qualifies as 'deserted': how many farmsteads on its site still prevent us from using this description? Christopher Taylor has discussed the difficulties of dating desertion in areas of dispersed settlements, but it is not much easier in the very different world of the chalklands, with its compact nucleated settlements.[64] Two general comments may be made. Desertion should not be treated in isolation from village shrinkage or other changes in the rural economy of the surrounding areas. Moreover, desertion could be the product of either long-term developments or a succession of changes that weakened a settlement and only at a much later stage resulted in its desertion.[65] Here shrinkage may have been a more common feature of the period than complete desertion.

Post-medieval developments also helped to cause depopulation. Away from the chalklands, the growth of the family farm economy encouraged the erosion of existing small open-field settlements,[66] replacing them by a more dispersed pattern of farmsteads. Within the chalklands the growing emphasis on the gentleman farmer may have helped to reduce some villages to the big house and a farm. In 1826, William Cobbett contrasted the large number of churches and manor houses in the valley of the Avon with its population. 'It is manifest enough that the population of this valley was at one time, many times over what it is now; for, in the first place what were the 29 churches built for?' Yet he noticed the process still continuing, with the disappearance of some of the gentry houses.[67] The population continued to decline in the late nineteenth and twentieth centuries (except where this was counterbalanced by the growing tentacles of suburban growth or the emergence of the army as a major source of employment), and led to continuing desertion, as at Snap.[68]

The scale and chronology of late medieval desertion can be seen clearly in two well-documented parishes in south Wiltshire. At Bishopstone, the three deserted or heavily shrunken settlements of Bishopstone, Faulston and Throope might suggest a classic example of settlements in narrow chalkland valleys that were abandoned for more prosperous lands elsewhere during the later Middle Ages. Throope, which was the poorest of the settlements in 1334 and the least populated in 1377, was an obvious candidate for the desertion that was indeed to come. Bishopstone was still a substantial settlement in 1377,[69] but Faulston, the third of the deserted villages, provides the most interesting contrast. Although it was the second poorest settlement in 1334 it had become one of the most populous of the six settlements of Bishopstone by 1377. It and Flamston seem to have been growing in importance in

---

64. Taylor, 'Three deserted medieval settlements', 39–45. See also Aston, 'Regional study', 109, 120–21, 127.
65. R.H. Hilton, *The English peasantry in the later Middle Ages* (Oxford, 1975), 161–73; Dyer, *Everyday life*, 41–5.
66. Kerridge, 'Agriculture 1500–1793', 47–52.
67. W. Cobbett, *Rural rides* (1830) (Harmondsworth, 1967), 311–14.
68. VCH *Wilts* 4, 'Table of population, 1801–51', 315–61; and VCH *Wilts* 12, 80; M.W. Smith, 'Snap: a modern example of depopulation', *WAM*, 57 (1960), 389–90.
69. Hare, 'Agriculture and rural settlement', fig. 7.2, 162.

the fourteenth century, and not declining.[70] This growth probably reflected that of the Ebble textile industry in the immediate hinterland of Salisbury. At Bishopstone itself the earthwork remains of a street of houses provides a dramatic example of planned village expansion and then shrinkage (see Plate 2.5). It probably represents the physical remains of the 18 half virgates holdings created to serve the new demesne there in the early thirteenth century, although it is difficult to track its subsequent decline. In 1409–10 eight half virgates were in the lord's hands but they were also released and this pattern continued in the first half of the fifteenth century. Subsequently, in the fifteenth or sixteenth century, the land attached to the 18 half virgates was added to the demesne, but even this did not necessarily imply full desertion: some tenements might have continued in use as labourers' cottages.[71]

Downton, by contrast to Bishopstone, included both river valley settlements and more dispersed ones, particularly on the clays and gravels to the east. It contained 12 taxable settlements in 1377, of which 5 were subsequently to be deserted. Two of these, Walton and Standlynch, were among the poorest in 1334, and among the smallest settlements in the 1377 taxation. Walton, with only 5 taxpayers, then had the second smallest population in the county. None of the other three settlements (Barford, Pensworth and Witherington) seem to have been particularly poor in 1334. Barford and Standlynch appear to have weakened by 1377, although Witherington, with 34 taxpayers, still seemed secure. With the possible exception of Standlynch they seem to have seen demesne and customary lands merged and amalgamated into a single holding in the course of the fifteenth century, suggesting that desertion was occurring. Witherington seems to have become largely deserted by 1474, when it was recorded that the tenants were dead or had fled the land and tenancies of the township, and it was leased as a single unit.[72] Barford has been treated as a victim of emparking,[73] but by 1500 it was restricted to two farmsteads and by about 1567 to only one.[74] Emparking was merely the final blow.

The chalkland landscape still provides much evidence of settlement shrinkage and desertion, some of which probably comes from this period, particular concentrations having been demonstrated in the valleys of the Salisbury Avon, the Bourne and the Till.[75] In the Avon valley, about which Cobbett had later commented, tenant numbers declined among the main arable tenements: at Durrington the number of customary tenants fell from 30 in the mid-fourteenth century to 19 at the end of the fifteenth. In this valley, the difficulties of comparing the assessment of wealth in 1334 with that of population in 1377 are accentuated by the lack of consistent grouping of settlements between the two assessments. But examination of the returns for the area between Upavon and Amesbury, excluding these two marketing centres, suggests that the

---

70. Beresford, 'Fifteenths and tenths', 299; 'Poll tax payers', 308; 'Poor parishes', 314. This and subsequent tax data for these settlements are tabulated in Hare, 'Agriculture and rural settlement'.
71. *Pipe roll 1409–10*; HRO 11 M59 B1/192 and 193; VCH *Wilts* 11, 11.
72. VCH *Wilts* 4, 294–314; VCH *Wilts* 11, 54, 71, 72–3, 76; HRO Eccl 2 15900/1/3.
73. e.g. J.H. Bettey, *Wessex from AD 1000* (London, 1986), 112.
74. VCH *Wilts* 11, 54.
75. M. Aston, *Medieval Village Research Group Report* 30 (1982), 11; and 31 (1983), 11; and his 'Regional study', 109.

future deserted villages of Knighton, Syrencot, Alton and Choulston were in groups of settlements that appeared to be in decline and vulnerable by 1377. By comparison with their neighbours they showed a particularly sharp drop between the assessments.[76] In the neighbouring Bourne valley, Gomeldon shrank substantially, with the number of tenants in Idmiston and Gomeldon falling from 32 in 1235/6 to 13 in 1518.[77] But Gomeldon was still not deserted and there were still at least 5 virgators in 1518.[78] Other chalkland settlements were probably deserted during this period, as at Shaw.[79]

Demographic decline probably produced some settlement shrinkage in areas where intense concentrations of houses had grown up along the chalkland valleys. The decline initially occurred in cottages and half virgates, some of which had been created to cope with the labour demands of a larger demesne arable by providing servile work services that were no longer required. Later, the merging of larger holdings generated further shrinkage. High downland sites may have been particularly vulnerable: in the valley villages, severe shrinkage could occur and still leave a viable pattern of agriculture.

Desertion or heavy shrinkage also occurred outside the chalklands in this period,[80] but it is even more difficult to trace the scale and chronology of change. Here villages tended to be smaller and the record base is much poorer, through both a relative lack of manorial documents and the difficulties of using tax and tithing materials. Here, too, the process was long drawn out and some future deserted villages continued for many years to operate an effective open-field system, as at Avon, in north Wiltshire, which was being enclosed in 1578.[81]

---

76. Calculations from figures in Beresford, 'Fifteenths and tenths', 296–302; 'Poll tax payers', 306–13; see also D. McOmish, D. Field and G. Brown, *The field archaeology of the Salisbury Plain training area* (Swindon, 2002), 110, 123–30.
77. Musty and Algar 'Excavations at Gomeldon', 129–30.
78. BL Harl MS 3961.
79. VCH *Wilts* 10, 10–11.
80. For discussion of this issue see Lewis, 'Patterns and processes', 183–4.
81. E. Kerridge, *Agrarian problems in the sixteenth century and after* (London, 1969), 165.

Chapter 3

Landlords and estates

Agriculture and rural society were shaped both by the land and by lordship. Moreover, most of our sources are manorial and were therefore the product of the application of lordship. Because these records are so fragmentary in their survival it is important to go beyond individual manors and take a county-wide view of lordship, both for ecclesiastical and for lay estates. Henry VIII's great survey of church land, the *Valor Ecclesiasticus* of 1535, provides a snapshot of the ecclesiastical estates at the end of our period. It should be used with caution, as it suffers from local inconsistencies and is less reliable in assessing items of income that fluctuate from year to year. Work elsewhere, however, suggests that it is reasonably accurate as an indication of the landed income of the various religious houses and institutions, since this was increasingly derived from fixed rentals and leases.[1] Moreover, the value of this source for the period under study is reinforced by work on individual Wiltshire manors which suggests that the rent totals had not changed dramatically since the mid-fifteenth century.

The 1412 tax assessment provides a cross section of the lay landed wealth in the county. Here, income assessments are based upon the county unit, and the manors and lands held by each significant landowner are valued. The assessment is of little general use for ecclesiastical estates, since they are included only where the land had been acquired after the Statute of Mortmain in 1279. It thus excludes most ecclesiastical land, so that it cannot be used for comparison between church and lay landlords. For the church, the later *Valor Ecclesiasticus* has been used in preference. The 1412 assessments should have been based on units of £20, although in the Wiltshire returns this was not always done.[2] Its valuations cannot be expected to provide anything other than an impression of the general scale and social hierarchy of land-holding. Where it has been possible to compare the Wiltshire assessments with the evidence of contemporary valors or account rolls it would suggest that the assessments of manorial income varied between the full annual value and half of that amount. Even with such a level of inaccuracy useful points of comparison may be made, and the evidence of these figures may be supplemented by other material. The returns record only the lands held in Wiltshire, but lords in Wiltshire often also held land elsewhere.[3]

---

1. A. Savine, *English monasteries on the eve of the dissolution* (Oxford, 1909), 190–99; J. Youings, *The dissolution of the monasteries* (London, 1971), 15.
2. J.M.W. Bean, 'Landlords', in Miller (ed.), *Agrarian history of England and Wales*, 526–86. The comparisons between Wiltshire and other counties have been based on his figures, and he also lists the counties for which these records survive. I have used the printed text in *Inquisitions and assessments relating to feudal aids. Vol. 6, York and additions* (London, 1920), 529–42.
3. e.g. the analysis of Dorset landowners in K.B. McFarlane, *England in the fifteenth century* (Oxford, 1981), 262–5; T.S. Purser, 'The county community of Hampshire, c.1300–c.1530, with special reference to the knights and esquires', PhD thesis (Southampton, 2001), 73–81.

The church

Wiltshire's landownership, and most of its surviving manorial documentation, was dominated by the ecclesiastical estates, most of which had begun in large pre-Conquest land grants. In Domesday Book the abbot of Glastonbury, the abbot of Malmesbury and the bishops of Salisbury and Winchester all had Wiltshire estates with valuations higher than those of the richest laymen.[4] These massive land grants to the church could result in large demesnes of 400 sown acres, flocks of over 1,000 sheep and rentals of over £15 of tenant land (excluding the demesne).

There were three local Anglo-Saxon foundations (Malmesbury, Wilton and Amesbury) but many of the ecclesiastical land grants had gone to institutions outside the county. Some of the latter possessed Wiltshire lands that placed them among the wealthiest lords in the county in the period under study. Shaftesbury Abbey has left its mark in the surviving buildings of its great manorial farm complexes at Tisbury and Bradford, a reminder in stone and timber that is as eloquent of the great scale of seigneurial activity as any manorial account roll (see Plates 2.6–2.7). At the end of the Middle Ages Glastonbury produced an income from its nine Wiltshire manors of over £435. Even more important were the lands belonging to the Hampshire monasteries that lay at the heart of Anglo-Saxon Wessex. Fortunately, a substantial amount of documentation survives for these, above all for the Wiltshire manors of Winchester Cathedral Priory and the two Wiltshire manors belonging to the nunnery of St Mary, Winchester (Urchfont and All Cannings). The Cathedral Priory records for Wiltshire and Hampshire, despite a gap in the mid-fourteenth century, provide a massive collection from a great estate in southern England. Its relative neglect by historians has probably resulted from the unique and overpowering scale of the records of the neighbouring bishops of Winchester.[5]

Two bishoprics – Salisbury and Winchester – had extensive Wiltshire estates in our period. The former was the more important within the county, but few of their estate records survive. The bishops of Winchester had several large manors in the south of the county, and this estate has, as intimated above, incomparable surviving documentation: an account survives for most manors from most years from 1208/9 onwards. Although the bishop had rich Wiltshire lands he was essentially an outsider, who only infrequently visited his estates there. This was in sharp contrast to the bishop of Salisbury, some of whose main residences were in the county.[6]

The Norman Conquest led to a spate of land grants to the church from the king and

---

4. R.R. Darlington, 'Introduction to the Wiltshire Domesday', in VCH *Wilts* 2, 1955, 52–3; on the pre-Conquest Wiltshire monasteries see VCH *Wilts* 3, 210–59.
5. On the bishopric records see R.H. Britnell, 'The Winchester pipe rolls and their historians', in Britnell (ed.), *The Winchester pipe rolls*, 1–19; and B.M.S. Campbell, 'A unique estate and a unique source: the Winchester pipe rolls in perspective', in Britnell (ed.), *The Winchester pipe rolls*, 21–43. For comparison of agriculture on the estates of the bishopric and the Cathedral Priory see J.N. Hare, 'The bishop and the prior: demesne agriculture in medieval Hampshire', *AHR*, 54 (2006), 187–212.
6. Especially Potterne, Ramsbury, Woodford and Salisbury.

the new lay nobility, often to monasteries abroad, such as Bec in Normandy.[7] Later, William II gave Bromham to the Conqueror's new foundation of Battle Abbey, that symbol of the success of himself and the new Anglo-Norman aristocracy. The twelfth and early thirteenth centuries saw the foundation of a series of new monasteries: Augustinian canons at Bradenstoke, Maiden Bradley and Ivychurch, Augustinian canonesses at Lacock, Cluniacs at Monkton Farleigh, Cistercians at Stanley and Benedictine nuns at Kington St Michael.[8] Most, according to the *Valor Ecclesiasticus*, achieved a similar level of wealth that contrasted with the much higher income of the earlier Anglo-Saxon foundations. The majority were founded away from the chalk, in the claylands and limestone of the vale, in areas that provided greater scope for colonisation. They gave a further boost to agricultural expansion in these areas. Their grants had been on a more modest scale than their predecessors, and a founder, by this date, would have had to look around for land to purchase: much depended on what was available. When Peter des Roches (1205–38) was planning to found Netley Abbey in Hampshire, for example, he purchased lands in Oxfordshire, Surrey, Dorset and Wiltshire, as well as Hampshire, both from gentry and from foreign monasteries who were prepared to sell. These holdings included the Wiltshire manor of Kingston Deverill, for which substantial later documentation has survived.[9]

By the thirteenth century the essential pattern of subsequent ecclesiastical landownership had been finalised. The last major changes to the pattern of ecclesiastical landowning came in the fourteenth century and resulted from foundations by two fourteenth-century bishops of Winchester. Bishop Edington (1346–66) established a monastery at Edington itself, and endowed it on a lavish scale. His successor, William of Wykeham (1367–1404), bought substantial amounts of Wiltshire land which he bequeathed to his new foundations of New College, Oxford, and Winchester College. The former received the manors of Colerne, Alton Barnes and Stert, while the latter received Durrington, Coombe Bisset and Downton Rectory; both preserve excellent and under-used documentation, and the Winchester College manors have been given a prominent place in this study. During the later fourteenth and the fifteenth century some of the lands earlier given to foreign abbeys, such as the lands which had formerly belonged to Bec Abbey in Normandy, were recycled to existing or new English ecclesiastical houses or were put to educational use.[10]

---

7. M. Morgan, *The English lands of the abbey of Bec* (Oxford, 1946); VCH *Wilts* 3, 392–7; for the wider context see D. Mathew, *The Norman monasteries and their English possessions* (Oxford, 1962), 26–70. Such gifts were both thank-offering and penitential in their roles: C. Harper-Bill, 'The piety of the Anglo-Norman knightly class', in *Proceedings of the Battle conference on Anglo-Norman studies*, 2 (Woodbridge, 1979), 63–7.
8. VCH *Wilts* 3, 275–316, 262–75, 259–61.
9. J.N. Hare, 'Netley Abbey: monastery, mansion and ruin', *Proceedings of the Hampshire Field Club and Archaeological Society*, 49 (1993), 207–16; C.A.F. Meekings, 'The early years of Netley Abbey', in his *Studies in thirteenth century justice and administration* (London, 1981), XVII, 1–37; N. Vincent, *Peter des Roches: an alien in English politics, 1205–38* (Cambridge, 1996), 65, 257, 358, 478.
10. Morgan, *Abbey of Bec*, 132; see also Mathew, *The Norman monasteries*, 108–42.

The crown and the nobility

The church estates dominate our picture of rural society, but surveys of land-holding such as the *Nomina Villarum* make clear that most manors belonged to the laity.[11] Such estates were generally on a smaller scale than their ecclesiastical counterparts, and have poorer surviving manorial documentation. No single great lord, other than the crown, held land in Wiltshire on a scale comparable with the great ecclesiastical establishments. Royal involvement in the area was particularly prominent in the thirteenth-century hunting palaces in the eastern part of the county at Marlborough, Ludgershall and Clarendon. Subsequently, these and other substantial royal residences tended to be granted to queens and royal relations, as, for example, at Marlborough and Ludgershall. In general, Wiltshire ceased to be part of the crown's main area of interest after the thirteenth century. Clarendon Palace, however, continued as a royal residence and was to achieve notoriety as the place where Henry VI was staying when he had a mental breakdown in 1453.

The Wiltshire lands of the greater nobility represented a small part of their total revenue and landed influence. Moreover, politics and inheritance led to some of these major estates falling into the hands of the crown. The dukes of Lancaster became kings of England from Henry IV onwards, and brought major lands to the crown, with good surviving documentation for the fifteenth century. For much of Henry VI's reign, until 1443, a large part of these duchy estates was in the hands of the feoffees, or trustees, appointed to carry out Henry V's will. The main Wiltshire manors used in this study belonged to this group (Trowbridge, Aldbourne, Everleigh, Collingbourne and Berwick).

The peripheral nature of the lands belonging to the greater nobility is reflected in the 1412 assessments. At that time 15.8 per cent of the lay wealth in Wiltshire belonged to the peerage, placing the county halfway down the rankings list among the counties whose assessments survive.[12] The most important non-ecclesiastical estates still outside royal control in 1412 were those of the Duke of York (£231) (mainly in northern Wiltshire), the Bohun inheritance (still held by the dowager Countess of Hereford, £120, and with other lands by the Queen, £158), the earldoms of Salisbury (£120), and of Arundel (£60), while Lord Botreaux had land assessed at £28.[13] Subsequently, parts of the Bohun inheritance descended to the earls of Stafford and dukes of Buckingham. None of these families was primarily based in Wiltshire. Nor was the county's land-holding generally dominated by a single family, with the exception, for a short period, of the Hungerfords, who in 1412 had not yet achieved the peerage. But, despite this, Wiltshire possessed a substantial and wealthy nobility. Of the 17 counties for which the 1412 returns survive, Wiltshire figures highly in terms of both the number of nobles (with 16, it was fourth in the ranking) and its wealth (with an average value of £56.4, it was fifth).

The pattern of land-holding was not a stable one, and individuals and families could

---

11. *Inquisitions and assessments relating to feudal aids. Vol. 5, Stafford to Worcester* (London, 1908), 199–212.
12. Bean,'Landlords', 532, which lists the counties.
13. McFarlane, *England in the fifteenth century*, 262–6.

shift between noble and non-noble. Even in 1412, these two groups were indistinguishable on grounds of wealth alone. The lay estates were much more transient than those of the church. They were subject to individual success and failure in politics and service, as well as the impact of marriage, mortality and inheritance. Something of these influences can be seen in the rise and fall of the Hungerford family, which rose from working gentry to national prominence and then fell back to be among the influential county families. Moreover, during the family's travails, an exceptional amount of its estate records found their way into the national archives.[14] The family had begun its rise with Sir Thomas Hungerford, an important estate administrator on a variety of lay estates in the later fourteenth century, and subsequently it prospered through successful royal service until it joined the nobility and achieved a major role in national affairs.[15] Thomas's son Sir Walter was a close ally of Henry V and an active fighter in foreign campaigns. He served Henry and his son in the posts of chief steward of the south parts of the duchy of Lancaster, steward of the royal household (1417–24), and eventually as Treasurer of the Exchequer (1426–35), and was made a peer in 1426. Sir Walter added to his lands by marriage – his first wife, Katherine Peverill, brought him extensive lands in the west country; his second, Eleanor, countess of Arundel, brought him 26 manors, of which 6 were in Wiltshire – and purchase – buying some 30 additional manors, 7 of which were in Wiltshire. He was able to arrange successful marriages for his sons, grandson and daughters. By 1449 his landed income had risen to some £1,800.[16] Although his lands were scattered through much of southern England, the core of his estates lay in Wiltshire and Somerset and his land purchases suggest a deliberate policy of consolidation of his interests in these two counties. He had his main residence at Farleigh Hungerford, on the border between the counties, and he concentrated his spending on religious houses in these two counties.[17] He was probably the only major magnate in our period for whom Wiltshire (along with neighbouring Somerset) was at the centre of his concerns.

Service and politics had enabled the Hungerfords to rise to national prominence, but now these proved to be their undoing. Walter's son lived out an uneventful life until 1459, but his eldest grandson, Robert Lord Moleyns, was captured at the battle of Castillon in 1453 and was then ransomed at the cost of about £8,000. This led to the mortgaging of the estates, some sales and severe financial constraints, but not to disaster. But this family crisis was then followed by the attainder and execution of Lord Moleyns for his involvement in the Lancastrian opposition to Edward IV in 1464, and by the execution of his son Thomas in 1469. This left the main estates to Thomas's

---

14. Used particularly by Dr Scott: R. Payne, 'Agrarian conditions on the Wiltshire estates of the duchy of Lancaster, the lords Hungerford and the bishopric of Winchester', PhD thesis (London, 1940); and R. Scott, 'Medieval agriculture', in VCH *Wilts* 4, 7–42.
15. R.B. Pugh, 'The commons of Wiltshire in medieval parliaments', in VCH *Wilts* 5, 76; J.S. Roskell, 'Three Wiltshire Speakers', *WAM*, 56 (1956), 274–94; J.S. Roskell, L. Clark and C. Rawcliffe, *The House of Commons, 1386–1421* (Stroud, 1992), 446–53.
16. Roskell, 'Three Wiltshire Speakers', 304.
17. M.A. Hicks, 'Chantries, obits and almshouses: the Hungerford foundations, 1325–1478', in Barron and Harper-Bill (eds), *Church in pre-Reformation society*, 125–6; idem, 'St Katherine's Hospital, Heytesbury: prehistory, foundation and refoundation, 1408–72', *WAM*, 78 (1984), 62–9.

daughter Mary, who took her inheritance to a prominent midland family, the Hastings, who were then absentee lords. Only part of the estate was left to her uncle Sir Walter Hungerford. The family now reverted in Wiltshire to the role of local county gentry.[18]

The gentry

Below the nobility, in the social and political hierarchy of late medieval Wiltshire, as elsewhere, lay the gentry. This class comprised a wide range of individuals. At the top were those who were indistinguishable in wealth from the lesser nobility. At the bottom were those who held land rather than manors, and who depended for their income on providing professional service and advice and receiving the profits of farming and administration. The 1412 assessments suggest a substantial gentry presence in the county with its ranking in terms of gentry number comparable to its ranking in terms of population in 1377. Despite the need for caution in using these assessments, they also provide an indication of the pyramid of landownership, with relatively few of the gentry possessing the larger estates. In total, 91 owners were assessed between £5 and £19, 77 between £20 and £39, 36 between £40 and £99 and 7 above £100.[19] This balance of landownership is reinforced by the Wiltshire *Inquisitions post mortem*, which between 1290 and 1310 show that about 55 per cent of demesnes were below 150 acres and 74 per cent were below 250.[20] Both pyramids reflect the untypically large size of many of the great manors and estates that figure so prominently in this study. Inevitably, we have had to follow the surviving documentation, but the limitations of the sources need to be remembered.

The Wiltshire gentry may usefully be divided into three overlapping groups. There were the greater gentry and knights, who held an interest in the county but for whom their Wiltshire estates were peripheral to their main concentrations of land and influence. Secondly, there was the well-established local gentry and knights of the county, the core of whose land and interests lay here. Finally, there were the lesser or professional gentry, who received much of their income from professional activities rather than from land. Here, the approach will be to examine specific examples rather than to quantify.

Some of the Wiltshire lands of the greater knightly class were peripheral parts of a wider estate. Castle Combe and its associated lands of Oxenford and Bathampton Wylye formed part of the estate of Sir John Fastolf, held by right of his wife, but his main interests lay in East Anglia. This distance did not stop Fastolf's council knowing what was going on in this important Wiltshire village. It raised entry fines in order to tap into the growing wealth of the cloth industry here, and was involved in negotiations over the valuation of the property of William Haynes, Fastolf's serf, when Haynes died and heriot was due. William Worcester, Fastolf's surveyor, helped to keep his master fully informed.[21] A second example is provided by the large manor of

---

18. M.A. Hicks, 'Counting the cost of war: the Moleyns ransom', *Southern History*, 8 (1986), 11–31.
19. The figures are taken from Bean, 'Landlords', 530–2. The comparative population has been taken from R.B. Dobson, *The peasants' revolt of 1381* (London, 1970), 55–7.
20. Calculated from *Wilts IPM* i.
21. G.P. Scrope, *History of the manor and ancient barony of Castle Combe* (privately printed, 1852), 169–70, 192–8; 247–50.

Warminster, which had been held by a local family, the Maudits, but passed towards the end of the fourteenth century through the heiress and by marriage to the Greene family of Northamptonshire. Although her son acted briefly as sheriff of Wiltshire, he was much more consistently involved in Northamptonshire, where his main interests lay. But his Wiltshire lands were the richest and best-documented part of his estate.[22]

Others members of the gentry class possessed a more local interest, whether county or regional. The lands of the Stourton family provide an example. These lay in south-west Wiltshire, Dorset and Somerset: William Stourton held land assessed in 1412 at £70 5s in Wiltshire, and the wider family held land assessed at £245 here and in Somerset and Dorset. The Stourtons rose to the peerage in 1448.[23] In the northeast of the county the Esturmys were long established. Their successors, the Seymours, with the help of a royal marriage, rose to national eminence in the sixteenth century. Little manorial documentation survives for either estate. The Baynards possessed a smaller estate, with surviving accounts for the manor of Hilmarton and with references to the household at Lackham. Together their two manors were assessed in 1412 at £40.

Gentility might be defined in terms of manorial lordship, but it is notable that a group of men emerged in the fifteenth century who either had no manorial land or for whom such land provided only a small part of their wealth. They were men of influence because of their administrative abilities and were part of 'the rise of the gentleman bureaucrat [which] was one of the most significant results of the growth of lay literacy'.[24] One such man was John Whittocksmede. We know little of his Wiltshire landholding, although he eventually became someone of considerable influence in the county. He probably came from a Bath family, as his father was MP for Bath city four times between 1399 and 1410 and his grandfather was elected seven times between 1361 and 1373. Although our John began as an MP for Bath, he usually sat for one of the various Wiltshire boroughs. He attended at least 13 parliaments between 1427 and 1472, serving as MP for the county in 1450. After training in the law he became an influential figure in estate administration and local government. He was frequently a justice of the peace: in 1457–8 he and John Benger were the most regular attenders at the Commission of Peace, and he served as JP almost continuously from then until his death in 1482. He was regularly found in estate administration: as a frequent feoffee in local land transactions; as steward of Chiseldon (for Hyde Abbey) and Bromham (for Battle Abbey); as bailiff of Salisbury (for the bishop of Salisbury); and as a councillor of the Hungerfords and of Sir Henry

---

22. Roskell et al., *The House of Commons*, 225–30; VCH *Wilts* 8, 97.
23. McFarlane, *England in the fifteenth century*, 262; Roskell et al., *The House of Commons*, 492–6.
24. McFarlane, *England in the fifteenth century*, 202.
25. Roskell et al., *The House of Commons*, 851; J. Wedgwood, *A history of parliament, I: biographies* (London, 1936), 944–5; R.B. Pugh, 'The king's government in the Middle Ages', in VCH *Wilts* 5, 34, and 'The Commons of Wiltshire in medieval parliaments', 78; J.T. Driver, 'The career of John Whittockesmede, a fifteeenth-century Wiltshire lawyer and parliamentary carpet bagger', *WAM*, 92 (1999), 94; TNA: PRO SC6/1048/15–23 and 1049/1; J.L. Kirby, 'The Hungerford family in the later Middle Ages', MA thesis (London, 1939), app. D; WRO 845/manorial papers/14. He was described as of Melksham in a grant of permission for an oratory in 1440 (Miscellanea A of Sir Thomas Philipps, Wiltshire Archaeological Society Library, Devizes). For a recent account see Driver, 'The career of John Whittockesmede', 92–9.

Greene.[25] The family settled in the small village of Beanacre in Melksham, where they continued in estate administration. Henry Whitoxsmede died there in 1526, and was earlier recorded with William Whittoksmede as bailiff of Trowbridge in 1509.[26]

Whittocksmede seems to be one of those men of business and the law who were increasingly required by local estates and central government during this period. Other Wiltshire examples include John Westbury,[27] Robert Andrew[28] and Thomas Tropenell.[29] The last deserves special note thanks to the survival of his particularly full and detailed cartulary.[30] Such men could have advised the lords on agricultural matters: John Stannford, for example, was stockman to the duchy of Lancaster estates. They could have acted as lessees, as did the Bengers. Sometimes they achieved the explicit description of gentleman: William Worcester, Sir John Fastolf's surveyor at Castle Combe, might not have received much in the way of financial benefit from his master, but Sir John's widow described him as a gentleman. He occupied a position on the fringes of the gentry 'as a member of that large and highly trained profession whose duty it was to manage the estates and households of the great'.[31]

Relatively few manorial account rolls survive for gentry families. Those that do suggest a considerable similarity between their policies and those of the better-documented great estates, with both showing the manorial lords retreating into the role of rentier. Where the lesser gentry involved themselves in direct cultivation, it would seem that they left little in the way of manorial account rolls.

The administration of the estates

A distinct group of professional lay estate administrators was emerging. Estates might be run from the centre, as were those of Winchester Cathedral Priory, from where the officials went round the estates to advise or to determine policy. A more distant and isolated manor might be left in the hands of a local steward or administrator, as at Bromham, owned by far-off Battle Abbey (Sussex). In the thirteenth century monk-officials had often run the ecclesiastical estates: this was the case in the cathedral priories of Winchester and Canterbury.[32] But in Wiltshire, as elsewhere by the fifteenth century, such estates increasingly depended on lay officials. At Battle Abbey

---

26. VCH *Wilts* 7, 99.
27. He was steward of Hungerford lands 1414–15, unless this was his father, and served under Sir Walter Hungerford in France in the 1417 campaign as well as being active in local government and attending 15 out of 21 days of the sessions of the peace in 1428–31, an attendance exceeded only by two others; Roskell et al., *The House of Commons*, 813–14; Kirby, 'The Hungerford family', app. D and 109; Pugh, 'The king's government', 34.
28. Roskell et al., *The House of Commons*, 35–8; he was receiver on the Stafford estates.
29. Wedgwood, *A history of parliament*; *Tropenell cartulary*, ed. J.S. Davies, Wiltshire Archaeological and Natural History Society (Devizes, 1908); Kirby, 'The Hungerford family', app. D – he was receiver of the Hungerford lands 1448–57. For a recent account of Tropenell see J.T. Driver, 'A "perillous covetous man": the career of Thomas Tropenell Esq. (*c.*1405–88), a Wiltshire lawyer, parliamentary burgess and builder of Great Chalfield', *WAM*, 93 (2000), 82–9.
30. *Tropenell cartulary*, ed. Davies.
31. McFarlane, *England in the fifteenth century*, 201.
32. R.A.L. Smith, *Canterbury Cathedral Priory* (Cambridge, 1943), 101–12.

the last of the monk-stewards held court in 1330, and thereafter this task was usually done by a succession of laymen who, as with Bartholomew Bolney, possessed legal training and often worked on other estates.[33] Much might depend on the personal attributes of individual monks and it may have been that monastic involvement in estate administration continued more fully on the estates of some of the smaller houses. This seems to have been the case at Netley, where on occasion the abbot or monks inspected the estates, and one monk acted as receiver, although at other times the receivers were laymen, such as the Langports.[34] By contrast, Winchester Cathedral Priory was very much in the hands of lay or clerical officials, rather than the monks. As befitted such an important house, its steward was usually a powerful figure in the area. Of the stewards between 1380 and 1415, three were sheriffs of Hampshire and two of these had also been MPs. Others, such as John Greenfield, formed part of a near-permanent group of officials, endlessly touring the manors of this great estate. Officials such as Greenfield and other figures met together as the prior's council, just as Whittocksmede and others had met as the council of the Hungerfords.[35] They and others, including Kingsmill and Froste in Hampshire or Twynho in Dorset, Somerset and Wiltshire, formed a section of professional gentry active in the running of estates and in the administration of royal government in the localities.[36]

Estate administration produced much of the manorial documentation on which this study is based, and these sources become much less valuable for the historian as the lords gave up direct cultivation. The accounts cease to be a source of figures for wages, prices, acreage sown and other indices of agricultural activity, rather they increasingly tend to repeat identical entries year after year, long after these had ceased to reflect the reality of the situation. On some, such as those of St Mary's nunnery, the standard entries were evidently copied up, leaving gaps for those items, such as the issues of the court, which varied from year to year. The official who drew

---

33. E. Searle, *Lordship and community: Battle Abbey and its banlieu* (Toronto, 1974), 418, 422–3; R.L. Storey, 'The foundation and medieval college, 1379–1530', in J. Buxton and P. Williams (eds), *New College Oxford, 1379–1979* (Oxford, 1979), 35; *The book of Bartholomew Bolney*, ed. M. Clough, Sussex Record Society 63 (Lewes, 1964).
34. Hare, 'Netley Abbey', 213.
35. J. Greatrex, 'St Swithun's Priory in the later Middle Ages', in J. Crook (ed), *Winchester Cathedral: nine hundred years 1093–1993* (Chichester, 1993), 155; Kirby, 'The Hungerford family'.
36. J.N. Hare, 'Regional prosperity in fifteenth-century England: some evidence from Wessex', in M. Hicks (ed.), *Revolution and consumption in late medieval England* (Woodbridge, 2001), 119; R.H. Fritze, 'Faith and faction: religious changes, national politics and the development of local factionalism in Hampshire, 1485–1570', PhD thesis (Cambridge, 1981) 66–8, 390, 403–4. On the Twynho family, members of whom included the abbess and receiver-general of Shaftesbury Abbey, men with strong Bristol and legal connections, and one who held several ecclesiastical posts, see J.H. Bettey, *The suppression of the monasteries in the west country* (Gloucester, 1989), 1–2; WRO 1728/70; *Somerset medieval wills (1383–1500)*, ed. F.W. Weaver, Somerset Record Society 16 (London, 1901), 284–5, 352; J. Hutchins, *The history and antiquities of the county of Dorset*, vol. 3 (1868; repr. Wakefield, 1973), 468–71; J. Sherborne, *William Canynges (1402–1474) mayor of Bristol and dean of Westbury College* (Bristol, 1985), 28; Wedgwood, *A history of parliament*, 886–8. On the stewards of Winchester College see W.A. Harwood, 'The household of Winchester College in the later Middle Ages', *PHFCAS*, 59 (2004), 171–3.

up the account would then fill in the gaps, as shown by his different handwriting. Within the account a single holding might appear as the rent itself, as a decayed rent in which the land is in the lord's hands and as part of a new lease or rent.[37] Moreover, the debts and arrears totalled up on the account may provide a grossly exaggerated view of the reality of the situation. Such arrears included short-term debts that would soon be paid off; long-term ones that would never be collected; debts that resulted from a single year; and those that accumulated year after year. Arrears represented both debts that were collectable by the lord and those that were not. This was a distinction that was familiar to contemporary administrators.[38] Seigneurial debts may have been more a product of the conservatism of administrators than of indebtedness. Urchfont provides a good example of these problems. In 1481 there might seem to have been a case of major seigneurial crisis, with arrears of £99 9s 1d compared with payment in cash to the lord in the previous year of only £62 12s 7d. But more than one-third of these arrears came from the accumulated debts over the years from three rent payments the annual value of which amounted to only 16s 3d. A second group of debts (£11 6s) went back to the difficult last days of seigneurial sheep farming, some to 1462. Most or all of the debts of the current officials of the manor (£43) were ultimately paid off. Of the original total arrears, less than £6 came from the debts of past lessees or rent collectors – a much more encouraging situation for the lord. Such a situation was by no means uncommon, particularly in the middle and later part of the period, and the distinction between good debts that would soon be paid and bad ones that would not has been shown in studies of the patterns of debt owed to the lord for Bromham, Enford, Wroughton and All Cannings.[39] Over and over again an impressive total of arrears resulted from uncollectable and long-lost rents that gentry and noble 'tenants' were refusing to pay, as at Stratton, Wexcombe and All Cannings. The uncollectable rent was accounted for year after year: to do anything else was to admit a loss of right. Arrears can be helpful, but only if we study the breakdown of these debts. The manorial account was not designed to make life easy for the historian, who needs to establish what the officials were trying to do; but they may tell us more about concientious and conservative officialdom than about economic disaster.

---

37. For a recent discussion of some of these issues see J.Z. Titow, 'Lost rents, vacant holdings and the contraction of peasant cultivation', *AHR*, 42 (1994), 97–114.
38. R.R. Davies, 'Baronial accounts, incomes and arrears in the later Middle Ages', *EcHR*, 2nd series 21 (1968), 221; C. Dyer, 'A redistribution of incomes in fifteenth-century England', in R.H. Hilton, *Peasant, knights and heretics* (Cambridge, 1976), 197–8.
39. This material is tabulated in Hare, 'Lord and tenant in Wiltshire, c.1380–1520, with particular reference to regional and seigneurial variations', PhD thesis (London, 1976), 162–4.

Chapter 4

Agriculture before the Black Death

By 1380, the demesnes on many manors had already been leased and direct management of seigneurial agriculture had become largely restricted to the Wiltshire chalklands. In order to examine regional differences it is necessary to look back to around the year 1300. Lords were still heavily involved in agricultural management throughout the county and extensive documentation survives. This chapter examines agriculture at the end of a long period of demographic growth and after about a century of active demesne agriculture. The comparison between manors has often been based on individual accounts for particular places and, although any single year's account may give an untypical picture, the use of evidence from a large number of manors provides a check against any such distortions. In addition, this chapter will place demesne farming in a wider context by examining some of the scant available material that deals with tenant agriculture.

It is generally accepted that at the end of the twelfth century or the beginning of the thirteenth most lords resumed direct cultivation of their demesnes after an earlier period of leasing out the land.[1] Such a change did not occur overnight and our sources hint at some of these chronological variations. By 1208/9 most of the bishopric of Winchester manors had resumed direct management, but the Cathedral Priory seems to have been slightly behind the bishopric in this regard. In a tax assessment for the church estates in 1210/11 the suspiciously round stock figures for some manors suggest the continued presence of stock and land leases. On the estate of the Cathedral Priory there were then 239 sheep at Hinton and 925 at Enford, but these figures contrast with the smaller and more regular 250 at Stockton, 250 at Alton, 100 at Ham, 400 at Overton and Fyfield and 100 at Wroughton. The latter figures represent the animals included at the beginning of the lease and returned at its end.[2] The subsidy assessment for 1225 also suggests that many ecclesiastical manors in south Wiltshire were still leased out.[3] The first quarter of the century was characterised by transition, with many estates still shifting over to direct cultivation. But, by the end of the thirteenth century, demesne agriculture had reached its peak. Lords had invested heavily in stock, arable expansion and buildings, as did the bishop, Winchester

---

1. *Pipe roll 27 Henry II, 1180–81* (PRS xxx 1909) 15; *Pipe roll 32 Henry II, 1185–6* (PRS xxxvi 1914), 166–7 (dealing with land belonging to the bishop of Salisbury, although he had already resumed cultivation at Cannings and Ramsbury); E. Miller, 'England in the twelfth and thirteenth century: an economic contrast', *EcHR*, 2nd series 24 (1971), 1–14; E. Miller and J. Hatcher, *Medieval England: rural society and economic change, 1086–1348* (London, 1978), 210–13; P.D.A. Harvey, 'The pipe rolls and the adoption of demesne farming in England', *EcHR*, 2nd series 27 (1974), 355–6.
2. 'Two royal surveys of Wiltshire during the Interdict', in *Interdict documents*, ed. P.M. Barnes and W.R. Powell, Pipe Roll Society 72 n.s. 34 (London, 1960), 23–5.
3. *Rolls of the fifteenth of the ninth year of the reign of Henry III for Cambridgeshire, Lincolnshire and Wiltshire; and, Rolls of the fortieth of the seventeenth year of the reign of Henry III for Kent*, ed. F.A. and A.P. Cazel, Pipe Roll Society 83, n.s. 45 (London, 1983), 46–106.

Table 4.1
Liveries of grain from the Wiltshire manors of Winchester Cathedral Priory.

	1310–11	1315–16
Alton Priors	248q	275q 3.5b
Enford	102q 2b	141q 4b
Overton	7q	103q 7b
Stockton	20q 4b	23q 5b
Westwood	No account	None
Wroughton	60q	26q
Total	437q 6b	569q 3.5b

Source: Composite manorial accounts: WCL Composite 1311, 1316. Figures in quarters and bushels.

Cathedral Priory and William of Colerne, abbot of Malmesbury.[4] It was an important and dramatic development.

This chapter and the next are essentially about production, but agriculture was also directly related to consumption, whether in the lords' households or through the market, and to those who brought the grains, animals and dairy products to market. The function of manors within an estate varied and this could affect management decisions on farming policies. Some manors belonged to monastic households, with relatively predictable food demands, while others belonged to the households of bishops and lay lords with more unpredictable demands for food as they moved across their estates. The Wiltshire manors of Winchester Cathedral Priory provided the monastery with large quantities of foodstuffs, whether the delicacies of swans (from Enford) or the everyday wheat, barley, oats, pork, beef and mutton. In addition, they sold foodstuffs and sent the resultant cash to the priory. Generally, however, the priory consumed more of its Wiltshire grain than it sold. Much grain was used on the manor itself, but generally the priory consumed more of its Wiltshire grain than it sold. It received at Winchester only 16 per cent of Wiltshire manorial oats production, but more of other crops (wheat 28 per cent, bere or winter barley 29 per cent and barley 24 per cent).[5] Alton was the most important producer of grain for the priory, followed by Enford and Overton. Wroughton and Stockton sent grain, but on a much smaller scale (Table 4.1). Much of the produce was consumed on the manors themselves: from 40 per cent of wheat production to 71 per cent of oats. Pigs and sheep were also sent to the priory. Pigs were recorded in the Wiltshire manorial accounts and in those of Chilbolton (Hampshire), where the Wiltshire pigs were fattened.[6] In 1340, 807 sheep were sent to the priory from manors throughout the estate: 10 per cent came from Overton alone, and another 10 per cent from Alton and Stockton together.[7] By contrast, the estates of the bishopric of Winchester sold a higher proportion of their

4. *Registrum Malmesburiense: the register of Malmesbury Abbey*, ed. J.S. Brewer and C.T. Martin, Rolls Series 72 (London, 1879–80), 365–7.
5. B. Harrison, 'Field systems and demesne farming on the Wiltshire estates of St Swithun's Priory, Winchester', *AHR*, 43 (1995), 17 (table 14).
6. 'The manor of Chilbolton', ed. J.S. Drew (unpublished typescript, 1945) (copies in WCL and Institute of Historical Research, London).
7. K.A. Hanna, 'An edition with introduction of the Winchester Cathedral custumal', MA thesis (London, 1954), 48.

crops, since there was no permanent static household to supply. A sample of documents showed that on its Wiltshire lands, in the thirteenth and fourteenth centuries, sales ranged from 60–90 per cent of wheat production to 30–60 per cent of the barley and over half the oats.[8] In 1302, on this estate as a whole, sales of demesne produce made up 58 per cent of its income of £5,188, with the greatest amount (63 per cent) coming from the sale of grain. On the single Wiltshire manor of Downton 36.6 per cent of its gross receipts came from the sale of grain and 31 per cent from the sale of other demesne produce.[9] The market lay at the heart of the bishopric's economic activity at this period.[10]

Arable farming

The two main farming regions within the county, the chalklands and the vale (together with its subdivisions), can already be distinguished before 1350, although these became clearer in later centuries (see Table 4.2). The chalklands were characterised by sheep–corn husbandry: large flocks that wandered the downs and great expanses of arable land. A useful distinction may be drawn between the chalkland proper and those manors that contained a larger than normal proportion of the underlying heavier greensand and lower chalk soils. These soils outcropped to the west beneath the great chalk escarpment and in the projecting vales of Pewsey and Tisbury, and here demesnes showed an increased emphasis on wheat. In the chalklands wheat usually accounted for about 30–40 per cent of the sown acreage, but this percentage rose on heavier or vale soils, as at Alton Priors in the vale of Pewsey, or Wroughton or East Knoyle.

The second most important chalkland crop was barley, which usually covered about 25–35 per cent of the sown acreage, in contrast with the Hampshire downlands of the bishopric, where the dominant crops were typically wheat and oats, with barley being of lesser importance.[11] The former situation was particularly noticeable in the immediate hinterland of Salisbury, where a group of manors cultivated barley on over 30 per cent of the sown arable. At Stockton, Enford and Durrington barley and its associated mixes constituted almost half of the sown acreage. This concentration suggests that agriculture was already being affected by local market factors such as the rapid growth of Salisbury and an increased demand for ale. Oats were also an important crop and covered about 20–35 per cent of the sown area, although less on those estates where wheat production was above average. Some manors with extensive downland cultivated exceptionally large areas of oats, suggesting that a large proportion of the poorer land was being ploughed up and cultivated. This large-scale cultivation of oats was also characteristic of the Hampshire downlands.

---

8. R. Payne, 'Agrarian conditions on the Wiltshire estates of the duchy of Lancaster, the lords Hungerford and the bishopric of Winchester', PhD thesis (London, 1940), 125.
9. *Pipe roll 1301–2*, xxii–xxiii.
10. For further consideration of the contrast between the bishopric and the priory estates see J.N. Hare, 'The bishop and the prior: demesne agriculture in medieval Hampshire', *AHR*, 54 (2006), 187–212.
11. J.Z. Titow, 'Field crops and their cultivation in Hampshire 1200–1350 in the light of documentary evidence', unpublished paper, HRO 93/M47/C1; Hare, 'The bishop and the prior', 194–7.

Table 4.2
Demesne crops: sown acreage. The crops have been expressed as a percentage of the total acreage sown.

Chalk downlands	Date	Wheat	Rye	Bere	Barley	Dredge	Oats	Peas etc	Total sown acreage
Enford	1311,16	28.7		14.6	33.7		15.0	8.0	561
Overton	1311,16	39.0			27.8		33.2		431
Stockton	1311,16	34.8			49.4		15.7		178
Bishopstone	1302	33.0			34.7		25.0	7.4	176
Great Ogbourne	1294	38.7			10.8	11.5	35.8	3.2	558
Little Ogbourne	1294	36.4			18.2	17.0	22.7	5.7	176
	1339	34.5		2.8	24.0	12.2	20.7	5.8	483.5
Clatford	1294	34.1			18.2		45.5	2.3	88
Homington	1294	50.6		18.4	19.5		9.2	2.3	43.5
Winterbourne Earls	1296	31.3		6.0	21.9		36.8	4.0	201
Amesbury	1296	32.0			29.0		35.5	3.5	318.5
Collingbourne Ducis	1314	37.1		0.9	35.0	5.6	17.8	3.6	337
Everleigh	1314	30.0		6.1	27.5	7.6	28.8		196.5
Edington	1289	44.4			13.1	6.4	35.2	1.0	613
Warminster	1349	49.4	3.9		34.4		12.3		243
Steeple Langford	1294	25.8			24.3	8.0	31.9	10.0	244.5
Damerham	1313	44.8			16.8		35.6	2.9	385
Idmiston	1313	29.2			27.8	9.1	30.5	3.4	219.5
Downton	1302	42.2			33.2		24.6		509
Durrington	1324–41	25.2		11.8	29.0	5.4	19.9	8.7	303.5

Vales of Pewsey and Wardour, and lower chalk

Alton Priors	1311,16	67.5			22.2		9.3	1.0	407.5
Wroughton	1311,16	47.5		4.5	31.3		13.3	3.4	278
East Knoyle	1302	34.2			23.9		36.5	5.5	238.5
Fonthill Bishop	1302	25.8		13.6	18.6		38.4	3.6	139.5
Upton Knoyle	1302	30.1			24.0		40.8	5.1	98
Mere	1297	49.1			10.6	6.5	32.4	1.4	216
Avebury	1294	40.0		8.8		32.9	13.5	4.7	170
Badbury	1313	45.3		9.4	18.3	5.0	12.2	9.7	139
Winterbourne Monkton	1313	29.1		30.0	7.4	4.7	27.4	1.5	340

Non-chalk Wiltshire

Westwood	1316	58.5			6.4	5.8	29.2		85.5
Thornhill	1294	50.0			15.4		28.6	6.1	140
Sevenhampton	1285,6,7	56.0			28.9		15.0		464
Kington	1313	43.4			11.3	7.0	38.3		128
Grittleton	1313	41.7			7.6	4.3	46.3		184.5
Nettleton	1313	63.0			7.1	15.7	14.2		127
Christian Malford	1313	53.9			6.9	0.9	38.4		174.5
Bromham	1345	18.8	25.4		21.1	24.1	6.8	3.8	236.5

Sources: WCL Composite accounts 1311, 1316; Pipe Roll 1301–2; TNA: PRO E106/2/3; KCM WB2/3; TNA: PRO DL29/1/1; DL29/1/3 m14; SC6/1052/1; WRO 845 manorial papers/14/1349; *Accounts and surveys of the Wiltshire lands of Adam de Stratton*, ed. M.W. Farr, Wiltshire Archaeological and Natural History Society Records Branch 14 (Devizes, 1959); TNA: PRO SC6/1045/14; *Ministers' accounts of the earldom of Cornwall, 1296–1297*, ed. L.M. Midgley, Camden Society 3rd series 66, 68 (London, 1942), 67; J.N. Hare, 'Durrington, a chalkland manor in the later Middle Ages', *WAM*, 74–5 (1979/80), 139; Longleat MSS 11216.

In the clay vale a different pattern was discernible, showing in an accentuated form the greater emphasis on wheat noted for the vales of Tisbury and Pewsey. In the vale manors wheat took up 46–62 per cent of the sown area, substantially more than in the chalklands. Oats was clearly the second crop, with 29–45 per cent, and barley trailed in a poor third. Bromham marks an exception to this pattern and was the only manor in the county where substantial amounts of rye have been found, grown on the sandy soils of the upper greensand. Here rye and barley were grown in the open fields, with oats and wheat grown in enclosed fields on the clay lands, as at 'le Cley'.[12]

Sheep farming

The mixed farming of the chalklands here, as in Hampshire, Dorset and Sussex, depended on large sheep flocks.[13] These animals provided a means of extracting wealth from the poor downland pastures, through both meat and wool; and in addition they played a key role in maintaining the fertility of the soil for arable production. The sheep ate the downland grasslands during the day and were folded on the arable fields, where their manure was deposited and trodden into the soil.[14]

Lords frequently maintained very large flocks. In 1211 the bishopric of Winchester already had 2,365 sheep at Knoyle and 1,238 at Downton, and numbers were to grow substantially. In the thirteenth century flocks of over 2,000 sheep were to be found in peak years on these manors and on three related Hampshire demesnes. Numbers fell at Knoyle and Downton in the latter part of the thirteenth century, but they grew at Bishopstone until the early fourteenth century. In 1302, which was not a peak year, the five Wiltshire manors alone held almost 5,000 sheep.[15] On the estate as a whole, flocks were kept under 20,000 from the late 1270s to the period of the Black Death and occasionally fell as low as 10,000 in the second quarter of the fourteenth century, but they were still on an exceptional scale.[16] Numbers fluctuated according to the mortality of sheep, and of the bishop, as at his death the livestock came into the possession of his executors and flock numbers had to be rebuilt. On the estate of the cathedral priory the thirteenth-century expansion was only just beginning in 1210, when there were 1,825 sheep on the five Wiltshire manors that subsequently made up the main priory estate here, and some manors were probably still leased on a stock and land lease. By the early fourteenth century numbers had risen to about 4,500 (Table 4.3).

Other lords maintained very large flocks on their documented downland manors.

---

12. See Chapter 2.
13. J.N. Hare, 'Agriculture and rural settlement in the chalklands of Wiltshire and Hampshire from c.1200 to c.1500', in Aston and Lewis (eds), *The medieval landscape of Wessex*, 160–61.
14. E. Newman, 'Medieval sheep-corn farming: how much grain yield could each sheep support?', *AHR*, 50 (2002), 164–80.
15. *Pipe roll 1210–11*, ed. N.H. Holt (Manchester, 1964); J.Z. Titow, 'Land and population on the bishop of Winchester's estates', PhD thesis (Cambridge, 1962), 49, and table IV; *Pipe roll 1301–2*, 53, 57, 61, 69–70, 76.
16. Titow, 'Land and population', 50; M.J. Stephenson, 'Wool yields in the medieval economy', *EcHR*, 2nd series 41 (1988), 385.

Table 4.3
Sheep flocks on the Wiltshire estates of Winchester Cathedral Priory.

Year	No. of years	Overton	Alton	Enford	Stockton	Wroughton
1210	1	400	250	925	250	
1247/8	2	2125	628	1463	364	172
1266/67	2	1210				
1279/83	5	729				
1298/1309	6†	1649	550			
1310/18	7*	1693	544	1641	525	
1372/73	2		576			
1389/91	3#	1893	612	1881	571	None
Post-1391			533	1567	427	
			(1394/5)	(1402/3)	(1399/1409)	

Notes: † average of 3 years for Alton; * average of 7 years for Overton, but 4 for the other manors; # average of only 2 years for Stockton. For fifteenth-century figures for Stockton see Table 6.1.
Sources: Interdict documents; WCL Composite accounts 1248–1318 (all available material has been used for Overton, but not for other manors); Alton 1373; WCL Stockbook; BL Harl Rl X/7; WRO Stockton Accs; HRO 111 M94 W N2/1, 2/2 (Alton).

The abbey of Bec had 1,750 sheep at the Ogbournes in 1210, rising to 2,419 in 1294.[17] Romsey Abbey had 1,608 sheep at Edington in 1284, Reading Abbey had 1,066 sheep at Whitsbury in 1210 and St Mary's nunnery, Winchester, had 1,344 at Urchfont in 1259. In 1333, Glastonbury Abbey had 967 sheep at Idmiston and 1,600 at Damerham, and there were 1,143 at Brixton Deverill in 1333/4.[18] On the great lay manors there were 1,352 sheep at Aldbourne, 1,511 at Amesbury and 1,329 at Mere in 1296.[19] Smaller, but still large, flocks were more characteristic of the chalklands. In 1282/3 Hyde Abbey, Winchester, had 4,869 sheep on its various manors, mainly in the chalklands, of which Collingbourne, Chisenbury, Pewsey and Micheldever (Hants) together kept over 2,800. Here, the estate had just been through a vacancy and the flocks were probably depleted. The reduced size of some other flocks probably reflected their smaller demesnes. There were 83 at Hanging Langford and 222 at Clatford in 1294. Durrington did not always have a demesne flock: there was no flock at the beginning of the century, but numbers rose sharply to a peak of 212 in 1350 and then declined. By 1359 there were only 25 sheep left. Nevertheless, it is clear that flocks of many hundreds were a familiar part of the agriculture of this area in the thirteenth century and afterwards.

The chalklands of southern England were among the greatest wool-producing areas of the country and possessed some of the largest flocks known anywhere in England. In the early fourteenth century the bishopric of Winchester possessed well over

---

17. Two later accounts for the two component manors, one in 1330 and the other in 1318, suggest that these levels were maintained into the fourteenth century, the two flocks totalling 2,867. KCM WB2/1; WB2/2.
18. TNA: PRO SC6/1052/1; Interdict documents, 25; VCH Wilts 5, facing 54; I.J.E. Keil, 'The estates of Glastonbury Abbey in the later Middle Ages', PhD thesis (Bristol, 1964), table 22; there were similar numbers at Idmiston in 1312/3, but lower at Damerham (average of 1152) (Longleat MS 11216).
19. TNA: PRO DL29/1/1; Ministers' accounts of the earldom of Cornwall, 1296–1297, ed. L.M. Midgley, Camden Society 3rd series 66, 68 (London, 1942), 67.

20,000 sheep, and Winchester Cathedral Priory seems to have owned at least that number.[20] In comparison, other large estates elsewhere seem to have kept fewer sheep: there were over 13,000 at Canterbury Cathedral Priory and on the duchy of Lancaster, about 12,000 at Rievaulx Abbey and 10,000 at Gloucester Abbey, with smaller figures at Croyland, Worcester and Peterborough.[21] Only Fountains seems also to have possessed as many as 20,000 sheep by the end of the thirteenth century.[22] Individual large manorial flocks have been found elsewhere in southern England, such as the 2,000 sheep at Battle Abbey's manor of Alciston (Sussex), but generally, even in sheep country like the Cotswolds, demesne sheep farming seems to have been on a much smaller scale than in the chalklands of Wiltshire.[23]

The manorial flocks were managed on an estate-wide basis. Already by 1300, sheep were moved between manors, although the scale of this was subsequently to increase. Thus at Overton flocks were moved between the neighbouring manors of Alton, Hinton, Patney and Wroughton. Later, towards the end of the fourteenth century, management of the priory flocks was characterised by movement of sheep over long distances. Sheep transfers are also recorded for the estates of the bishopric of Winchester and, later, of Shaftesbury Abbey (1367).[24] The wool from the larger estates was sent to a centre from where it could be sold in a single large transaction, in order to maximise the price: the bishop of Winchester sent his wool to Wolvesey, at Winchester, and the estates of Winchester Cathedral Priory and Shaftesbury Abbey sent their wool to their respective monasteries.[25] Wool provided an important but very variable part of the manorial revenues; in 1334–5 wool sales recorded on the central receivers' accounts on the estate of the Cathedral Priory ranged, as a percentage of individual manorial revenues, from 10 per cent at Wroughton to 83 per cent at Overton. On the lands of Bec Abbey, at the Ogbournes, 14 per cent of the manorial revenue came from wool sales.[26] Occasionally, even on these large estates, the sale

---

20. E. Power, *The wool trade in English medieval history* (Oxford, 1941), 34: the source of the reference is not clear, but the later-fourteenth-century figure was very similar (see below, Table 6), and figures for individual manors suggest fourteenth-century stability.
21. R.A. Smith, *Canterbury Cathedral Priory* (Cambridge, 1943), 152–3; Power, *The English wool trade*, 35; B. Waites, *Monasteries and landscape in north-east England* (Oakham, 1997), 139; R.H. Hilton, *A medieval society: the west midlands at the end of the thirteenth century* (London, 1966), 84; F.M. Page, '"Bidentes Hoylandie": a medieval sheep farm', *Economic History*, 1 (1929), 605; C. Dyer, *Lords and peasants in a changing society: the estates of the bishopric of Worcester, 680–1540* (Cambridge, 1980), 134–6.
22. B.M.S. Campbell, *English seigniorial agriculture, 1250–1450* (Cambridge, 2000), 158 citing R. Trow-Smith, *A history of British livestock husbandry to 1700* (London, 1957), 139.
23. J.A. Brent, 'Alciston manor in the later Middle Ages', *Sussex Archaeological Collections*, 106 (1968), 90; Hilton, *A medieval society*, 83–4.
24. *Pipe roll 1301–2*, 53, 84, 110; R.B. Harvey and B.K. Harvey, 'Bradford-on-Avon in the fourteenth century', *WAM*, 86 (1993), 124–5.
25. e.g. Overton, 1311; *Pipe roll 1301–2*, 53, 61, 70, 76; Scott, R., 'Medieval agriculture', in VCH *Wilts* 4, 20; Harvey and Harvey, 'Bradford on Avon', 125.
26. *Compotus rolls of the obedientaries of St. Swithun's Priory, Winchester*, ed. G.W. Kitchen, Hampshire Record Society 7 (Winchester, 1892), 226–7. The figure for Overton may be very high because of grain produced on the manor being sent to Winchester rather than sold, thus reducing the apparent income of the manor; M. Morgan, *The English lands of the abbey of Bec* (Oxford, 1946), 45–6.

of the manorial wool was dealt with separately, as at the Cathedral Priory's manor of Littleton (Hants) in 1400, when the wool was exported via Chichester.[27]

These large flocks of sheep were kept, sheltered and fed on hay during winter in permanent sheep houses, or *bercaria*, around which lay a large enclosed yard (Plate 4.1). Their earthwork remains, consisting of large and often rectangular enclosures or pennings, are visible on the downlands today. Sheep houses are known elsewhere, but those from the Gloucestershire Cotswolds seem to lack the large rectangular enclosures so typical of those in the chalklands of Wiltshire and Hampshire.[28] The sheep house was usually surrounded by a ditch and bank with surmounting hedge (the cheaper alternative), or in some cases a stone wall.[29] The sheep shed itself was usually timber-framed on timber or stone footings. It would have been a substantial building of several bays and with two or more doors. Occasionally stone was used, as at Enford.[30] The buildings were almost always roofed in thatch, which was both cheap and provided better insulation than tiles (as at Overton, All Cannings and Kingston Deverill).[31] In 1318 one of three such buildings was built at Overton. The account shows that it had seven bays and stone footings constructed by a mason, and three doors, and was thatched with straw from 36 acres of stubble. Wooden racks and mangers were purchased at a cost of £3 4s 3½d.[32] The accounts for the sheep house at nearby Raddon also show minor repairs and the digging of ditches and the planting of the banks with thorn bushes in order to create a hedge in 1311.[33] At Raddon a neighbouring and probably associated farmhouse has been excavated. The excavations showed that there had been a timber building which was replaced by a longhouse (sheltering livestock and humans under the same roof) and then, in the later thirteenth century, by a complex of more specialist buildings. The accounts suggest that the farmstead and the shepherd were key elements in the running of the priory flocks at Raddon, as well as providing a satellite farm on the edge of the manor.[34]

By the mid-nineteenth century these sheep enclosures were apparently a thing of the past, but still part of folk memory. Dean Merewether noted that the term 'the Pennings' was not a farmyard and adjacent fold, but 'belongs to a disused enclosure adjoining, of a double square in form, and of some extent, surrounded by a slight ditch and mound, on which still grow many stunted whitehorn bushes. The term pennings

---

27. WCL Littleton 1400.
28. For a general survey of sheepcotes see C. Dyer, 'Sheepcotes: evidence for medieval sheep farming', *Medieval Archaeology*, 39 (1995), 136–64 and 138–47 for the Cotswold structures. See also his *Lords and peasants*, 138. Hare, 'Agriculture and rural settlement', 161–2, provides discussion of some of the Hampshire documentation; and 'Agriculture and land use on the manor', in Fowler, *Landscape plotted and pieced*, 157–9; for those at Overton (Wilts). See also D. McOmish, D. Field and G. Brown, *The field archaeology of the Salisbury Plain training area* (Swindon, 2002), 115–17; Stephenson, 'Wool yields', 384; Hare, 'The bishop and the prior', 196–7.
29. BL Harl Rl X/7 Enford, although the reference may be to the sheephouse itself.
30. BL Harl Rl X/16.
31. WRO 192/28/1451; 192/32/1419.
32. WCL composite 1318.
33. WCL composite 1311.
34. P.J. Fowler, *Landscape plotted and pieced: landscape history and local archaeology in Fyfield and Overton, Wiltshire* (London, 2000), 118–28; Hare, 'Agriculture and land use', 157–8.

Plate 4.1 The enclosure belonging to a sheep house, or *bercaria*, in Bishops Cannings. Such earthworks were a common feature of the chalk downlands. During the winter months the large sheep flocks were kept in a permanent timber-framed sheep house within the enclosure, and could be easily released into the yard in a controlled fashion.

is applied by husbandmen to other similar enclosures and earthworks.'[35] By their very nature such earthworks are difficult to date, but there is a group of large rectangular enclosures, often in sheltered or south-facing combes, that would seem likely to have been such sheep houses, or pennings. Few have been excavated, and with disappointing results: the timber structures would have left ephemeral remains, easily missed by narrow trenches or limited excavations.[36] One earthwork, near Morgan's Hill in Bishops Cannings, had an outer enclosure with a continuous bank and ditch (although later both were interrupted with a series of openings) and a small inner enclosure.[37] At Barbury, there is evidence of stone walls ten feet apart.[38] On large manors such as Overton the various parts of the main flock (ewes, wethers and hoggasters) were frequently separated and given distinct pastures as well as their own buildings. Here there were sheep houses at Raddon and others at Hackpen and Attele (Audeley's Cottage, south of the river Kennet), while neighbouring Wroughton had one at Wyke.[39]

---

35. RCHM, *Stonehenge and its environs* (Edinburgh, 1979), xxi.
36. M.E. Cunnington, 'A medieval earthwork near Morgan's Hill', *WAM*, 36 (1910), 590–98; A.D. Passmore, 'Medieval enclosures at Barbury and Blunsdon', *WAM*, 50 (1943), 194–5; P.J. Fowler, J.W.G. Musty and C.C. Taylor, 'Some earthwork enclosures in Wiltshire', *WAM*, 60 (1965), 1–23.
37. Cunnington, 'A medieval earthwork', 591–6.
38. Passmore, 'Medieval enclosures', 194.
39. Hare, 'Agriculture and land use', 157.

In the Cotswolds and on some of the islands of lighter soil that broke up the clay vale sheep were kept, but on a much smaller scale, frequently numbering fewer than 300. The Glastonbury Abbey manors of Grittleton and Kington had, in the early fourteenth century, substantially fewer than any other of the abbey's Wiltshire estates. Elsewhere, in the vale Bromham had a flock of over 370 in 1345, Sevenhampton had 565, and Trowbridge had 160 in 1296, while at the manor of Stratton St Margaret and Sevenhampton the flocks started off at about 200 or fewer, but rose to over 700, with a peak of 767 in 1286.[40]

Sheep provided a range of benefits, as noted above. They produced wool, meat and cheese, but they also both generated and spread their own manure, and this provided a vital means of reinforcing the fertility of the soil.[41] Already by the thirteenth century the sheep were being concentrated into small areas for folding, or manuring. When custumals record the shepherd's right to the manure of the demesne flocks on his strips, as at Downton, Bishopstone, Knoyle and Badbury,[42] they presuppose a situation in which the flock were penned into a small area rather than being left free to wander over the open field. This would also account for the frequent requirements for customary labour to produce hurdles, or for these to be bought by the lord.[43]

Sheep flocks thus contributed to the large-scale capital-intensive agriculture which was characteristic of the chalklands. In other parts of the county, with a few noticeable exceptions, such as Bradford, agriculture and flocks were on a smaller scale. It was a contrast that became increasingly visible and helped to shape the regional nature of agriculture. Wool brought in the main profits of the flock, but sheep offered wider benefits: for instance, meat and cheese brought in cash. The milking of demesne sheep was widely prevalent and firmly established in the early fourteenth century on the estates of the bishopric of Winchester and the Cathedral Priory, continuing at Bradford up to at least 1367 and at Enford to 1403, although in general it declined in the later fourteenth century.[44]

Pigs and cattle

Pigs were found on most manors throughout the county, but their number varied between regions. The largest demesne herds were found in the chalkland, although this included areas of woodlands that lay on the covering clay-with-flints, as at Overton. In 1294 81 pigs were to be found at Ogbourne St George, and 84 in 1331. In 1259 there was a smaller herd of 28 pigs at Urchfont.[45] On the manors of Winchester Cathedral Priory the herds rose at Overton from 18 in the 1240s to an average of 58 in 1298–1309. At the beginning of the fourteenth century the estate's other largest Wiltshire herd was also located on the chalkland at Enford (62), and there were smaller

---

40. TNA: PRO DL29/682/11039; for 1333–4, Keil,'Estates of Glastonbury', and, in 1312–13, Longleat MS 11216; TNA: PRO SC6/1045/14; TNA: PRO DL29/1/1; *Accounts and surveys of the Wiltshire lands of Adam de Stratton*, ed. M.W. Farr (WRS xiv, 1959).
41. Newman,'Medieval sheep-corn farming', 164–80.
42. Scott,'Medieval agriculture', 23.
43. Ibid., 21–2; WRO 1742/6786; BL Harl Rl X7..
44. *Pipe roll 1301–2*, 53, 70, 76.
45. TNA: PRO E106/2/3; KCM WB2/1; VCH *Wilts* 5, facing 54.

numbers at Wroughton (39) and Alton (15).[46] On the bishopric of Winchester estates in 1301/2, three large herds were kept on manors which included both chalkland and woodland, with average figures of 69 at East Knoyle, 54 at Bishops Fonthill and 109 at Downton, but none were kept on the smaller demesnes of Bishopstone and Upton.[47] Pigs seem to have been less important on Glastonbury Abbey's Wiltshire manors, although there was a large herd on the great chalkland manor of Damerham (77 and 32), and a smaller but substantial one at Winterbourne Monkton.[48] Pigs could scavenge for food in woodlands, but they might also be fed with grain. In Enford in 1311 almost 7 quarters of bere were used to fatten 83 pigs previously bought at Chippenham in the clay vale.[49] The pigs of the Wiltshire manors of the Cathedral Priory were sometimes rested and fattened at Chilbolton (Hants) on their way to Winchester.[50] At Bradford, later in the fourteenth century, pigs were fattened on barley and beans.[51] Within an estate pigs might be moved from manor to manor (as between Alton, Overton and Enford).[52] They both generated cash from sale (the three Wiltshire herds of the bishopric produced £12 4s 1d from this source in 1302) and provided essential foodstuffs for the household.[53]

Outside the chalklands sizeable herds of pigs made use of the woodland pastures of the clay vale: thus, in 1294, Corsham had 32 and Chippenham 53, while until the 1390s Bromham kept a herd of over 50 pigs, and in 1356 there were 48 on the small lay manor of Hilmarton. Glastonbury Abbey possessed a large herd at Christian Malford and a substantial one at Grittleton in 1313.[54] But none, except Bradford with 96 pigs, approached the size of the largest chalkland herds.[55] Chippenham developed as a large-scale market for pigs and other livestock, as can be seen both in the purchase there of pigs for Winchester Cathedral Priory and for Enford, noted previously, and by the substantial number of butchers recorded there in the poll tax of 1379.

In the later thirteenth century oxen provided the main draught power, particularly outside the chalkland: thus in 1294 there were 24 oxen and no horses at Chippenham, and 23 oxen and no horses at Slaughterford. A regional distinction seems to have been evolving between the chalklands and the rest of the county. The hilly terrain of the former and the great and difficult distances between the manorial centre and some of the fields may have encouraged the use of horses there. Thus, in 1294, 34 horses and 43 oxen were listed at Ogbourne St George, 19 horses at Ogbourne St

---

46. WCL Composite 1311, 1316; HRO 111 M94 W N2/1 & 2/2.
47. *Pipe roll 1301–2*, 76.
48. Longleat MS 11216. Its eight Wiltshire manors averaged 26 pigs each.
49. WCL composite 1311.
50. 'The manor of Chilbolton', ed. Drew, 180 (1267, pigs from Overton), 319 (1318, from Overton, Stockton and Enford); 334 and 351 (1325 and 1326 Wroughton and Overton); 385 (1339 Enford and Wroughton).
51. Harvey and Harvey, 'Bradford-on-Avon', 125.
52. HRO 111 M94 W N2/1 and 2.
53. *Pipe roll 1301–2*, 47–8, 57, 63.
54. Longleat MS 11216: Christian Malford 44 and 33 pigs; Grittleton 27 and 22 respectively.
55. TNA: PRO E106/2/3; Bromham accounts; Bad.Mun. 110/5/3; Harvey and Harvey, 'Bradford-on Avon', 124.

Andrew and 8 horses and 22 oxen at Avebury.[56] There are signs of an increasing use of horses, with 28 used at Ogbourne St Andrew in 1339.[57] On the bishopric of Winchester's estates oxen provided most traction, although the balance varied from manor to manor. In the vale of Wardour and at Bishopstone horses made up less than 13 per cent of the numbers of mature oxen in 1301/2, but they were over 40 per cent at Downton, perhaps reflecting an association between horse traction and enclosure of distant thin soils. This is probably also the case on the bishopric lands in Hampshire.[58] On the estates of Winchester Cathedral Priory there seems less regional contrast, but a significant growth took place in the number of horses at the end of the thirteenth century.[59] The estates of Glastonbury Abbey in 1313 remained dominated by oxen, but horses were again more important in the chalklands than elsewhere, as at Damerham and Idmiston.[60]

The herds of cows varied in size, although with little clear regional significance. Few manors kept more than 10 cows, and the presence of large herds appears to be determined by both the presence of local rich grazing lands and estate policy. On the estates of the bishopric of Winchester the manors of East Knoyle and Downton, with rich pastures in the vale of Tisbury and the Avon valley, possessed large herds of cows. In 1301/2 they averaged 37 and 38 cows respectively. Such chief dairying centres frequently produced over £10 profit in the first half of the thirteenth century and the beginning of the fourteenth century.[61] The smaller manor of Bishopstone had 11 cows, Upton and Fonthill none. There was another large chalkland valley herd on the Bec estates at Ogbourne St George, with 24 cows in 1296, although this herd subsequently declined in number.[62] Winchester Cathedral Priory had smaller herds averaging 10 at Wroughton and at Overton and 5 at Alton in the first decade of the fourteenth century, while earlier, in 1259, there had been 17 at Urchfont.[63] In 1312/13 Glastonbury Abbey also showed very limited cow herds on its Wiltshire manors except at Badbury and Damerham (where the number of cows averaged 16 and 12.5 respectively). There was a small herd at Grittleton (3 and 8), but elsewhere Glastonbury had no more than 1 cow and frequently none.[64] Here, as elsewhere, some substantial manors had very few cows: Slaughterford had 1 in 1294, Thornhill 2 in 1294 and Mere none in 1296.[65] We possess little evidence from the clay vale itself, the future cheese country, a reflection of the relative weakness of manorial structures here; but this area would have provided opportunities for the expansion of cattle rearing, as demonstrated by the royal grant to Bradenstoke Priory of pasture for 40 cows and one-year-old calves within the forest, together with the timber for the cattle sheds.[66]

---

56. TNA: PRO E106/2/3.
57. KCM WB2/1.
58. Hare, 'The bishop and the prior', 198–200.
59. Harrison, 'Field systems and demesne farming', 16.
60. Longleat MS 11216.
61. Scott, 'Medieval agriculture', 21; *Pipe roll 1301–2*, 52, 57, 61, 69, 75.
62. TNA: PRO E106/2/3; KCM/WB2/1.
63. Figures from WCL 1310 and 1316 composite accounts; VCH *Wilts* 5, facing 54.
64. Longleat MS 11216.
65. TNA: PRO E106/2/3; *Ministers' accounts of the earldom of Cornwall*, 67.
66. VCH *Wilts* 3, 277.

Deer parks and the rearing of deer comprised a type of pastoral farming that rarely appears in the manorial accounts. The existence of such parks in Wiltshire is revealed both by documents and by earthworks.[67] Geographically they reflect the contrasting regions of the county, being concentrated in the clay vale, the claylands of the vale of Wardour and those of the east of the county. They were virtually all in existence by the middle of the fourteenth century. Such parkland would have generated additional occupations based on the timber (such as felling, sawing, managing underwood, or making shingles and charcoal), using the clay of the forest (in pottery and tile manufacture), as well as the pastoral farming of cattle, horses, pigs and deer.[68]

Peasant and tenant agriculture

Studies of medieval agriculture have traditionally been dominated by the lord, since his demesnes produced most of our surviving documentation. A picture of peasant agriculture has to be reconstructed from stray fragments of evidence, and these fragments are also fuller in the period before the Black Death than afterwards. Two major sources will be considered here: some records of tithe collection and the returns from parts of south Wiltshire for the fifteenth of 1225. These records help place demesne agriculture in a wider context.

Both medieval villagers and lords were required to pay tithes to their church, and in the course of the Middle Ages many of these rights to tithes fell into the hands of major ecclesiastical lords. Occasionally tithes are recorded in surviving accounts, allowing us to compare the lord's production with that of his tenants. These sources are relatively scarce and need to be used cautiously, but they deal with an important topic and have recently become of greater concern.[69] The fluctuations from year to year shown in the records of tithes found in the manorial accounts, suggest that the figures are useful and that meaningful comparisons can be made. Five Wiltshire places possess such records. Three belonged to Winchester Cathedral Priory and lay in the chalklands (Alton Priors, Enford and Overton). Two lay outside: Inglesham (belonging to Beaulieu Abbey, in the Thames valley) and Stratton St Margaret (belonging to Merton College, Oxford on the corallian limestone and adjacent claylands). These latter are more restricted in their information, and do not distinguish between the produce of the tenants and that of the demesne.

The accounts for the three manors of the Cathedral Priory, however, record both the tithe crops coming from the demesne and those coming from the rest of the

---

67. J. Bond, 'Forests, chases, warrens and parks in medieval Wessex', in Aston and Lewis (eds), *The medieval landscape of Wessex*, 134–44.
68. See also E. Roberts, 'The bishop of Winchester's deer parks in Hampshire', *PHFCAS*, 44 (1983), 67–86; J. Birrell, 'Personal craftsmen in the medieval forest', *AHR*, 16 (1969), 91–107.
69. The value of the tithe records is discussed in a forthcoming paper, J.N. Hare, 'Lord, tenant and the market: some tithe evidence from the Wessex region', in B. Dodds and R.H. Britnell, *Agriculture and rural society after the Black Death: common themes and regional variations* (Hertford, 2008), 132–46. See also, for the tithes of Durham cathedral priory, B. Dodds, 'Estimating arable output using Durham Priory tithe receipts, 1341–1450', *EcHR*, 57 (2004), 245–85 and idem, 'Managing tithes in the late Middle Ages', *AHR*, 53 (2005), 125–40.

Table 4.4
Parish and demesne tithes, c.1270–c.1320.

	Parish (crop as a percentage of the parish total)							Demesne (crop as a percentage of the demesne total)						
	Wheat	Bere	Rye	Barley	Oats	Dredge	Vetch, Peas, Beans		Wheat	Bere	Rye	Barley	Oats	Dredge	Vetch, Peas, Beans
Alton Priors															
1303	51.1		2.5	34	1.8	4.4	6.2		61.4		29.4	9		0.2	
1304	54.6		2.5	32.8		5.7	4.4		68.8		30.5		5.7	0.7	
1309	50.6			40.8	7.7		0.9		65.8		24.3	8.6		1.3	
1311	40.4			41.9	1.7	14.0	3.8		56.4		32.1	11.0		0.5	
1316	50.8			48.5	0.7		0.0		56.5		33.0	8.9			
Enford															
1309	21.8			51.9	12.5		5.3		19.6		5.8	44.9	26.3		3.3
1311	19.5	6.8		56.2	9.3		8.3		17.8		15.3	41	17		9
Overton															
1307	32.3	10.5		48.3		8.8			34.7		8.2	21.2	24.6	9.1	2.3
1311	20.5	6.1		57.8	2.4	7.6	5.5		17.7		8.7	40.2	23.1	6.6	4.5
1312	32.7	3.3		48.4	8.4	4.4	3		25.8		6.6	35.9	20.6	5.1	
1316	24.7	8.4		47.1	6.1	13.6			30.2		1.3	30	30.3	8.2	5.9
Stratton (parish and demesne together)															
1294	30.2			29.1	24.3	8.3	8.1		*56.0			*28.9	*15.0		
1295	37.6			22.8	29.7	0.8	9.1								
1299	21.8			45	6.8	20.3	6.1								
Inglesham															
1270	30.1			57			12		46.2			40.7	10	3.1	

Notes: The produce of each crop is expressed as a percentage of the total production of the parish (the non demesne produce) or of the demesne enabling comparison between the two sectors. Tithe returns are not always recorded in the same way. At Enford in 1309, the parish figures are for the parish and demesne together, and the demesne figure has been taken from the demesne accounts. At Alton in 1309, the oats and dredge figures are recorded together. The Stratton figures do not distinguish between parish and demesne. The Stratton figures in the last column are for beans and not peas and vetch.
* The figures are those for a large manor within the parish, that of Sevenhampton between 1285–6, 86–7 and 87–8. They are not strictly comparable with those of the parish as a whole.

parish, enabling the cropping of the lord to be compared with that of the tenants. To facilitate this comparison the tithes of each crop have been converted into a percentage of the volume of the tithes, firstly for the demesne and secondly for the tenant land. A tabulation of some of the same material based on cash valuation has been published elsewhere by Harrison.[70] Calculations based on market price, however, tend to increase the importance of the expensive wheat and diminish the importance of barley and oats. Alton Priors was the smallest of the three parishes, although it possessed a large demesne of about 400 sown acres. Lying in the vale of Pewsey, Alton showed a different emphasis in its demesne cropping to the other two Priory manors, with two-thirds of its sown acreage used for wheat. This high figure reflected its more fertile soils and lower proportion of downland compared with the Priory manors of Overton (in the Kennet valley) and Enford (in the Avon valley). The latter were more typical chalkland manors, except in their large size. They possessed demesnes of over 500 acres, extensive colonisation of the downlands (certainly at Overton) and a roughly even balance between the main crops of wheat, barley and oats. Both manors showed large-scale sheep–corn husbandry, with a close integration between the great sheep flocks and the arable farming (see Table 4.3). Such manors are representative of the great ecclesiastical manors so dominant in the agrarian economy of chalkland Wiltshire, but they also show the importance of tenant production. In 1311, the demesne crops at Alton produced 44 per cent of the total production of the parish, as measured by the tithes. By contrast, Overton and Enford produced much less: 29 per cent and 17 per cent respectively. It would be wrong, however, to regard the rest of the production as the work of the peasantry. Parish production included that of sub-manors and, as at Enford, the tenants included men of gentry status. Parish tithes have therefore been described as tenant rather than peasant production. They remind us that even the greatest of landowners were responsible for only a minority of total production.

In general, demesne and parish tithes show a similar balance of crops, suggesting that the evidence from demesne agriculture about cropping patterns may be of wider application. But there were differences (Table 4.4); at Alton the dominance of wheat was greater on the demesne than on the tenants' land. Barley was very much the second crop in importance but was much more widespread as a tenant crop. Oats were relatively insignificant, particularly among the tenantry. On the downland proper, Enford and Overton showed a greater emphasis on the poorer crops of barley and oats, with oats becoming particularly important on the demesne. At Enford wheat was much less important (under half the proportion of barley). Here, too, the tenants grew relatively more barley and less oats than the lord. At Overton, wheat was relatively low in importance (about a quarter of the tithe grain) with no significant difference between the cropping of the tenants and the demesne. But here the situation was different for barley and oats. Barley was by far the most important crop on the tenant lands but was much less important on the demesne (18 per cent less). By contrast, oats were more important on the demesne than on the tenant land. This may represent the large-scale production of oats on the thin downland soils, where the lord had expanded his cultivation on a massive scale in the thirteenth century. The tithe

---

70. Harrison, 'Field systems and demesne farming', table 6.

figures suggest that the evidence of the demesne may seriously overemphasise the importance of oats within the village economy, and that the large-scale demesne cultivation of oats was untypical of the manor as a whole.

Outside the chalklands the evidence is more limited. At Inglesham, in the Thames valley, cultivation was dominated by wheat and barley, with barley more important than wheat on the tenants' land. Here, as in the chalklands, oats was more important as a demesne crop than as a tenant one, while vetch and beans were more important as tenant crops. At Stratton St Margaret, the accounts provide figures only for the total tithe issues of the parish (i.e. the demesne and the tenants combined). The accounts suggest that in 1294 and 1295 wheat was the most important crop, followed fairly closely by barley and then oats. Oats, with about a quarter of the parish production, was more important than anywhere else apart from the demesne lands at Overton. By comparison, a large documented demesne within the parish (Stratton and Sevenhampton) shows that there was greater emphasis on wheat, with barley slightly less important and oats less so again. Comparison of the demesne and parish figures suggests that at Stratton, more than elsewhere, tenants may have concentrated on the cultivation of oats.

This limited Wiltshire evidence warrants comparison with similar material from neighbouring counties: Beaulieu Abbey's Coxwell (Berks) (1269–70); Bec Abbey's Combe (Hants) (1305–8 and 1332–3), Winchester Cathedral Priory's manor of Wootton (Hants) (1325–6 and 1337–8) and the bishopric of Winchester's possessions of Hambledon and East Meon (Hants) (1305–14).[71] This material also emphasises the role of wheat as the main cash crop, as at Great Coxwell and in Hambledon and East Meon (east Hampshire). It was not always, however, the most important crop (as at Combe and Wootton in north Hampshire). These two manors also showed that in the north Hampshire chalklands, as in Wiltshire, barley, together with bere, comprised the second most important crop. But barley was less prevalent in east Hampshire, at Hambledon and East Meon, reflecting the greater predominance of wheat and oats combinations on the Hampshire demesnes. In Wiltshire, oats were generally much less extensive as a crop than wheat or barley, except on some of the demesnes, but the situation was very different in Hampshire.[72] Here oats were the second most important tenant crop in east and north Hampshire, as well as frequently the largest one on the demesne. Rye was unusual in Wiltshire, with a small amount produced on the parish lands of Alton, but it was found in Berkshire and north and east Hampshire. The mixtures of dredge and bere were found in relatively small quantities on most manors in Wiltshire and elsewhere.

These variations in cropping were probably influenced by geographical and environmental factors, as well as the impact of the market and society. Wheat seems to have been the main cash crop, with greater specialisation in certain places. Barley was more important on the Wiltshire manors than on those in Hampshire, and was generally more important on the tenant lands than on the demesne lands. Was this

---

71. I am grateful to Dr Jan Titow for the East Meon and Hambledon figures ('Field crops and their cultivation' – HRO 97M97/C1). The figures for the non-Wiltshire manors are included in Hare, 'Lord, tenant and the market', 132–46.
72. Hare, 'The bishop and the prior', 194–6.

because it was the main subsistence crop, or was it a sign of growing demand for ale to which the peasantry were more responsive? It may have been an advantage of barley that it could serve both purposes and allow a shift between consumption and sale depending on the circumstances and harvests of the year. The greater prevalence of oats on the demesnes may have reflected the lord's cultivation of large areas of poor soil that lay outside the open field and were dependent on large sheep flocks to maintain fertility.

We lack comparable tithe evidence for chalkland sheep and, in its absence, we need to turn to the assessment for the fifteenth of 1225. This has for long made a key contribution to discussion of medieval agriculture, thanks to an important article by M.M. Postan.[73] The assessment covers parts of south Wiltshire, mainly in the chalklands: a group of manors in the Ebble valley; the downland manors of Damerham and Martin belonging to Glastonbury Abbey; a group of downland manors overlooking the upper Nadder; and a group of villages in the vale of Wardour. It contains a list of the stock of the villagers and of the demesnes. Given that the assessment comes from an area that contained much chalk downland, it was the relative lack of sheep and livestock that impressed Postan. He suggested that the number of sheep in the area in 1225 was about one-fifth or one-third of that which the well-informed eighteenth-century agricultural writer, Thomas Davies, had regarded as adequate to dung the lands.[74] For Postan, it supported the model of thirteenth-century society which had become dangerously dominated by grain production: 'in which population was abundant and growing, land was scarce and getting scarcer, and men in search of sustenance were forced to till the lands which in other and more spacious periods would and should have been used as pasture'. To summarise, it was 'an age in which the frontier between corn and hoof had moved very far, indeed too far, cornwards'.[75]

Such a gloomy picture needs qualification. Despite the very fragmentary nature of our evidence we can compare these figures with later ones for a few of the same demesnes and look at what was happening elsewhere at the same time. Such a comparison suggests that these demesne flocks were untypically small in size. Elsewhere in Wiltshire some chalkland estates already maintained large flocks of over 1,000 sheep, as at Knoyle, Downton, the Ogbournes and Whitsbury.[76] Other flocks, as at Overton, grew massively during the thirteenth century. But such large flocks did not yet exist in the area covered by the assessments, while many of the demesnes appear to have still been leased out in 1225. The largest flock was at Damerham, where 570 sheep were kept, and the next highest was only 400 (at Berwick).[77] The Damerham figure was comparable to the figures recorded a few years before in 1210, but was only one-third of that a century later (1,600 and 1,531 in 1333–4). We do not possess any later figures for Tisbury and Donhead until the fifteenth century, but they

---

73. M.M. Postan, 'Village livestock in the thirteenth century', reprinted in his *Essays on medieval agriculture and general problems of the medieval economy* (Cambridge, 1973), 214–48.
74. Ibid., 235–7; the document was subsequently published: *Rolls of the fifteenth of the ninth year of the reign of Henry III*, 46–106.
75. Postan, *Essays on medieval agriculture*, 247.
76. *Pipe roll 1210–11*, 91–2, 36; TNA: PRO E106/2/2 and 2/3; *Interdict documents*, 25.
77. *Rolls of the fifteenth of the ninth year of the reign of Henry III*, 91, 69.

suggest that here the demesne flocks subsequently grew substantially.[78] To the student of later demesne sheep farming it is the relatively small scale of these flocks that is such a remarkable feature of these assessments, but the situation in 1225 was probably untypical of the thirteenth century as a whole and would underestimate the later availability of manure. Although we can make comparisons only for the demesne, the growth here is likely to have reflected a parallel growth among the tenantry, as market demand increased for sheep and wool. Moreover, while some of the demesne manure may have been concentrated on enclosed portions of the demesne some would have helped to enrich peasant arable production.

Flocks grew in the later Middle Ages, but they also increased dramatically in subsequent centuries. By post-medieval standards these flocks of 1225 were very small, but medieval farmers were constrained by the availability of winter feed. Here the great agricultural breakthrough arose from the development of the artificial floated water-meadows in the seventeenth century. These allowed more hay and an earlier growth of meadow, and thus enormously increased the size of flock that could be maintained during the winter. Larger flocks in turn meant more dung and higher arable yields.[79] What was regarded as essential stocking in the eighteenth century would have been unimaginable before this development.

---

78. Ibid., 71, 76; Keil, 'Estates of Glastonbury', table 22; VCH *Wilts* 13, 226 & 148.
79. E. Kerridge, 'Agriculture, 1500–1793', in VCH *Wilts* 4, 282–9.

Chapter 5

Agriculture *c.* 1380–*c.* 1440

The leasing of the English demesnes was already well underway by 1380, but in the chalklands of southern England demesne agriculture remained in a resilient state. Here it survived, albeit on a slightly smaller scale, until about the 1430s, while many lords continued to keep large demesne flocks for much longer. By 1380, however, agriculture faced very different conditions. Society had been freed from demographic pressure by the devastation of the Black Death, by continued epidemics and by possible changes in fertility. Agriculture now needed to be refocused to cater for different commercial conditions and demands: living standards had risen as the balance of land and labour had shifted in the interests of labour. In Wiltshire these national and international trends were reinforced by the growing cloth industry, which both generated demands for more labour and produced a population with more money to spend on food and drink: more meat, better-quality grains, or the relatively wasteful conversion of grain to drink. Here, the last half-century of seigneurial agriculture was not a phase of sad decline, but a time when lords were still heavily engaged in direct cultivation and necessary buildings, or varied their crops and the balance between pastoral and arable farming according to changing market pressures. In the last decades of the fourteenth century lords used their large capital resources to maintain arable production and to develop pastoral farming. In the fifteenth century they stabilised their activity at a generally lower level until they gave up direct cultivation. Moreover, when leasing occurred, particularly in the chalklands, the new tenants continued the existing pattern of large-scale agriculture. Here leasing did not generally lead to a reduction in the scale of agriculture, to a break-up of the demesne or to a shift towards a more subsistence economy.[1]

While this chapter is largely about the better-documented agriculture of the chalklands, it also looks at the limited available evidence on peasant agriculture and at signs of the emerging pastoral economy that was to be such a feature of the clay vale in subsequent centuries.[2] With the exception of the estates of the bishopric of Winchester, most of the surviving documentation about agriculture belongs to the early fifteenth century, so this chapter is mainly concerned with the period before about 1440. The treatment of the clay vale draws upon the limited material from the whole of the fifteenth century. The later continuation of sheep farming and the leasing of the chalkland demesnes are dealt with in the next chapter.

---

1. J.N. Hare, 'Regional prosperity in fifteenth-century England: some evidence from Wessex', in M. Hicks (ed.), *Revolution and consumption in late medieval England* (Woodbridge, 2001), 115–9, and for a more pessimistic view, M.M. Postan, *Essays on medieval agriculture and general problems of the medieval economy* (Cambridge, 1973), 48, 44; M.M. Postan, *The medieval economy and society* (Harmondsworth, 1975), 158. For examples of continuities elsewhere see, e.g. C. Dyer, *Warwickshire farming, 1349–c.1520: preparations for agricultural revolution*, Dugdale Society Occasional Papers (Oxford, 1981).
2. E. Kerridge, 'Agriculture 1500–1793', in VCH *Wilts* 4, 43–64.

Arable farming

The chalklands of Wiltshire continued to be characterised by large-scale demesne agriculture and a sheep–corn husbandry that was dominated by large sheep flocks. There was little evidence of the shrinkage of demesne arable except on the estates of the bishopric of Winchester. By 1408–11 Downton was cultivating only 56 per cent of its early-fourteenth-century acreage and Bishopstone 78 per cent. Knoyle and Fonthill were both now leased, but their previous decline in demesne sowing had followed the trend at Downton.[3] But this decline was already underway at the end of the thirteenth century and continued in the first half of the fourteenth century and afterwards.[4] Lords could use the high demand for land, and therefore high rents, to lease some land to the peasantry, and some of the most dramatic shrinkage of the demesne occurred before, not after, the Black Death; on the eve of this cataclysm the demesne at Downton cultivated only 39 per cent of its early-thirteenth-century acreage.[5] In general, the long-term shrinkage of acreage resulted from a reduction in the cultivation of marginal downland, as at Edington (belonging to Romsey Abbey) (Table 5.1). The manors of the Cathedral Priory, by contrast, showed much less reduction in grain acreages: it had already leased the demesnes at Stockton and Wroughton, but its main Wiltshire manors of Enford and Alton showed little sign of demesne shrinkage and this was also generally the case on most of its Hampshire manors.[6]

The relative importance of the different crops changed during the fourteenth century (see Table 5.1). The national picture shows a growing concentration on the high-quality crops, whether wheat for bread or barley for ale, and these developments are found in Wiltshire.[7] Oats and the poorer mixed crops became much less important, both nationally and locally. The proportion of land given over to barley either expanded or remained constant. As shown in the previous chapter, there were already signs of an increased demand for barley in Salisbury's hinterland in the early fourteenth century, at Bishopstone and Enford. Such specialisation grew with the expansion of the west Wiltshire cloth industry: the most dramatic increases were at Edington, Alton Priors and East Knoyle, on the fringes of this area. At Bishopstone and Enford the importance of barley remained high but did not grow significantly in relation to other crops, and at Enford it even declined. The chalk soils of the valleys were highly suitable for barley production and now emerged into the role which they maintained for the next few centuries, as a major producer of malted barley, enhancing the demand for labour and the value of the product. At Urchfont barley was

---

3. D.L. Farmer, 'Grain yields on the Winchester manors in the later Middle Ages', *EcHR*, 2nd series 30 (1977), 562.
4. J.N. Hare, 'The bishop and the prior: demesne agriculture in medieval Hampshire', *AHR*, 54 (2006), 193, 200–1.
5. J.Z. Titow, *Winchester yields: a study in medieval agricultural productivity* (Cambridge, 1972), 139.
6. No late account rolls are known for Overton; Hare, 'The bishop and the prior', 193, 201–2.
7. B.M.S. Campbell, K.C. Bartley and J.P. Power, 'The demesne-farming systems of post-Black Death England: a classification', *AHR*, 44 (1996), 131–79. See also now Campbell's *English seigniorial agriculture, 1250–1450* (Cambridge, 2000); J.A. Galloway, 'London's grain supply: changes in production, distribution and consumption during the fourteenth century', *Franco-British Studies*, 20 (1995), 31–2.

Table 5.1
Demesne crops after 1380.

Chalk downlands	Date	Wheat	Rye	Barley	Dredge	Oats	Peas etc.	Total (acres)	%age of pre-Black Death acreage*
Enford	1403	37.9		36.3		25.9		470	83.8
Durrington	1354–9	30.9		39.3	12.9	7.2	9.6	230.5	75.9
Bishopstone	1410	36.4		31.8		15.2	16.7	132	75.0
Downton	1410	32.9		43.9		10.3	12.9	155	30.5
Edington	1414	51.3		24.1	7.5	15.0	2.1	468	76.3
Warminster	1379–80	49.3		31.9		18.8		213	
Winterbourne Stoke	1409	41.2		41.9	7.4	9.5		148	
Heytesbury	1409	45.3		31.5	5.2	16.0	2.0	600	
Ebbesbourne Wake	1381	39.9		38.5		16.1	5.5	218	
	1383	40.5		36.2		23.3		81.5	
Longbridge Deverill (parsonage)	1393,94	31.5		37.4	19.6	22.7		48.5	

Vales of Pewsey and Wardour and lower chalk

Alton Priors	1373, 95	55.3	33.0	3.9	7.8			427	104.8
Potterne	1426	56.7		16.3	7.9	11.2	7.9	178	
East Knoyle	1375, 95	41.8		27.1		27.8	3.3	184.3	77.3
Fonthill Bishop	1375, 95	34.6		36.7		20.4	8.3	105.6	75.7
Upton Knoyle	1375, 95	35.7		28.1		28.9	7.3	65.8	67.1
Teffont	1404	41.5		25.4	13.1	16.9	3.1	130	60.2

Non chalk

Bromham	1381	36.8	12.7	20.1	10.8	17.6	2.0	204	86.3
	1402	35.1	14.0	19.3	7.0	21.9		114	48.2
Homegrange, Stanley	1415	31.1		10.4		48.8	9.7	149.5	
Bradford	1368	41.7		14.5	12.9	31.0		326.3	
Kington St Michael	1450	32.3		19.9	18.6	29.4		102	

Notes: * This figure represents the total acreage given as a percentage of the pre-Black Death acreage (see Table 4.2).
Sources: BL Harl Rl X/7; WCM 5944; Pipe Roll 1409–10; TNA: PRO SC6/1052/2; WRO 845/manorial papers/14/1380; I.J.E. Keil, 'Impropriator and benefice in the later Middle Ages', WAM, 58 (1963), 359; WCL Alton 1373, 1395; SDC press 3 Potterne; R. Payne, 'Agrarian conditions on the Wiltshire estates of the duchy of Lancaster, the lords Hungerford and the bishopric of Winchester', PhD thesis (London, 1940), Appendix I; J.N. Hare, 'Lord and tenant in Wiltshire, c.1380–1520, with particular reference to regional and seigneurial variations', PhD thesis (London, 1976), appendix table III, 349; TNA: PRO SC6/1054/9; WRO 1742/6786 (Bradford); BL Add Rl 15142 (Kington).

still sent to St Mary's Abbey, Winchester, but now its value rose from £8 for the grain to £9 for the malted barley.[8] At Downton the tithe returns show that already by the early fifteenth century, small landowners and tenant farmers were shifting to barley on a larger scale than their lord, the bishop of Winchester, thus suggesting that the demesne figures may underestimate the scale of this agricultural change. At Enford barley was already important in 1403, but the evidence of a later stock and land lease suggests that by 1485 it was perceived to be the largest crop, comprising just under half the seed grain provided for the lease.

Wheat and barley remained the pre-eminent crops in chalkland Wiltshire, even though wheat, traditionally the main demesne crop, was now occasionally overtaken by barley. Oats, a crop widely sown on thin downland soils, showed some dramatic falls, particularly at Bishopstone and Edington, and in neighbouring Hampshire. As the demesne acreage fell demand shifted to the better-quality bread and ale grains (wheat and barley) now preferred for human consumption.[9]

At Bromham, away from the chalklands, comparison of an account for 1344–5 with those for the 1380s suggests that here barley remained constant but wheat and oats came to occupy a significantly larger part of the arable. This was one of the few Wiltshire manors to grow rye, but this crop now declined sharply and ultimately disappeared. Other accounts for the manor suggest that the fall occurred particularly after 1377 and that the crop had ceased to be grown by 1422.[10] In general, legumes seemed to be of little importance. At Bradford, also away from the chalklands, wheat and oats were pre-eminent and barley constituted the third crop.

The crop preferences for this period seem to be confirmed by the evidence from those manors for which documentation survives for the later period only. On the Hungerford manors of Heytesbury and Teffont Ewias, and the lay manor of Ebbesborne Wake, wheat was the largest crop, with about 40 per cent of the sown acreage; barley came second, although it was substantially more important on the latter manor, and oats trailed a distant third. It was rare for oats to occupy as much as 20 per cent of the demesne acreage, whereas in the early part of the century other manors suggest that figures in the 25–40 per cent range were common (see Table 4.2). Such figures indicate both similarities and contrasts to the wider picture of seigneurial agricultural production that is emerging from national figures.[11] Both national and local evidence shows an increased emphasis on the quality grains and their products, with an increase in wheaten bread and malted barley and a decline in oats. There is no general evidence of increased areas of legumes, although individual manors may show significant change. The great downland pastures may provide an explanation for the contrast with other areas. Not only did their grass provide

---

8. BL Add Rl 19728.
9. Hare, 'The bishop and the prior', 195–6, 202–3.
10. Rye acreages 1345: 60a; 1377: 53a; 1381: 26a; 1421: 14a; 1432 no rye but demesne arable continued. See below table 6.3 and J.N. Hare, 'Lord and tenant in Wiltshire, c.1380–1520, with particular reference to regional and seigneurial variations', PhD thesis (London, 1976), Appendix table III, 349.
11. Campbell et al., 'Demesne-farming systems', 131–7.

admirable foodstuffs for the animals, but the manure renewed the fertility of the soils without the use of legumes.[12]

On some manors agriculture was geared to the domestic needs of lords and the revival of demesne agriculture on some of the estates of the lords Hungerford may have partly reflected household needs, although large quantities of grain continued to be sold.[13] Winchester Cathedral Priory continued to be a major consumer of manorial produce, receiving an annual minimum of about 1,500 quarters of estate grain in the opening decade of the century.[14] Of this grain, wheat made up 38 per cent, barley 43 per cent, oats 14 per cent and dredge 6 per cent. Almost all the barley was used for brewing, being sent to the cellarer for the prior's brewery, in contrast to the wheat, oats, some very small quantities of barley, and livestock, which were all sent to the curtarian for the kitchen.[15]

Sheep and wool farming

Sheep flocks expanded dramatically in the fourteenth century. Campbell's national sample showed an 87 per cent increase in the century after the Black Death.[16] In Wiltshire, and especially in the chalklands, the demesne flocks at the end of the century were as large as before and remained of national importance, but their growth was at a lower level.

On the estates of the bishopric of Winchester (in Wiltshire, Hampshire and beyond) numbers grew dramatically after the Black Death, after which stability was reached at a new level. During the 1340s the numbers of sheep on the estate as a whole had fluctuated around 14,000, but they rose from the later 1340s to peak in 1369 at 35,000. After a period of decline and recovery, the flocks averaged 33,000 between 1388 and 1397. Bishop Wykeham's death led to a fall of about 8,000, as stock was sold by his executors, after which a levelling off followed in the early fifteenth century. Flocks were larger than in the immediately preceding period, and greater than those of the early fourteenth century.[17] On the Cathedral Priory estate, expansion seems to have been significant but less dramatic, and its Wiltshire manors

---

12. E. Newman, 'Medieval sheep-corn farming: how much grain yield could each sheep support?' *Agricultural History Review*, 50 (2002), 164–80.
13. R. Scott, 'Medieval agriculture', in VCH *Wilts* 4, 16. Between 1340 and 1429, a quarter to two thirds of the grain was sold at Heytesbury, and between 1400 and 1450 a third to a half of the grain was sold at Winterbourne Stoke including half the wheat and half the barley.
14. Hare, 'The bishop and the prior', 189. The figures are both an approximation and an underestimate. Total 1,580 quarters: wheat 601, barley 672, oats 219, dredge 88.
15. Calculated from J. Greatrex, 'The administration of Winchester Cathedral Priory in the time of Cardinal Beaufort', PhD thesis (Ottawa, 1972). The distinction between grain for the cellarer and for the curtarian had not been noted systematically, but, where there was any doubt, I checked the originals.
16. Campbell et al., 'Demesne-farming systems', 134.
17. M.J. Stephenson, 'Wool yields in the medieval economy', *EcHR*, 2nd series 41 (1988), 385–6; with Wykeham's death the flock of East Knoyle was disposed of and not initially resumed: *Pipe roll 1409–10*; Hare, 'The bishop and the prior', 204.

generated an increase of less than 20 per cent between c.1300 and 1389/91, appreciably less than Campbell's national figures.[18]

Winchester Cathedral Priory was second only to the bishopric as a sheep master, and possessed the second largest flock known in southern England. Moreover, the fortunate survival of its stockbook allows us to see the estate as a whole at the peak of its sheep farming.[19] This source provides summaries of the livestock on each priory manor, including the sheep, drawn up mainly during a mid-yearly inspection in April, for the years between 1389 and 1392. It provides much of the information that would be available in countless manorial stock accounts, but covering the whole estate. This remarkably valuable and unusual source allows us to view the Wiltshire manors within the context of the wider estate (Table 5.2). In 1390, the priory's main estate contained 20 different flocks scattered throughout Wiltshire and Hampshire with a total of 20,357 sheep. By way of comparison, there were 4,638 on the estate of the bishopric of Worcester in 1389.[20] None of the other estates with manors in Wiltshire seems likely to have come near the scale of the priory flock.

The Wiltshire manors of the Cathedral Priory played an important role in the organisation of the estate. Overton and Enford possessed the largest flocks on the estate, apart from the huge home manor of Barton, next to Winchester itself. Stockton and Alton had much smaller flocks, the former being a small manor and the latter, in the vale of Pewsey, having less chalkland pasture. Wroughton lay just off the chalklands and had no flock of its own, although its land might have been used by those of neighbouring Overton.

Within the scattered estate, sheep were driven from one manor to another. Such transfers were partly aimed at correcting temporary deficiencies, such as when murrain struck particularly hard at an individual flock, or when a manor had a surplus of one kind of sheep. But there were also places where a specialist flock was kept: the manor concentrating on breeding flocks of ewes, the larger wool crop of wethers or the immature hoggasters. In the early part of the century Stockton had possessed a breeding flock, but this had ceased by 1390. It was now provided with young sheep from other manors, and concentrated on a downland flock producing wool and meat. In the later fourteenth century such new stock usually came from the Cathedral Priory manors of Alton, Enford and Overton. By contrast, Alton, in the more sheltered vale of Pewsey and with much less high downland, had no wethers but maintained a breeding flock. Similar contrasts could be seen on the Hampshire manors, with the

---

18. Was growth less obvious in those areas where sheep had already become a key part of the rural economy or were his figures over-influenced by the fluctuations on the well-documented estates of the bishopric of Winchester or of Norfolk?
19. The comment that this was the peak of its production is based on comparison with individual manorial accounts of the Wiltshire manors for the early fourteenth century (see also table 4.3, and the longer runs for a few of the Hampshire manors tabulated in the works of J.S. Drew: 'The manor of Chilbolton', 'The manor of Silkstead', 'The manor of Houghton', and 'The manor of Michelmersh' (unpublished typescripts, 1945, 1947, 1943, 1943)). See also Hare, 'The bishop and the prior', 198–9 and 204. Some manors show occasional higher figures, but the generalisation remains valid.
20. C. Dyer, *Lords and peasants in a changing society: the estates of the bishopric of Worcester, 680–1540* (Cambridge, 1980), 134.

Table 5.2
Livestock on the Wiltshire manors of Winchester Cathedral Priory, 1390.

	Cart horses	Plough horses	Horses	Total Horses	Oxen	Bull	Cow	Bullock	One year	Calves	Total Cattle	Wethers	Rams	Ewes	Lambs	Total sheep	Pigs	Piglets	Total Pigs
Stockton	5			5	14						14	505			111	616	44	39	83
Enford	4	12		16	20	2	10	7	6	6	51	952	18	556	356	1882	44	52	96
Overton	5	3		8	27	1	10	8	8	8	62	975	19	556	350	1900	76	57	133
Alton	4	4		8	32	1	8	6	5	6	58		12	454	148	614	45	42	87
Wroughton	4			4	16		12	9			37								
Total	93	99	3	195	405	19	189	92	97	109	911	9216	223	6932	3996	20367	975	834	1809

Source: WCL Stockbook. The figures for the whole estate in 1390 are given in J.N. Hare, 'The bishop and the prior: demesne agriculture in medieval Hampshire', AHR, 54 (2006), 206.

breeding flocks on the more sheltered pastures and the hardier wether flocks kept on the upper downland pastures. While most of the movements were short-distance others went much further, and sheep from Wiltshire ended up at Winchester or the manors of east Hampshire. Thus, in 1391, sheep from Alton went to Stockton, Sutton and Hannington; from Overton to Mapledurham, Wonston and Hurstbourne; and from Enford to Stockton, Hannington and Hurstbourne.

The Cathedral Priory was exceptional in the scale of its flocks and the documentation of its stockbook, but it was not exceptional in the size of its individual manorial flocks. Downland sheep flocks remained large until beyond the end of the fourteenth century. On two of the most extensive manors of St Mary's Abbey, Winchester, the abbess maintained a flock of over 1,200 sheep at Urchfont in the period from the 1450s to the 1470s and a flock of between 700 and 900 sheep at All Cannings (see Table 6.1). The abbess of Romsey had over 2,000 sheep at Edington in 1414, a substantial rise from the 1,700/1,608 in 1284.[21] On the estates of the lords Hungerford there were flocks of 1,800–2,400 at Heytesbury and 940–1,330 at Winterborne Stoke in the fifteenth century. There were more than 1,000 sheep at Alton Barnes in 1391, although the number had fallen substantially by 1401.[22] In the small Deverill valley and its extensive downland beyond, there were flocks of over 1,000 at each of Brixton Deverill, Kingston Deverill and Monkton Deverill, and over 800 at Longbridge Deverill.[23] Not all lords maintained large flocks and that at Durrington largely ceased in the 1350s, having only 28 sheep by 1358; but its three-field system may suggest that its agriculture was already much less focused on the large sheep flocks, although tenants and the lessee would still have provided sheep manure.[24]

Chalkland demesne flocks were stable or expanded during the fourteenth century, but in other parts of the county they frequently declined. At Trowbridge the flock had disappeared by 1381. At Hilmarton a flock was introduced, or reintroduced, by 1365, but had ceased by 1385.[25] At Bromham there were 387 sheep in 1345, but flock numbers fell markedly to 113 in 1376. Despite a period of recovery in the 1380s and 1390s, when the flock size reached over 200, numbers fell by 1398 and again after 1412, before the flock was incorporated in the demesne lease in 1424. By then, however, only 25 sheep were included (see Table 6.2).[26] The largest flock found so far

---

21. TNA: PRO SC6/1052/2; SC6/1052/1.
22. KCM WB2/1; Scott, 'Medieval agriculture', 25; NCA 5827.
23. Brixton Deverill: 1386–7, 1,195 and 1,062; 1398–9, 834 and 899 (KCM WB2/1 & 2/2); Kingston Deverill: the highest known figure was 1,015 in 1407 (see also table 6.1); Monkton Deverill: 1333–4, 886 and 523 (I.J.E. Keil, 'The estates of Glastonbury Abbey in the later Middle Ages', PhD thesis (Bristol, 1964), Table 22); increased after Black Death until a flock of 1,000 became common. Longbridge Deverill 400–300 after second half of the fifteenth century, but 846 in 1420 (Ibid., 133; D. Farmer, 'The famuli in the later Middle Ages', in R.H. Britnell and J. Hatcher (eds), *Progress and problems in medieval England: essays in honour of Edward Miller* (Cambridge, 1996), 221).
24. Hare, 'Durrington', 139–40.
25. Bad.Mun. 110/5/3.
26. Hare, 'Lord and tenant', Appendix, 347–8.

in this area (and itself comparable to some of the great downland flocks) was at Bradford, a huge ecclesiastical estate, where there were 910 sheep in 1367 and 1,072 in 1372.[27]

The close integration of the flocks and the transfer of sheep between specialist flocks, seen on the Cathedral Priory estate, was also found on many other estates, such as the bishoprics of Winchester and Salisbury.[28] On the Hungerford and Burgassh lands the breeding flocks were maintained on the Somerset manors of Farleigh, Holt and Wellow, which then sent lambs to the Wiltshire manors. On occasion, two manors operated together with a breeding flock in one place and the wether flock at the other, as on the duchy of Lancaster manors of Collingbourne and Everleigh, the Glastonbury manors of Longbridge and Monkton Deverill or the distant Netley manors of Kingston Deverill and Waddon (Dorset). Romsey Abbey's manor of Edington kept breeding and wool flocks, but there was also a related breeding flock at Ashton, to which Edington supplied ewes and from which it received lambs.[29] But the flocks were clearly linked to individual manors. Some manors became increasingly dependent on the market for replacement stock, getting rid of their breeding flock, as at Urchfont after 1443 and at Aldbourne between 1295/6 and 1400.[30]

The great estates, as noted in Chapter 4, usually sent their wool to a central store from which it was sold in a single transaction in order to maximise the price.[31] This also happened on the estates of Winchester Cathedral Priory, the abbeys of St Mary at Winchester, Hyde, Wilton and Romsey, the bishoprics of Winchester and Salisbury and the lords Hungerford.[32] Sometimes it was sold locally, where a manor was relatively isolated from the rest of the estate, as with Kingston Deverill (Netley Abbey) or Bromham (Battle Abbey). On the duchy of Lancaster estate there was no central store, but the wool may have been sold through a central transaction, as in 1407, when the duchy sold the wool of the four main wool-producing Wiltshire manors in a single transaction.[33]

Sheep farming also produced meat, whether for the household or for sale. On the estates of the Cathedral Priory only a small proportion of the flock separated as kebbs for fattening and disposal would have gone to the priory itself: in 1391, 3,794 sheep were so separated and only 600 of these were to be sent to the lord's household. At Enford in 1403 five times as many sheep were sold locally, for the markets of Salisbury and west Wiltshire, as were sent to Winchester.[34] The large size of the

---

27. R.B. Harvey and B.K. Harvey, 'Bradford-on-Avon in the fourteenth century', *Wiltshire Archaeological and Natural History Magazine*, 86 (1993), 124; BL Harl Rl X/7.
28. R. Payne, 'Agrarian conditions on the Wiltshire estates of the duchy of Lancaster, the lords Hungerford and the bishopric of Winchester', PhD thesis (London, 1940); the few surviving accounts for the bishopric of Salisbury show movements between the manors of Potterne, Cannings and Lavington: SDC Potterne.
29. Scott, 'Medieval agriculture'; TNA: PRO DL29/683/11068-, 684/11074; Keil, 'Estates of Glastonbury', 127; WRO 192/32; TNA: PRO SC6/1052/2.
30. HRO 83M85 W/1; TNA: PRO DL29/1/1.
31. An exception to this occurred at Littleton in 1400 (WCL Littleton 1400).
32. SDC Potterne 1426; Scott, 'Medieval agriculture', 20.
33. TNA: PRO DL29/710/11432; Payne, 'Agrarian conditions', 215.
34. WCL, Stockbook; BL Harl Rl X/7.

flocks suggests that the manors were producing more than a single household would have required. Sheep continued to be milked for the manufacture of cheese,[35] although this practice was becoming less common.[36] Finally, sheep provided some of the raw materials for the leather industry and the large-scale export of hides.

Although contemporaries may not yet have perceived manure to be the most valuable product of the sheep, as in the eighteenth century,[37] they were evidently aware of the value of systematic folding, whereby the flocks were concentrated on a limited area within wattle hurdles and moved from place to place for concentrated manuring. At Durrington in 1389 the lessee had to fold the demesne lands in order to maintain them in a suitable state, and in 1435 he had to deposit all dung coming from the demesne lands on the same land and to manure these lands sufficiently with the fold. At Downton the manure from the demesne was to be deposited on it, and the land was to be kept manured and sown properly. Upon the commencement of the lease the lessee received twelve well-fallowed acres, of which six were manured with the fold and domestic manure (*fimo domestic*). A lease of 1455 at the Ogbournes required land to be manured from the demesne flocks. The lessee was to put the folds on the demense land and received an allowance in the first and last year for the cost of doing this. The scale of this allowance, 26s 8d, suggests that this was a regular burden.[38] At Urchfont a shepherd was allowed to keep the flock outside the fold, presumably on his own lands, for four nights.[39] At other times the flock's manure was leased out. Thus at Warminster £6 12s 8d came from the lease of various demesne lands, but in addition £1 14s 8d came from manuring these lands, with differential rates for those lands with wheat and those with oats, while another £3 18s 4d came from manuring various other places with the fold. In an open-field system we must be looking at a situation in which the flocks were being enclosed within separate strips and not left to wander over the fields. Lords also rented out the manure of the flock at Monkton Deverill, Kingston Deverill and Aldbourne.[40] Both at Aldbourne and at Warminster this annual rent came to over £5, a substantial sum, suggesting that the manure was highly appreciated. All these examples come from valley and downland manors, but even when the lord gave up demesne arable the integration of arable and pasture remained. This was not a sheep monoculture.

How profitable were these large sheep flocks? It is difficult to resolve this question because the income from wool sales was often not included in the manorial accounts. These sales were carried out as a central estate transaction but formed an important part of the manorial profitability, as is suggested by comparison of the annual wool sales with the rent paid to the lord for the lease of the demesne arable. On three

---

35. e.g. BL Harl Rl X/7.
36. E. Miller, 'Farming practice and technique. I: The southern counties', in *The agrarian history of England and Wales*, 3, 295–6.
37. T. Davis, *General view of the agriculture of Wiltshire* (London, 1794).
38. WCM 5650m; 22992 f.115, f.110; KCM Ledger Book I, f.VIII.
39. WRO 192/20c m3.
40. e.g. TNA: PRO DL29/728/11991; WRO 845 Warminster accounts; I.J.E. Keil, 'Impropriator and benefice in the later Middle Ages', *WAM*, 58 (1963), 351–61; WRO 192/32; TNA: PRO DL29/730/12007; for other examples see Miller, 'Farming practice and techniques', 290.

Table 5.3
The finances of sheep farming on the manors of the duchy of Lancaster (averages for the years 1400–1406 and 1435–9).

	No. of sheep	Sale of wool	Sale of stock	Expenses*	Purchase	Profit ** of stock
Aldbourne						
1400–6	981	£26.2	£7.8	£3.4	£9.7	£20.9
1435–9	781	£20.1	£8.3	£2.4	£15.0	£11.0
Collingbourne & Everleigh						
1400–6	1443	£32.8	£12.5	£3.3		£40.9
1435–9	1104	£15.1	£4.9	£7.6	Nil	£12.8

Notes: *These calculations are based on manorial accounts and on the duchy valors and receivers' accounts. It is difficult to establish a complete list of expenses since some are listed under headings that incorporate expenditure on other aspects of the manor. There is either no separate section of shepherds' wages or it is not consistently adhered to. I have not therefore included the shepherds' wages. The limitations of this column would not affect either the fall in sales or the general movement of profits.
** See the above note appended to Table 5.1 emphasising that this column excludes some expenditure such as the shepherd's wages. It will therefore slightly exaggerate the profit levels.
Sources: TNA: PRO DL29/728/11991, 729/11993, 11994, 11997, 11999, 12002, 12005; 730/12007; 731/12023; 732/12034; 733/12037, 120939, 12040, 12041.

manors of the duchy of Lancaster in 1400 and 1406 the wool sales represented about three times the rent of the lease of the demesne arable at Aldbourne and Everleigh and about twice that at Collingbourne.[41] At Kingston Deverill in the same decade we find 41 per cent and 24 per cent of the total valor of the manor coming from the sale of wool, the latter low figure resulting from unusually high sales of sheep which increased the total income of the manor and thus diminished the proportion that came from wool. Similar comparison of wool sales and total valor on the duchy of Lancaster manors produces comparable figures.[42]

Such figures provide a rather more optimistic assessment of the profits of seigneurial sheep farming than that put forward by T.H. Lloyd, who, among other manors, made use of many of the same duchy of Lancaster estates. He argued that in the 1430s the duchy was making a loss on sheep farming in Aldbourne, Berwick and Chipping Lambourne (Berks.), while at Collingbourne and Everleigh there were only very narrow profit margins. But although income fell, and there were evident short-term difficulties, the flocks still earned significant revenues in difficult times. At Aldbourne the profitability of sheep farming changed dramatically between the first and fourth decades of the century. Wool sales were high and sheep farming highly profitable at the beginning of the century, producing an average net income between 1400 and 1406 of about £21. The annual balance varied substantially from £6.7 to £41.5, partly as a result of the scale and irregularity of livestock purchases required. In

---

41. The figure in 1400 was also twice the demesne lease for the Hampshire manor of Somborne but only two-thirds that for the Dorset manor of Shapwick (TNA: PRO DL29/728/11991).
42. Hare, 'Lord and tenant', table VI. With the exception of Everleigh in 1406 where the relative importance of the wool sales was reduced by high sales of stock and low sales of wool, wool sales fluctuated between 27% and 44% of the annual valor.

1407 an exceptionally large amount was spent on new stock (£44 16s 8d). By the 1430s the situation had been transformed and the income from sheep had fallen to about half[43] (Table 5.3). The fall at the linked manors of Collingbourne and Everleigh was even greater, to almost a third of the earlier total. The reasons were varied. The fall in the flock size to about 80 per cent at Aldbourne and Collingbourne and about 70 per cent at Everleigh cut the revenue from wool sales. This may have been the key element at Aldbourne, where the wool sales fell approximately in line with the decline in sheep numbers and the income from stock sales showed no drop. Revenues were affected by the vulnerability of the breeding flocks, as at Collingbourne where in 1435 an illness (slynkittes) meant that over half the ewes had still births, leading to a drop both in its total flock and in that of Everleigh in the following year.[44] An alternative approach was to buy rather than breed replacement stock, although this did not avoid the problems of falling wool prices or fleece yields.[45] But more and more lords ceased to maintain a flock of ewes and depended on the market for restocking, as at Urchfont by 1443.

Nevertheless, sheep farming remained attractive. When John Stannford, or Stamford, first leased the pastures of Everleigh and Collingbourne in 1443 the rent of the demesnes rose by £12 6s 8d to take into account the rent of the pasture but not the sheep (which had been sold to him). But Stannford had for many years been stockman to the duchy manors in this area, and was surely in a better position than most to assess the likely profitability of pastures. He presumably expected them to produce more than his new rent and to justify his purchase of large flocks of sheep. Despite depressed wool prices and lower wool yields the readiness of such men to undertake the leasing of the great demesne pastures suggests that sheep farming could still produce worthwhile profits. Moreover, not all the great estates had given up sheep farming by the end of the century, as in south Wiltshire and Dorset on ecclesiastical estates such as those of Shaftesbury and Wilton Abbeys.[46]

Pigs, cattle and other chalkland livestock

Historians have frequently neglected the other demesne animals that were an important part of chalkland farming. The stockbook of Winchester Cathedral Priory can again be used to provide a snapshot of all the livestock on a large estate in the chalklands of southern England. In 1390, in addition to the 20,357 sheep, there were 1808 pigs, 929 cattle and 209 horses. Comparison with the near-contemporary account of the bishop of Worcester for 1389 shows the distinctiveness of chalkland agriculture compared with agriculture elsewhere, in this case the west midlands. Sheep and horses were relatively more important on the Winchester estate; pigs and cattle were more important on that of the bishops of Worcester. Nevertheless, pigs

---

43. See also E.M. Fryde, *Peasants and landlords in later medieval England, c.1380–c.1525* (Stroud, 1996), 109–10.
44. TNA: PRO DL29/683/11068.
45. D.L. Farmer, 'Prices and wages, 1350–1500', in Miller, *Agrarian History of England and Wales*, 513–14; Stephenson, 'Wool yields', 388.
46. Hare, 'Regional prosperity', 118–19.

and cattle were prominent on the Cathedral Priory's chalkland manors. In Wiltshire, the manors of Enford, Alton and Overton possessed some of the largest herds on the estate.

Substantial demesne herds of pigs were kept in the early fourteenth century. They seem to have expanded later in the century, when growing individual prosperity allowed greater consumption of meat. On the estates of the Cathedral Priory, pig production seems to have been at its peak. On the four Wiltshire manors in the stockbook that kept pigs, Overton had increased its stock from about 50 around the beginning of the century (with a maximum known size of 74 in 1315), to 130 in 1390–91, when its herd was second only to the great home manor of Barton (Hants). At Alton production had previously been small and erratic (averaging only 11 in the period 1302–6, from six years' figures), but it now rose to 87. This was not an isolated example, as shown by figures for 1372/3 and 1394/5, which averaged 94 and 75.5 respectively. At Stockton the herd increased from 36 in 1311/16 to 83 in 1390, a particularly noteworthy figure for a small manor, which probably reflected demand from Salisbury and the industrial workforce of south and west Wiltshire. At Enford the increase was less dramatic but still substantial, from 62 (1311/16) to 96, giving it the eighth largest herd on the estate. In Wiltshire there is an absence of mid-fourteenth-century records, but the evidence of the better-documented Hampshire manors suggests that such growth occurred over much of the estate.[47] Much, but not all, of this expansion went to feed the priory household. The estate provided it with 499 pigs in 1390 and 469 in 1391, while at Alton in 1395 35 pigs were fattened for the priory's larder.[48] Here was a household where the eating of pork was evidently occurring on a large scale. By contrast, Canterbury Cathedral Priory consumed only 90 pigs in 1484–5 and Syon Abbey an average of 67 between 1446 and 1461.[49]

The large scale of pig-keeping was not a peculiarity of the Cathedral Priory. Elsewhere, Romsey Abbey possessed a herd of between 91 and 100 pigs at Edington in 1413–14, a substantial rise from the thirteenth-century level.[50] In the late fourteenth century at Warminster piglets were bought and fattened in large numbers before being sold as pigs, with a total herd of about 1000, again reflecting the demands of the market. Perhaps significantly, large-scale expansion of pig production was particularly evident in the vicinity of industrial or urban areas, as at Bromham, Stockton and Warminster.

Such large-scale pig farming contrasts with the situation on the Glastonbury estate, where there was a decline on most manors in the later Middle Ages, while the chamberlain had drastically reduced the size of the herd at Longbridge Deverill in the 1330s.[51] On the bishopric of Winchester estates pig farming seems to have been traditionally on a smaller scale than that of the priory, and had virtually ceased on many manors by 1410. There were then substantial herds at only seven manors, in Wiltshire

---

47. Hare, 'The bishop and the prior', 207–8.
48. WCL Stockbook.
49. M. Mate, 'Pastoral farming in south-east England in the fifteenth century', *EcHR*, 2nd series 40 (1987), 523–36.
50. TNA: PRO SC6/1052/2 and 1.
51. Keil, 'Estates of Glastonbury', 126.

and Hampshire.[52] The growth of pig production on the priory estate is clearly also much greater than Campbell's national figures would suggest. He found a 3 per cent increase in his core demesnes and 10 per cent in those of the London area.[53] There was an evident growth in demand for an animal that provided a rapid means of generating meat.

No substantial shift from oxen to horses or decline in the number of oxen can be established. But, as before, horses were more likely to be found in the chalkland than the clayland. This was part of a long-term process that was to lead to the later emphasis on the use of horse power in the chalklands.[54] In Wiltshire, Enford was heavily dependent on horse traction, but this was much less the case on the priory's other manors. In part this stability of means of traction reflects the stability of demesne acreages (particularly in comparison with Campbell's national trends)[55] and the continued demand for animals necessitated by the decline in ploughing works.

Contrasting with the large scale of sheep and pig rearing, demesne cattle herds tended to decline. On the Cathedral Priory estate its Wiltshire chalkland manors did not figure prominently for cows and immature cattle (see Table 5.3), and on the bishopric of Winchester's manors in 1409 there were eight cows in Downton and only two at Bishopstone. Many manors probably managed without a demesne breeding herd, as at the Deverills, and depended on the market for restocking with cattle.[56]

The growth of rabbit farming

Faced with a contraction of downland arable, many lords looked for new profitable ways to exploit the potential of the poorer pastures. As well as expanding sheep flocks and swine herds, lords invested in rabbit production. The presence of rabbit warrens within parks was nothing new, but here on the downlands of southern England, as on the sandy soils of the East Anglian breckland,[57] lords developed large-scale commercial warrens in the late fourteenth century. Nowhere was this more evident than in east Wiltshire, on the great expanses of downland distant from the richer river valleys.

The industry was particularly large-scale at Aldbourne, on the estates of the duchy of Lancaster. In some years, the three demesne warrens produced over 5,000 rabbits for sale, and when the warren was leased it still generated the very large sum of £30 per year. In 1425/6 it was leased for £40 for the first three years and £50 for subsequent years; in practice £50 was never raised, but the revenue nevertheless rose to £42 by the end of the seventh year.[58] In the fifteenth century a third to a half of the revenue of this great manor came from rabbit sales.[59] These usually

---

52. *Pipe roll 1409–10*.
53. Campbell et al., 'Demesne-farming systems', 134.
54. E. Kerridge, *The agricultural revolution* (London, 1967), 49–50.
55. Campbell et al., 'Demesne-farming systems', 134.
56. WCL, Stockbook; *Pipe roll 1409–10*; Longleat MSS 10696.
57. M. Bailey, 'The rabbit and the medieval East Anglian economy', *AHR*, 36 (1988), 1–20.
58. Payne, 'Agrarian conditions', 277.
59. TNA: PRO DL29/728/11991, -734/12044; 710/11456; 687/11134, 11137; 737/12073, 12076, 12078, 12086; DL28/12A f.34a; Payne, 'Agrarian conditions', 277.

substantially exceeded the sales of wool and other livestock together.[60] Many rabbits ended up in the royal household, figuring prominently in the early fifteenth century, as shown by the lists of debtors.[61]

Aldbourne may have been untypical in its size but there were other large warrens on the downlands of east Wiltshire at Everleigh, Mildenhall and Marlborough (which produced £6 13s 4d, £4 13s 4d and £14 respectively per year), and Sherston was leased for 6s 8d in 1437.[62] Further west and south on the chalklands there were warrens at Heytesbury, Amesbury, Winterbourne Stoke and Teffont. There was also an extensive warren at Clarendon.[63] Such warrens were a frequent feature of downland agriculture in southern England: the bishop of Winchester, for example, developed them on some of his downland manors in north Hampshire at Highclere and Ashmansworth,[64] and above all at Overton and Longwood Warren (both of which could produce over 1,000 rabbits in a single year); and the duchy of Lancaster had warrens at King's Somborne (Hants) and Lambourne (Berks), and a transient one at East Garston (Berks).[65] Warrens provided a means of converting the poor downland soils and difficult terrain into a valuable and easily produced crop with low labour costs.

The conversion of land to rabbit warrens was underway at Overton (Hants) by the 1360s and at Aldbourne in the previous decade.[66] There were significant cost implications in this change of land use. The medieval rabbit seems to have been less tough than its descendants,[67] and was therefore kept in artificially protected warrens with disturbed and well-drained soils and built-in burrows. The management of the warren might also involve the roofing of the rabbit holes with scrub and bushes, as at Merdon (Hants),[68] and the management of the burrows or *les buryes* is also referred to in a lease of Longwood Warren (Hants).[69] They have left their traces on the landscape as pillow mounds, or as groups of banked ridges,[70] although these are difficult to date. In some cases they overlie medieval ploughing, but this may merely suggest that they post-date the peak period of medieval cultivation: they could be of late-fourteenth- or fifteenth-century date, or significantly later. The larger warrens also had lodges for those running the warren, as at Overton (Hants).[71]

---

60. Figures in Payne, 'Agrarian conditions', 328.
61. TNA: PRO DL29/737/12073, 12076, 12078, 12085.
62. TNA: PRO DL29/732/12034; SC6/1056/14; Scott, 'Medieval agriculture', 18; WRO 192/34.
63. Scott, 'Medieval agriculture', 18; TNA: PRO SC6/1062/6; A. Richardson, *The forest, park and palace of Clarendon, c.1200–c.1650* (Oxford, 2005), 8–9.
64. e.g. HRO Eccl 2 159422; *The register of the common seal of the Priory of St. Swithun, Winchester, 1345–1497*, ed. J. Greatrex, Hampshire Record Series 2 (Winchester, 1978), 193.
65. TNA: PRO DL29/728/11991 (£3 0s 9d) and 687/11137.
66. E. Roberts, 'The bishop of Winchester's deer parks in Hampshire', *PHFCAS*, 44 (1988), 78; *Wilts IPM* ii, 181, 299; a neighbouring lord to Aldbourne received compensation for damage from the warren in 1378 (*Lacock Abbey charters*, ed. K.H. Rogers, Wiltshire Record Society 34 (Devizes, 1979), 78).
67. O. Rackham, *The history of the countryside* (London, 1987), 47.
68. *Register of the common seal*, 180.
69. *Register of the common seal*, 150.
70. J.N. Hare, 'Agriculture and rural settlement in the chalklands of Wiltshire and Hampshire from c.1200 to c.1500', in Aston and Lewis (eds), *The medieval landscape of Wessex*, 164–5.
71. VCH *Hants* 4, 213.

On the cost side it should also be noted that death and escapes could have a dramatic effect on the profits of the warren, and thus of the estate as a whole. The warren at Aldbourne produced nothing in 1437, 1438 and 1439, and only £10 in 1451 and 1465. The difficulties of the 1430s had resulted from the impact of a very severe winter and spring in 1435/6, with so much frost and snow that for three years that there could be no sales in case the rabbits died out altogether.[72] But these were exceptional years. Rabbits were kept in large numbers because they offered the opportunity of turning poor chalk soils into high cash sales; they could make an important addition to manorial revenues as well as serving the needs of royal, noble and episcopal households, and the warrens would help open up the market for rabbit meat and furs to a much wider clientele than hitherto. Prices were steady in the fifteenth century, generally at 4d a couple and only in two decades (1401–10 and 1421–30) did Thorold Rogers' decennial averages rise to 5d or more. These stagnant prices suggest a relatively plentiful supply for most of the period.[73]

Tenant agriculture in a chalkland valley: Downton and its tithes

Although the study of medieval agriculture is usually dominated by the manorial demesnes, something can be established about peasant land-holding and the large-scale agriculture of many customary tenants or demesne lessees. Court rolls provide one such source. Occasionally, however, records of tithe collections allow us to compare the agriculture of the great estate with that of the parish as a whole, and Chapter 4 examined these sources from five Wiltshire manors in the thirteenth and earlier fourteenth century. For the period of this study there is an exceptional and largely complete run for almost half a century at Downton, and here the well-documented demesne of the bishopric of Winchester provides a valuable point of comparison. The tithe evidence must be treated with caution, as discussed in the previous chapter, but despite possible evasion and concealment, the figures seem to have reflected changes in real production. Production fluctuated from year to year and varied widely between different crops. We would not expect such wide divergences if the prime variable was the lord's ability to collect his due. When tithe receipts fell dramatically in the 1420s it was solely the result of the fall in barley receipts, while wheat was constant and oats grew. Similar considerations suggest that the figures of lamb tithes may also be of value, albeit needing cautious assessment. Here the totals can also be broken down into the tithings, or sub-divisions, of the parish, and neither the totals nor the tithings suggest that the figures had become static (see Table 5.9). They varied from year to year and different tithings show distinct patterns, as would be expected given the lottery in survival represented by the birth of a lamb. The evidence of the manorial accounts reinforces the impression of ecclesiastical sources that there was no general resistance to the payment of tithes.[74]

Downton consisted of a series of villages on both sides of the Avon valley linked in

---

72. TNA: PRO DL29/683/11070; 684/11072, 74; Payne, 'Agrarian conditions', 277, 338.
73. J.E.T. Rogers, *A history of agriculture and prices*, vol. 4 (Oxford, 1882), 355.
74. A.D. Brown, *Popular piety in late medieval England: the diocese of Salisbury, 1200–1550* (Oxford, 1995), 81; on the tithe evidence from Wiltshire and Hampshire see also J.N. Hare, 'Lord, tenant

Table 5.4
Downton: demesne and tenant production, 1407–12.

Crop	Parish crops (%)	Demesne crops (%)
Wheat	16.8	18.0
Barley	75.4	65.8
Oats	7.8	16.2

Sources: The production of the individual grain is expressed as a percentage of the total grain production of the demesne or the parish. The figures are calculated for the years 1407, 1410, 1411 and 1412. The figures for the parish are taken from the rectory accounts, WCM 5385, 5388, 5389, 5390, and would have included the produce of bishopric demesne. The figures for the bishopric are taken from the pipe rolls: HRO 11 M59 B1/154, 157, 158; *Pipe roll 1409–10*, 65–6. To ensure comparability the demesne figures have been calculated on the basis of these three crops. In the tithes vetch and peas were paid for in cash, and curral was rarely included. The bishopric figures including these extra items would have been 17.2, 62.8 and 16 per cent of the total grain produced.

the early thirteenth century by a new market town. Beyond the valley there were areas of clayland with their own distinct economies. The rector had his own demesne, rents in East Downton and tithes from all the settlements. He was responsible for the maintenance of the chancel of the parish church and the chapels of Stanlynch, Nunton and Witherington.[75] In 1385, Bishop Wykeham gave the rectory to Winchester College, in whose manorial accounts the tithe returns survive. Although we possess an almost complete sequence of accounts the tithes were not always collected directly and when they were leased they cease to be informative. Nevertheless they record direct collection for 1369, 1384–9, 1401–29 and 1454, and allow us to recognise short-term trends. The figures exclude the settlements in the former woodland – Pendleworth, Redlynch and Hamptworth – where tithes were sold in sheaves, presumably to the peasant cultivators themselves.[76] Pulse was generally sold in the fields, although whether before or after harvesting is unclear.[77] The tithe returns thus largely relate to settlements in a rich wide chalkland valley and to its main crops. Despite their limitations, they provide a rare opportunity to compare the production of different crops on the great estate and in the parish as a whole and over a substantial period of time. The largest landowner here was the bishop of Winchester, and his production would continue to influence the tithe figures for the parish as a whole.

Barley production was particularly important both on the demesne and in the parish (Table 5.4). As has already been seen, it had increased on the bishop's demesne by the beginning of the fifteenth century, reflecting wider trends.[78] In 1410, 44 per cent

---

74 *cont.*
   and the market: some tithe evidence from the Wessex region', in B. Dodds and R.H. Britnell, *Agriculture and rural society after the Black Death: common themes and regional variations* (Hertford, 2008), 132–46.
75. And evidently spent on their maintenance, e.g. WCM 5426, 5427, 5431, 5445.
76. WCM 5365, 5380.
77. WCM 5382.
78. Campbell et al.,'The demesne-farming systems', 133–4; Galloway,'London's grain supply', 31–2.

of the sown acreage of the bishopric demesne was given over to barley, one of highest percentages yet located in the county at any time in the Middle Ages (see Table 5.1). But the tithe evidence suggests that tenants at Downton attached even greater importance to barley than did the bishop's officials. Barley constituted 63 per cent of the grain produced on the bishop's demesne, but about 77 per cent for the parish (despite the parish production being influenced by that of the demesne). Moreover, on the much smaller parsonage demesne the college grew nothing but barley in 1405, 1406 and 1408, or barley with a few acres of oats in 1386 and 1389. This specialism in barley affected the local economy, generating extra labour demands for malting, although this demand would be under-represented by the demesne records. Such extreme specialism on the tenant and small demesne lands seemed to have been a feature untypical of the Salisbury area. Elsewhere, as at the parsonage of Longbridge Deverill, the proportion dedicated to barley (about 30–40 per cent) was much less.[79] Moreover, in east Hampshire, barley was, at best, the second largest crop on the chalkland manors of East Meon and Hambledon.[80]

The Downton tithe returns also allow us to examine the trends in grain production in the parish as a whole (excluding the eastern tithings) over a period of more than half a century. The 1380s seem to be a period of high output at levels that do not appear to have been reached again in the period for which documents survive. The first two decades of the fifteenth century were periods of stability followed by one of dramatic decline in the 1420s, with a fall of about 20 per cent. But crucially, this fall was not uniform and occurred largely in one crop, barley, which fell to 64.8 per cent of the figure for 1400–1415. Wheat and oats, by contrast, retained their earlier level, and oats even increased in the later 1420s (Tables 5.5 and 5.6).

Why had such a dramatic development occurred, and why in a single crop? Weather conditions probably hit barley more than other crops, and there seem to have been difficult barley harvests in 1423, 1426 and 1429. By the later 1420s this led to reductions in the sown acreage of barley on the bishop's demesne, to 87 per cent of its early-fifteenth-century figure. Wheat and oats acreages remained constant (Tables 5.7 and 5.8). The difficulties of the 1420s were widespread beyond Downton, but they would particularly have affected those people who had become dependent on the demands of the market.[81] From the bishop downwards, cultivators shifted away from their earlier dependence on barley. On the much smaller and more typical parsonage demesne, the almost exclusive preoccupation with barley in the first decade of the century had given way to a more balanced regime in which barley remained the most important crop, but others were also grown. Between 1401–6 and 1424–9 the sown acreage given over to barley fell from 88 to 66 per cent while wheat rose from 6 to 23 per cent. The latter was still very much the lesser crop, but there had been a significant shift in scale. Oats showed little change.

Evidence from the nearby demesnes reinforces the presence of substantial

---

79. Keil, 'Impropriator and benefice', 359.
80. Hare, 'Lord, tenant and the market', tables 8.2 and 8.3, 141 and 144. The Harmondsworth figures for 1451 were lost in the editorial process and should be added. Parish: wheat 49.6, barley 50.4. Demesne: wheat 45.1 and barley 54.9. The oats and vetch figures refer to 1398, 1407 and 1451 respectively.
81. See Chapter 12 for the difficulties of the 1420s.

Agriculture c. 1380–c. 1440

Table 5.5
Downton: tithe grain production, 1384–1454.

Date	Wheat	Barley	Oats	Total (qtrs)
1384–9 (4)	68	320	18	406.3
1401–6 (6)	46	267	32	340.9
1407–12 (6)	57	290	28	374.4
1413–15 (3)	70	265	32	367.0
1420–3 (4)	52	188	30	269.7
1424–8 (5)	60	167	50	277.7

Notes: Number of annual figures given in brackets.
Sources: WCM 5364–5430; HRO 11 M59 B1/136.

Table 5.6
Downton: barley tithes in 1420s (in qtrs).

Year(s)	No. qtrs
1413–15	264.9
1420	151.3
1421	233.9
1422	210.8
1423	156.6
1424	222.6
1425	157.0
1426	139.1
1427	110.4
1428	204.4

Source: WCM 5406–5430.

Table 5.7
Downton: crop production on the bishop's demesne, 1407–28 (% of total production of wheat, barley and oats).

	1407–12(4) % of wheat, barley & oats	acres	1424–8(5) % of wheat, barley & oats	acres
Wheat	15.4	56	23.4	56
Barley	77.1	70	59.4	61
Oats	7.5	25	17.2	25
Peas		4		7
Vetch		12		10

Notes: Number of annual figures given in brackets.
Source: HRO 11 M59 B1/154, 157, 158, 168–172; Pipe Roll 1409–10.

A Prospering Society

Table 5.8
Downton: crops sown on the parsonage demesne, 1369–1429 (acres).

	Wheat	Barley	Oats	Pulse
1369	16	16	7	
1384–89 (5)	9.2	32.4	7.1	
1401–6 (6)	3	44.3	3	
1407–12 (6)	2.3	22.2	3	
1413–15 (3)	18.3	32	2.7	
1420–22 (3)	12	38.3		1.7
1424–29 (5)	10.9	31.2	3.6	1.6

Notes: Number of annual figures given in brackets.
Source: WCM 5362–5430; HRO 11 M59 B1/136.

Table 5.9
Downton: tithes of lambs.

Years	No. lambs
1369 (1)	260
1384–9 (5)	187
1399–1406 (8)	129
1407–15 (9)	124
1420–28 (9)	119

Notes: Number of annual figures given in brackets.
Sources: WCM 5362–5430; HRO 11 M59 B1/136.

agrarian difficulties in a group of manors south of Salisbury in the 1420s. At Coombe Bisset, the demesne rent was cut by £2 in 1421 and there were reductions in rents of virgate holdings. At Downton and Coombe Bisset the income of the manors was cut between second and third decades, at the latter by 12 per cent (including a 14 per cent cut in the rent). These difficulties probably resulted from contracting demand in the cloth industry of Salisbury and its immediate hinterland, as well as the weather and harvest conditions. Such difficulties would have been exacerbated by the earlier boom conditions and the resultant over-dependence on barley. The area does not seem to have recovered during the century. By contrast, north of the city the growth of the west Wiltshire industrial area would have compensated for any decline in the Salisbury area. But urban Downton showed some signs of recovery, as reflected in Winchester College's investments in building tenements there in the 1440s.

The tithe returns also provide figures for the size of the village lamb flocks and allow comparison between the seigneurial and tenant lamb flocks in 1405–11, enabling us to establish the totals of lambs produced and surviving until weaning. Between 1403 and 1410 the figures are even divided up among the various tithings, or sub-divisions, of the parish. Unfortunately the five earliest figures are too erratic to produce a reliable fourteenth-century base with which to compare the later figures.[82]

At Downton the demesne flocks were low in 1405 and 1406, and this probably reflected necessary rebuilding after the death of Wykeham and Beaufort's acquisition of the see and estate.[83] During the period 1407 to 1411 the bishopric flocks produced

---

82. 260 lambs in 1369; 169 in 1384; 202 in 1385; 258 in 1386; 118 in 1389.
83. Hare, 'The bishop and the prior', 303–4.

only 21.7 per cent of the tithe lambs, and the figures were similar in 1424–8, at 20.3 per cent.[84] The bishop still owned more sheep than any other individual, with over 1200 sheep in Downton in 1411,[85] but, even then, only a fifth of the parish lambs were his. If the flocks of the bishopric and the parish had a comparable age structure, the rest of the parish would have had flocks of about 5000.

These figures raise questions about earlier calculations of tenant flocks based on rights to free pasture and rents for pasturing on the demesne. Scott suggested a figure for the tenant flocks of only 800 to 1000 for the thirteenth century, although she accepted that such figures represented minimum figures rather than total tenant flocks.[86] This would seem to be a serious underestimate, as are her figures for the much smaller chalkland manor of Bishopstone.[87]

The large scale of parish sheep flocks is demonstrated by several sources. Court rolls suggest the presence of large tenant flocks and overstocking at Durrington and Coombe Bisset.[88] At Warminster the agistment of lambs on Cow Down (not necessarily the total tenant flock) shows that there were 1,070 non-seigneurial lambs compared with the 90 belonging to the lord.[89] Tithe evidence also supports this view of the large size of tenant flocks, and can occasionally allow comparison of the demesne and parish flocks, a vital task in assessing the typicality of the demesne records. Downton, with substantial sub-manors in its area, probably had a particularly large parish flock in relation to the demesne. East Meon in Hampshire was also a complex manor and provides an exceptional case where records survive of both the tithes of the lambs and of the fleeces, enabling calculations of the total parish flock as a whole, and not just of the lambs. This suggests that the demesne lambs made up about 17 per cent of those of the parish and the rest of the demesne flock about 18 per cent of the parish in 1410.[90] At Monkton and Longbridge Deverill, by contrast, the demesne flock was more important, contributing half the parish lambs.[91]

Moreover, the peasantry, however elusive, seem to have been increasing their role in sheep farming. When the lords gave up their breeding flocks, as the nuns of St Mary did in 1443, they had to purchase new stock from others, essentially from the peasantry, lessees and other substantial cultivators. As the duchy of Lancaster found, it was a convenient but more expensive option. The demesne had become dependent on the breeding of tenant flocks.

---

84. This figure has been calculated combining the bishopric and rectory accounts WCM 5385–5430; HRO 11 M59 B1/154; 157; 158; 168–72; *Pipe roll 1409–10*. In 1385, the figure was similar but lower at 19% (HRO 11M59 B1/136).
85. 1239 and 1269 respectively; *Pipe roll 1409–10*, 66–7.
86. Scott,'Medieval agriculture', 26–7.
87. e.g. 208 in 1296, and 26 in 1395: VCH *Wilts* 4, 26–7; for demesne flocks see *Pipe roll 1301–2*, 75; *Pipe roll 1409–10*, 82–3.
88. e.g. WCM 4396g; 5656 d, e, h, j.
89. WRO Warminster accounts 845/.
90. Calculated from *Pipe roll 1409–10*. The tithe figures for this year are similar to others from the first two decades of the fifteenth century, when the parish flocks were at their peak, HRO 11M59/B2/18/11–38. There is no indication that East Meon church paid tithes on its wool, so another 224 should probably be added to the total sheep population of the parish.
91. Longleat MSS, 10699, 9599–9605. Average 1394–1402: E. Monkton, demesne 25.4 and for vill 9.9; [Longbridge] Deverill, demesne 17.5, vill 34.5.

The pastoral economy of the clay vale

Most of this chapter has been based on the chalklands, reflecting the origins of most of the sources. All farming tended to be mixed farming, but the balance varied from region to region. In the chalklands both large-scale farming and sheep flocks were increasingly characteristic of the agriculture of both the demesne and the peasantry. In the sixteenth century and afterwards the clay vale was to take on a distinctive pastoral and dairying role, characterised by small-scale family units. The evidence from this area is as yet too limited for us to be able to argue with confidence that this was already fully established in the period of study, but manors had been weak and demesne cultivation given up early. There was already evidence of increased pastoral farming in this area, and this grew in the period under study. Our evidence of demesne cultivation, moreover, tends to come not from the clay vale proper, but from those manors which, even in the eighteenth century, were to remain areas of mixed farming. In addition, it was as a family rather than a seigneurial enterprise that dairying developed, and it thus did so without documentation. There are, however, already signs that changes were afoot and that the clay vale was increasingly dominated by pastoral farming. Evidence has been drawn from the whole period c.1380 to c.1520.

The incomplete poll tax returns from 1379 show concentrations of butchers in particular places, but almost exclusively in the vale, suggesting an emphasis on pastoral farming there. In the north of the county there was a group at Cricklade (Cricklade (10) and Ashton (5)), and another at Malmesbury (4). In west Wiltshire the concentration included Bradford (4), Rowde (4), Devizes (1), Bromham (5), Worton (1), Calne (2) and Chippenham (at least 4). In the south there was a smaller group in the vale of Wardour: Hatch (2), Ansty (1), Fonthill (1) and Hindon (incomplete, 2). In the chalklands there was a group in the east of the county (Marlborough (3 butchers), Ogbourne St George (1) and Aldbourne (3)).[92]

In the vale, sheep farming was less important, but herds of cows and pigs were characteristic. At Bromham, Battle Abbey maintained a herd of between 46 and 77 pigs in the 1380s, falling to 30–39 in the 1390s and thereafter to about 25–35. Here cattle were kept long after a demesne sheep flock had ceased to be maintained. The pigs and cattle were kept for sale rather than for any household requirements (see Table 6.4). At Bradford there were 96 pigs and 30 to 32 cows, together with 47 to 31 young stock in 1368.[93] On the estates of Stanley Abbey the Homegrange maintained a substantial breeding herd, with 34 to 38 cows in 1415, and produced 750lb of cheese. Monkton Farleigh Priory cultivated a small demesne at Chippenham in 1402, but this included 72 to 69 pigs and a breeding herd of between 16 and 18 cows.[94] The prospering pastoral sector was also reflected later when, by 1528, Stanley Abbey resumed direct cultivation of several major pastures for the abbot's greater profit.[95] There were signs of significant specialisation at Coleshill, over the Berkshire border,

---

92. TNA: PRO E179/239/193/III; /239/193/V, Vb, XIII; /196/52a; /196/42a.
93. WRO 1742/6786. Each account provides a total at the start of the account and at the end, hence the two figures in each of the subsequent references.
94. TNA: PRO SC6/1054/9; WRO 192/29.
95. TNA: PRO SC6/1054/9; SC6/Hen VIII/3958.

where, as the lord diminished his arable cultivation and absorbed tenancies into the demesne, he increased the size of his demesne cattle herds, trebling them between the 1390s and the mid-fifteenth century.[96]

Peasants and tenants kept many animals. Lords who owned parks might lease out the pasturage, and these leases reveal details of some of the livestock owned by the peasants. At Vastern Park (Wootton Basset) there was a substantial herd of tenant horses and cattle, the agistment including 99 bullocks and 262 horses belonging to about 64 people, suggesting an average of one and a half cattle and four horses each. Occasionally inventories and indications of individual peasant livestock survive and suggest the growth of a substantial pastoral economy. In 1500, Robert Carter, a tenant of the abbot of Malmesbury, claimed that the abbot had confiscated his livestock, which included 5 bullocks, 10 cows, 9 calves and 109 sheep. The abbot disputed the figures, but the suggestion is of stock rearing on a substantial scale.[97] At Wroughton in 1480, Richard Smith, a tenant who had fled the manor, left behind 12 oxen, 12 cows, a bull, 10 bullocks and yearlings, 7 horses, 53 ewes and 33 lambs together with 68 quarters of crops of various sorts;[98] 10 to 12 cows would have been worthy of a substantial monastic demesne in the chalklands, and Smith's livestock holdings resemble those found in fifteenth-century Warwickshire.[99]

Peasants kept many sheep in the limestone islands in the vale. At Eastrop 3,370 sheep were presented for overstocking the demesne in 1466. They ranged from 30 to the 800 of R. Vyncent of Sevenhampton, husbandman. Most flocks were of fewer than 200 sheep, but there were ten above 300.[100] Many of the sheep belonged to local graziers from neighbouring villages such as Hampton, Westrop, Highworth, Inglesham, Sevenhampton and Shrivenham: 'The really important people in Eastrop were not those with most land but those with most sheep, and these, by the end of the fifteenth century, had come to dominate the economy of the village.'[101] At Coleshill the lord both increased his own herds and made increasing gains from renting pastures to others.[102]

By the start of the sixteenth century the contrasting worlds of chalk and cheese, of large-scale sheep–corn husbandry and the family-based pastoral economy, had already emerged. The fragmentary sources suggest the development of a specialised pastoral area such as was emerging elsewhere in England – in the west midlands, for example.[103] Similar developments were also occurring on a smaller scale in southern England, in the Hampshire basin and in the Thames valley. This can be seen in south Hampshire, on the bishopric of Winchester's estate at Bitterne, on the Titchfield

---

96. R. Faith, 'Berkshire: fourteenth and fifteenth centuries', in Harvey, *The peasant land market*, 171.
97. R.H. Hilton, *The decline of serfdom in medieval England* (Basingstoke, 1969), 54–5.
98. WCL Wroughton court roll, 1480.
99. Dyer, *Warwickshire farming*, 30.
100. Faith, 'The peasant land market in Berkshire in the later Middle Ages', PhD thesis (Leicester, 1962), table III; eadem, 'Berkshire', 172.
101. Faith, 'Berkshire', 149, 171–2.
102. Ibid., 169–72.
103. C. Dyer, 'Farming practice and techniques. E: the west midlands', in Miller (ed.), *The agrarian history of England and Wales*, 236–7.

Abbey estate and in Leland's emphasis on pastoral farming in 1542. Further north, in the London basin, the Cathedral Priory possessed 24 cows at Crondal in 1390.[104] These are not well-documented areas, but they suggest the growing specialisation of agriculture that was to become so characteristic of future agrarian development, in Wiltshire and beyond.

---

104. Hare, 'The bishop and the prior'; 206, 208; VCH *Hants* 2, 185; *John Leland's itinerary*, ed. J. Chandler (Stroud, 1993), 202.

Chapter 6

The leasing of the demesnes

The process of leasing

The leasing of the demesnes was the most obvious change in the organisation of agriculture in this period. It represented 'a sharp break with a long tradition'. In Dyer's words, 'It is the scale of the change, in a few decades, which gives it an almost revolutionary quality. The leasing of the demesnes put new people in control of landed resources, established new relationships between lords and tenants, and the farmers brought new methods of production and management.'[1] The lords withdrew from direct cultivation in agriculture and retreated again into the role of rent collectors. In Wiltshire, this development both reflected and reinforced the existing contrasts in agriculture, and its impact considerably outlasted our period. Leasing here showed both parallels and contrasts with the pattern elsewhere in England. On a national level, the leasing of the demesnes had largely taken place by 1400.[2] But in the chalklands of Wiltshire most large ecclesiastical demesnes, such as those that figure so prominently in this study, maintained direct involvement in arable farming until about 1430. Why did lords now give up cultivation of the demesne when it seemed to have favoured them so well, and why were the changes so delayed here? In order to answer these questions it is first necessary to establish a chronology of the process by examining the progress of leasing at several different times.

This chapter excludes examination of some of the essentially non-agricultural elements that might bring revenues to the lord and which might be leased separately, such as quarries, mills and warrens, manorial courts and rectories. Such items might be included, however, in a general manorial lease: some smaller manors incorporated all the revenue elements, including the rents and sometimes the court. Usually, however, the leases did not include the manorial courts, although the lessee might have some responsibilities connected with them, such as providing accommodation for the appropriate officials.

The process of leasing was not a steady, consistent or permanent one. This uncertainty can clearly be seen on two of our Wiltshire manors. At Battle Abbey's manor of Bromham, the demesne was leased in the 1400s and the 1420s, but direct cultivation agriculture was then resumed and it was not until 1442 that permanent leasing occurred; while at Kingston Deveril there was a complex chronological intermixture of demesne lease and cultivation, particularly between 1420 and 1440. These two estates also show similar transient shifts of policy on manors outside

---

1. C. Dyer, *Making a living in the Middle Ages: the people of Britain, 850–1520* (New Haven, CT, and London, 2002), 332, 346.
2. E. Miller (ed.), *The agrarian history of England and Wales: vol. 3, 1348–1500* (Cambridge, 1991), 13; for the west Midlands see R.H. Hilton, *The English peasantry in the later Middle Ages* (Oxford, 1975), 60.

Wiltshire, as in the late fourteenth century at Battle Abbey's Apuldram (Sussex), Brightwalton (Berks) and Hotton (Essex), and at Netley Abbey's Roydon (Hants).[3] A comparable process can also be observed on local lay manors, as on those which were to make up the estates of the Hungerford family, where some lands that had previously been leased were taken into hand again in the fifteenth century. Heytesbury was leased in 1360, taken into hand in the 1390s and by 1408/9, and leased again in 1443/4. Teffont was leased in 1381 but cultivation had resumed by 1403 and, after another intermission, was resumed again in 1443.[4] Similar reversals of policy have also been seen elsewhere, as on the estates of Canterbury Cathedral Priory or Westminster Abbey, at Methwold (Norfolk), or with the flocks of the bishopric of Winchester at Witney and Adderbury (Oxfordshire).[5]

Leasing in the fourteenth century

Wiltshire's seigneurial agriculture in the early fourteenth century had been dominated by extensive demesne cultivation. Places such as Corsham and Patney, where the lord leased the demesne in the late thirteenth or early fourteenth century, were very much the exception.[6] Moreover, the demesnes generally remained intact and were then leased as a single unit. There are cases where small portions were earlier leased out on a piecemeal basis, as at Downton (belonging to the bishop of Winchester) or Bromham (Battle Abbey), but such leasing was limited in scale and unusual.[7]

By 1380 the development of leasing already showed a distinct regional pattern, as it occurred earlier outside the chalklands. In the Cotswolds demesnes were leased in Castle Combe by 1352 and at Westwood by 1364. In the lighter soils that outcropped within the clay vale they were leased at Stratton by 1368, Tockenham by 1372, Trowbridge by 1372, Chelworth by 1372, Sevenhampton by 1376 and Stanton fitz Warren by 1382.[8] Of these, both Stratton and Sevenhampton had extensive demesne

---

3. J.N. Hare, 'The monks as landlords: the leasing of the demesnes in southern England', in Barron and Harper-Bill (eds), *Church in pre-reformation society*, 82–94; and 'Netley Abbey: monastery, mansion and ruin', *PHFCAS*, 49 (1993), 214–15.
4. R. Payne, 'Agrarian conditions on the Wiltshire estates of the duchy of Lancaster, the lords Hungerford and the bishopric of Winchester', PhD thesis (London, 1940), 300–301; TNA: PRO SC6/1053/12; SC6/1054/4; SC6/1059/2, and 24.
5. M. Mate, 'The farming out of manors: a new look at the evidence from Canterbury Cathedral Priory', *Journal of Medieval History*, 9 (1983), 337–42; B. Harvey, 'The leasing of the abbot of Westminster's demesnes in the later Middle Ages', *EcHR*, 2nd series 22 (1969), 19; G.A. Holmes, *The estates of the higher nobility in fourteenth-century England* (Cambridge, 1957), 119, 128; Miller (ed.), *Agrarian history*, 264–5. See also F.R.H. Du Boulay, *The lordship of Canterbury* (London, 1966), 224. Occasionally the expected temporary nature of leasing is specifically articulated, e.g. Hilton, *English peasantry*, 66.
6. *Tropenell cartulary*, ed. J.S. Davies, Wiltshire Archaeological and Natural History Society (Devizes, 1908), 3; B. Harrison, 'Field systems and demesne farming on the Wiltshire estates of St Swithun's Priory, Winchester', *AHR*, 43 (1995), 12.
7. J.Z. Titow, *English rural society, 1200–1350* (London, 1969), 115; TNA: PRO SC6/1045/23.
8. E.M. Carus-Wilson, 'Evidences of industrial growth on some fifteenth century manors', in Carus-Wilson, *Essays in economic history*, 160; WCL Westwood 1365 39/1; TNA: PRO SC6/1058/15; DL29/682/11039; SC6/1049/9 and 11; SC6/1057/22; BL Add Ch 66520.

cultivation at the end of the thirteenth century.[9] Teffont, in the Nadder valley, was leased by 1381.[10] Direct cultivation still occurred at Chippenham, Box and Hilmarton, in the Cotswolds and the vale, in areas where leasing had developed early. In some cases, as at Castle Combe and Trowbridge, the demesne was leased to a group rather than to an individual, a feature that does not seem to be found where leasing began later. Such group leases continued to be a feature of the claylands in the fifteenth century, as at Oaksey and Poole.[11]

By contrast, leasing made slower progress in the chalklands, where account rolls show continued direct cultivation at the end of the fourteenth century and after 1400. The exceptions seem generally to be among the smaller lay manors: West Chisingbury was leased by 1362, Coombe Bisset by 1372, although Heytesbury, which was leased by 1360, does not fit into this category.[12] The poll tax of 1379 was supposed to distinguish 'farmers of manors and parsonages',[13] and the incomplete Wiltshire series records 7, most of which seem to be leases of small chalkland manors: Laverstock, Winterborne Dauntsey, Milton or Fyfield, Wexcombe or Wilton, Fonthill, Hindon and Chisbury.[14] A second generalisation that can be made about this early leasing is that it did not occur on the ecclesiastical estates. Out of 26 ecclesiastical demesnes examined, only 1 or possibly 2 had been leased by 1380.[15]

These regional and seigneurial contrasts were reinforced by 1400. The process of leasing had continued in non-chalk Wiltshire: Wroughton was leased then, and possibly earlier, as was Box, probably in 1395, Bremhill in 1391 and Colerne in 1394.[16] All were on estates where other manors were retained in hand. To these should probably be added Oaksey and Poole Keynes, in the far north of the county.[17] Only Hilmarton, Bromham, Chippenham, Lacock and Stanley Abbey's Homegrange have been found continuing cultivation into the fifteenth century in these areas.[18] By contrast, in the chalklands, although further leasing continued, direct cultivation remained the norm. Small manors continued to be the most likely to be leased: Kingston Deverill by 1396, Durrington in 1389, Ebbesborne Wake between 1383 and 1402 and Stockton from 1399.[19] Ecclesiastical estates remained more conservative in their policies than lay ones. Although leasing had occurred on some ecclesiastical manors, it tended to be among the smaller ones.

---

9. *Accounts and surveys of the Wiltshire lands of Adam de Stratton*, ed. M.W. Farr, Wiltshire Archaeological and Natural History Society Records Branch 14 (Devizes, 1959).
10. Payne, 'Agrarian conditions', 300–302.
11. Ibid., 302–6.
12. WRO 212B/2290; WCM 43516; Payne, 'Agrarian conditions', 300.
13. R.B. Dobson, *The peasants' revolt of 1381* (London, 1970), 108.
14. TNA: PRO E179/239/193 vi, xxi a; 194/42a.
15. Westwood by 1364, and Wroughton leased between 1373 and 1387: WCL Westwood; WCL Wroughton court rolls.
16. TNA: PRO SC6/1045/10; BL Add Mss 6165 (transcript); NCA 5960.
17. R. Scott, 'Medieval agriculture', in VCH *Wilts* 4, 36; TNA: PRO DL43/14/4.
18. Bad. Mun 110/5/4; J.N. Hare, 'Lord and tenant in Wiltshire, *c.*1380–1520, with particular reference to regional and seigneurial variations', PhD thesis (London, 1976), appendix 338–50; TNA: PRO SC6/1062/9 and 13; Hare, 'Monks as landlords', 87; TNA: PRO SC6/1054/9.
19. WRO 192/32; WCM 5650 m; WRO 492/14 and 17; BL Add Rl 24395.

In Wiltshire, as elsewhere, there were considerable variations within a single estate. On that of Winchester Cathedral Priory direct cultivation was still very much the norm in 1400. It was the smaller and sometimes peripheral manors or demesnes that had been leased, as with Westwood, Wroughton and Stockton or the Hampshire manors of Hannington and Silkstead.[20] The chronology among the lay estates is difficult to establish. The scale of leasing may have been underestimated, for the duchy of Lancaster and Bohun estates lack evidence for most of the fourteenth century. By the time that documentation survives, at the beginning of the fifteenth century, there was little demesne cultivation left. On the duchy of Lancaster estates the demesne arable (except on the manor of Berwick) had probably become leased by 1388 and certainly by 1393,[21] and on the earl of Derby's manor of Upavon the demesne was leased by 1384.[22] Only 3 out of 25 documented lay manors retained their demesne in hand during the decade 1400–1410: Hilmarton, for which documentation ceases in 1411, Heytesbury, which was leased temporarily by 1420 and more permanently by 1436, and Winterbourne Stoke, which was leased between 1448 and 1464.

Leasing in the fifteenth century

By about 1400 the lay estates in Wiltshire had ceased to be actively involved in direct cultivation. The ecclesiastical estates in the chalklands of the county continued with the old methods, and were generally leased after 1420. Such continued activity was widely paralleled on the chalklands of southern England, as on the Hampshire lands of Winchester Cathedral Priory, the bishopric of Winchester and Romsey Abbey, or the Sussex lands of Battle Abbey at Barnhorn, Alciston and Lullington.[23] But this chalkland pattern contrasts with developments elsewhere in England, where leasing was already the norm, as on the estates of Canterbury, Coventry or Durham Cathedral Priories, Westminster or Ramsey Abbeys, or the bishopric of Worcester.[24]

On the ecclesiastical estates in the chalklands it was the 1430s and 1440s that saw the lord's main retreat from direct cultivation: New College Oxford's Stert was leased in 1431 and Alton Barnes in 1433; Battle Abbey's Bromham was finally leased

---

20. Hare, 'Monks as landlords', 86–7.
21. TNA: PRO DL43 15/2, 15/6.
22. TNA: PRO DL29/682/11044.
23. Hare, 'Monks as landlords', 85; J. Greatrex, 'The administration of Winchester Cathedral Priory in the time of Cardinal Beaufort', PhD thesis (Ottawa, 1972); P.F. Brandon, 'Cereal yields on the Sussex estates of Battle Abbey during the later Middle Ages', *EcHR*, 2nd series 25 (1972), 412; J.N. Hare, 'The bishop and the prior: demesne agriculture in medieval Hampshire', *AHR*, 54 (2006), 209–11.
24. R.A. Smith, *Canterbury Cathedral Priory* (Cambridge, 1943), 192; C. Dyer, *Warwickshire farming, 1349–c.1520: preparations for agricultural revolution*, Dugdale Society Occasional Papers (Oxford, 1981), 4; R.A. Lomas, 'The priory of Durham and its demesnes in the fourteenth and fifteenth centuries', *EcHR*, 2nd series 31 (1978), 345; B. Harvey, *Westminster Abbey and its estates* (Oxford, 1977), 150–51; J.A. Raftis, *The estates of Ramsey Abbey* (Toronto, 1957); C. Dyer, *Lords and peasants in a changing society: the estates of the bishopric of Worcester, 680–1540* (Cambridge, 1980), 147–50.

by 1443; Winchester Cathedral Priory's Enford between 1428 and 1431; and St Mary's Abbey's Urchfont between 1434 and 1441 and All Cannings by 1449.[25] By contrast, direct management had become unusual on the lay estates and sometimes reflected the individual concerns, activities and enthusiasms of a particular lord or council, as with the resumption of demesne agriculture on some of the Hungerford estates. At other times the reasons for local variation within a single estate may be unclear. On the duchy of Lancaster estate sheep farming continued or was resumed at Berwick St James and Somborne (Hants) long after the flocks had been given up on the rest of the manors in 1443.[26]

The leasing of the chalkland demesnes did not mean an end to the lord's direct agricultural activities, for the demesne sheep flocks remained characteristic of this region long after the end of demesne arable. Large flocks continued to be maintained on some of the lay manors, such as on those of the duchy of Lancaster at Aldbourne, Everleigh and Collingbourne until 1443, and on the estates of the lords Hungerford. This was also the case on the Wiltshire monastic estates of Winchester Cathedral Priory, St Mary's Abbey, Winchester, Netley, Lacock and Wilton Abbeys and the bishoprics of Winchester and Salisbury (Table 6.1). These large flocks were not a peculiarity of the Wiltshire downlands but were found elsewhere where large-scale sheep farming had been the norm, as on the southern chalkland manors of the duchy of Lancaster estates in Hampshire, Dorset and Berkshire, or those of the bishops of Winchester, Winchester Cathedral Priory (Hampshire), Battle Abbey and Netley Abbey; or on the Cotswolds lands of Winchcombe Abbey, Westminster Abbey and the bishop of Worcester.[27] The lords' continued involvement in pastoral agriculture was also seen in rabbit farming, where some of the great warrens remained under direct seigneurial control.[28]

On these great chalkland estates the sheep flocks were mainly leased between 1440 and 1475, probably reflecting the impact of the mid-fifteenth-century depression and the fall in wool prices. On the duchy of Lancaster estate the sheep were sold off in Collingbourne, Everleigh and Aldbourne together with those of some of its estates in Hampshire and Dorset in 1443, the timing seeming to reflect the reacquisition by the duchy of those of its lands previously granted out to the feoffees of Henry V's will. These feoffees had included Henry Beaufort and Lord Hungerford, on both of whose

---

25. T.A.R. Evans and R. Faith, 'College estates and university finances, 1350–1500', in J. Catto and R. Evans, *The history of the university of Oxford, ii: late medieval Oxford* (Oxford, 1992), 375; Hare, 'Lord and tenant', appendix 338–50; BL Harl Rl W19 and W20; WRO 192/20 (court rolls); WRO 192/28.
26. Payne, 'Agrarian conditions', 120–26; flocks were maintained at Berwick and Somborne until at least 1462: TNA: PRO DL29/687/11134 and 5.
27. TNA: PRO DL29/728/11991, 732/12034, 733/12041; *Pipe roll 1409–10*; Hare, 'Netley Abbey', 216; idem, 'Monks as landlords', 85–6; idem, 'The bishop and the prior', 211; idem, 'Regional prosperity in fifteenth-century England: some evidence from Wessex', in M. Hicks (ed.), *Revolution and consumption in late medieval England* (Woodbridge, 2001), 117–19; R.H. Hilton, 'Winchcombe Abbey and the manor of Sherborne', in H.P.R. Finberg (ed.), *Gloucestershire studies* (Leicester, 1957), 111; Harvey, *Westminster Abbey*, 150–51; Dyer, *Lords and peasants*, 150.
28. Above, Chapter 5.

Table 6.1
Sheep flocks on four ecclesiastical demesnes.

	Stockton	Kingston Deverill	All Cannings	Urchfont
1399–1405	440.6 (7)			
1405–1415	374.2 (9)	885.7 (7)		
1416–27	214.1 (9)	784.7 (7)		
1428–42	132.8 (13)	232.0 (2)		
1442–51	196.8 (5)	828.5 (4)	839.7 (3)	1,277 (2)
1452–66	171.0 (3)		819.7 (3)	1,306 (11)
1466–76			746.5	1,295

Notes: For comparison with earlier figures see Table 4.3 for Stockton, and for Urchfont in 1259 1,344 sheep (BL Add Rl 66602). The flocks were later leased: Stockton with 159 sheep by 1472 (after 1456); Kingston Deverill by 1446; All Cannings 503 in 1478; Urchfont 1000 sheep by 1478 and after 1471. After the full leasing of Kingston Deverill various items in the accounts suggest that substantial transactions in sheep took place between Kingston Deverill and Netley Abbey's manor of Waddon (Dorset), lambs going to Waddon and hoggasters and sometimes ewes coming to Kingston Deverill, in order to maintain substantial flocks. £13 6s 8d was regularly allowed for lambs for Waddon and occasional payments included: 1462 (for 100 ewes, 165 hoggasters), 1464 (63 hoggasters), 1466 (100 hoggasters), 1487 (100 hoggasters), 1490 (124 hoggasters).
Sources: Stockton BL Add Rl 24395–19, WRO 906/SC7–10; Kingston Deverill WRO 192/32; All Cannings WRO 192/28; Urchfont WRO 192/36b–24/2e, BL Add Rl 19717, 19718, 19719, 19720, 19721, JRL Rylands Charter 170.

estates large-scale sheep farming had been retained.[29] Now the estate policies could be rethought to fit with changing circumstances, and the flocks were leased. At Kingston Deverill Netley Abbey leased the pastures after 1449. On the Cathedral Priory's estate the flock was leased at Enford between 1455 and 1463, and at Stockton between 1458 and 1472, together with the Hampshire manors of Silkstead by 1468, Wootton between 1471 and 1475 and Whitchurch between 1471 and 1483. The abbey of St Mary's at Winchester probably leased its great flocks of Urchfont and All Cannings in 1478. Lacock maintained a large flock at Chitterne, although it seems already to have given up arable farming there, while Wilton Abbey may have maintained its sheep flocks for much longer. It maintained a flock at nearby Brudcombe in 1486, and in 1521 the abbess was engaged in a legal case that revolved around her disputed failure to provide £180 of wool from the abbey wool house.[30] Ecclesiastical landlords remained active in sheep cultivation in Dorset, particularly in the chalklands, until the bitter end in the 1530s, when flocks were recorded in the *Valor Ecclesiasticus*. Moreover, on one of these estates, that of Shaftesbury, a surviving account for 1518 confirms that here, at least, the figures provided for sheep pasture represent flocks that had still been under direct control 20 years before. Wilton may have reflected this Dorset pattern rather than that of other old-established monastic estates elsewhere in Wiltshire.[31] Elsewhere, the bishopric of Winchester continued with some of its Hampshire flocks after it had leased those in Wiltshire, but this practice had ceased by 1489.[32]

---

29. R. Somerville, *History of the duchy of Lancaster*, vol. 1 (London, 1953).
30. TNA: PRO Wards 2/94c/9; WRO 492/8, VCH *Wilts* 3, 237.
31. Hare, 'Regional prosperity', 118–19; WRO 1728/70, *Valor ecclesiasticus temp. Henr. VIII*, vol. 1, ed. J. Caley and J. Hunter (London, 1810), 277–9.
32. Hare, 'The bishop and the prior', 211.

By the middle of the fifteenth century lords had generally given up direct cultivation of demesne land. Many lords, however, particularly ecclesiastical ones, continued to cultivate a small fragment of their land, which produced part of their food requirements. Thus a valor of 1476 suggests that Lacock Abbey continued to maintain a manor under direct management for arable and pasture, and it maintained a mixed home farm at Lacock itself until the Dissolution.[33] Monkton Farleigh kept a home farm until 1526, although it had also continued to cultivate the nearby demesne at Chippenham until at least 1461.[34] This late survival of a home farm or of cultivation on nearby manors is a familiar feature elsewhere in southern England, as on the estates of Winchester Cathedral Priory, Netley Abbey and Battle Abbey.[35]

Although the great lords were now dependent almost exclusively on rent, the role or function of individual manors within the estate might remain constant. On some of the great monastic estates, particular manors had traditionally had a key role as food producers, while others had been exclusively cash producers. Enford, together with the Wiltshire manors of Overton and Alton, had long been among the main food suppliers to Winchester Cathedral Priory, and in 1403 it produced 337 quarters of grain (a substantial increase on the early-fourteenth-century figures) as well as 2 calves, 30 wethers, 36 pigs, 8 cheeses, 12 geese, 12 swans, 12 capons and 12 hens. After the demesne had been leased the manor continued to produce foodstuffs, rendering 106 quarters of grain together with 21 pigs and 12 each of geese, capons and hens as the rent payment for the demesne arable.[36] By contrast, the priory's manors of Wroughton, Westwood and Stockton had previously been unimportant as food providers, and were let for a cash rent.[37] On the estate of St Mary's Abbey, Winchester, Urchfont had long been a major food provider and both it and neighbouring All Cannings continued in this role, paying rents in kind for the demesne arable (sending 236 quarters of grain as rent to the abbey each year).[38] The barley was first malted, generating an increase in value of 12.5 per cent.[39] This rent in kind continued to be sent from Urchfont to Winchester until the early sixteenth century.[40] The distinction between cash and food producers was still apparent too on the Wilton Abbey estates at the Dissolution, the *Valor Ecclesiasticus* enabling us to see that the more distant manors were leased for cash while the nearer chalkland manors of south Wiltshire produced rents in kind.[41]

---

33. TNA: PRO Wards 2/94c/9; Hare,'Monks as landlord', 87.
34. WRO 192/29.
35. Hare,'Monks as landlords', 86–7.
36. BL Harl Rl X/8.
37. Hare,'Lord and tenant', table I, 118; WCL composite 1311, 1316.
38. BL Add Rl 66602, 19717; WRO 192/28.
39. The barley was assessed at £8, the malting at £1 (BL Add Rl 19728).
40. Urchfont: wheat until after 1521, and barley until sometime after 1500 and before 1502–3; All Cannings from 1490 (WRO 192/28 (1490)).
41. *Valor Ecclesiasticus*, vol. 2 109; such a distinction can also be found elsewhere, as at Coventry (Dyer, *Making a living*, 334).

Types of leases

Leasehold arrangements varied a great deal. In the chalklands most leased demesnes went to a single tenant and were often of the stock and land type, in which the tenant received a fixed quantity of livestock and grain at the start of the lease and had to return the same quantities at the end. This would have helped the tenants to take on the responsibility for large chalkland demesnes and reflects one way in which the large and traditional scale of chalkland farming was kept intact. For example, at Enford the lord had sown 524.5 acres in 1403 before he gave up cultivation and leased the demesne, and his pastoral economy was on a similar large scale; even the better-off village farmers would surely have found it difficult to produce the capital required for such extensive agriculture, and a stock and land lease was provided from 1463. Outside the chalklands, some leases were to a group of tenants and thus served both to weaken manorial structures still further and to increase the contrast between the traditional patterns of the chalklands and those elsewhere.

The terms of leases varied both from manor to manor and from time to time, depending on the demands of the estate and the availability of suitable lessees. At Enford, where direct cultivation had been maintained in 1403, the initial lease was expected to produce an annual rent of £40, together with 106 quarters of grain and other food. In return the tenant received the rents of the tenantry which were payable to the manor, and livestock, but no sheep. The latter remained the direct responsibility of the lord. This pattern continued until after 1455. By 1463 the sheep flocks had been leased while a similar quantity of grain continued to be sent to the priory, but now the lord had resumed the direct collection of rent from his other tenants. Finally, by 1485 the whole demesne was leased for a cash rent of £45 16s 8d. The lord still supported the tenant through a stock and land lease including 351 quarters of grain (of which 167 was of barley) and 1,362 sheep, but had now divorced himself from the manorial grain supplies and would have to purchase alternatives from the market. There were evidently tenants who could undertake the high risks of cultivating such a demesne and buying and selling such large quantities of produce, even though they needed help with stocking at the start.[42]

Initially the duration of leases varied considerably, although frequently the account will tell us nothing more than that the lease was held 'for a term of years'. An analysis of 75 leases[43] shows that the vast majority, 71 per cent, were for terms of between 5 and 14 years in length. Among the earliest leases on each manor none provide for terms longer than 12 years. In general, leases were short, and there was no progressive lengthening of the lease in the sample, compared with those on the estates of Canterbury Cathedral Priory, Westminster Abbey or the bishopric of Worcester.[44] There are signs, however, that the situation may have been changing at the end of the fifteenth century and the beginning of the sixteenth. In general, those manors with long-term leases tend to be the smaller ones: of the four manors with leases over 21 years in length, Westwood (40 years and 3 lives), Stockton (24 years

---

42. BL Harl Rl X/8; X/13; X/14.
43. As listed in Hare, 'Lord and tenant', 123.
44. Harvey, *Westminster Abbey*, 157; Dyer, *Lords and peasants*, 210–11.

and 1 life) and Homington (1 life) fitted into this category. Only Collingbourne (31 years) was a large one. There are also signs of such lengthening of terms on the estate of the bishopric of Winchester (not included in the sample) at the end of the fifteenth century. Thus, in 1499, the tenant was in the ninth year of a 21-year lease at Downton, the eighth year of a 41-year lease at Bishopstone and the fifth year of a 41-year lease at Fonthill Bishop.[45] On the estates of Winchester Cathedral Priory the 1490s were to see an increased enrolment of leases in the chapter register, and they were often much longer than the previous norm, frequently being for 40 years.[46]

On the ecclesiastical estates of southern England, the 1490s marked a significant stage in the process of leasing. A series of long-term leases was produced and such landlords showed an increased concern for enrolling the leases, as may be seen elsewhere at the time on the estates of Westminster Abbey and the archbishop of Canterbury.[47] Evidence elsewhere suggests substantial contemporary building programmes for farmhouses, as at Littleton (Hants) and Overton (Hants), on the estates of Winchester Cathedral Priory and the bishopric of Winchester respectively.[48] So far, the small and very untypical manor house of Westwood provides the only documented Wiltshire parallel.[49] Elsewhere in the south of England the 1490s saw a further stage in the process of leasing, with most of the few remaining demesnes being leased on the estates of Battle, Glastonbury and Tavistock Abbeys.[50] Leasing had now become a permanent feature of estate policy. It was ironic that this was happening on the eve of what was to be a long period of inflation, when long leases would not be in the landlords' interests. Finally, as the dissolution of the monasteries approached, some much longer leases were found, as with the demesne at Lacock, which was leased in 1533 to the brother-in-law of the abbess for 99 years. But, by then, there were more than economic factors at stake, and the abbess may have been looking after family interests at a time when monastic estates may have begun to seem less secure.

The leasing of the demesne did not mark an end to the lord's involvement in the manorial economy. Large-scale building could still be his responsibility, as shown by the construction of new barns at Ludgershall (1429–34), Durrington (1412–13), Downton (1410) and Coombe Bisset (1398–1400), of a substantial new hall and chamber at Stockton (1416–17), and in the roofing repairs to the great barn at All Cannings (1471). Such projects might cost £50 or more.[51] This was not unique to the county, as the great surviving Hampshire barns of Overton and Burghclere make

---

45. Payne, 'Agrarian conditions', 307–8.
46. *The register of the common seal of the Priory of St. Swithun, Winchester, 1345–1497*, ed. J. Greatrex, Hampshire Record Series 2 (Winchester, 1978), *passim*; WCL Register of the common seal, vol 2, *passim*.
47. Harvey, *Westminster Abbey*, 153; F.R.H. Du Boulay, 'A rentier economy in the later Middle Ages: the archbishopric of Canterbury', *EcHR*, 2nd series 16 (1964), 266; *Register of the common seal*, passim; WCL Register of the common seal, vol. 2, *passim*.
48. Hare, 'The bishop and the prior', 211.
49. E. Roberts, 'Overton Court Farm and late-medieval farmhouses of demesne lessees in Hampshire', *PHFCAS*, 51 (1996), 91–5, 103–4; D. Sutton, *Westwood Manor* (London, 1962).
50. Hare, 'Monks as landlords', 87.
51. TNA: PRO SC6/1054/25; WCM 5967 and 8 (£42 13s 3d); 4628–30 (£10 15s 3d), 5388 (£56 9s 6 ½d); BL Add Rl 24407 and 8; WRO 192/28 (1471).

clear.[52] As in subsequent centuries, landlords were expected to invest in their estates, in farmhouses and buildings, although the lessee had responsibility for maintenance.[53] But, when circumstances permitted, cultivation could be resumed, whether in order to find a new tenant or to enhance the lord's own profits. By 1528 the abbot of Stanley had resumed control over some of his pasture leases, which he was now reoccupying for what was stated to be his greater profit.[54]

Why did leasing occur?

Why, then, had leasing occurred? Unfortunately there is little evidence of the last days of demesne agriculture from most of the lay or church estates, apart from the bishopric of Winchester, making it difficult to resolve this question. The general economic arguments are clear, but do not provide a complete explanation. The later fourteenth century was a period when the long-term economic situation was no longer as advantageous to the lord. Rising wages increased the cost of arable farming, while static or falling prices and falling yields together destroyed the profitability that had made possible this exceptional period of high farming. This did not immediately occur: grain yields and prices dropped to new levels in the 1380s,[55] but little leasing had occurred by 1400 on the church estates in the chalklands. We are left to explain both why leasing occurred and why the old system was retained for so long. We should also remember that in the many centuries of English seigneurial agriculture the period of direct cultivation by the lord might be seen as an important but transient development. Both before and after this phase, lords leased out their land to tenant farmers and agricultural improvement occurred in partnership with these tenants.

Only one of the manors that has been systematically studied, Bromham, provides us with a great deal of information about the latter stages of demesne arable farming. This manor, however, lay away from the chalklands and cannot claim to be typical. Here demesne agriculture remained relatively stable until the 1390s, only to be followed in the fifteenth century by a period of reduction and uncertainty with intermittent periods of leasing and direct cultivation. The sown acreage remained high until 1400 (225 acres, varying between 168 and 301 acres), but thereafter the arable was on a much smaller scale. Although both the acreage and livestock remained at a lower level, this was not a period of continuous decline, and totals remained at a consistent level of about 100–130 acres (Tables 6.2 and 6.3). This shrinkage, however, concealed a worsening of the financial position of demesne agriculture: income from sales fell, but wages remained at the higher total they had reached in the later

---

52. Roberts, 'Overton Court Farm', 102–3; Overton and Burghclere both belonged to the bishopric of Winchester.
53. As in the nineteenth century, T.W. Beastall, 'Landlords and tenants', in G.W. Mingay (ed), *The Victorian countryside* (London, 1981), 428–9.
54. TNA: PRO SC6/Hen VIII/3958.
55. See Miller (ed.), *Agrarian history*. The evidence of the bishopric of Winchester prices suggests that in Wiltshire the price fall had already occurred by 1380 (LSE, Beveridge prices and wages collection Box B2, grain prices from bishopric of Winchester pipe rolls. The wheat figures are graphed in Hare, 'Lord and tenant', fig. III).

fourteenth century, despite the reduced size of the demesne (Table 6.4). One important factor in the declining revenue from demesne agriculture lay in falling yields, with a major drop between the 1380s and the 1420s and 30s (Table 6.5). A reduction in grain sales transformed the finances of agriculture in 1399 and 1400. In these two years only 30 quarters and 29 quarters were sold, compared with almost 77 quarters in 1392. In part this represents the impact of falling yields, which here were dramatic. The figures for the 1380s suggest a much higher productivity by comparison both with later figures and with those for the bishopric of Winchester estate (Table 6.5). But the Winchester material suggests that the 1380s was a period of particularly high productivity, as do the figures for Heytesbury, so that the use of this period, determined by the surviving yield calculations of the documents, may produce an untypical picture of high production.[56] These good times could not last, but the long-term trends were perhaps less dramatic than the figures suggests.

At Bromham the scale of demesne agriculture shrank in the fifteenth century. The fall in arable farming was accompanied by a check in livestock levels after the 1380s, which maintained a lower level in the fifteenth century; sheep disappeared after 1424 (see Table 6.3). There were, however, signs of a limited revival of pig and cattle herds in the 1430s, particularly in 1435. The general shrinkage threatened the financial viability of demesne agriculture, although this was worsened by the repeated shifts in policy from leasing to direct cultivation. Restocking was expensive. Acreages fell faster than the wage bill. Lords were perhaps increasingly open to alternatives, and estate policy showed a new flexibility to short-term trends. Here all three attempts at leasing occurred after short spells of low prices. If the lord gave up agriculture because of low prices it was as a result of short-term rather than of long-term factors. But when leasing finally occurred it does not seem to have made any dramatic impact on the finances of the manor of Bromham. Here the product of the demesne was sold and the cash then sent to Battle, so that the profits of the demesne were incorporated in the annual cash livery. The annual value of the livery in the first five years after leasing (1443–8) was less than 1.4 per cent lower than in the previous six years, but even this fall may not have resulted entirely from the demesne lands, but from changes in other parts of the lord's revenue.[57]

The contracting size of demesne agriculture at Bromham was not typical. In the chalklands, arable acreages remained stable. Any changes there were long-term and had occurred well before leasing. The early fifteenth century was to be a period of difficulties, despite the general rural prosperity and the resilient demand for foodstuffs, but it does not seem to have been a time of crisis. On the bishopric of Winchester estates in the Wiltshire and Hampshire downlands yields seem to have been lower in the period after 1411 than in the 30 years before, particularly in barley, and this was also seen at Bromham.[58] Given the general background of low profits, short-term problems may have encouraged lords to reappraise their agricultural policies. The 1420s seem to have been a particularly troublesome period for barley

---

56. D.L. Farmer, 'Grain yields on the Winchester manors in the later Middle Ages', *EcHR*, 2nd series 30 (1977), 555–66; Payne, 'Agrarian conditions', 122–4.
57. TNA: PRO SC6/1047/15–23, 1048/5.
58. Farmer, 'Grain yields', 557–61.

Table 6.2
Bromham: the decline of demesne agriculture, arable sown area.

Date	Wheat	Rye	Barley	Dredge	Peas	Oats	Total
1345	44	60	50	57	9	16	236
1377	93	53	40	42.5	20*	53	301
1381	75	26	41	22	4	36	204
1392	70	32	45	18	5	41	211
1402	40	16	22	8		28	114
1411	44	24	26.5	5.5		36	136
1421	53	14	27	4		9	107
1432	52		24	24		19	119
1442	60		26		6	40	132

* includes beans
Source: TNA: PRO SC6/1045/14, /1047/2.

Table 6.3
Bromham, the decline of demesne agriculture, livestock.

Date	Horses	Oxen	Other cattle	Sheep	Pigs
1345	5	6	56	387	50
1377	4	21	26	147	45
1381	5	20	34	222	46
1386	6	21	33	195	61
1392	5	25	34	221	32
1399	7	19	36	150	39
1402	5	10	13	85	15
1411	9	9	21	103	14
1416	5	11	23	35	21
1421	2	11	23	21	33
1424#	2	11	18	25	-
1432	2	13	17	-	14
1437	5	18	21	-	
1442#	1	10	14	-	22

includes stock delivered to lessee.
Source: simplified from J.N. Hare, 'Lord and tenant in Wiltshire, c.1380–1520, with particular reference to regional and seigneurial variations', PhD thesis (London, 1976), Appendix table I, 347–8. The original table covers all 37 accounts in PRO from 1345 to 1442 with figures for 51 years (TNA: PRO SC6 1045/14–1047/2).

production, which had already become a much more important aspect of the rural economy of the county and especially of the chalklands. If such a period of difficulty did not lead directly to lords giving up the demesne, the problems may at least have helped to ensure that the lords and their councils looked again at alternatives.

Leasing was thus encouraged by underlying economic developments: long-term trends in wages, prices and yields created difficulties that made the old system of arable demesne farming vulnerable. But it is difficult to explain the precise motivation that led to the leasing of the demesnes, and we also need to explain the contrasts that emerged. Why were there regional variations in leasing, with the process taking place earlier outside the chalklands, while direct farming continued into the second quarter of the fifteenth century in the chalklands and sheep farming was maintained long after arable farming had ceased? Finally, why were the ecclesiastical estates so much more conservative in their leasing policy than comparable lay estates?

Table 6.4
Bromham: the finances of demesne agriculture.

Date	Acreage sown	Sale of grain	Sale of stock	Purchase of stock	Wages
1345	236	£19 13s 6d	£7 9s 0d	£1 4s 2d	£4 4s 5d
1377	301	£2 9s 4d	£5 15s 1d	£3 9s 2½d	£2 5s 4½d
1381	204	£8 7s 6½d	£4 3s 10d	£2 16s 8½d	£3 14s 2d
1386	197	£20 8s 6¾d	£3 14s 1d	10s 10d	
1392	211	£16 0s 2d	£5 5s 1d	10s 0d	£6 4s 9½d
1399	225	£5 7s 2d	£3 12s 2d	£6 1s 10d	
1402	114	£6 19s 10d	£18 0s 10d	£5 0s 0d	£6 8s 10d
1411	136	£8 12s 1½d	£1 16s 8d	14s 1d	£5 6s 11½d
1416	154	£5 5s 0d	£2 12s 0d	£1 10s 2½d	£4 12s 3½d
1421	107	£9 0s 9d	£4 1s 0d	12s 7d	£5 1s 9d
1425	None	£0 17s 0d	£3 6s 9d	15s 6d	
1432	119	£3 9s 0½d	£1 4s 0d	5s 4d	£4 5s 0d
1437	160	£4 13s 8d	£2 10s 10d	3s 0d	£3 18s 10d
1442	132	£7 10s 11d	£3 5s 9d		

Notes: on calculation of the wage total: occasional wage items are found scattered throughout the many sections of the expense account. This total is not exhaustive, therefore, but is based on the following principles: it includes the entries for threshing and winowing, weeding and mowing, harvesting and those parts of the wage and stipend entries which concern agriculture (the steward's fees have been excluded). Sale of hides and wool occur under the heading of the issues of the manor, and have not been included. The demesne was leased after 1402, when stock was being reduced, in 1425 and in 1443. During the first period of leasing from 1404 to 1410 the harvest works were commuted, increasing the amount of wage labour that would subsequently be required. The dating of the Bromham accounts for the reign of Henry IV: those for 1400 and 1401 have taken the regnal year as beginning on 30 September; thereafter they begin on 29 September, so that the last account is from Michaelmas 14 Henry IV. The change can be dated to the 1402 account, since the account for 3–4 Henry IV must on internal evidence immediately follow that from 1–2 Henry IV. A similar change seems to have happened elsewhere on the Battle estate, as shown on the cellarers' accounts: *Accounts of the cellarers of Battle Abbey 1275–1513*, ed. E. Searle and B. Ross (Sydney, 1967). Source: simplified from J.N. Hare, 'Lord and tenant in Wiltshire, c.1380–1520, with particular reference to regional and seigneurial variations', PhD thesis (London, 1976), Appendix table I, 347–8. The original table covers all 37 accounts in PRO from 1345 to 1442 with figures from all surviving accounts (PRO SC6 1045/14- 1047/2).

Table 6.5
Bromham, grain yields.

	Wheat	Rye	Winter barley	Spring barley	Dredge	Oats	Peas
1384–9	7 (3)	4.5 (5)	4.7 (5)	4.7 (6)	4.3 (6)	3.4 (4)	
1419–23	4.8 (3)	3.8 (3)		3 (3)	4 (1)	2 (1)	
1433–40	3.8 (2)	3.3 (3)		3.1 (5)	2.5 (1)	3.5 (4)	3.5 (3)

Notes: The figures have been calculated from 15 account rolls. The yield renders are not recorded systematically in the account rolls, either for all accounts or within a single account. In addition, many have been lost through damage to the left-hand margin of the account roll. The number of entries used has been listed in brackets.
Source: TNA: PRO SC6/1045/24; 1046/1, 2, 3, 4, 5, 21, 22, 24; 1047/1, 3, 4, 15, 18, 20.

Certainly, the new system was administratively more convenient. Administrators now had to ensure merely that the rent for the lease was paid; previously they had had the more difficult task of checking that the reeve had not cheated the lord on any single item of sales or wage payments. Nowhere is the impact of this change seen more clearly than in the size of the new account rolls. No longer were parchment accounts with many hundreds of entries required. Administrative simplification had already begun on some estates, where lords had sought to fix yields. This was particularly seen in the fixing of the expected yields of calves, milk and piglets on, for example, the estates of the Cathedral Priory and the bishopric of Winchester.[59] If the yield was higher than expected the tenant took the surplus. Leasing marked the end of a long period of struggle.[60]

Moreover, this administrative convenience could be achieved without the drawback of a severe financial loss. Unfortunately the Wiltshire evidence rarely allows us to make a strict comparison of the financial system before and after leasing, but it can be done for Bromham and for the manors of New College, Oxford, at Alton Barnes and Stert, all in a similar area, and where the liveries were not confused by rent in kind. At Bromham grain yields had fallen substantially by the 1420s and 1430s and the net income from demesne agriculture showed extensive variation and uncertainty in its last few decades (see Tables 6.2–6.5). Leasing provided the lord with a settled secure income in place of considerable fluctuations. This would have been the case also at Stert and Alton Barnes, which were leased at a similar time (1431, 1433). Both, before this leasing, had seen a very fluctuating and generally lower income. At Stert the income after leasing was slightly reduced but more stable; at Alton Barnes it saw some recovery after a few particularly difficult years, and at a more stable level.[61]

There were some large demesnes outside the chalklands, but in general their smaller size and the lack of large sheep flocks may have made it easier for the lord to lease the demesnes there and even to lease to a group of tenants. The economic factors may have been little different, but the change in practice was less risky for lord and tenant alike. In explaining this later survival and flourishing of demesne agriculture in the chalklands, it is also necessary to remember the conservatism of the ecclesiastical estates. It was a conservatism partly encouraged by the different functions of respective parts of the estate. A monastic house required the reliable provision of food, and the large estates of the chalklands regularly performed such a role. This may help to contribute to the longevity of demesne agriculture on the estates of Winchester Cathedral Priory or of St Mary's Abbey, Winchester, where their Wiltshire estates had previously served as food producers, and often continued to do so after leasing. But the need for food was not always such a significant factor. Bromham had long produced cash, not food, for distant Battle Abbey, but it continued to be cultivated long after most of the abbey's more central manors had ceased cultivation. Nor would the need for food explain the long-continued production on the estates of the bishopric of Winchester: they also sold the produce and sent cash to

---

59. J.S. Drew, 'Manorial accounts of St Swithun's Priory Winchester', in Carus-Wilson, *Essays in economic history*, 2, 12–31; *Pipe roll 1409–10*, xx.
60. Drew, 'Manorial accounts', 29.
61. Evans and Faith, 'College estates', 675.

the lord. There may have been a general conservatism about clerical estate policies but too much should not be made of this. Such estates shared officials with their lay counterparts; they were part of the same world of estate administration. The highly capital-intensive sheep farming of the duchy of Lancaster in the early fifteenth century brought together the policies being pursued by an ecclesiastical lord, Henry Beaufort (the bishop of Winchester), and the secular Lord Hungerford, both of whom were among the feoffees of the duchy of Lancaster manors. Moreover, the leasing policies pursued by the ecclesiastical landowners contrasted with those of similar landowners elsewhere. It is perhaps more appropriate to see this as a regional development produced by agrarian prosperity and underpinned by the need for large sheep flocks and thus the necessity for large capital investment in those flocks. The ecclesiastical estates were relatively compact by comparison with their lay counterparts: even the vast estates of the bishopric of Winchester did not stretch beyond southern England, and the core of their estates lay in the chalklands of that area. They may have found it easier to develop a distinct regional policy than the greater lay estates, in which such manors formed a very small part of the wider whole, scattered over many counties.

Moreover, a limited element of conservatism could have led to a substantial difference in policy. An estate that maintained direct cultivation until the 1390s would have run into a period characterised by the growth of the cloth industry and an expanding demand for meat, grain and wool, circumstances which encouraged continued direct cultivation. Even a lay estate like that of the Hungerfords might resume cultivation on some of its manors. In such a situation the policies of ecclesiastical lords may have owed as much to a perception of economic reality as to any innate conservatism: or the former may have reinforced the latter.

On many chalkland manors lords maintained their sheep flocks long after they had leased their arable lands. The profits of sheep farming were probably more secure: wool and meat were in great demand in the early fifteenth century, and low labour demands reduced the impact of rising wages. The large sheep flocks were an essential feature of the fertility and the profitability of the arable sector, as the animals were required for their manure. Finally, the large scale of the demesne sheep flocks and the higher risk of sheep farming, compared with arable, may have led to an initial inability to find people who were prepared or able to lease these flocks, hence in some cases leading to the use of stock and land leases. The lords were able to apply their great strength: the ability to raise high capital investments and to finance the large flocks.

Yet within a few decades this had all changed. In 1440 most of the chalkland demesnes studied here continued to maintain their sheep flocks, but by 1480 most had given up these flocks. This wide-scale cessation of demesne sheep farming would seem to have been linked to short-term low wool prices in the mid-century and particular local manorial difficulties, as well as the underlying longer-term problems of falling wool yields and the increased dependence on peasant flocks for renewal. Having a flock that had to be renewed by purchase was a simpler but more expensive option. Sheep farming could still make substantial profits in the early fifteenth century, but the finances were more vulnerable and some estates gave up their flocks before the impact of the mid-fifteenth-century crisis. This occurred in the 1430s and 1440s at both Kingston Deverill and Alton Barnes. In both cases the decision followed a short-term fall in prices, although these did not reach record depths. The difficulties of the duchy estates and the end of sheep cultivation have already been examined, and may have resulted from administrative restructuring as well as the declining profitablity of the sheep flocks.[62] Subsequently, the decades from the 1450s to the 1470s saw dramatic difficulties for sheep cultivation across England. Prices fell and lords in the second half of the century received an average 25 per cent less than in the first half, while in seven years prices fell to below 2s per stone: in 1452–3, 1455–6, 1459–60, 1474–5, 1475–6, 1476–7 and 1478–9. Lords such as Syon Abbey found it impossible to sell the year's wool crop at a suitable price and kept the wool in store, but this in turn generated financial losses.[63] It was not surprising that gradually in this period many lords, including Winchester Cathedral Priory and St Mary's Abbey, Winchester, would reappraise their sheep-farming activities and lease the flocks. By the end of the century direct cultivation of flocks was largely confined to some of the ecclesiastical manors in southern Wiltshire and Dorset, as on the estates of Wilton and Shaftesbury Abbeys.

The leasing of the demesnes reflected the regional nature of Wiltshire farming and its long-inherited patterns of landownership. The chronology of the process shows that its chalkland estates tended to lag far behind comparable estates elsewhere in the vale of Wiltshire and indeed in England. This conservatism reflected the large-scale nature of chalkland agriculture, and above all of the sheep flocks, as well as the prosperity engendered by the growth of the cloth industry in the later Middle Ages and the increased demands for agricultural produce. The landlords now resumed their role as rentiers: they were concerned at how their tenants looked after the land but were not directly involved in agriculture themselves. It was a role which they would continue to play in succeeding centuries. The process also produced a regional impact: there was no break-up of the demesnes in the chalklands, but such a subdivision occurred on some manors elsewhere in the county. The process thus reinforced the regional contrasts, but left the chalklands with the large-scale agriculture that was to remain its dominant characteristic in succeeding centuries.

---

62. See Chapter 5.
63. J. Hatcher, 'The great slump of the mid-fifteenth century', in R.H. Britnell and J. Hatcher (eds), *Progress and problems in medieval England: essays in honour of Edward Miller* (Cambridge, 1996), 236–72; D.L. Farmer, 'Prices and wages, 1350–1500', in Miller, *Agrarian History of England and Wales*, 431–525; M. Mate, 'Pastoral farming in south-east England in the fifteenth century', *EcHR*, 2nd series 40 (1987), 525–6.

Chapter 7

The demesne lessees

During this period the great lords ceased to cultivate their demesne lands and began instead to rent them out for a specified and regular amount of cash or produce. Such a development offered enormous opportunities for tenants who were not manorial lords to expand their agricultural production, but who was it who benefited? Did the process help to produce a social transformation in the countryside? Were the great lords replaced as cultivators by large numbers of village peasants,[1] by wealthy outsiders or by men who were already much superior in wealth and social status to the rest of the village population?[2] Was there a shift over time from peasant lessees to gentry ones?[3] Previous work has tended to focus on the study of individual estates. But how typical were the estates of the archbishop of Canterbury or of the abbey of Westminster? Were the gentry lessees on such estates the beneficiaries of patronage rather than the profiteers of the open market? Were they an exceptional minority or a more significant group? There were clearly lessees who, whatever their origin, were evidently now farming on a substantial scale and who can no longer usefully be described as peasants. These were men who were not able to cultivate using family labour alone, but were employers of much labour, and who produced extensively for the market. People like Roger Heritage of Burton Dassett (Warks.) can aptly be described as capitalists.[4] Here in Wiltshire, a pattern of large-scale tenancies emerges, particularly in the chalklands. Whatever the social origin of these families, they became economically separated from the peasant population of the village, and often increasingly socially distinct as well.

This attempt to establish who were leasing the demesnes has been based on building up as detailed a picture as possible of the individual lessees on 14 Wiltshire manors before 1510, focusing on the men who were leasing wholesale the demesne lands. As in the previous chapter, other manorial resources, such as rabbit warrens, mills, quarries and rectory tithes, have not been included as they would have

---

1. e.g. J.E.T. Rogers, *Six centuries of work and wages* (Oxford, 1906), 274f; A.R. Bridbury, *Economic growth: England in the later Middle Ages*, 2nd edn (London, 1975), 41–2. M.M. Postan, 'The fifteenth century' and 'Medieval agrarian society in its prime: England', in M.M. Postan (ed.), *The Cambridge economic history of Europe*, i, *The agrarian life of the Middle Ages*, 2nd edn (Cambridge, 1966), 42–4 and 630–2.
2. e.g. F.R.H. Du Boulay, 'Who were farming the English demesnes at the end of the Middle Ages?' *EcHR*, 2nd series 17 (1965), 443–55; B. Harvey, 'The leasing of the abbot of Westminster's demesnes in the later Middle Ages', *EcHR*, 2nd series 22 (1969), 21, though neither writer suggests that peasant lessees were not important. See also B. Harvey, *Westminster Abbey and its estates* (Oxford, 1977), 151–2. See also now C. Dyer, *An age of transition? Economy and society in the later Middle Ages* (Oxford, 2005), 197–210.
3. As on the bishopric of Worcester estates: C. Dyer, *Lords and peasants in a changing society: the estates of the bishopric of Worcester, 680–1540* (Cambridge, 1980), 211. The term 'lessee', rather than the term 'farmer', has been used in order to avoid the ambiguity of the latter term.
4. C. Dyer, *Everyday life in medieval England* (London, 1994), 315–22.

distracted attention from the main issue: who took over the agricultural land of the manor. It also excludes those manors where the demesne was leased to a group of peasants, as this would have distorted the figures by involving too many individuals from a single manor. In Wiltshire these group or multiple leases were largely to be found away from the chalklands, as at Oaksey, thus emphasising the growing contrast between farming in the chalklands and elsewhere. The sample includes a wide variety of manors, although with a preponderance of certain types: of large manors, of those on large estates and particularly of chalkland manors. The sample includes large and small, lay and ecclesiastical, chalkland and non-chalkland manors. The documentation is at its best for the chalklands. Other known lessees from beyond the sample manors have been included in the discussion.

In building up a picture of our lessees and their families the evidence of the manorial records (account rolls, court rolls and rentals) has been supplemented by other sources, such as wills, taxation returns, receivers' accounts and individual leases and deeds. To establish a picture of the background of each lessee it was necessary to look first at the activities of earlier members of the family; our material is far too limited to depend on information about the individual lessee himself. But the sources rarely provide us with any direct evidence about family relationships, and surnames have therefore had to be used as an indicator of his family connections. Relationships through the mother are missed. But the problem of name duplication does not seem to be serious. In the manors examined in Wiltshire it was rare for there to be more than two families with the same name, and when this did occur, a distinguishing alias was usually added. Thus the Weylot family of Durrington also produced a Weylot alias Carter and a Weylot alias Barbour family, although in the latter case the family seems later to have dropped the original name and became known by the alias alone. Families with the same name but occurring on different manors have not been linked, unless there is positive evidence suggesting a relationship between them. Thus when a Benger of Alton Barnes acted as a pledge for another Benger, an outsider who leased the demesne at Durrington, it suggests the likelihood of a family link. It is important, however, to stress the fragmentary nature of our documentation. Our knowledge of individual families must inevitably be based on occasional glimpses into their land-holding or other activities. But this should not deter us from trying to ascertain what sort of men leased the Wiltshire demesnes.

The 14 manors in our sample are Enford, Stockton, Westwood, Wroughton, Aldbourne, Collingbourne (Ducis), Everleigh, Upavon, Durrington, Coombe Bissett, All Cannings, Urchfont, Kingston Deverill and Bromham. Together they provide a list of 88 lessees from 67 different families. For some of these, little about them could be discovered except for their leasing activities: we know nothing about 13 of these families save that they leased a particular manor at a particular time. In attempting any quantitative analysis of these lessees a choice had to be made between the family and the individual, as 14 of the families produced 2 or more lessees. In view of the limitations of the evidence it was considered that analysis in terms of individuals might have distorted the results by giving undue prominence to a few well-documented families. Calculations have therefore been based on families (Table 7.1).

Table 7.1
Leasing families on fourteen Wiltshire manors: their origins

Local (active in the village before they leased the demesne)	
Customary tenants	26
Unknown status	8
Foreign (from families based outside the village)	
Customary tenants	1
Leased demesnes elsewhere	2
Gentlemen	1
Unknown origin	
Unknown before they leased	14
Unknown before and after they leased	13
Total	68

Note: 67 families are known to have leased on the fourteen manors up to 1510, and 14 of these also leased elsewhere. The Harvests have been included both as a local customary family (for Urchfont) and as a family of foreign lessees (for All Cannings and Durrington). This accounts for the additional entry in the total.

The village or peasant lessees

Despite the enormous variety of lessees an analysis of the sample, summarised in Table 7.1, highlights the importance of one particular group: of 67 families in the survey, at least 26 were drawn from the ranks of local customary tenants. Moreover, while this figure constitutes 39 per cent of the sample, it almost certainly underestimates the importance of this group. The use of the surname provides an indication of descent through fathers, but would miss out on descent through mothers. Furthermore, the documentary limitations conceal the local origins of some lessees. A further 8 lessees can be shown to have been active in their respective village before they leased the demesne there, although no record survives of their tenurial status. Finally, nothing is known about 27 lessees and their families in the period before they undertook the leasing of the demesne. Occasionally, enough documents survive for a particular manor to suggest that the family had indeed come from outside the manor. This is confirmed by other sources for the Bengers and Harvests, who both first came to Durrington as lessees and who were linked to families based on Alton Barnes and Urchfont respectively. But such cases are rare. For most manors, the documentary evidence is too fragmentary for us to attach significance to any lack of earlier references. It is clear, therefore, that at least a large minority, and probably a majority, of the leasing families had previously been customary tenants of the manor where they later leased the demesne.

A fuller picture of some of the lives and backgrounds of these lessees can be established. Some of the families were to be found on their manor a century or more before they became lessees, and for some this long-standing tenure on the manor was symbolised in their continued burden of serfdom. At least five families of demesne lessees retained their unfree status into the fifteenth century, at a time when such survival was unusual. In the case of the Gerveys and the Mascall families, they can be seen gaining their manumission. But as would be expected, in view of the mobility of the tenant population in this period,[5] other lessees were drawn from among relatively recent immigrants to the village. Families such as the Langfords of Durrington did not appear there until the fifteenth century, and therefore were not subjected to the personal disabilities of serfdom.

In general, these lessees and their families came from among the tenants of the large standard customary tenements, whether these were virgates, as at Durrington, or half-virgates, as at Stockton. At Stockton in the 1350s two ancestors of later lessees both held half-virgates.[6] At Durrington the 1388 rental includes the families of three future lessees. One had accumulated a virgate and an additional cottage and few acres, another was temporarily holding two virgates, while a third held no more than a single virgate.[7] The lessees thus came from among the more substantial families of the village, but from a broad village minority and not necessarily from the customary tenants with the largest holdings. Occasionally the family included someone who was a cottager, but not for long. A newcomer might start as a cottager, either as a craftsman or agricultural labourer, while the son of a substantial tenant farmer might take his first step to independence by setting up home in a cottage. But the ready availability of land meant that such men, and certainly those capable of leasing a demesne, soon moved on to a standard customary tenement.

These lessees came from families whose members were accustomed to playing an active role in village life: eight of our lessees had earlier acted as reeve; one had acted as rent collector; and another had a father who had been reeve.[8] These 10 examples may not appear particularly significant when compared with the 67 families in the sample or even with the 24 families of local customary tenants. But this figure is a clear underestimate, as very few account rolls survive for Wiltshire manors in the last days of seigneurial cultivation, so that we have few surviving names for those who acted as reeve on these manors in the later fourteenth and early fifteenth centuries.

These lessees also held other positions of responsibility. They were to be found in charge of the lord's flocks, as a juror for the collection of a royal subsidy and as reap reeves. Others can be seen playing an active role in the administration of law and order in the village, acting as, for example, pledges and tithing men.[9] In addition to the routine pledging these families are also occasionally seen supporting other lessees. When Richard atte Mere leased Durrington in 1389 John Gilberd was one of two other men who pledged themselves for £100 to secure Richard's lease.[10] Such a task

---

5. Below, Chapter 8.
6. BL Add Rl 24394.
7. WCM 5596; 5950, 5954, 5956.
8. Thomas Goddard and John Runte at Aldbourne, Richard Cantelowe, Richard Batte and Richard Webbe at Collingbourne, John Daniel at Kingston Deverill, Robert atte Mere at Durrington and Nicholas atte Mulle at Coombe Bissett (R. Payne, 'Agrarian conditions on the Wiltshire estates of the duchy of Lancaster, the lords Hungerford and the bishopric of Winchester', PhD thesis (London, 1940), 284; TNA: PRO DL29/710/11446, 737/12071, 737/12076; WRO 192/32; WCM 5650a, 4622); John Colet at All Cannings (WRO 192/28); John Gerveys at Enford (WCL Register of the Dean and Chapter, formerly of the Cathedral Priory, i, fo.33).
9. TNA: PRO DL29/683/11061; BL Add Rl 19719; *Inquisitions and assessments relating to feudal aids. Vol. 5, Stafford to Worcester* (London, 1908), 233; WCM 5650 k.
10. WCM 5650m. For another example see TNA: PRO DL29/685/11087, m2.

clearly required men of greater wealth and repute than the normal pledge. Later John himself became a lessee. Similarly, when John Stannford leased Collingbourne in 1443 his two pledges were both future lessees. Other lessees performed prominent roles in the village: for example, they are commonly found as brewers who regularly broke the assize. The social origins of this group of lessees are to be found among the substantial tenants of the village whose judicial and administrative activities formed an essential part of the smooth running of the community. Such lessees' wealth and experience was well suited to the challenge of taking on the responsibilities of leasing the demesnes.

A well-documented example of such a local lessee is John Hickes, who took on the demesne at Durrington from 1401 until his death in 1413/14.[11] He came of a long-established family of Durrington customary tenants that had held a virgate or more in 1334/35, 1359 and 1388. In 1411/12 John Hickes had three virgates and with two other tenants shared an additional virgate.[12] Already before he had leased the demesne he had raised himself far above most of the other customary tenants (although this was not typical of the lessees), but the family was not to last. After his death his lands passed to his son or brother William, but the latter in turn died soon afterwards and in 1428 his widow surrendered her lands.[13] The Hickes family was certainly no stranger to responsibility: John Hickes was reeve in 1357–9, and John Hickes, the future lessee, served as rent collector from 1399 to 1401.[14] The family also held other influential posts in the local community, such as tithing man and assessor to the manorial court.[15] Members of the family could often be found as pledges, including for another lessee.[16] As in the 1390s, they were regularly to be found as brewers; but legally the family remained a villein one.[17] A similar picture of the background and activity of a leasing family could be provided for the Mascalls and Shilvingstoles of Stockton, or for the atte Meres of Durrington, or, outside our sample, for the Alweys of Colerne.[18]

In origin, at least, these men may aptly be described as peasants. But the leasing of the demesnes and the extensive scale of their agriculture provided the opportunities for men to rise above the rest of their village neighbours. Thus, when later in 1545 a very selective benevolence was levied, its contributors included a number who were descended from the customary 'peasant' lessees: a Mascal at Stockton, a Goddard and a Shepherd at Aldbourne and a Cerle at Enford.[19] Not all prospered, however, and Robert Hopkyns alias Shilvingstole of Stockton provides a

---

11. WCM 5956–5969.
12. WCM 5601a, 5601Ca, 5596, 13373.
13. WCM 5655q.
14. WCM Index (Durrington account rolls); WCM 5954–5.
15. WCM 5650a, 5655t.
16. WCM 5650r & m.
17. WCM 5650k & p.
18. The Mascals and Shilvingstole families are discussed in J.N. Hare, 'Lord and tenant in Wiltshire, c.1380–1520, with particular reference to regional and seigneurial variations', PhD thesis (London, 1976), 209–12. For the atte Meres see the Durrington records in WCM, and, for the Alweys, below Chapter 8.
19. *Two sixteenth century taxation lists, 1545 and 1576*, ed. G.D. Ramsay, Wiltshire Record Society 10 (Devizes, 1954).

cautionary corrective. When he died, a few years after having leased the demesne there, nothing could be raised for his heriot, 'for he had no goods or chattels'.[20] Even if we should not take this phrase literally, it suggests that, at the very least, Robert's position was not a very prosperous one.

Some lessees in the records are shadowy figures who come into view only when they leased the demesne. There are 13 families about which nothing is known prior to the start of the lease or subsequent to its termination. In part, such ignorance may result from the fragmentary nature of the documentation, but in other cases they were probably substantial 'foreigners' whose involvement in the village was only temporary. Not surprisingly, some of these 'foreign' lessees were drawn from the tenants, customary or otherwise, of neighbouring manors, and often came from a similar social environment to the customary tenants that have already been considered. The Pynkeney family who leased the demesne at Upavon in the late fifteenth century were initially described as 'of Rushall' (a neighbouring village).[21] John Gyffgor was a customary tenant at Durrington, but also leased the demesne at neighbouring Knighton.[22] Other examples include John Thurborne of Amesbury, who leased at Durrington,[23] and the Potter family at Coombe Bissett.[24]

Some lessees came from much further away, although we can then rarely say anything about their social and economic background. But the origins of one of them is particularly well documented. Thomas Weylot alias Barbour, who leased the demesne at Coombe Bissett in the period 1491–1523 and established a family there, certainly came from a family of customary tenants.[25] He was a newcomer to the manor, and was absent from any of the plentiful earlier records. But he was evidently a villein of one of Winchester College's other manors, for the College administration took exceptional pains to stress his personal servility, and even described him on the account rolls as a bondman by blood. No doubt it feared that the change of scene might lead Thomas to be regarded, like other outsiders, as a freeman. Fortunately, the records for the College's manor of Durrington, 12 miles away, show where he came from, and enable us to examine his family background before he moved to Coombe Bissett. The Durrington records show the presence of a family with both the same surname and the same alias – Weylot alias Barbour. Here the Weylots provided many of the substantial and influential members of the village community. They figure regularly on the rentals from 1359/60, holding a half-virgate then and in 1388/89. In 1411/12 one of them held a virgate and another a virgate and additional few acres. Thereafter, the family seems to have proliferated, and in 1444 six members of the family were included on the rental. John Weylot alias Barbour then held two cottages

---

20. BL Add Rl 24382.
21. Payne, 'Agrarian conditions', 304, TNA: PRO Prob 11/14/20.
22. WCM 5655n.
23. WCM 5655u & p, 5603d, 20013.
24. WCM 4646–93, 4351b, 13373, 4396–7; *Wilts IPM* i, 332; *The register of John Chandler, Dean of Salisbury 1407–17*, ed. T.C.B. Timmins, Wiltshire Record Society 39 (Devizes, 1984), 118. The Potter family subsequently became one of the main families on the college manor, as seen in the late-fifteenth-century court rolls.
25. WCM 4721–52, 4354; TNA: PRO Prob 11/21/12.

and eight acres, much less than the others.[26] The Weylots played an active part in village administration, acting as hayward, ale taster, tithing-man, assessor to the manorial court and rent collectors. They were also to be found acting as pledges for, and on one occasion as executor to, other members of the village community.[27] With so many younger sons to support, the Weylots were to be found in several occupations other than those of customary tenant. They provided servants for other lessees: there were a shepherd, a barber and a carter, and several who broke the assize of ale.[28] The family was still a bond, or villein, one and remained so in the later fifteenth century, although parts of the family struggled to achieve, eventually successfully, their freedom.[29]

It is rare for the social origins of our foreign lessees to be so well documented, but this example shows how they could be drawn from among the customary tenantry elsewhere, and how they could move some distance in order to take on a demesne.

The richer lessees

The lessees so far considered generally came from among the more substantial members of the village community, but they were not markedly distinguishable in wealth, tenure or personal status from the rest of the village population. While this group probably provided the bulk of the Wiltshire lessees, there were also men whose wealth and range of interests clearly separated them from the rest of the village community. This is the case despite the general absence of the highest ranks of county society; in our sample only one lessee was described as a gentleman or a knight,[30] and the limited involvement of such men was probably typical of the county as a whole. The many additional records that have been consulted have revealed no other knight leasing a demesne, only one esquire (John Fferres at Oaksey), and only seven who were described as gentlemen.[31]

Below this small group of lessees was a group of men who, although they were not described as gentlemen, cannot be described as peasants. They were men of substance and standing beyond the boundaries of the village where they leased the demesne. The stewards, for example, were freemen of more than parochial standing who held the manorial court and maintained the lord's judicial rights. But they were also to be found

---

26. WCM 5601Ca, 5596, 13373, 5603d.
27. WCM 5601Ca, 5596, 13373, 5603d.
28. e.g. WCM 5950, 5655e, n, j, 5650s, 5656e.
29. See Chapter 8 for the family's gradual escape from serfdom.
30. Sir Walter Hungerford at Everleigh, TNA: PRO DL29/694/11235.
31. John Fferres: Payne, 'Agrarian conditions', 304. Thomas Horton at Westwood after 1518, Richard Hugys alias Baker at Cricklade, John Westley, John Pareham, William Powey and Richard Page at Brixton Deverill, and Richard Dobyn at Stratton St Margaret: WCL Westwood accounts; SDC Chapter Act book Reg. Burgh fo.18; KCM Ledger Book I, fo.28, 48, 187 and 5; T.A.R. Evans and R. Faith (eds), 'College estates and university finances, 1350–1500' in J. Catto and R. Evans (eds), *The history of the university of Oxford, ii: late medieval Oxford* (Oxford, 1992), 687. On Page, who was not described as a gentleman on the lease, see J.N. Hare, 'The Wiltshire risings of 1450: political and economic discontent in mid-fifteenth century England', *Southern History*, 4 (1982),

acting as lessees, as with John Westbury at Kingston Deverill[32] and Thomas Terrante at Enford.[33] Members of baronial households or estate officials also acted as lessees: on the Hungerford estate the lessees included the receiver-general (Gregory Westeby at Winterborne Stoke) and the stockman (John Clayden at Sutton Veny).[34]

The wealth and range of activities of such greater yeomen or petty gentry may be seen in the life of John Stannford (although he may also have been a cleric), whose scale of operations lifted him above the local village population. Interestingly, John or someone with the identical name was rector of Rushall, making him, in this respect, an unusual example of this type of lessee.[35] Although he was described as 'of Rosshale'[36] his activities spread far beyond that small Wiltshire village. The family may have been local, for a John Stannford had leased at Milton and Fyfield in 1379, and a William Stannford was also recorded there.[37] John was an important figure in the administration of the duchy of Lancaster estates, for he was stockman of the southern parts of the duchy. Moreover, this was at a time when the sheep-rearing and grazing activities of these manors became most centralised and co-ordinated under the direction of the feoffees of Henry V's will. His responsibility covered the Wiltshire manors of Aldbourne, Berwick, Collingbourne and Everleigh, and also manors in Dorset, Hampshire and Somerset. He had to tour these manors, seeing to the upkeep of the stock, selling wool and sheep and buying new stock. Something of the scale of his responsibilities may be gauged from the amounts of money he expended on new stock: in 1432/33 he spent £85 8s 4d (buying 846 wethers) and in 1436/37 £67 13s 4d.[38] When, a few years later, the duchy ended its direct involvement in pastoral farming and leased out its pastures, it was not surprising that he should have leased the large demesnes of Collingbourne and Everleigh. To stock these he bought the existing duchy flocks there, and was to pay £76 17s 3d for 1,074 sheep.[39] Stannford's leasing operations were, moreover, even more extensive. He was already leasing the sheep pastures at Upavon from 1423, and by 1448 he leased the whole of the western part of Upavon.[40] In 1439 he secured a seven-year grant of custody on the manor of an alien priory at Charlton.[41] Then came the leases at Collingbourne and Everleigh, and finally in the period 1439–52 he leased Rushall.[42] It is noticeable that all

---

32. WRO 192/32. The Westburys were an important local gentry family. J.L. Kirby, 'The Hungerford family in the later Middle Ages', MA thesis (London, 1939), appendix D; VCH *Wilts* 5, 1957, p 34; *Tropenell cartulary*, ed. J.S. Davies, Wiltshire Archaeological and Natural History Society (Devizes, 1908), *passim*.
33. BL Harl Rl V22.
34. Payne, 'Agrarian conditions', 280–81. Westeby's lease, however, was granted as a financial reward as he lived rent-free on the demesne. For similar examples of estate administrators on the bishopric of Worcester, see Dyer, *Lords and peasants*, 211.
35. T. Phillipps, *Institutiones Clericorum in Comitatu Wiltoniae, 1297–1810*, privately printed, 1825, 129.
36. e.g. TNA: PRO DL29/685/11087; *Cal Close Rl Hen VI*, iii, 495.
37. TNA: PRO E179/194/42a.
38. TNA: PRO DL29/710/11433, 11436.
39. TNA: PRO DL29/685/11087.
40. TNA: PRO DL29/682/11058.
41. *Cal Close Rl, Hen VI*, iii, 495.
42. TNA: PRO SC6/1057/1, 2.

these manors are to be found in a very restricted part of the county, with each manor lying adjacent, or almost adjacent, to a manor on which he had already secured a lease. The scale of his agricultural activities thus certainly marked him off from the peasant lessees or from the rest of the village population. As to his origins, earlier references to a Stannford family in this area suggest that he came from a family of substantial freemen.[43] The family remained prominent in this area in the later fifteenth century (Figure 7.1).[44]

There were also other lessees whose interests lay outside the manor because they were primarily merchants or industrialists. None has so far been found among the lessees in our sample, but work on other manors has shown the involvement of such men. Thomas Horton leased the manor of Westwood in 1518–42, just outside the sample period. He was noted in this part of the country as a great clothier, and was one of three specifically mentioned by Leland as pre-eminent in the Bradford–Trowbridge cloth area.[45] The family's fortunes seem to have been established by his father, John, who had moved his cloth-making activities from Somerset to west Wiltshire and had evidently flourished. By the time of his death he was able to make generous benefactions to churches and his family. His cloth-making interests passed to his second son, the Thomas Horton of our lease. Thomas evidently flourished in the trade, rising to great wealth and fame as one of the most important cloth producers of his time. He built lavishly, including houses, a chantry and almshouses in Bradford and Trowbridge, and added to the manor house and church at Westwood (Plate 11.2). He achieved gentry status and is examined more fully in a later chapter.[46]

The other merchants who leased demesnes are much more shadowy figures. A John Goddard of Marlborough leased at Mildenhall in 1439.[47] He was probably the same as the John Goddard of Poulton, a small village near Marlborough and Mildenhall, whose will was drawn up in 1443 and proved in 1454.[48] This will shows a man of great wealth with very close connections to Marlborough, one of the largest towns in the county and an important industrial, trading and cloth-producing centre. His bequests included £16 13s 4d to various churches in the area and to the cathedral. He left to his son all his lands and rents in Marlborough, £140 in cash, a debt of £20 still owed to him and an extensive list of silverware and chests. His daughter was to receive various household goods and 500 sheep, and the cash alone given away to his friends, executors and servants totalled £19. We do not know precisely how John had acquired such wealth, although the strength of his Marlborough connections and a link with a mercer of London suggest that his fortunes may have come from trade and probably from the cloth industry. Robert Baron, an important London mercer, who was

---

43. *Abstracts of feet of fines relating to Wiltshire for the reign of Edward III*, ed. C.R. Elrington, Wiltshire Record Society 29 (Devizes, 1974), 145; TNA: PRO E179/194/42a.
44. William Stannford leased at Upavon from 1455 (TNA: PRO DL37/53) and there are frequent references to him in the Tropenell cartulary from 1458 to 1485.
45. WCL Westwood. On Horton see E.M. Carus-Wilson, 'The woollen industry before 1550', 141–2, and below, Chapter 11.
46. See below, Chapter 11.
47. TNA: PRO SC6/1056/10.
48. TNA: PRO Prob 11/1/10 fo.78v.

A Prospering Society

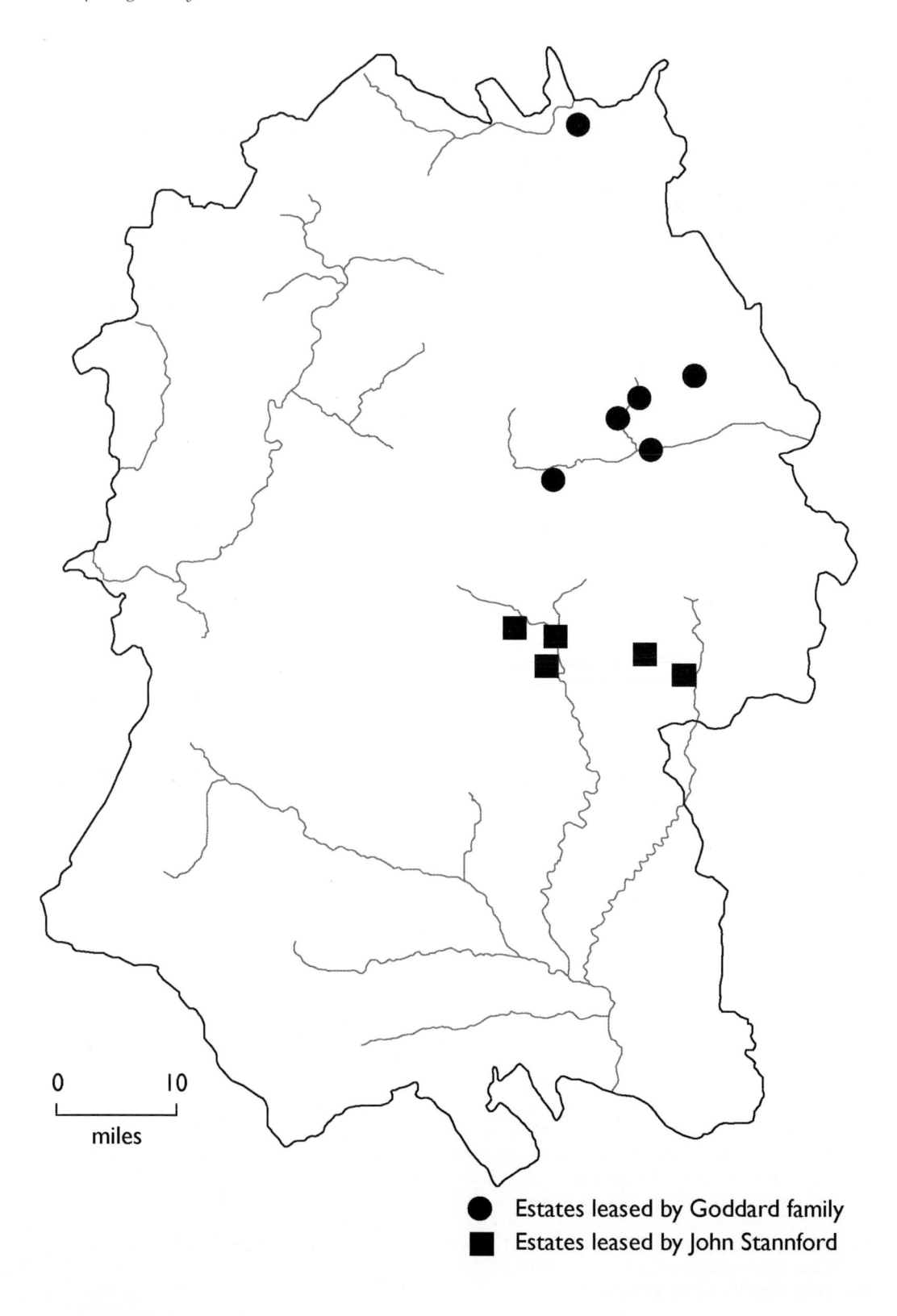

Figure 7.1 Two leasing families: the Goddards and Stannfords

warden of the mercers in 1446–7 and again in 1454–5, was sufficiently close for Robert to hold £100 of John's money and to be one of his executors.[49] William Dolman of Marlborough was another of his executors, holding a further £100 of his money. His son-in-law was a citizen of the town. John's largest bequests to churches (after that to Aldbourne, which was probably his village of origin) went to the three parochial churches of Marlborough and to the Carmelites there. Finally, if his son and daughter died without heir, his lands and rents in Marlborough were to pass to the mayor and commonalty of the town.[50]

Three Salisbury merchants have been identified as lessees in the county: Nicholas Noble leased Homington, as did William Bryt, while John Welles, a butcher, leased at Little Durnford.[51] Richard Page of Warminster, who leased Brixton Deverill in 1455, was presumably the same person as Richard Page of Warminster, merchant, who had leased some land there from the chapter of Salisbury cathedral a few years before.[52] Since there was little value in specifying the lessee's occupation on the account roll, or even on the lease, this small group must surely provide an underestimate of mercantile involvement in leasing. Some of our unknown 'foreign' lessees were probably merchants.

A few families repeatedly leased demesnes: we find some who leased on several different manors, and others who leased on one manor but for several generations. Such families might already have been involved in agriculture on a larger scale than that of the rest of the village. Although they may have started as customary tenant families, their interests soon spread beyond that of their native village, and no doubt they were helped to acquire a lease by earlier experience of large-scale agriculture or by support from their family.

The Goddards of Aldbourne provide a good example of a family who leased on several different manors. They came from a long-established family of Aldbourne tenants: in 1379 Walter Goddard was a free tenant there and three other Goddards contributed to the poll tax.[53] They had also held customary land, as the 1431 account roll refers to a Richard Goddard who had earlier held a messuage and virgate for rent and works.[54] This may have been the same Richard Goddard who bequeathed a bell

---

49. Typescript, 'The Wardens accounts 1348, 1390–1464', information from the archivist, the Mercers' Company, London.
50. An Agnes Dolman remained in Marlborough in 1524 (TNA: PRO E179/197/161 m3). No connection has yet been established with the Dolmans who were noted cloth producers in sixteenth-century Newbury, although this must remain a possibility.
51. Nicholas Noble, a Salisbury mercer and mayor in 1476, initially leased with Stephen Mowdner of Homington, husbandman, and subsequently leased by himself (KCM Ledger Book I, fo.61, 72, 91); R. Benson and H. Hatcher, *Old and New Sarum or Salisbury*, being vol. VI of Sir R.C. Hoare, *A history of modern Wiltshire* (London, 1843), 695; William Bryt is described of Salisbury, but with no occupation provided (KCM Ledger Book I, fo.282). For Welles see *Tropenell cartulary*, vol. 2, 281.
52. KCM Ledger Book I, fol 5; SDC Chapter Act book Reg Burgh, 11.
53. TNA: PRO E179/239/193/IIa: Walter (6d), Geoffrey (4d), John (4d), William (4d). Walter was sufficiently engaged in large-scale farming to have his own shepherd.
54. TNA: PRO DL29/683/11061.

on behalf of himself and his two wives to Aldbourne church in 1416, and the same family that was subsequently accused of being villeins.[55] The family were probably among the early demesne lessees, for in 1398 a Thomas Goddard was leasing the neighbouring manor of Hinton.[56] In the middle of the following century the family provided two lessees: both men of substance, but whose wealth had probably been derived from very different sources.

The probable urban and trading links of John Goddard of Marlborough and Poulton have already been considered. He, or his son, also leased the demesne at Mildenhall from 1451 until at least 1456,[57] and was eventually succeeded by a John Goddard of Lydiard. His link with the Aldbourne family of the same name is suggested by his will, for its church was to have his largest single religious bequest, while several Aldbourne men were also among the beneficiaries. His interests seem to have mainly been in trade, but his contemporary, a Thomas Goddard of Aldbourne, apparently concentrated on agriculture. The latter acted as lessee and reeve at Aldbourne from 1443, where he had earlier been a reeve,[58] and was evidently a man of means. When he became lessee he undertook to pay £61 17s 6d for the 825 wethers of the existing duchy flock, and in the same year he acted as a pledge for the new lessee of the duchy manor of Chipping Lambourne in Berkshire.[59] Finally, in 1445 he, or a relation with the same name, undertook the leasing of the demesnes at neighbouring Ogbourne for an annual rent of £50.[60] There was certainly a later connection between the two families, although the Goddard family were already influential at Ogbourne in the early fifteenth century, when William Goddard was accused of withholding tithes there and appeared among a select group of parishioners who were questioned by the Dean in his visitation.[61]

By 1460 Thomas had ceased to be lessee at Aldbourne, but this position was retaken by the Goddards in 1468 and they then retained it into the sixteenth century. Richard Goddard leased Aldbourne until 1507, when he was succeeded by a John Goddard.[62] At Ogbourne, Richard's brother John became the lessee in 1500, with Richard acting as a pledge for him.[63] A gap in the documentary evidence prevents us establishing whether the family had held the lease between 1445 and 1500, but at his death in 1501 John was also leasing the manor of Eaton.[64] In the sixteenth century the family continued to dominate the lease at Ogbourne, with a Thomas securing it in 1510 and Anthony and another Thomas in 1520 (Plate 7.1).[65] Finally, a Thomas

---

55. E.D. Webb, 'Notes on Aldbourne church', *WAM*, 28 (1895), 159; Wilts Archaeological Society MSS vol 241, 61.
56. TNA: PRO DL29/737/12073.
57. TNA: PRO SC6/1056/13–14.
58. Payne, 'Agrarian conditions', 284.
59. TNA: PRO DL29/685/11087.
60. KCM Ledger Book I, fo.8.
61. *The register of John Chandler*, 36, 37, 99.
62. Payne, 'Agrarian conditions', 302; TNA: PRO DL29/693/11226, 11229.
63. KCM Ledger Book I, fo.172. It is possible that John had already been leasing the demesne before this (the 1478 case refers to a John Godard of Ogbourne St George) and that the Godards had dominated the lease for most or part of the intervening period.
64. TNA: PRO Prob 11/12/23.
65. KCM Ledger Book I, f.226, 241. Thomas had died in 1517, according to his brass: Plate 7.1.

The demesne lessees

Plate 7.1 A Wiltshire lessee: the brass of Thomas Goddard from Ogbourne St George church.

Goddard leased the large manor of Overton, belonging to Winchester Cathedral Priory, in 1512.[66] As with John Stannford, the Goddard family shows how an individual's or family's leasing activities were concentrated in one part of the county (see Figure 7.1).

The Goddards rose to exceptional wealth, such as may have come from trade and industry. In the 1525 lay subsidy returns John Goddard of Aldbourne was credited with

---

66. WCL Register of Dean and Chapter, ii, fo.74.

goods to the value of £440, while Thomas Goddard at Ogbourne was assessed on £640, figures that put them well beyond most lessees.[67] The former may well have been the John Goddard who sold £30 of wool in one transaction to a wealthy Wiltshire clothier.[68] With this increase in wealth came an accompanying rise in status, though this was rather delayed. Throughout the fifteenth century the Goddards were referred to merely as husbandmen and in 1478 they were even accused of being villeins.[69] But by 1510 Thomas Goddard of Ogbourne was described as a gentleman.[70] The family's links with trade have already been noted above, with the career of John Goddard of Marlborough, and in the 1478 legal case about their villeinage the list of Goddards included a William Goddard of London. But the interaction between trade and agriculture, and the importance of family, can perhaps be seen most clearly in the will of a Richard Goddard who died in far-off London in 1505, apprenticed to John Peyntour, a grocer. Peyntour was an important figure in the city of London from c.1496 until his death in 1506: he was a member of the Common Council and MP for London in 1504, and represented the city in dealings with the crown and foreign trade. As a rising member of such a powerful company he would have required a high premium to allow Richard Goddard to be apprenticed to him.[71] Moreover, although Richard was merely an apprentice, he had two sizeable bequests to dispose of: the 100 sheep and 2 cows left by his father, which were in the possession of his cousin Thomas Goddard of Ogbourne; and the 100 sheep and 2 sacks of wool bequeathed by his uncle Richard.[72]

The Harvest family also leased several manors in a concentrated area. They were a family of customary tenants at Urchfont, active in village life and apparently little different in origin from the rest of the village population.[73] They leased the demesne, with one possible exception, from at least 1452 to 1510. This was a large-scale commitment for which they paid £14 11s 8d annually for the rent of 1,000 sheep, and rent in kind of 50 quarters of wheat and 50 quarters of barley for brewing. In addition, other members of the family leased the demesne at Durrington from 1478 to 1512, and at All Cannings from 1498 to at least 1517.[74] Another example of a family leasing

---

67. TNA: PRO E179/197/161. Dyer, *Age of transition?* 209, suggests a range of £13–£100 for the wealth of the lessees, and the Wiltshire evidence reinforces this with figures of £20 to £100: e.g. E179/197/156. The Goddards and Thomas Horton, the rich clothier, with his assessment on goods of £450 stand out as exceptions (TNA: PRO E179/197/155).
68. G.D. Ramsay, *The Wiltshire woollen industries in the sixteenth and seventeenth centuries* (Oxford, 1943), 6.
69. The Goddard Family (Wiltshire Archaeological Society MSS, vol 241) provides a transcript of the case taken from the *de banco* roll for 18 Edward 1V.
70. KCM Ledger Book I, fo.226.
71. My comments on Peyntour are based on information supplied by Dr Pamela Nightingale, to whom I am most grateful. See also J. Wedgwood, *A history of parliament, I: biographies* (London, 1936).
72. TNA: PRO Prob 11/15/20.
73. e.g. WRO 192/20 c, mm. 3, 5, 30; 11 21, 23; HRO 83M85 W/1; see also Hare, 'Lord and tenant', 229–31.
74. The only exception at Urchfont was Robert Wylkins, although he probably married into the family (Hare, 'Lord and tenant', 230). BL Add Rl 19722. For Durrington see WCM: 6034–66, 20015, 22992 fo.158 v, and for All Cannings WRO 192/28.

several demesnes, although coming from a rather different social background, is provided by the Benger family of Alton Barnes, a family of freeholders there who were probably linked to a prominent local gentry family of the same name. They leased the demesne in Alton Barnes in 1484 and 1531.[75] In addition, Thomas Benger and then Richard Benger leased at Durrington from 1512 to 1525. When Thomas first undertook the lease he was supported by Richard Benger of Alton Barnes, who acted as his pledge.[76] Finally, the Martyn family of Durrington leased the demesnes at Brigmerston, Enford and Amesbury Earls.[77] Given the inherent difficulties in documenting more than one of a family's leases (since our evidence does not come from the family's own muniments), our five families become much more significant. This tendency for individuals and families to lease from several different lords, usually in a limited area, suggests that a regrouping of agricultural production was taking place: one that is concealed by the traditional emphasis on the individual estate.

The significant length of time for which some leasing families were able to maintain control of the demesnes must also have helped to separate the lessees from the rest of the village. The Goddards and the Harvests leased the demesnes at Aldbourne and Urchfont almost continuously from the 1450s well into the sixteenth century. In our sample 14 families are found who provided at least 2 successive lessees, and some of these more than 2. At Collingbourne Ducis, 3 members of the Diper family leased the demesne from 1461 to 1522.[78] Finally, at Kingston Deverill, John Danyell, his wife and then Stephen Danyell leased the demesne from 1446 to 1487. It was then held by a newcomer, although he had probably already married Stephen's widow, for he is found in this position shortly afterwards.[79]

Conclusions

Who, then, were leasing the Wiltshire demesnes? The evidence clearly points to the great diversity of such men, ranging from villeins to a knight, from peasant farmers to wealthy merchants. We can conclude that the leasing of the demesnes provided great opportunities for the peasantry to expand their scale of agriculture, and it was the peasant families who, above all else, took advantage of this leasing. Local customary tenants provided by far the largest group (and probably the majority) of leasing families. In addition, men from a similar background were leasing demesnes outside their own village. Such men came from the substantial village tenantry, the holders of

---

75. TNA: PRO Prob 11/21/29; J.E.T. Rogers, *A history of agriculture and prices* (Oxford, 1866–82), vol. 3, 709–10. The Bengers were a prominent local legal and gentry family active in local government (R.B. Pugh, 'The King's government in the Middle Ages', in VCH *Wilts* 5, 34).
76. WCM 22992 fo.167 v, & 6068.
77. WCM 5656b; BL Harl Rl X/18–22; R.B. Pugh, 'The early history of the manors in Amesbury', *WAM*, 52 (1947), 98. Although in these cases it is the identical combinations of names and their close proximity to Durrington that suggests the link of these lessees to the Durrington family.
78. TNA: PRO DL29/687/11134–694/11246. In the latter year he was still leasing the demesne and had eight years left of his thirty-one-year lease.
79. WRO 192/32. The relationship is suggested by their wills (TNA: PRO Prob 11/8/11 and 17/25). Bartram came from outside, probably from Winterbourne Martyn in Dorset, where he had intended to found a chantry using lands he possessed there.

the larger standard tenements, who had played an active part in village life and had often already had experience as manorial and village officials. Such developments are familiar elsewhere, as in the midlands. In Warwickshire, 19 out of 75 were local peasants, leading Dyer to conclude that probably the great majority of the demesnes were leased to such men. And on the bishopric of Worcester estate the initial peasant predominance gradually shifted to a gentry pre-eminence by the early sixteenth century.[80]

By contrast, the higher ranks of county society, the knights and esquires and those described as gentlemen, provided few lessees in Wiltshire. We thus have a very different picture from that on the estates of the Archbishop of Canterbury, where under Archbishop Warham (1502–32) about a third were so described.[81] In Warwickshire, 18 examples of gentry lessees were found in comparison with the 1 Wiltshire example from our sample and a few others located from the rest of the county. Wiltshire, however, showed an important intermediate group: men who, although they as yet lacked the recognition of gentility, were clearly men of influence and standing beyond the confines of their own local community or village. Whatever their social origins may have been, they were now men of substance who would have to be treated with respect by the manorial lord and his administration.[82] Some were men who took part in the administration of the great estates, some were involved in industry and trade, while others were involved in large-scale agriculture. Some had emerged out of the ranks of the village peasantry, but now towered over the rest of the village community in wealth and had extended their influence and activities into the neighbouring villages.

Very little is known about the conduct of agriculture on the demesne once it had been leased. Very few leases survive, but these often specifically forbid sub-leasing without the lord's consent.[83] The detailed provisions concerning the maintenance of the demesne also suggest that at least the greater part of the demesne remained under the direct cultivation of the lessee. Moreover, where sub-letting took place, this could be of the whole demesne or manor, as occurred on one occasion at Durrington. When William Harvest renewed his lease here in 1498 he was allowed to sub-lease it, but only to his brother John: it was, in effect, a clause allowing reversion.[84] In the same year, William left Durrington to lease the larger demesne at All Cannings and John became lessee at Durrington. The wills of the lessees also suggest that they were involved in agriculture on a large scale. That of John Goddard of Ogbourne, for example, refers specifically to 1,100 sheep which belonged to him and which were held in three flocks,[85] while Stephen Danyell, a lessee at Kingston Deverill, bequeathed at least 500 sheep.[86] Such benefactions do not represent the total size of their flocks. The large sheep purchases made from the duchy of Lancaster by John Stannford and Thomas Goddard when they first leased the duchy demesnes supports

---

80. Dyer, *Lords and peasants*, 211; and on Roger Heritage, Dyer, *Everyday life*, 319.
81. Du Boulay, 'Who were farming?', 450.
82. Ibid., 444–5.
83. WCM 22992, fo.58 v.
84. Ibid., fo.158.
85. TNA: PRO Prob 11/12/13.
86. TNA: PRO Prob 11/8/11.

the belief that the farmers kept very large flocks. The lessees seem to have been practising farmers.

This evidence reflects the large scale of chalkland farming. The lessee could potentially increase the profit which the lord had been able to make as his administrative overheads were much less: he had to maintain neither a large administrative machine nor a far-flung estate. It is significant that when one person is found leasing several demesnes, as with John Stannford, they were all concentrated in one small part of the county. Because he could maintain a close eye on his lands he was probably able to do without employing an official, or he could keep a much closer eye on those that he did employ. He was able to escape the great and expensive burden of 'paperwork' that the old system had imposed.[87]

Moreover, leasing provided opportunities for investment in agriculture at a time when agriculture remained a major source of profit and when the instinct to acquire land remained unabated. Merchants and other successful men wished to acquire land and its prestige. The culmination of mercantile dreams was the establishment of their families as country gentlemen who were no longer required to work in trade or industry.[88] Leasing thus brought incalculable social returns, providing opportunities for the large-scale, if temporary, acquisition of land at a time when land was of considerable importance for social status. When Thomas Horton leased Westwood was he really concerned with the financial returns of this small manor, or did its attractions lie in his being, in effect, a manorial lord?

The leasing of the demesnes was producing a group of men who were cultivating on a scale far beyond that of the customary peasant farmers, but this development must not be seen in a vacuum. The large-scale character of this agriculture was also being reinforced by the accumulation of holdings within the population of customary tenants of the chalkland manors more generally. Here was emerging a group of men who cultivated two or more customary virgates. Both these developments helped to characterise the chalklands in the sixteenth century as an area of large-scale capital-intensive agriculture.[89] This was reflected in the 1524 taxation returns, which showed a concentration of wealthier taxpayers in this region, particularly in the area of the Marlborough Downs.[90]

The economic prosperity of the lessees and of these new greater tenants lead to social change in the chalklands, and to the gradual development that was to prove so significant in the later evolution of Wiltshire agriculture. This was the emergence of the gentleman farmer of the succeeding centuries, 'a man of education and leisure, who might take part in the government of a borough or serve as a steward to some great landowner'. It was a type that was to be so characteristic of the later farming in

---

87. For a similar example of such concentration from the bishopric of Worcester's estate see Dyer, *Lords and peasants*, 215.
88. A familiar story exemplified in Wiltshire, at a slightly later date, in the career of William Stumpe: below Chapter 11.
89. E. Kerridge, 'Agriculture 1500–1793', in VCH *Wilts* 4, 57–8, 64.
90. This is based on the maps in J. Sheail, *The regional distribution of wealth in England as indicated in the 1524/5 lay subsidy returns*, ed. R.W. Hoyle, List and index society, special series 28 (Richmond, 1998), 345ff.

the 'sheep and corn' parts of the county.[91] Although our lessees were rarely described as gentlemen, and were not among the most important men of the county, they were emerging as a group distinct from the rest of the village population and with some of the attributes of the group that succeeded them. Their activities and horizons had already spread far beyond the agriculture and life of their village. We find them with influential and time-consuming tasks as baronial or royal officials. They could be active in the law. They were often concerned to provide a formal education for their children, so that we find representatives from several leasing families among the Wiltshire entrants to Winchester College and New College, Oxford.[92] They mixed with families who were clearly gentry ones. We cannot provide a clear picture of the activities and social milieu of such families, but the scraps of evidence that survive suggest that there was a substantial group of lessees who cannot usefully be described as peasants, and for whom the term 'gentleman-farmer' was becoming more appropriate. This process was not just the product of the leasing of the demesnes, for it also resulted from general changes within the rural population: from the growing stratification of the tenant population and the declining social distinctions between free, customary and leasehold tenures. It was a process that was well underway throughout the fifteenth century.

---

91. Kerridge,'Agriculture, 1500–1793', 64 (the quotation is his).
92. I am very grateful to Guy Lytle for providing me with a list of the Wiltshire entrants to these colleges.

Chapter 8

Tenant mobility and the decline of serfdom

Customary tenure

The earlier part of this study has been primarily concerned with agriculture, particularly that of the lord's demesne, and was primarily based on the evidence of manorial account rolls. The following sections focus more specifically on the peasantry and largely draw upon the evidence of another important source, the manorial court rolls, supplemented by rentals and tax records. It should be emphasised that these court rolls are more limited in their scope than their thirteenth-century predecessors, making it more difficult to reconstruct the relationships within the village population. This chapter examines the nature of peasant tenure and the mobility and readiness of the tenantry to move elsewhere. It then explores the decline of serfdom, that lack of personal freedom so widely prevalent among the peasantry of the thirteenth century. Changing economic conditions now meant that lords could no longer force the financial and personal burdens of servility on new tenants. The study has been based on a small group of well-documented manors, including examples drawn from the major regional divisions of the county: Durrington, Coombe Bisset, Enford and Stockton, from the chalklands; and Wroughton, Bromham and Stratton from the northern vale. These have been supplemented by the work of other scholars on Eastrop, Castle Combe and Coleshill (Berks., but just over the border).[1] The sample includes both agricultural and industrial villages.

The pattern of land-holding in medieval England varied considerably from region to region. In Wiltshire, as in areas like the midlands, manorial structures were strong, with large manors closely linked to tithing, and parish and with a long-established customary unit of tenant land, the virgate. By contrast, some other areas, above all East Anglia, showed a very different pattern, with land held within a looser manorial structure, and with land-holding based on a market in individual acres rather than the formal virgate unit.[2] Within this highly manorialised structure, Wiltshire land had been held in return for rent paid both in service and in cash, as well as often involving the personal legal constraints of serfdom. Now this villein tenure evolved into the more limited customary or copyhold tenure that dominated the agrarian holdings of the next few centuries, but its essential traditional nature remained unchanged. The court rolls describe the tenants as holding land 'according to the customs of the manor' and, later, 'by copy of the court'. This copyhold tenure allowed the use of the land for a life

---

1. R. Faith, 'The peasant land market in Berkshire in the later Middle Ages', PhD thesis (Leicester, 1962); and eadem, 'Berkshire: fourteenth and fifteenth centuries', in Harvey, *The peasant land market*, 106–77; L.C. Latham, 'The decay of the manorial system', MA thesis (London, 1928), E.M. Carus-Wilson, 'Evidences of industrial growth on some fifteenth century manors', in Carus-Wilson, *Essays in economic history*, 159–67.
2. J. Whittle and M. Yates, '"Pays réel or pays légal": contrasting patterns of land tenure and social structure in eastern Norfolk and western Berkshire, 1450–1600', *AHR*, 48 (2000), 12–26.

or more without freehold but with effective security. But behind this essential continuity, however, lords were unable to maintain some of the characteristics of villein tenure. Most regular labour services now disappeared, as did most of the personal burdens associated with serfdom and inherited villeinage. On a few manors, notably those of the bishopric of Winchester or at Bromham, the contraction of the demesne opened up an additional substantial market in small holdings.

The patterns of land-holding were influenced by geography. In the later Middle Ages the well-established units of land-holding, the manor and customary virgates, remained least disturbed in the chalklands, which coincidentally also provides much of the best documentation. By contrast, the recently colonised and more poorly documented woodlands of the clay vales showed a wider range of small enclosed fields. Here the traditional framework was both weaker and was being eroded, though our sources are mainly from the older core settlements. On a chalkland manor like Durrington only a small amount of demesne was leased out and this occurred in small acreages. Elsewhere, away from the chalk, there was more free tenure, demesnes and virgates were more likely to be broken up and there were more assarts, enclosed from the woodlands. In such areas a greater market in acres was more likely to emerge, as at Corsham and Eastrop, near Highworth. At Eastrop in 1473 free tenants made up 26 out of the 38 tenants. Demesnes tended to be smaller and, as at Oaksey and Castle Combe, they were often leased to a group of tenants, so encouraging a further shift in the balance between tenant land and demesne.

The contrast between land-holding in the chalklands and elsewhere is shown by a comparison of Durrington and Bromham. At chalkland Durrington, the traditional customary structure of land-holding still survived and the rental continued to serve as a reliable indicator of land-holding. Of the 17 virgates in 1441, 16 remained, and 1 had been broken up into a half and 2 quarters, while all the half-virgates remained. Some of the cottages had now disappeared but no significant amount of land was available in small plots. Land-holding continued to be dominated by customary tenements and by the demesne. By contrast, at Bromham, in the mixed soils of the northern vale, the rental (1430) needs to be reinforced by the evidence from the contemporary account roll (1431). Together they show that most of the lord's total net income from land came from assised rents, from the sale of works and minor rents, but that a substantial amount came from the piecemeal leasing of land or meadow that had previously either been part of the demesne or of customary tenements. The tenement called 'Slapertone', for example, had been 'in the lord's hands' for a long time and was leased out piecemeal in seven pieces with rents from 2s 6d to 2d. Such leases made up approximately 12 per cent of the seigneurial net rent of £23 17s 7¼d and had a considerable impact on individual land-holding. Henry and Agnes Kyng held land with an annual payment of 8s 4d recorded on the rental, but in addition they paid an annual rent of 6s 9d for leased land. The importance of the traditional structure of customary tenements was being eroded.[3]

The general prevalence in the chalkland of customary virgate tenements meant

---

3. TNA: PRO E315/56; SC6/1047/9, for a fuller analysis of land-holding here in 1450–51 see J.N. Hare, 'Lord and tenant in Wiltshire, c.1380–1520, with particular reference to regional and seigneurial variations', PhD thesis (London, 1976), 291.

that the land market was characterised by large and relatively inflexible units. It was not a world in which minor shifts in family fortunes could be reflected by the acquisition or loss of an extra acre or two.[4] Holdings came onto the market relatively rarely and were eventually transferred in the one or two courts held each year. The customary tenements usually consisted of virgates, half virgates and cottages. The virgate varied in size from manor to manor: at Durrington it was about 28 acres, and at Coombe Bisset only 20. The standard holding was usually but not always a virgate, being half a virgate at Stockton. Each virgate consisted of a series of strips scattered across the open fields: thus John Smyth's virgate at Durrington contained 28½ acres and was spread across 19 different fields or furlongs.[5] The land was owned by the lord, but the tenant could hold it for life as long as he did not break the customs of the manor. At the tenant's death his wife retained a life interest in the whole tenement as long as she remained single. A heriot was paid at the death of a tenant, and an entry fine when the new tenant (but not the widow) took up the land. If the widow remarried the tenement was forfeit, but it could usually be retaken in combination with her new husband. The son or heir had no legal rights to the holding, although in practice he could expect to succeed if he wished. Families who sought to maintain the holding could pay for a reversionary right, most of these payments being for a holding already held by a family member.[6] In mid-century Durrington, a small group of holdings was held for three lives (husband, wife and named son or daughter), as when in 1461 Thomas Clerk, Margery his wife and William their son took a messuage and three virgates.[7] Customary holdings were described as being held by copy of the court roll at Bromham[8], but this was very unusual and the tenure does not seem to have been different in its terms to customary tenure elsewhere in the county.

In the thirteenth century, regular labour services had varied greatly from manor to manor, as between nearby manors of the abbeys of Bec and Glastonbury at the Ogbournes, Winterbourne and Badbury, and at the Deverills, but were often substantial.[9] By the fifteenth century, regular week work had long ceased to be part of the burdens of customary tenure. A few light labour services survived, the most common in the chalklands involving the washing and shearing of the sheep, as at Stockton, Heytesbury and Bromham (just beyond the chalklands). Work rents were already being reduced in the early fourteenth century and their commutation for cash can be shown on most documented manors in the second half of the century. This occurred at Hilmarton by 1352, at Castle Combe in 1352, at Coombe Bisset before 1372, at Durrington between 1359 and 1388 and at Alton Priors by 1373.[10] Most

---

4. e.g. J. Whittle, 'Individualism and the family-land bond: a reassessment of land transfer patterns among the English peasantry c.1270–1580', *Past and Present*, 160 (1998), 28–9, 44–5.
5. WCM 5601Cc.
6. WCM 5650o, p.
7. WCM 5655a.
8. e.g. TNA: PRO SC6/1047/8, 9, 13, 19.
9. M. Morgan, *The English lands of the abbey of Bec* (Oxford, 1946), 82; *Wilts IPM* i.
10. Bad.Mun. 110/5/3; Carus-Wilson, 'Evidences of industrial growth', 160; WCM 4350, 4351b; WCM 5601 Ca, 5596 (the half virgators who did regular ploughing works had their services commuted in 1389 – WCM 5650m) WCL, Alton Priors accounts, 1389.

manors possess surviving documentation only from the fifteenth century, but by this time virtually all manors seem to have commuted their regular labour services and it was only exceptionally, as at Bromham, that general commutation had to wait until later (between 1404 and 1410).

The evidence of court rolls and rentals may have been distorted by sub-leasing that might not appear in traditional court records. Occasional references to sub-leasing occur, as when this created an offence because it had been done without the lord's permission.[11] A licence to sub-let was given at Coombe Bisset in 1469 and in 1476 (both for seven years).[12] But if parts of a virgate were commonly sub-let we might expect complications when a virgate was surrendered to the lord and taken by a new tenant, yet none has been found. Given the repeated and endless complaints of the courts against, for example, the decay of buildings, the rarity of complaints about sub-leasing suggests that the latter was not a substantial phenomenon and should not challenge the evidence of court rolls and rentals. This conclusion echoes Dyer in his remark that 'My general impression is that concealed sub-letting was not so widespread that conclusions based on records of "official" tenants are invalid.' Howell at Kibworth Harcourt also saw a general absence of sub-tenancies.[13] It seems a very different situation from that in the late sixteenth and early seventeenth century described by Kerridge in which sub-tenancies for leases, copyholds and under-tenancies are both frequent and significantly well-documented; moreoever, many of his examples were drawn from Wiltshire.[14]

A second set of qualifications results from the need to use family surnames as an indicator of family identity. This clearly ignores family links through daughters, and court rolls cannot be relied on to provide consistent and reliable family links through the female line. Secondly, confusion might arise from a variety of families with the same name. But this does not seem to be a great problem, particularly on the Wiltshire manors. Where there might have been such confusion the court also had an interest in clarifying the situation and added distinctive alias names, as with the Weylots of Durrington. Very few multi-branch families have been found (the Mascals at Stockton and the Weylots and possibly Gyfgo or Gugos at Durrington, and the Wrottes at Idmiston).[15]

Some of the influences on the passage of land – death, widowhood, family and the presence of apparent outsiders – are highlighted by the study of a single pair of virgate holdings at Durrington. This pair became, in effect, a double virgate, their story

---

11. Or occasionally the offence was specified as that of leasing to a man 'of suspect and bad disposition' (BL Harl Rl V21. For some other examples of illegal subleasing at Stockton see BL Harl Rl V53, Add Rl 24351, 24377 & 24378.
12. Probably for the same tenement, although for the second time to someone from Salisbury, 5656b, d. For other examples from Stockton and Wroughton see BL Add. Rl. 24356, WRO 906/SC3, WCL Wroughton 1476.
13. C. Dyer, 'Changes in the size of peasant holdings in some west midland villages' in Smith (ed.), *Land, kinship and lifecycle*, 279; C. Howell, 'Peasant inheritance customs in the midlands, 1280–1700', in J. Goody, J. Thirsk and E.P. Thompson (eds), *Family and inheritance* (Cambridge, 1976), 112–55; C. Howell, *Land, family and inheritance in transition: Kibworth Harcourt, 1280–1700* (Cambridge, 1983), 252–3.
14. E. Kerridge, *Agrarian problems in the sixteenth century and after* (London, 1969), 48–53.
15. For the Wrottes, BL Harl Mss 3961.

reminding us both of the accumulation of holdings that was taking place at this time and of the importance of women in land-holding. The two virgates can be tracked throughout the fifteenth century as formerly John (or sometimes as formerly Jane) Hyckys and formerly Salysbury. John Hickes senior had first brought these two virgates together. In 1401 he surrendered them on account of his illness: one messuage reverted to the lord and the other, in which he had lived, was subject to an earlier reversionary fine and was therefore taken by his son John.[16] John later leased the demesne from 1402 to 1413/4. He was succeeded by William Hyckys, who still held the two messuages and two virgates when he died. The two virgates passed to his widow Agnes, who surrendered them in the following court in 1430[17] to the use of John Weylot, a member of a well-known local villein family.[18] Was he a son-in-law? He in turn granted her the chamber at the east end of the kitchen of one of the holdings, together with the right to take water from the kitchen. John Welot, alias Carter, died in 1445, still holding the two tenements and land, which now went to his widow Joanna.[19] At the next court (4 May 1446), John Pereham, who probably came from outside the manor, paid a fine for marrying her and receiving her lands. He also took on responsibility for at least one child; a few years later, in 1453, Edith, daughter of John Welot Carter, was about ten years old and was recorded as staying with him. We know nothing about Joanna's death, but John may not have been a great success as a farmer: when he surrendered the holding in 1458 he left the tenements in a state of decay.[20] John Kepenell, probably another outsider, took the virgates in 1460 and held them until his death in 1465, when they passed to his wife Leticia.[21] When she died, over 20 years later in 1488, she still held one – but only one – of the virgates, and this was then taken by her son John Kyppenell.[22] He may have already held the second virgate, with the twin holdings having been divided between his mother and himself: for he held both of them when he died in 1496. His widow, Joanna, now came and claimed them. Subsequently, in 1497, John Perker, probably another outsider, took the two holdings, but it is not clear what had happened to Joanna.[23]

Peasant mobility

Villagers were not rooted to the place of their birth.[24] Much of their movement was probably short-distance, but long-distance migration also existed, as shown by the presence of the Irish and the French in fifteenth-century Wiltshire (see Chapter 12). Increased local industrial employment created movements of population across the county, and there were also short-distance movements to and from neighbouring

---

16. WCM 5601b, 5650p.
17. WCM 5655q.
18. For the Weylottes, see above, Chapter 7.
19. WCM 5655j.
20. WCM 5655b, 5655a.
21. WCM 5655j, d, c, b; 5656a.
22. WCM 5656h.
23. WCM 5656j.
24. For a recent discussion see C. Dyer, 'Were late medieval English villages "self-contained"?' in C. Dyer (ed.), *The self contained village* (Hertford, 2007), 6–7.

A Prospering Society

Table 8.1
The disappearance of tenant families.

Durrington

	1334–59	1359–88	1388–1411	1411–41	1441–72*	1472*–82*	1482*–1506
(a) Number of families	38	36	38	26	26	27	23#
(b) Disappeared families	22	11	14	15	7	12	14
(b) as %age of (a)	71	37	54	65	41	50	74
Annual rate of disappearance	2.8	1.3	2.2	2.3	1.3	5.0	3.1

Coombe Bisset

	1307–72	1372–89	1389–1411	1411–50
(a) Number of families	29	32	29	28†
(b) Disappeared families	12	6	14	22
(b) as %age of (a)	52	21	54	81
Annual rate of disappearance	0.8	1.2	2.4	2.1

Notes: *The rentals are undated but can be dated on internal evidence to 1472–3 and 1480–83. # 20 in 1506; † 20 in 1450
Sources: Durrington: WCM 5601Aa; 5601Ca; 5596; 13373; 5603d; 5603A; 5603e; 5603Aa; 5604; Coombe Bisset: WCM 4350; 4351b; 4355; 13373; 4353; 4354.

villages. It is, however, desirable to try to estimate the scale and chronology of such mobility. Normally such questions can only be answered through a painstaking study of a complete set of court rolls. In Wiltshire, two of Winchester College's manors (Durrington and Coombe Bisset) provide enough rentals to allow us to sketch the trends in the mobility and survival of the land-holding families. To these have been added Faith's work on Coleshill in the clay vale, just over the border in Berkshire.

Both Durrington and Coombe Bisset were chalkland villages, the former in the Avon valley, north of Salisbury, and the latter in the smaller Ebble valley to the southwest of the same city. Both manors saw a reduction in the tenant population, falling most dramatically at Durrington, from 38 in 1334/5 to 23 in 1480/3 with the greatest period of change around 1400, from 38 in 1388 to 26 in 1411/2. Over the Berkshire border at Coleshill the tenant population fell even more sharply, from 44 in 1395 to 18 in 1424.[25] The difference probably reflects the impact on an agricultural area of the increasing demand for labour in the expanding textile industries beyond. Coombe Bisset showed a much more stable situation, reflecting the increased demand generated by the cloth industry locally. (Table 8.1).

Tenant mobility can be assessed through the disappearance of families in the male line between each rental. Such calculations need to be used with care. The figures for Coombe Bisset from 1307 to 1372 underestimate mobility because during such a long period some people are likely to have settled and departed without ever having appeared on any one of the rentals. Moreover, each manor included a group of freeholders in addition to the customary tenements. At Durrington, it has been possible to exclude these free tenants, who included such important figures as the prioress of Amesbury and a local gentry family who held a sub-manor, but at Coombe

---

25. Faith, 'Berkshire', 161.

Bisset the nature of the later rentals means that this could not be done, and the figures for this manor thus include all tenants. Fortunately, here the amount of free land was small and it was held by men whose economic position seems much closer to that of the customary tenants than in Durrington.

The most obvious feature of this table is the high turnover rate in the tenant population, a general trend of the period.[26] Even when the population was at its most stable and in villages that were not being deserted a generation of 30 years would have seen the disappearance of a third of the tenant families. Such movement to and from these villages was quite typical. There were, however, chronological variations (real or apparent) in the rate of change. At Durrington the period spanning the Black Death showed a high rate of disappearance, while the low figure at Coombe Bisset probably underestimates the amount of movement because of the long period between rentals. The period from the 1360s to 1380s seems to have been one of relative stability. By contrast, the 1390s and the first half of the fifteenth century showed much greater change.[27] In part, this development reflected trends elsewhere, although here it was also influenced by the mobility generated by the growing cloth industry, whether immigration at Coombe Bisset or emigration at Durrington. Both manors show a remarkable similarity (Table 8.1). By contrast, Coleshill showed a much higher turnover, particularly in the period 1379–1424 (with figures of 4 per cent and 3 per cent each year) but beginning earlier than on the other two manors. Coleshill seems to have been more obviously in decline. The growth of the Wiltshire cloth industry would have helped to generate a new mobility in the land market throughout the county, both encouraging movement to new jobs and influencing the demand for foodstuffs. In this situation of greater fluidity some manors would have found it much more difficult to hang on to their tenants, and Coleshill seems to have been one of these. From the mid-fifteenth century we are dependent on the Durrington evidence, which suggests that a mid-fifteenth-century stability was followed by greater change. This stability may represent a by-product of the difficulties of agriculture and industry, when there was less incentive to move. Later the decline in the number of tenants may have made the figures over-dependent on too few families.

Greater mobility could indicate a period of change rather than necessarily one of decline, with people wanting to enter the manor as well as wishing to leave, and moving between neighbouring villages. When, in 1454, the Durrington court roll listed the places of residence of the children of serfs, one was to be found at Bulford, on the opposite side of the river, and another at Tidworth, not far away, while the mother of two of them married a man from Wishford, a few miles away, when she was widowed in the same year. The growth in tenant movement from the 1390s fits in with the expansion of the industrial areas, which both sucked in population from the agricultural hinterland and continued to maintain the attractiveness of the agricultural areas around. At other times, the explanations for this mobility are more ambiguous.

---

26. e.g. ibid.; Z. Razi, 'The myth of the immutable English family', *Past and Present*, 140 (1993), 33; Howell, 'Peasant inheritance customs in the Midlands', 123, 131.
27. For examples of growing peasant mobility in the late fourteenth and early fifteenth centuries see Razi, 'The myth of the immutable English family', 28–30, 35; Dyer, 'Were late medieval English villages "self-contained"?' 15.

The decline of serfdom

In Wiltshire, as elsewhere, this increased mobility ushered in one of the most important legal changes in the conditions of the medieval peasantry, the end of serfdom. Previously, customary tenants had been burdened with personal servility, or lack of freedom. Now, the much lower population meant that lords were unable to enforce servility upon new tenants, while at the same time there were fewer surviving traditional families that remained subject to these restrictions. Some serf families died out in the male line, and others left for the vacant land that was now available elsewhere or bought their freedom. Individual sons escaped for education or for the church, and daughters married and moved elsewhere. Serfdom declined and, by the sixteenth century, such families were a tiny minority, although this did not diminish the irksome character of the restraints or of the extra financial impositions. At the same time, holding customary or bond land no longer brought with it the burdens of serfdom and most tenants were now legally free.[28]

The decline of serfdom can clearly be seen on individual manors. At Durrington 71 per cent of the old tenant families who had combined the holding of bond land with the personal burdens of servile status disappeared from the manor between 1334 and 1359. In the latter year a note was made on the rental as to which of the tenant families were free and which were of villein blood: only 5 of the 9 virgaters fell into the latter category, and three of these had gone by 1411/2.[29] Similarly, at Coombe Bisset by about 1380 only 4 of the 14 customary virgators were described as bondmen by blood.[30] Villein families continued to disappear in the fourteenth century, helped by the failure of lords to keep serfs on their land. The steady trickle of villeins who were repeatedly fined for being outside the lordship is reflected in the five examples from the small manor of Hilmarton and those from manors like Hannington, Stockton and Wroughton.[31] The lord knew where they were, but he could do little apart from recording it. Although villeinage continued to decline, the Wiltshire evidence suggests that it had ceased to affect more than a small minority of the tenant population by the end of the fourteenth century.

Serfs were thus a declining minority and were distinguished by legal factors rather than wealth. Tenure and legal status had now become separated: freemen now held bond or customary land, and serfs held specifically free tenures. But serfs suffered greater financial burdens than others: the requirement to pay a fine if they wished to stay outside the lordship, for the marriage of their daughters or at death. The scale of such payments may be seen at Stockton, where in 1390 the lord received 6s 8d for

---

28. R.H. Hilton, *The decline of serfdom in medieval England* (Basingstoke, 1969); A. Savine, 'Bondmen under the Tudors', *Transactions of the Royal Historical Society*, 17 (1903), 235–89; D. MacCulloch, 'Bondmen under the Tudors', in C. Cross, D. Loades and J.J. Scarisbrick (eds), *Law and government under the Tudors* (Cambridge, 1988), 91–109; J. Hatcher, 'English serfdom and villeinage: towards a reassessment', *Past and Present*, 90 (1981), 3–39; C. Dyer, 'Tenant farming and tenant farmers. the West Midlands', in Miller (ed.), *Agrarian History of England and Wales*, 638–9.
29. WCM 5601Ca.
30. WCM 4352.
31. Bad.Mun. 110/5/3; C.B. Fry, *Hannington: the records of a Wiltshire village* (Gloucester, 1935), 101; BL Add Rl 24345; WCL Box 52,. Wroughton court rolls.

one merchet (marriage fine) and 23s 4d for the merchet of four daughters of Thomas Self. In 1397 William Palmer paid 8s for his two daughters.[32] Serfdom seems to have survived rather more fully in the chalklands, reflecting the greater traditionalism of this area in its agricultural and social organisation. Chalkland manors such as Enford, Stockton, Wroughton, Urchfont and Durrington possessed a small but significant group of villeins. The estates of Winchester Cathedral Priory contained at least four distinct villein family groupings at Enford, and there were five or six villein families at Wroughton. On the eight Wiltshire manors of Glastonbury Abbey in 1518 the rental's scribe took care to record the tenant's servility, the description *nativus de sanguine* being written in a different-coloured ink. Outside the chalklands, only one manor had a villein family (Nettleton with one), whereas within the chalklands the manors of Idmiston and Damerham recorded eighteen bondmen from seven families.[33] Off the chalk, at places like Bromham, Abyndscourt, Eastrop, Purton and over the Berkshire border at Coleshill, personal servility appeared virtually or absolutely non-existent.[34]

The survival of serfdom does not seem to have been greatly affected by the distinction between lay and ecclesiastical estates, the influence of markets or towns, or any relationship to trends in economic prosperity or decline. Some of the factors affecting its continuance were – like family fertility – beyond the control of estate owners. Both lay and ecclesiastical estates were run by the same administrators, such as John Whittocksmede, and this should have helped to produce common policies towards serfdom. There was, moreover, an accidental element to the survival of serfdom. If some serf families died out in the male line, others grew. When surveys of bondmen were made at Durrington in 1453 and 1454, 6 such families were recorded representing the descendants of only 3 earlier ones.[35] Some serfs purchased their freedom, and on one large estate, that of Winchester Cathedral Priory, a chronology can be established.[36] Of the 46 known manumissions on its Wiltshire and Hampshire manors, the vast majority (37) occurred within the period 1390–1450, with the highest concentration in the decade 1410–19, when 15 grants were made. The paucity of manumissions after 1450 probably reflects the fact that by then there were few villein families remaining. Manumissions on this estate seem to have preceded the main period of activity on the estates of the bishopric of Worcester and probably also of Ramsey Abbey. At the latter the evidence begins in the 1430s but thereafter manumissions remained consistently higher than on the cathedral priory estate.[37] Although there are only 8 recorded manumissions in the priory register for the Wiltshire manors they seem to parallel the pattern of the estate as a whole.

But although serfdom affected only a small part of the tenant population, landlords were keen to maintain its financial benefits. Lords as diverse as Sir John Fastolf,

---

32. BL Add Rl 24349, 24355.
33. BL Harl Mss 3961. Not all the chalkland manors possessed serfs.
34. Latham, 'Decay of the manorial system', 80–83; TNA: PRO SC2/208/18, 19, 21–6.
35. WCM 5655d & c.
36. Based on WCL Register of the Dean and Chapter vol I & II; and *The register of the common seal of the Priory of St. Swithun, Winchester, 1345–1497*, ed. J. Greatrex, Hampshire Record Series 2 (Winchester, 1978).
37. C. Dyer, *Lords and peasants in a changing society: the estates of the bishopric of Worcester, 680–1540* (Cambridge, 1980), 272; J.A. Raftis, *Tenure and mobility* (Toronto, 1964), 184–5.

Winchester College and Glastonbury Abbey took care to record which of the customary tenants were legally unfree, or sought to keep a note of the movements of their villeins. In 1423 Winchester Cathedral Priory's court at Wroughton recorded that Robert Jumpere had fled the lordship. As Robert was a comparative newcomer to Wroughton this might not have been of great significance to the lord, except that Jumpere was a villein belonging to another of its manors, at Houghton in Hampshire.[38] It was therefore important to establish his movements so that he could be prevented from acquiring his freedom by default.

As serfdom was a legal not an economic state, it could apply to rich and poor alike. Landlords can be found attacking men of wealth: if the latter were their bondman, then the lord would have a right to his property. One notable example was John Halle, one of the dominant figures in the economic and political life of the great city of Salisbury in the mid-fifteenth century.[39] He was accused by the prioress of Amesbury of being her bondman and her officials went as far as seizing some of his property. In the end the case was resolved in 1468 by the arbitration of no less a personage than the king's brother, George, duke of Clarence.[40] The accusation of serfdom may have been a long-standing one, as suggested by the decision of the city council in 1456 that its members should not engage in personal invective singling out John Halle and his rival William Swayne. Among the specific banned words were 'ceorl' and 'knave', both of which could imply villeinage and unfree status as well as being more general terms of abuse.[41]

Another, but better-known, example of villeinage affecting the rich was found at Castle Combe, a flourishing centre of the cloth industry. While many of the men who benefited from this prosperity were outsiders and freemen, William Haynes belonged to a local family who were already called 'villein by blood' in 1392. He was a wealthy clothier, a man of standing in the local community and a former church warden.[42] As a bondman, his property theoretically belonged to his lord. At his death, the council of Sir John Fastolf, his lord, valued his goods and chattels at 3,000 marks (£2,000). Even the more lenient local jury still assessed his movables, debts, household goods, merchandise, stock and all else at 300 marks (£200), after allowing for the payment of outstanding commitments, such as the bequest to the new bell tower of the parish church. In view of later developments, the jury seems to have underestimated his wealth, for in the following years his widow was able to pay Fastolf £140 in order to gain possession of his lands and for permission to hold them and marry. Moreover, the new husband also had to pay a fine of £40 for admission to his wife's property.[43]

---

38. WCL Wroughton court rolls, 1423; WCL Book of Common Seal, vols i, ii, 1424.
39. On Halle see below, Chapter 10.
40. WRO 214/8; M.A. Hicks, 'Restraint, mediation and private justice: George, Duke of Clarence as "good lord"', *Journal of Legal History*, 4 (1983), 56–72.
41. WRO G23/1/2 (Ledger Book B) f. 31 r & v. Faith, 'Berkshire', records an attempt by a Wiltshire lord (Edington Priory) to secure the return of a villein worth 1,000 marks from a town, Newbury, to its manor of Coleshill (Berks), 174–5.
42. G.P. Scrope, *History of the manor and ancient barony of Castle Combe* (privately printed, 1852), 165; Latham, 'Decay of the manorial system', 188; Carus-Wilson, 'Evidences of industrial growth', 162–3.
43. BL Add Mss 18478 m.10; Scrope, *Castle Combe*, 223–5; Carus-Wilson, 'Evidences of industrial growth', 162–3; see also below, Chapter 11.

Haynes and Halle may have gained most of their wealth from industry or trade, but there were also rich villeins who had acquired their wealth from agriculture and the increasing opportunities in Wiltshire for self-advancement, whether through accumulating agricultural holdings, through the leasing of the demesnes or through involvement in trade. The Goddards became major lessees and, by 1510, Thomas Goddard of Ogbourne was being formally referred to as a gentleman; his wealth was reflected in the 1525 lay subsidy returns, in which he was assessed at £640. But in 1478 the family were accused of being villeins when John Yorke, late of Ramsbury, seized £50 of the family's goods and chattels on the grounds that they were his villeins of the manor of Upham. The Goddards sued Yorke and eventually the jury declared in their favour.[44]

A smaller and later case is provided by the abbot of Malmesbury's seizure of Robert Carter's stock on the grounds of the latter's bondage. He possessed a sizeable number of livestock, whether it was the 109 sheep, 5 bullocks, 10 cows and 9 calves that he claimed had been seized, or the 53 sheep, 8 lambs and the same number of cattle claimed by the abbot.[45] Some families remained unfree well into the sixteenth century, as with the Alweys of Colerne. The family had long been an important and wealthy one there. They served their lord, New College Oxford, as serjeants or reeves of the manor from at least 1394 and held the post until at least 1400, and again from 1422 to 1432, and possibly in between. Richard Alweys, who is found in early-fifteenth-century documents, was probably the son of the sergeant. He was evidently also a figure of substance: in 1435 he was fined 20s for the marriage of his daughter and in 1436 £6 13s 4d for the messuage and land that his father had held. There may have been an element of friction in his relations with New College, and he is found accused of keeping greyhounds and using them in the lord's warren. His son, Robert, paid a fine of £6 13s 4d in 1457 for his father's land and served as serjeant and bailiff from 1456, the year before his father's death, until at least 1479.[46] Their long service did not, however, help them secure their freedom. They tried to secure their manumission from New College under Henry VIII and were able to secure the support of influential figures such as Sir Henry Long, the bishop of Winchester, the archbishop of Canterbury and, later, Thomas Cromwell himself. The warden, however, refused, claiming that the statutes of his college prevented him from making such a grant.[47]

Such cases serve to remind us of the limited and, to the lord, essentially financial benefits of villeinage in the fifteenth century. The abbess of Amesbury would not have been interested in having John Halle, a rich Salisbury merchant, to serve as an extra tenant or ploughman. Nor should Fastolf's financial success in the case of William Haynes allow us to forget that serfdom was dying out at Castle Combe. Haynes had died in 1434, but already many of the other villein families had disappeared. A few years later, in 1443/4, a list of the surviving villeins was compiled.[48] There were then only three remaining in Castle Combe, of whom two belonged to one family (the

---

44. On the Goddards see above, Chapter 7; Wiltshire Archaeological Society MSS vol 241, 61.
45. Hilton, *Decline of serfdom*, 54–5.
46. NCA 2734, 5960, 5963, 5964.
47. Savine, 'Bondmen under the Tudors', 277; Letters & Papers, Henry VIII, xiii, i, 108.
48. BL Add Mss 28208 f.32v; Scrope, *Castle Combe*, 217.

Newmans). The third member of this family then lived at nearby Slaughterford. Another villein lived at Hawkesbury (Glos.) and another was with his family at Tetbury (Glos.). As for William Haynes, he had left three children, of whom only the son remained at Castle Combe. A fine was paid for the marriage of his two daughters in 1434 and both left Castle Combe, significantly for two Wiltshire cloth towns, Trowbridge and Malmesbury. The family's survival as one of bond status depended on William's son Thomas, who had previously left the manor but now returned to Castle Combe and who in 1455 paid a fine to inherit his father's land.[49] He had, perhaps, too much to lose by leaving the manor forever. Fastolf's council might try to squeeze the maximum financial returns from villeinage and from the Haynes family, but they could not stop the decline of serfdom. Only the Newmans and Thomas Haynes remained, and not for long: Thomas Haynes purchased his freedom in 1463, and a William Newman and his son did the same in 1482.[50] Such families remind us that a silent struggle was going on, and that the lords were losing it, often accepting the inevitable by taking the short-term benefit of manumission in return for the long-term loss of a serf.

The Weylot family of Durrington provides another good example of the lord's losing battle to maintain serfdom. The family arrived after the Black Death but before 1388,[51] and were evidently and specifically regarded as unfree during the fifteenth century, so it seems likely that they had come from one of the other Winchester College manors. They constituted one of the active and influential families of the village in the fifteenth century and, by 1453, there were three resident branches.[52] Gradually they sought and achieved their freedom. Thomas Weylot was probably the first to accomplish this, since he headed the free jurors in 1484 and 1485.[53] By 1502 another Thomas Weilot was staying outside the lordship at the neighbouring village of Fittleton. His death, along with the fact that he had three sons who were also bondmen, was carefully recorded in the Durrington manorial court of 1509: two sons remained with their mother at Fittleton and another had moved on to the nearby village of Alton.[54] Thomas was evidently a man of substance, leaving bequests to five of the local churches and making specific bequests of 274 sheep together with 1 sheep for each of his godchildren. Despite his unfree status his will was proved at the Prerogative Court of Canterbury, like that of any freeman.[55] A third Thomas Weilot (alias Barbour) moved from Durrington to Coombe Bisset, another Winchester College manor. There he leased the demesne from 1491 until 1523 and established his family. Although his place of origin is never noted on the Coombe Bisset records comparison of the documents from the two manors make it clear that he had come from Durrington, where the same surname and alias was to be found. Despite his being a newcomer to Coombe Bisset and not appearing on any of the earlier rentals, the college took

---

49. Scrope, *Castle Combe*, 225.
50. Ibid., 226, 289.
51. WCM 5596.
52. WCM 5655d.
53. WCM 5656g.
54. WCM 5656l & m.
55. TNA: PRO Prob 11/16/14.

particular pains to record his servile status, even on the account rolls, as *nativus de sanguine* (villein by blood). The lord was evidently concerned that his move should not lead to his servile status being forgotten. But all this effort was in vain and, at his death, he too was treated like a freeman when his will was proved at the Prerogative Court of Canterbury.[56] Since there were four or five sons and a daughter, Winchester College was the loser. Another member of the Barbor branch of this family remained at Durrington, but evidently flourished. Robert Weylott or Barbor held three virgates in 1505–6 and was rent collector from 1518 until his death in 1525.[57]

Occasionally the struggle over serfdom may have flared into violence, as at Faccombe just over the border in north-west Hampshire. In 1425, 3 of the lord's bondmen by blood assaulted him, and in 1426, 2 of them removed sheep and corn earlier seized on behalf of the lord. One of these serfs, Richard Gosyn, had already sought to reject his villein status: he refused to do his labour services and married his daughter outside the lordship without permission, an action concealed by the homage. Subsequently, he and others prevented the steward holding the manorial court, 4 villeins left the manor and, in 1426, he, members of his family and others dragged the lord outside the manor house and killed him. The list of tenants drawn up in 1427, in the aftermath of these disturbances, suggest that serfdom was particularly strong in this village, with as many as 13 villeins by blood. There were then 4 vacancies resulting from hanging, forfeiture or flight. Eight villeins had fled, although some later reappeared. It is not clear how far the trouble was caused by the exceptional scale of serfdom here. The battle seemed to have ended in victory for the lord; in 1427, 3 of the vacant holdings were filled and 2 of the villeins returned, formally accepting their position as 'the lord's villein by blood, together with their offspring born or to be born thereafter'. It may, however, have been a pyrrhic victory, for villeinage declined: in 1433 there were 5 grants of manumission and after 1435 incidents involving villeins became less frequent.[58]

Serfdom was thus a matter of concern for landlords, for whom it could mean extra payments or money for manumission, and it would have been of great concern and irritation to those families who had to suffer its financial, social or mental costs. It had a tendency to hit the richer villagers more than the poorer, as the latter had little to tie them to the manor and could easily become free by leaving. It was the richer villeins who were faced with the difficult choice between staying or returning: inheriting both their father's goods and his servility, or achieving freedom by moving elsewhere and losing their inheritance. William Hayne's son Thomas left Castle Combe but felt it worthwhile to return, despite the legal humiliation, in order to take over the lands and goods from his mother. But examination of the richer peasant farmers of the Wiltshire villages reveals families like the Goddards who were accused of villeinage, families

---

56. TNA: PRO Prob 11/21/12.
57. WCM 5606Aa; 6073–9; the surviving inventory (WCM 4359) may reflect his servile status.
58. R.H. Hilton, *The English peasantry in the later Middle Ages* (Oxford, 1975), 63. The Faccombe case is based upon Latham, 'Decay of the manorial system', 176–81. See also J.N. Hare, 'The lords and their tenants: conflict and stability in fifteenth century Wiltshire', in B. Stapleton, *Conflict and community in southern England* (Stroud, 1992), 24–5.

like the Martyns of Durrington who bought their freedom and the vast majority for whom there is no hint of villeinage. It was to be the same among the rest of the tenantry. For the mass of the population, even in the conservative chalklands, serfdom had become irrelevant: it had withered away.

Chapter 9

The land market and the village economy

The family and the land market

This chapter examines three aspects of the relationship between the tenants and their village communities. The first concerns the link between the family and the tenement: how far did this period see a decline in the family–land bond and the role of inheritance in the land market? Secondly, what was happening to the size of peasant landholdings? How far was this a period dominated by greater differentiation of landholding within the peasantry or was it a case of relatively more people now having the opportunity to hold a standard tenement? Finally, how far was there an internal village economy and growing specialisation within the countryside or was village trade organised exclusively around the towns?[1]

Wiltshire and its land market generally fits into the heavily manorialised 'midland' pattern in which the settlement was organised into a single or sometimes two manors, and most of the land was held by tenants in large-scale customary units, or virgates, although there was also land held as free tenure or as cottages. Here relatively few transactions came to the court, in contrast to the situation in the weakly manorialised world of East Anglia, with its much greater market emphasis on acres and small units, its larger numbers of transactions and its larger numbers of lords.[2] In Wiltshire there may have been a greater market in small holdings in quasi-urban and suburban contexts within the county[3] and a greater market in freehold tenures away from the chalk in the vale. The manors studied here were essentially rural ones and included chalkland examples (Durrington, Coombe Bisset, Enford and Stockton) and others from the vale (Stratton, Bromham and Wroughton).

Land transactions concerning the customary holdings were regulated through and recorded in the manorial courts. The holding was surrendered and then, or later, taken by a new tenant and the transaction recorded. A summary of these entries for seven manors is included in Table 9.1. They have been analysed in standard 30-year periods in order to provide the opportunity to see long-term trends and to observe a sample of adequate size. The chronological divisions – 1390–1419; 1420–49; 1450–79; and

---

1. For discussions on the use of court rolls and the peasant land market see P.D.A. Harvey (ed), *The peasant land market in medieval England* (Oxford, 1984); R.M. Smith (ed.), *Land, kinship and lifecycle* (Cambridge, 1984); and P.D.A. Harvey, 'The peasant land market in medieval England' and Z. Razi and R.M. Smith, 'The historiography of the manorial court rolls', both in Razi and Smith, *Medieval society and the manor court*; M. Mate, 'The East Sussex land market and the agrarian class structure in the late Middle Ages', *Past and Present*, 139 (1993), 46–65.
2. e.g. J. Whittle, 'Individualism and the family-land bond: a reassessment of land transfer patterns among the English peasantry c.1270–1580', *Past and Present*, 160 (1998), 49–59; Whittle and Yates, '"Pays réel or pays légal": contrasting patterns of land tenure and social structure in eastern Norfolk and western Berkshire, 1450–1600', *AHR*, 48 (2000), 1–3.
3. *Tropenell cartulary*, ed. J.S. Davies, Wiltshire Archaeological and Natural History Society (Devizes, 1908), e.g. Corsham.

Table 9.1
Land transactions.

	No. of courts	No. of transactions	Land into court by death	Land passing to family (other than to widow)	Land passing to widow
Enford					
1333–45	2	3	1 (33%)	2 (67%)	
1354–72	8	12	2 (17%)	1 (8%)	
1428–39	5	6	1 (17%)	1 (17%)	
1450–79	8	6	6 (100%)	1 (17%)	1 (17%)
1480–1509	16	13	6 (46%)	3 (23%)	4 (31%)
Total	39	40			
Stockton					
1377–1419	46	39	20 (41%)	3 (8%)	4 (10%)
1420–49	13	7	5 (71%)		1 (14%)
1450–80	16	7	1 (14%)		
1480–1520	25	6	4 (67%)		5 (83%)
Total	100	59			
Wroughton					
1372–1416	8	10	8 (80%)	1 (10%)	3 (30%)
1423–36	5	12	2 (17%)	1 (8%)	
1454–73	11	28	10 (36%)	1 (4%)	6 (21%)
1485–1507	10	17	6 (35%)	2 (11%)	3 (18%)
Total	34	67			
Bromham					
1386–1419	33	33	15 (45%)	1 (3%)	7 (21%)
1420–39	22	19	15 (79%)		9 (47%)
Total	55	52			
Stratton St Margaret					
1407–22	24	18	3 (17%)	3 (17%)	1 (6%)
1442–48	17	26	2 (8%)		2 (8%)
Total	41	44			
Coombe Bisset					
1391–1420	35	20	10 (50%)	2 (7%)	8 (30%)
1431–49	34	14	5 (36%)	2 (10%)	5 (24%)
1450–79	37	29	9 (33%)	4 (15%)	4 (19%)
1480–1519	27	45	16 (36%)	2 (4%)	5 (11%)
Total	131				
Durrington					
1377–1420	50	49	18 (37%)	6 (17%)	6 (12%)
1420–49	26	36	13 (36%)	3 (8%)	7 (19%)
1450–79	23	42	15 (38%)	4 (10%)	6 (14%)
1480–1510	22	28	16 (57%)	5 (18%)	7 (25%)
Total	121	155			

Notes: The figures have been calculated as a percentage of the total number of transactions. The prevalence of inheritance and the family have been assessed by calculating the proportion of holdings that came into the court through death, and of those that then went to the family or to a widow, rather than to others from outside the family. Sometimes family relationships are specified, at other times inferred from a common surname. They will regrettably have been generally missed when the land passed to a son-in-law, and the figures for family transactions are therefore an under-estimate. Figures for transactions outside the family have not been calculated, since in many cases the land was not taken up within the same court, and with the exception of Durrington and Coombe Bisset we lack long complete sequences.
Sources: Enford: BL Harl Rl W8–30; V20–29; Stockton: BL Add Rl 24330–57; 24716; WRO 906/SC3–5; SC11–14; BL Add Rl 24376–80; WRO 906 SC16; BL Add Rl 24381–2; WRO 906 SC18; Wroughton: WCL Box 52 (Wroughton court rolls); Bromham: TNA: PRO SC2 208/16–26; Stratton: MCM 4322h, i; 4323a–c; 4324 c; Coombe Bissset: WCM 4398a–j; 4400ee–a; 4402, 4403, 4404 (not a complete coverage of the surviving rolls); Durrington: WCM 5650a–r; 5651a–b; 5652a–d; 5653 d–f; 5655u–a; 5656a–m.

1480–1510 – have been chosen both to provide an evenness of documentary coverage and to link to the chronology of economic change shown by other sources.

Studies of peasant land-holding have emphasised that, before the Black Death, there was both a clear presence of a land market and the general prevalence of the passage of land within the family from one generation to another. During the later Middle Ages there was an evident decline in the link that had existed between an individual holding and a specific family, although the passage of land through inheritance remained in a minority of cases.[4] Such a picture is reinforced by the Wiltshire evidence.

The limited known pre-Black Death figures must be used with caution but suggest a greater prevalence of land passing within the family.[5] On the great estate of the bishops of Winchester, covering land in Wiltshire and much of southern England, 46 per cent of cases were transferred within the family and 34 per cent by inheritance.[6] The fragmentary early evidence from Enford (Table 9.1) and from Bromham, where Faith saw the court rolls of Edward I as suggesting that family inheritance was 'firmly established', reinforces the importance of family transmission.[7]

Our Wiltshire evidence is largely from the fifteenth century and suggests that here, as elsewhere, a substantial minority of the tenant population maintained their holding until death.[8] Usually at least a third of the transactions came into the court as a result of death, and often substantially more, although rarely above half. Moreover, in a substantial minority of cases the land passed to a widow or a member of the family, with a quarter or a third generally going to such relations. The proportion of tenancies which passed to a member of the family other than a widow is comparable to the 10 to 20 per cent found on some midland manors.[9] This may have reflected the large units of land that came into the court in Wiltshire: a tenement was more likely to be

---

4. R. Faith, 'Peasant inheritance customs in medieval England', *AHR*, 14 (1966), 86–92, and 'Berkshire: fourteenth and fifteenth centuries', in Harvey, *The peasant land market*, 132, 158–65; C. Dyer, *Lords and peasants in a changing society: the estates of the bishopric of Worcester, 680–1540* (Cambridge, 1980), 304–5; E. Miller, 'Tenant farming and tenant farmers. I: the southern counties', in Miller (ed.), *Agrarian History of England and Wales*, 717–18; C. Howell, *Land, family and inheritance in transition: Kibworth Harcourt, 1280–1700* (Cambridge, 1983), 248–54; Z. Razi 'The myth of the immutable English family', *Past and Present*, 140 (1993), 3–44; A. Macfarlane, *The origins of English individualism: the farming, property and social transition* (Oxford, 1978), 94–100; J. Whittle, 'Individualism and the family-land bond', 25–63; for the bishopric of Winchester now see M. Page, 'The peasant land market in southern England: the estate of the bishops of Winchester', in L. Feller and C. Wickham (eds), *Le marché de la terre au Moyen Age* (Rome, 2005), 315–40, and idem, 'The transfer of customary land on the estates of the bishopric of Winchester before the Black Death', in Britnell, *Winchester pipe rolls*, 62–5; J. Mullan, 'The transfer of customary land on the estates of the bishop of Winchester between the Black Death and the plague of 1361', in Britnell, *Winchester pipe rolls*, 87–91; and most recently J. Mullan and R. Britnell, *Land and Family* (Hatfield, 2010)
5. Faith, 'Peasant inheritance customs', 77–95.
6. Page, 'The peasant land market', 63.
7. Faith, 'Peasant inheritance customs', 88.
8. C. Howell, 'Peasant inheritance customs in the midlands, 1280–1700', in J. Goody, J. Thirsk and E.P. Thompson (eds), *Family and inheritance* (Cambridge, 1976), 126.
9. Razi, 'The myth of the immutable English family', 29; C. Dyer, 'Were late medieval English villages "self-contained"?' in C. Dyer (ed.), *The self contained village* (Hertford, 2007), 9.

retained as a unit until death, rather than broken up to fit in with the changing demands of a family during a tenant's lifetime. Already before the Black Death family and inheritance were particularly strong influences on the estates of the bishopric of Winchester.[10]

There were chronological and regional variations within the county. Land seems to have been retained until death most consistently on those manors where there was economic growth and demand for land (as in early-fifteenth-century Bromham, which also showed a growth of inheritance by widows), or at those manors where the market was dominated by large customary holdings (such as Enford and Durrington in the later fifteenth century), where such tenants might stay put and pass on their inheritance, making the most of their capital investment even in difficult times. The tenants' retention of land until death and family inheritance seem to have been least common in areas where other evidence suggests that there were economic difficulties, such as would generate greater exodus from the manor, as at Stratton and Wroughton in the early fifteenth century. Both manors also showed substantial drops in the passage of lands to widows or other members of the family in 1420–49. As tenants moved elsewhere, so they created vacancies. At Wroughton tenure until death had been high at the end of the fourteenth century, but then declined sharply. At Stockton and Coombe Bisset, two small chalkland manors in the immediate hinterland of Salisbury, tenants in the later fourteenth and early fifteenth centuries seem more likely to have held their land until death than later in the fifteenth century. On some chalkland manors there seems to have been an increase in the amount of land going to the widow at the end of the century. In such places, prosperity and high demand may have encouraged the tenant to hold on to his assets, but left strong competition for land when the holding eventually became vacant. By contrast, in the later fifteenth century the relatively few transactions at Stockton show a revival of family inheritance, but the larger number at Coombe Bisset show an increased tendency for the land to come into the court before death and without passing to another family member. The latter trend may well reflect signs of economic difficulties in this area. There were variations between the Wiltshire manors, but, despite these, the evidence here reflects a more stable familial situation than that found in some other parts of the country, as at Halesowen (Worc.), where family transactions varied in the period 1431–1500 between 7.5 and 18.9 per cent.[11] Wiltshire's relative stability may, again, have reflected the large-scale units of land that came into the court: a tenement was more likely to be retained as a unit until death than to be broken up to fit in with the changing demands of a family during a tenant's lifetime.

As court rolls record, a widow retained the right to hold the tenements after her husband's death and to receive the complete holding without having to pay an entry fine as long as she remained single. At Durrington such transactions varied between 12 and 25 per cent of the total, and this range seems fairly typical of the county. The widow might decide to maintain her tenure or to surrender it to someone else. If she remarried the tenement would technically be forfeit, but she could then re-enter it with her new husband. She thus had a variety of choices. In the Durrington example

---

10. Page, 'The peasant land market', 340.
11. Calculated from Razi, 'The myth of the immutable English family', 29.

already cited Agnes Hickes gave up the holding but lived in retirement in a room next to the kitchen, Joanna Weylot had swiftly remarried outside the manor and Leticia Kepenell had continued as an independent tenant for another 28 years after her husband's death.

With the exception of Leticia the Durrington wives rarely outlived their husbands for more than a decade, and there seems little evidence to suggest that there was any substantial age difference between husband and wife such as has been seen on some of the bishopric of Winchester manors during acute land pressure in the thirteenth century.[12] The distorting effects of demographic pressures on the marriage market had now gone, and it was easier for widows to choose between the various options open to them. Alice Gyfgo acquired a customary virgate on the death of her husband William in May 1449 and held it until her death almost exactly 10 years later in 1459.[13] Robert Packet's widow survived him from 1449 to 1458; and Edith, widow of Nicholas Gilberd, held her husband's virgate from 1453 to 1456. Some surrendered the holdings, as did Edith, widow of John Weilot junior, who remarried Robert Vissher of Wishford and left Durrington. Those who married a widow acquired land and a fully stocked farm as well as a wife. The widow was free to make a choice, but we do not find the 'almost complete absence of marriage with widows' found at Woolstone (Berks).[14] The court rolls and rentals reflect a male-centred world.

Whatever the reality of their respective roles within the household it was the man who was legally the landholder and widowhood, as long as she remained single, seems to have been the only opportunity a woman might have to hold land. As in neighbouring Berkshire, few women were recorded as tenants in the surviving fifteenth century rentals, although in both counties there were apparently more before the Black Death.[15] At Durrington in 1334/5 there were 9 women tenants (with 4 virgators and 5 cottagers), while three fifteenth-century rentals produced a maximum of only 2. Such a change can only be partly due to a shrinkage in the number of cottage tenements, since women in the fourteenth century had also held the main agricultural tenancies. At Castle Combe there were a substantial number of women virgate tenants (5 out of a total of 11 in 1340), but a later rental shows a very different pattern compared with both the earlier account and the later ones for Durrington. In 1454 there were a few women virgate holders at Castle Combe, although they included the rich widows of farmer-clothiers in Agnes Halleway and Margery Haynes (widow of both William Haynes and, by now, her second husband);[16] but more unusual is the list of 19 cottages, of which 11 were held by women,[17] suggesting perhaps that within the industrial villages and towns the opportunities for women's

---

12. J.Z. Titow, 'Some difference between manors and their effects on the condition of the peasants in the thirteenth century', *AHR*, 10 (1962), 1–13, repr. in W.E. Minchinton (ed), *Essays in agrarian history*, vol. 1 (Newton Abbot, 1968) 39–51.
13. WCM 5655a.
14. Faith, 'Berkshire', 114.
15. Ibid., 161.
16. E.M. Carus-Wilson, 'Evidences of industrial growth on some fifteenth century manors', in Carus-Wilson, *Essays in economic history*, 163–4; G.P. Scrope, *History of the manor and ancient barony of Castle Combe* (privately printed, 1852).
17. Scrope, *Castle Combe*, 214–16.

independence and self-employment were greater than among the large farms of Durrington. Moreover, while in urban or quasi-urban contexts the conditions of the later Middle Ages opened up more opportunities for women this may not have been the case in the world of farming.[18]

Some tenants showed evidence of growth and decline in the size of their holdings, but it is generally not possible to relate this to any changing demands of a family lifecycle. The customary virgate was too large and inflexible: tenants could not reduce its size as they became older and less active or had more restricting family commitments. Some tenants, as we have seen, retained their collection of holdings at their death, or died in possession of a cottage or other single tenement. Thus at Durrington in 1438 John Palmer took a cottage and curtilage which had belonged to the late John Hyne for the lives of himself, his wife Agnes, and son William.[19] John died in 1484, almost half a century later, holding the same cottage and adjacent garden, together with two acres, which now went to his widow Agnes.[20] By contrast, in 1434 a new tenant took over a tenement while his predecessor retained a chamber at the south end of the cottage, but in 1440 the tenant forfeited it for lack of repairs.[21]

The relative abundance of available land during this period coupled with the increased mobility of the peasant population reduced the amount of land that passed through the family. But the concern for inheritance remained a significant element in peasant attitudes towards the descent of land, both in numbers and in individual cases. Where people purchased the reversionary rights to a holding the sitting tenant was often already a member of the family, suggesting either a concern to build a family tradition or to gain long-term security for a capital investment. Occasionally we can see family succession to a son-in-law, despite the change in surname. Alice Gyffgo held her husband's land for a decade after his death and, when she died, the tenement was taken by John Rowys and his wife Margery (Alice's daughter). Only one of the two grants to John records this relationship, although, perhaps significantly, this is the one that concerned the surrender of his father-in-law's tenements at the latter's death.[22] A more complex but still familial series of transactions occurred at Urchfont in 1414. Christina, widow of William West, a bondman, surrendered his messuage and half a hide to their son. But the son already had a smaller virgate holding, and he now surrendered this for the use of his own brother or son.[23] Elsewhere a tenant might have more than one holding and at his death one would go to the son and one to the widow. The links between a family and land are also reflected in the survival of serfdom. Families such as the Haynes and the Alweys continued in their own village despite the personal cost of continuing to accept their lack of freedom (see Chapter 8), whether on grounds of sentiment or hard-nosed economics and the advantages of inheriting the accumulated family possessions.

---

18. C.M. Barron, 'London, 1300–1540' in Palliser (ed), *The Cambridge urban history of Britain*, 427–8; P.J.P. Goldberg, *Women, work and life cycle in a medieval economy* (Oxford, 1992).
19. WCM 5655m.
20. WCM 5656g.
21. WCM 5656p & m.
22. WCM 5655a.
23. HRO 83M85 W,1.

The accumulation of holdings among the peasantry

The population decline of the later Middle Ages opened up considerable opportunities for the acquisition of extra land by the survivors. The land market showed a tripartite pattern of land-holding familiar elsewhere: a middle range of tenancies (here usually a virgate); a smaller and growing group who held more than this; and a substantial but generally shrinking group who held a cottage and a few acres, or a half virgate.[24] The main change was the accumulation of holdings in a single hand, above and beyond that of the standard tenement. This process was neither a simple case of the upgrading or 'economic promotion' of smaller holders into large ones (the cottager becoming a virgator), nor was it one of a growing differentiation between rich and poor peasants.[25]

The initial impact of the Black Death and subsequent plagues produced a general upgrading of peasant holdings rather than the emergence of a new class of large landholders. It was the cottage holdings that tended to be left empty or held by a virgator or half-virgator as an additional holding. At Upavon, a rental of 1397[26] shows that many people now held several properties, but extremely few held more than one virgate or half-virgate. Thus Walter Bryggeman's holding consisted of a cottage, a purpresture, half an acre, a messuage and a virgate, an acre of demesne, a parcel of meadow and an acre. At Durrington by 1388, 16 out of 33 bond tenants possessed more than one holding, but the additions were minor: extra acres, a cottage or the land of a deserted toft. Only Robert Erneys held more than the single standard holdings together with his other property, and he overshadowed the rest of the village. His annual rent of 46s 2d compared with 25s for his nearest rival.[27]

Here as elsewhere, the fifteenth century saw another and different development, with the emergence of a group of tenants who held several standard tenements and became a new landed class within the village, separated from the members of the elite who merely held a single large holding. We move from an age of economic promotion to one of increased differentiation; from peasant landholding to larger-scale 'proto-capitalist' holdings. In the fourteenth century the main distinction had been between those who held a virgate and those who had a cottage, not between those who held one virgate and those with more. In the fifteenth century a new distinction had emerged, between those who held several virgates and those who held only one. At Durrington, by 1411, one tenant held a cottage and two virgates, and another held three messuages and three virgates together with a shared portion of another virgate. By 1441, four men each held two virgates. By 1506 three men held two virgates and two held three. The virgators had once been the leading figures of the village, now the

---

24. R.H. Hilton, *The English peasantry in the later Middle Ages* (Oxford, 1975), 40.
25. For general discussion and differing approaches see, for example, M.M. Postan, *The medieval economy and society* (Harmondsworth, 1975), 176–8; and 'Medieval society in its prime: England', in M.M. Postan (ed.), *The Cambridge economic history of Europe*, i, *The agrarian life of the Middle Ages*, 2nd edn (Cambridge, 1966), 630–32; R.H. Hilton, *The economic development of some Leicestershire estates in the fourteenth and fifteenth centuries* (Oxford, 1947), 94–105; Dyer, *Lords and peasants*, 298.
26. TNA: PRO DL43/9/34.
27. WCM 5596.

Table 9.2
Land-holding and tenant differentiation at Durrington and Coombe Bisset.

	3 or more virgates	Between 2 and 3 virgates	2 virgates	Between 1 and 2 virgates	1 virgate	Between ½ and 1 virgate	½ virgate	Less than ½ virgate
Durrington								
1334/5				17			19	
1359			1	4	7		4	16
1411/12	1		1	1	7		2	12
1441		2	2	3	5	2		9
1505/6	2		3	3	2	2		14
Coombe Bisset								
1307				1	12		2	14
1372				5	8	3	2	12
1411/12			1	2	9		2	11
1450			1	4	9	1	2	6
1552	1		3		6	2	10	

Sources: Durrington: WCM 5601Aa; 5601Ca; 13373; 5603d; 5606Aa; Coombe Bisset: WCM 4350;

five who remained with only a single virgate were relatively small-scale agricultural producers (Table 9.2). Here the evolution of the customary land market accentuated the development of the chalklands of Wiltshire into an area of large-scale tenant agriculture.

At Coombe Bisset, a similar comparison can be made for the period up to 1449. In 1411/2 there was limited evidence of the accumulation of large standard holdings, with only a single pair of virgates. The 1450 rental suggests that, here, it was more a case of adding small extra holdings rather than throwing together the traditional standard holdings: of the 27 bond or customary tenants, 6 held compound holdings, but only one a double virgate. But, by the middle of the sixteenth century, a situation similar to that of Durrington had developed. Of the 15 virgates, 9 were now held by 4 men. The court rolls, however, suggest that this process had not gone far by 1500, as few compound holdings, other than of cottages, came through the court. This chronological contrast may result from the presence of the cloth industry in the Ebble valley, and the nearby Salisbury market in the late fourteenth and early fifteenth century, generating increased demand for land and discouraging accumulation. Tenant numbers declined in the later fourteenth century at Durrington, but less so at Coombe Bisset (see Table 8.1). This reduction reflected the decline in the number of small holdings. Subsequently tenant numbers stabilised in the fifteenth century at Durrington and to a lesser extent at Coombe Bisset, where numbers fell between 1412 and 1450, with 4 vacant tofts present in the latter year.[28]

Elsewhere, manorial court rolls provide further evidence for the accumulation of holdings. They show how much land a tenant had when he died or when he surrendered his tenements. Such records provide a less reliable indicator of the size of tenant holdings, since a tenant might not surrender all his land at the same time and

---

28. WCM 4353.

might have given up some land before his death. But the court rolls reinforce the view that the fifteenth century was a period of growing accumulation and an increasing contrast between the rich and poor of the village, and of variable rates of change. At Enford, near Durrington, there were 13 documented transactions in which holdings fell into the lord's hands between 1480 and 1501. Of these, the great majority were compound holdings, with 9 at one and a half virgates or more. The gulf between the larger tenement and the standard one had grown, but it was less than that at Durrington. At Enford, most half virgates seem to have ceased as independent tenements, being absorbed by virgators. There are only 6 surviving entries for the early part of the century, but the development was probably already underway: 4 of these were for compound holdings, of which 3 were for one and a half virgates or more. At Stockton, as at Coombe Bisset, the process of accumulation was slower: only 3 out of 24 transactions were for such holdings in the first half of the century, and 3 out of 7 in the second half. Again, the difference may have resulted from the contrast in the chalklands between essentially agricultural manors and those small manors in the valleys around Salisbury where the cloth industry had developed. Nor had accumulation happened in the early fifteenth century on any substantial scale away from the chalk, as at Wroughton and Stratton. At Wroughton such accumulation may have occurred later, since just over a third of cases passing through its court in the second half of the century were for compound holdings.

An inventory of a Durrington tenant in 1525 hints at the comfort that might be enjoyed and the agricultural activities that might be undertaken by such wealthy tenant farmers. Robert Weylot, alias Barbour, came from a serf family that had risen to local prominence. In 1505–6 he held three virgates and a bakehouse, and he acted as rent collector for Winchester College from 1517 until his death. He then possessed a house with kitchen, an alehouse, a hall decorated with three different painted cloths and seven candle sticks, a chamber with three pairs of sheets and 20lb of wool, and an upper chamber with six pairs of sheets and one painted cloth. His farming stock comprised 126 sheep, 2 cows, 4 younger cattle, 3 horses, 9 pigs, a plough and cart, 12 quarters of wheat, 50 quarters of barley and 20 quarters of oats, showing mixed farming and large quantities of barley and sheep. It was not a world of extravagance, but nor was it one of subsistence or poverty.[29]

The development of this peasant aristocracy reflects wider changes that were to be of extreme importance for the future of agriculture in the chalklands of Wiltshire and beyond.[30] Together, large-scale customary tenants and the demesne lessees formed a new village elite, whose scale of activities raised them far above the traditional virgator. The term 'peasant' no longer seems a useful term. They can surely justify the term 'capitalist farmers': employing labour, producing large surpluses for the market – of meat, wool, wheat, barley and malt – and expanding in new markets.

---

29. WCM 5606Aa; 6072–6079; 4359.
30. For similar trends in the Hampshire manor of Ramridge see J.P. Genet, 'Economie et société rurale en Angleterre au XVè siècle d'après les comptes de l'hôpital d'Ewelme', *Annales Économies Sociétés, Civilisations*, 27 (1972), 157–8.

The internal market of the village

Villages were not self-contained. They depended on neighbouring towns for the purchase of goods and for access to specialised labour, as well as a place in which to sell their agricultural surpluses (see Chapter 10). But there were also informal markets within the village and between the villagers themselves. Most villages included some specialists who catered for its own and neighbouring inhabitants: crafts were carried out both in conjunction with agricultural activities and as full-time employments. In addition, there were regional specialisations that occupied many villagers, such as cloth manufacturing, quarrying in the Cotswolds or the manufacture of tiles and other woodland occupations. Such activities are shown by fines recorded in the court rolls and others by the lists of specialist occupations in the incomplete 1379 poll tax returns (Table 9.3 and below, Chapter 10). The latter provide a minimal figure for those who were sufficiently well-off to be assessed above the basic rate of taxation.[31] The largest group of non-agricultural rural workers were the cloth workers, who are discussed in a later chapter.

Brewers produced a food product that was a virtual necessity in both town and village society. The Wiltshire chalkland provided good soils for barley, and it remained an area prominent for barley and malt in subsequent centuries. In the 1379 poll tax figures, 15 villages in the county accounted for 17 brewers, making it one of the larger specified occupation groups. In the manorial courts the brewers appear when they broke the assize of ale. This was such a regular item that it seems to have been akin to a licence payment for brewing and selling regardless of wealth and frequency of offending.[32] There was also a separate offence on some manors of using false measures for the sale of ale, which usually punished both the brewers and a few other individuals, probably outsiders who came into the village to sell their wares.

Brewing no longer appears as a predominantly female occupation, and women were rarely fined here.[33] At Coombe Bisset in 1391 there were only 2 women among the 17 people fined, and in 1425 there were none out of 25. At Bromham, in the decade 1410–19, women produced an average of less than 2 fines per court out of an average total of 11. This may, however, conceal the reality of the situation, in which women may have been doing the brewing while the men appeared in court to pay the fine for a wife: but this cannot be established.[34] This tendency for men to be fined may have been encouraged by the infrequency (generally twice yearly) with which the court met and the presence at the court of many of the male heads of household. The figures for women's brewing activity are lower than those for Alrewas (Staffs.) in the

---

31. Mapped in Hare, 'Lord and tenant in Wiltshire, c.1380–1520, with particular reference to regional and seigneurial variations', PhD thesis (London, 1976), 78. For consideration of the evidence elsewhere, see R.H. Hilton, *Bond men made free: medieval peasant movements and the English rising of 1381* (London, 1973), 171–4.
32. Hilton, *The English peasantry*, 45–6, 104–5.
33. On the decline of the brewsters in general see J.M. Bennett, *Ale, beer and brewsters in England: women's work in a changing world, 1300–1600* (New York and Oxford, 1996), and on their decline at Stockton since the thirteenth century see ibid., 51.
34. H. Graham, '"A woman's work...": labour and gender in the late medieval countryside', in Goldberg, *Women in medieval English society*, 138–44.

Table 9.3
Village craftsmen in the 1379 poll tax records.

Occupation	No. and %	
Cloth workers		
Weaver	63	
Fuller	22	
Other cloth worker	12	
Tailor	68	
Drapers and cloth seller	6	
Total	171	(49.3%)
Leather workers	23	
Total	23	(6.6%)
Building workers		
Mason	15	
Carpenter	41	
Thatcher	4	
Tiler	13	
Total	73	(21%)
The food industry		
Butcher	31	
Brewer	17	
Other food maker/seller	32	
Total	80	(23.1%)

Sources: TNA: PRO E179 239/193; 194/42; 196/42a, 52; 196/44, 52a. For a distribution map of places with surviving records see Hare, Lord and Tenant, 78. The percentages are of the total number of specified occupations. Towns have been excluded.

fourteenth century and, more particularly, the thirteenth century.[35] But we should not assume that women dominated rural brewing.[36] The brewers came from a variety of backgrounds, and included rich tenant farmers, demesne lessees, cottagers and wage-earners. In 1412, 18 brewers were fined at Coombe Bisset, including the church, for a church ale, 4 holders of standard virgate tenements, a miller and William Potter, who was to become the demesne lessee in 1415 (although his base was probably then in the village's other manor[37]), as well as tenants who were largely dependent on wages, with six cottagers and one half-virgator. None of the six who were fined for selling but not brewing appear on the contemporary rental, suggesting that this offence may have involved outsiders. There were also a number of related but distinct offences: hostellers at Stockton and a taverner at Coombe Bisset.[38] There seems to have been a greater prevalence of brewing in the chalklands than elsewhere in the county, reflecting the regional emphasis on barley. The populous manor of

---

35. Ibid., 137, 140; D. Postles, 'Brewing and the peasant economy: some manors in late medieval Devon', *Rural History*, 2 (1992), 140–41.
36. Discussed in Hilton, *The English peasantry*, 104–5.
37. The family subsequently became a key part of the college manor.
38. WCM 4396; on inns and inn keepers see below, Chapter 10.

Bromham had substantially fewer brewers, for instance, than the smaller chalkland manor of Durrington, and in four courts in 1441–3 the Cotswold manor of Colerne averaged fewer than four brewers per court.[39]

There were also signs of regional specialisation in brewing in the immediate hinterland of Salisbury, where several small villages seem to have particular high concentrations of brewers, as at Stockton, with 39 brewers in 1349 and 14 to 25 between 1368 and 1385,[40] and at Coombe Bisset, with 20 brewers and sellers in 1391. The presence of such an industry might have accounted for the unexpected use of Coombe as a market for grain from the Deverills in west Wiltshire three times in the early fourteenth century.[41] Moreover, the tithe returns for Downton show how much barley production seems to have dominated peasant and tenant agriculture in this area, a product both of Salisbury and of the concentration of cloth workers in the area.[42]

The period saw a noticeable decline in the number of brewers, although this may not be a product of a fall in consumption. At Coombe Bisset the 20 brewers and sellers in 1391 fell to about 10 around 1420 and 4 to 6 in the 1450s; there were generally at least 7 from the 1480s. At Durrington in the 1370s and 80s there were usually about 12 to 20 presentments; these appeared to reach a peak in the 1420s, with over 20 being consistently fined. Thereafter the number fell to well under 20 in the 1430s and 1440s, and with a further fall to well under 10 from the mid-1450s and in the 1460s. In the 1490s and 1500s there were generally between 1 and 4 per court. At Bromham numbers seem to have fallen from the end of the 1420s and at Stockton in the first decade of the century. In conclusion, the fifteenth century saw a long-term decline in the number of brewers, with a further short-term fall in the mid-fifteenth-century recession. This may have reflected a variety of factors. In the case of Stockton and Coombe Bisset the decline occurred early and may have resulted from the difficulties evident in agriculture and the cloth industry in the Salisbury area in the early fifteenth century. Durrington was also part of the immediate Salisbury hinterland, but any reduced demand from Salisbury would have been counterbalanced here by the growing demands of the west of Wiltshire, to which it also had access. In the long term other legal, social or economic factors may have reduced the numbers. The decline in the activities of the manorial court may have made it less able to tax all of the brewing industry. A growing concentration of the village market in the hands of a few large producers (who might have still only paid once) would give us a false view of decline, as would any concentration of the industries in a few large centres other than those examined in this study. A concentration of production within the village, as fewer brewers operated on a larger scale, has been suggested for Stoke Fleming in Devon for the late fifteenth and early sixteenth centuries, and also for the west Midlands.[43] In Wiltshire, however, brewing may have continued as an addition to the

---

39. NCA 2734.
40. BL Add Rl 24335, 37, 38, 24340, WRO 906/SC5. By 1479 there were only two brewers: Bennett, *Ale, beer and brewsters*, 48.
41. D.L. Farmer, 'Two Wiltshire manors and their markets', *AHR*, 37 (1989), 7.
42. See above, Chapter 5.
43. Postles, 'Brewing', 137–9; Dyer, *Lords and peasants*, 346–9; Bennett, *Ale, beer and brewsters*, 46.

agrarian economy of the large-scale farmer, such as the Martyns of Durrington, rather than as a single occupation:[44] malting and brewing had become an increasingly specialised part of agricultural production, which the large-scale tenant farmers could more easily control. This was a process that may have been further encouraged by the use of hops, which allowed larger-scale production.

The villages showed a variety of occupations that remind us of 'the sophistication of the late medieval economy'.[45] There were 31 village butchers in the poll tax figures, but while most were scattered one to a village, some villages had several, suggesting the development of regional specialisation in the clay vales: Rowde had 4 butchers, Bromham 5 and Ashton 5. Butchers are occasionally fined in the court rolls for selling meat, as at Stockton, Bromham and, later, Coombe Bisset (from 1450), Durrington (from 1435) and Enford. Fish dealers or poachers were fined at Durrington and Enford, on the river Avon.[46] On some manors, millers were regularly fined for infringement of regulations, as with the 3 millers of Bromham, or those of Coombe Bisset or Durrington, where it seems to have become a regular payment. Bakers were fined at Bromham and Enford.[47] It would be dangerous to read occupations into surnames, but the use of distinguishing alias names may be more useful, as with the proliferation of the Weylot family and the addition there of the distinctive occupations of carter and barber. Such people presumably served a group of neighbouring villages, as with the tailor of Knighton (a tiny neighbouring village) found on the court rolls of Durrington. Tailors were the largest single village group, making up about a fifth of the specified occupations. Many were concentrated in the main clothing areas and should be seen as an offshoot of that industry, as in Heytesbury hundred, where 18 were recorded among the villages (or 21 if Heytesbury itself is included). But many were also scattered isolated craftsmen who served the needs of several villages.

There were also full-time servants, probably frequently living in during their earlier years. Like their social betters, the children of the villagers were often put out as servants to another family. In a survey made of the villeins of Durrington in 1453 and 1454 all but one of the ten children aged between 9 and 16 years were listed as staying with someone else. Where there were several children within a family they were divided up between different tenants. Robert Martyn, a large tenant farmer from the other Durrington manor, had two such child servants: Thomas the son of John Welot, barbour, and Edith daughter of John Weylot alias Carter. We are evidently looking at patterns of service in an economy that could not be based exclusively on family labour.[48] Occasionally someone is described as a servant of someone else, but, as elsewhere, the references to servants and labourers on the court rolls are few and far between.[49]

The building trade also provided employment. When a lord wanted the construction of a major building he might draw upon expertise from a distance; thus,

---

44. Cf. Dyer, *Lords and peasants*, 348.
45. Ibid., 349.
46. e.g. WCM 5655e, d; BL Harl Rl V20, W20, W26, W28.
47. e.g. BL Harl Rl W28.
48. WCM 5655d & c.
49. See also Hilton, *The English peasantry*, 35.

when Winchester Cathedral Priory decided it needed a new manorial hall and chamber block at Stockton it sent William Ykenham, a leading Winchester carpenter, who was active in the service of the bishop of Winchester and Winchester College, as well as the cathedral priory, to issue instructions.[50] Winchester College employed Thomas Mason of Salisbury to build a new grange and porch at Coombe Bisset in 1400, and brought a carpenter from Salisbury to provide advice and supervise repairs to the mill in 1455.[51] Meanwhile, local craftsmen, scattered around the villages, catered for the construction and repair of the villagers' houses.

Peasant housing, as in other parts of England, did not consist of poorly constructed buildings, but was built by professionals. The houses consisted of several different rooms and were sufficiently well built for some of them still to survive, as both the documents and the surviving buildings make clear.[52] The usual peasant homestead was timber-framed, with wattle and daub infill, stone footings and a thatched roof. It had a hall with one or two storeys of chambers, and a kitchen adjacent. In addition, the associated farm buildings included at least a barn or grange. Such buildings are occasionally documented in the manorial account and court rolls. Sometimes the lord invested in new accommodation and payments for tenant building were frequent at Durrington, where the cost of a tenement went up to almost £6 or £7,[53] and over the Berkshire border at Coleshill, where sums of up to £10 were spent on rebuilding individual tenements.[54] These were not insignificant amounts of money and the occasional details reinforce their presence as substantial timber-framed constructions with stone foundations. In 1467 a house, or at least the timber-framing, was bought at Bulford, a neighbouring village just across the river, and then brought to Durrington for erection. In 1436 stone was purchased from the quarries of Chilmark for the footings of a peasant house, suggesting the presence of properly constructed footings, while at other times the footings were constructed with flint from the surrounding fields. The whole price of construction of this house, with its three doors and four windows, came to £6 18s 9d.[55] In 1434 John Aubrey took possession of a cottage[56] and was also the carpenter responsible for new buildings on one of the lord's tenements.[57] In 1434 a new tenant took up a ruined tenancy at Coombe Bisset and agreed to build a new hall with upper and lower chamber, kitchen and outer buildings. The lord gave him £6 and six cart loads of timber.[58] Occasionally, legal agreements include specific reference to particular rooms, as at Durrington in 1430, when a chamber at the east

---

50. BL Add Rl 24407, 1416; J. Harvey, *English medieval architects*, 2nd edn (Gloucester, 1984); J.N. Hare, 'Bishop's Waltham palace, Hampshire: William of Wykeham, Henry Beaufort and the transformation of a medieval episcopal palace', *Archaeological Journal*, 148 (1988), 240.
51. WCM 5630, 4684.
52. C. Dyer, *Everyday life in medieval England* (London, 1994), 133–65; for a study of the buildings of a neighbouring county with many dates from dendrochronology, see E. Roberts, *1200–1700, their dating and development* (Winchester, 2003).
53. WCM 5974, 5970, 5971, 5979, 5983, 6018, 6021.
54. Faith, 'Berkshire', 174.
55. WCM 5989–91.
56. WCM 5655p.
57. WCM 5989.
58. WCM 4400bb.

part of the kitchen was to be left for the previous owner.[59] In 1525 the inventory of Robert Weylott, a Durrington villein, recorded a house with kitchen, alehouse, a hall, chamber and an upper chamber.[60] Winchester College spent on all its Wiltshire properties, including at Downton, where it employed a carpenter from the nearby village of Britford.[61]

Conclusion

Life in the late medieval village was shaped as much by the world outside the village as that within. The operation of the land market encouraged contrasts between the rich customary tenants of the village and other members of the community and produced a decline in the influence of the family in determining land-holding. The labour and land markets were influenced by the conflicting impact of late medieval population decline and the growth of the cloth industry. Within the village fewer people each held more land and a growing number of village craftsmen and traders supplemented their agricultural activities with trading within or beyond the village. A capitalist agriculturalist class had emerged that was very different from the peasantry that typified the thirteenth-century village.

At Durrington Robert Martyn and his family could perhaps be taken as characteristic of this changing village society, and of the growth of a new larger-scale commercial farming. He was a former serf from the Dean and Chapter of Salisbury's manor of Durrington, where he had become its lessee and gained manumission. He, or a father with the same name, figured prominently in the court rolls of the Winchester College manor there, in the mid- and later fifteenth century, where he was frequently a butt of complaint for overstocking the common pastures or damaging the property of the college tenants. His servants included two of the children of the college villeins.[62] He himself was a substantial sheep grazier, stocking the college meadow with 800 sheep in 1478. By 1506–7 the family had become the greatest tenants on the Winchester College manor, John Martyn the elder holding three virgates and John Martyn the younger another two virgates. The elder John was fined regularly as a brewer and a butcher, but he also served the college and manor as assessor and head of the freemen of the court. Other Martyns are found active in the area as cottagers in Durrington or as demesne farmers in the nearby villages.[63] One of these, his cousin Robert from the Dean and Chapter manor at Durrington, drew up a will in 1509, and it reflects the world of the large-scale agricultural farmer that John would no doubt have recognised. He made bequests to his local church at Durrington and to that at Amesbury, the nearby town, but he made others too, to the Grey Friars of Salisbury and the church of Upavon and to every church or chapel along the Avon

---

59. See also R. Smith in M. Aston, *Medieval Village Research Group Report* 30 (1982).
60. WCM 4359; on the Weylotts see also above, Chapter 7.
61. e.g. WCM 5431, 5435, 5441, 5446 (1445, at a cost of over £34 for two cottages, at this price they may have been urban houses in Downton), 5449, 5450.
62. SDC Chapter Act books, x, 107, 114, vol xii, p.137; WCM 5655e–c, 5656d–f.
63. WCM 5603e; 5656b; BL Harl Rl X/18–X/22; WCL Book of the Common Seal, ii, 40–41; TNA: PRO SC6/Hen VIII/3822. For a general discussion of capitalist agriculture see Dyer, *Everyday life*, 306–16.

valley between Upavon and Salisbury. But he also looked westwards to the west Wiltshire cloth industry with bequests to Tilshead and to Steeple Ashton, a market and cloth centre whose importance is reflected in their receiving twice his normal bequest to the other churches.[64]

---

64. Printed in C.S. Ruddle, 'Notes on Durrington', *WAM*, 31 (1901), 339–40.

Chapter 10

Towns and trade

So far, the emphasis of this study has been on the countryside and the manor, but these did not operate in isolation. Both the peasant and the manorial lord worked within a commercial framework, producing for their own needs, but also buying and selling within a wider market. The towns were consumers of agricultural surpluses, but also provided goods and services for the countryside and acted as intermediaries between the villages and more distant markets at home and abroad. The peasants' assessment of the market demand and of their own requirements affected decisions about which crops to produce or which livestock to rear. Peasants, lords and other farmers were part of a wider commercial structure in which town, village, consumer, producer and market were closely integrated. This chapter seeks to examine the role of the towns and the patterns of commerce (Figure 10.1).

In recent years there has been an increased emphasis on the vital importance of the small towns in medieval urban life, as seen in the work of R.H. Hilton and C. Dyer.[1] In assessing the national importance of the urban sector the latter has calculated the urban population of Wiltshire in 1377 (including the small towns) at 19.5 per cent of the county's population, a proportion comparable with that of a sample of other counties.[2] It is, however, unclear whether the urban population that escaped or evaded the tax balanced those townspeople who made their living from agriculture. Many of the Wiltshire towns lay in the west of the county, in parishes whose rural settlements had grown through woodland clearance. By contrast, in some parishes industrial growth had produced a quasi-urban population in what had hitherto been rural villages. The figures need to be treated with caution, and seem more likely to be an overestimate than an underestimate, but nevertheless they reflect the vital importance of towns in late medieval society. As Dyer has commented, there is little evidence of any long-term 'deurbanization or shrinkage of [town] population'.[3] The urban population may have shrunk in line with the general population decline, but it still flourished.

The 1377 and 1379 poll tax figures provide us with a valuable starting point in examining the hierarchy of towns. The records of the 1377 tax, which was levied at a standard rate on every person over the age of 14 years, are almost complete and provide a snapshot of the distribution of population and of the main centres of

---

1. R.H. Hilton, *The English peasantry in the later Middle Ages* (Oxford, 1975), 76–94; C. Dyer, 'How urbanized was medieval England?', in. J.-M. Duvosquel and E. Thoen (eds), *Peasants and towns in medieval Europe* (Gent, 1995), 169–83; idem, 'Small towns, 1270–1540', in Palliser (ed), *The Cambridge urban history of Britain*, 505–37.
2. A. Dyer, *Decline and growth in English towns, 1400–1640* (Basingstoke, 1991), 175.
3. Dyer, 'How urbanized was medieval England?' 180.

A Prospering Society

Figure 10.1 Wiltshire: towns

population.[4] Children and some adults were exempt, so that, in order to convert the number of taxpayers into an approximate urban population, the figures should be doubled.[5] Many of the most populous parishes were essentially the result of earlier rural growth, so that towns cannot be defined simply through the size of their population.

The assessments for the 1379 poll tax survive for about half of the county.[6] This was a graduated tax, so that the collectors had to produce lists with occupation or status labels for those who had to pay more than the basic rate of 4d. Labourers and servants are also sometimes noted. Unfortunately the new scheme was narrower in its application: it included the adult population above 16 years of age (compared with those above 14 in 1377) and married women were exempt. The result was an apparent but misleading fall in population.[7] In addition, only the better-off taxpayers would be likely to have a higher assessment and therefore a recorded occupation, but these records can provide a crude indication of the range and geographical spread of particular occupations.[8]

Although other tax assessments provide the possibility of ranking towns, prime attention has been given to the poll tax of 1377, supported by the occupational descriptions in 1379. Other assessments of wealth are provided by the fifteenths and tenths of 1334, and assessments of wealth and taxpayers survive for the 1524/5 lay subsidies. The latter may have been distorted for individual places by the exceptional wealth of a single rich farmer or clothier, whose fortune may have derived from the country villages around, as with Thomas Horton of Westwood.[9] But these returns suggest both change and greater urban continuity than elsewhere. Marlborough grew and was now the second wealthiest town in the county with an assessment at £85, but there were no other towns in this league. Devizes, next in the list, was assessed at under £50. No Wiltshire town, apart from Salisbury (7) and Marlborough (43), was in the top 50 English towns which were assessed above £72; Devizes came seventy-fourth.[10] The growth of the cloth industry does not appear to have produced new rich towns, which parallels the situation in Somerset but contrasts with that in Suffolk, Devon or north Hampshire. In these latter places it was perhaps rural labour in a highly capitalised industry that generated such huge 'urban' wealth, as with the Springs of Lavenham and in such growing towns as Hadleigh and Long Melford (Suffolk) or Alton

---

4. M.W. Beresford, 'Poll tax payers of 1377', in VCH *Wilts* 4; mapped in J.N. Hare, 'Lord and tenant in Wiltshire, c.1380–1520, with particular reference to regional and seigneurial variations', PhD thesis (London, 1976), 17, and C. Lewis, 'Patterns and processes in the medieval settlement of Wiltshire', in Aston and Lewis (eds), *The medieval landscape of Wessex*, 180.
5. I have adopted the multiplier of 2 for conversion into a total population, see Dyer, 'Small towns', 536; the Wiltshire figures are taken from Beresford, 'Poll tax payers of 1377', 306–11.
6. Mapped in Hare, 'Lord and tenant', 78.
7. C.C. Fenwick, *The poll taxes of 1377, 1379 and 1381*, Records of Social and Economic History, new series, 27, 29 (London, 1998–), xxv–vi; at Marlborough the taxed population fell from 543 in 1377 to 267 and at Compton Basset from 126 to 76, and these examples are not extreme.
8. All comments on the Wiltshire material are based on my own work. Publication of this important national source is now well underway, creating a new and more secure basis for its use and allowing comparison with other counties. Fenwick, *Poll taxes*, i–iii.
9. See below, Chapter 11.
10. A. Dyer, 'Ranking lists of English medieval towns', in Palliser (ed.), *The Cambridge urban history of Britain*, 756–7.

and Basingstoke (Hants). Did Wiltshire's apparent lack of rapid urban growth represent a different, more stable structure for the industry that had grown up in the late fourteenth and early fifteenth centuries? Was there less of a gulf between rich and poor, or were the rich just spread among more villages? Was the comparatively recent dramatic increase of the industry based on a different commercial structure?[11]

Most of the Wiltshire towns would count as small towns and these were both part of rural society and distinct from it. Urban life was distinguished by a variety of elements, including the size of population, the range of occupations and specialisations, urban traditions, communal activities and self-government, legal rights of burgage tenure and market holding reflected in street and property plans, additional religious institutions beyond the single parish, wide-ranging non-agrarian employments and evidence of marketing. Not all places would have possessed all these elements and often evidence has not survived. No single element will provide an adequate definition of a town. But together they allow an attempt to sketch the variety of urban life within the county, to establish something of the urban hierarchy and to demonstrate the importance of towns in the economic and social life of the county. Wiltshire was a land of many small towns, even by medieval standards. But in Salisbury it also possessed one of the greatest of late medieval English cities. In 1377 the taxable population of Salisbury and the suburb of Fisherton was five times greater than that of Wilton, the next largest town. Although the gulf had been reduced by 1523/4 it was still four times that of the second largest town, now Marlborough. Salisbury will therefore be treated separately, albeit briefly. It warrants a full study in its own right, and no attempt has been made here to tackle the large quantity of its surviving documentation.

Salisbury

Salisbury overshadowed all other towns in the county. It was among the greatest cities in the kingdom and was the most successful of the many new towns that had been created in the twelfth and thirteenth centuries (Plate 10.1). It was one of two regional capitals that influenced the economy of Wiltshire, the other being Bristol. It had grown with remarkable speed from its beginnings in 1219: in 1220 the foundation stone of the new cathedral was laid in the valley, replacing the crowded and inconvenient hilltop site of its predecessor; in 1227 the king recognised the new town. It had started on a small scale, but grew in a series of stages from agricultural manor to urban greatness. The topographical expansion was completed by 1269, with the creation of a great new parish of St Edmund. Salisbury rose dramatically in the urban national hierarchy and by 1334 possessed the eleventh highest tax assessment outside London. It continued to grow and by 1377 it was the sixth largest provincial town, with a taxpaying population of 3,226 (3,373 including the suburb of Fisherton

---

11. A. Betterton and D. Dymond, *Lavenham: industrial town* (Lavenham, 1989), 42; E.M. Carus-Wilson, *The expansion of Exeter* (Exeter, 1961). For the growing cloth towns of Basingstoke and Alton see J.N. Hare, 'Regional prosperity in fifteenth-century England: some evidence from Wessex', in M. Hicks (ed.), *Revolution and consumption in late medieval England* (Woodbridge, 2001), 111–15; idem, 'Church-building and urban prosperity on the eve of the reformation: Basingstoke and its parish church', *PHFCAS*, 62 (2007), 185–91.

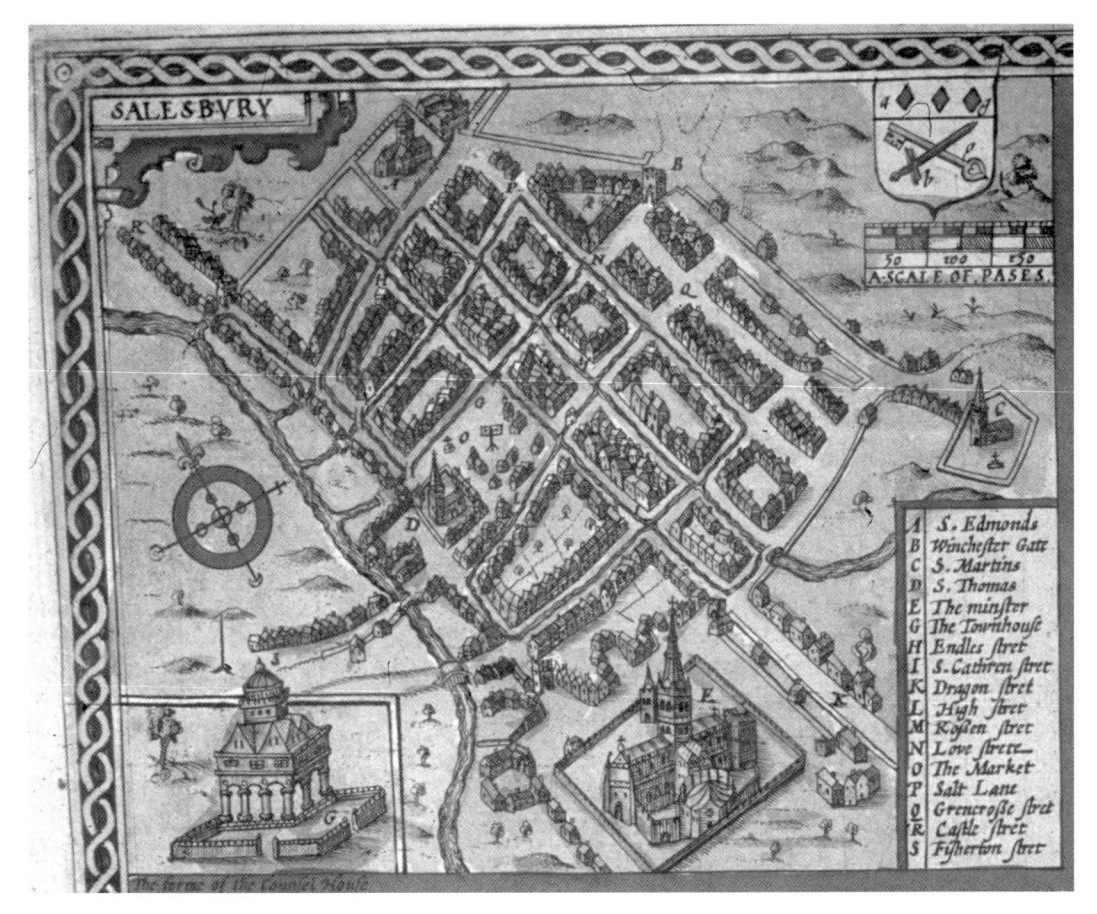

Plate 10.1 Salisbury in 1611, from John Speed's map of Wiltshire, showing the street grid of the medieval town.

Anger), representing a total population of about 6,400–6,700. Salisbury retained this national prominence throughout the later Middle Ages, as reflected in taxation and royal loans. In 1397, it was the sixth largest urban contributor to a royal loan and in 1422 it was third; it seemed to retain a similarly high standing throughout the fifteenth century. In the new subsidies of 1525 it was the fifth most highly assessed provincial town and the fourth in terms of number of taxpayers.[12] Like other towns, it may have suffered from the general decline in population, and from short-term recessions, but in general it prospered and maintained its relative importance throughout the period.[13]

---

12. M.K. Dale, 'The city of New Salisbury', in VCH *Wilts* 6, 104, 124, 129; K.H. Rogers, 'Salisbury', in M.D. Lobel (ed.), *Historic towns*, vol. 1 (London, 1969), 4; Dyer, *Decline and growth*, 64–71. Newcastle-upon-Tyne (not taxed) may have pushed Salisbury into sixth place for wealth, and Newcastle and underestimates for York and Coventry may push it down to seventh by population: Dyer, 'Ranking lists', 761–7.
13. A.R. Bridbury, 'English provincial towns in the later Middle Ages', *EcHR*, 2nd series 34 (1981), 8. On short-term problems of the city see below, Chapter 12.

Salisbury had risen to greatness with remarkable rapidity. Although the bishop's prime concern when he chose the site was its location on his own land the city was well placed for growth. It was a route centre in an area of rich well-populated river valleys that was short of towns, apart from Wilton: the five river valleys of southern Wiltshire come together in its vicinity. In addition, the intervening chalkland ridges which provided some of the main transport routes converged more directly on the site. Salisbury was thus ideally suited to become the marketing centre for southern Wiltshire. Bridge-building helped this growth, above all the construction of Harnham Bridge in 1244, which opened up the area to the city's south and west and meant that the long-distance trade from the west no longer had to go via the river crossing at Wilton. The presence of the bishop and chapter and the city's role as an ecclesiastical centre would also have brought visitors and officials into the city. In its early years, the city benefited from the construction of the new cathedral and associated buildings, and the frequent presence of the royal court at nearby Clarendon Palace.

Salisbury rapidly emerged as a major market for the agricultural produce – primarily wool and grain – of its hinterland. Its merchants were prominent in the wool trade: Robert of Knoyle, mayor in 1309–14, for instance, exported 5,665 wool fells in 1314–15 and purchased the wool of Monkton and Longbridge Deverill in 1304 and 1308.[14] The city's hinterland was extensive, with two of its citizens purchasing the wool of Gloucester Abbey for three years in the early fourteenth century.[15] Wool could be exported through Southampton or traded with the Italian merchants who came for this purpose.[16] Salisbury's merchants also exported the grain of the hinterland: William Gys and Elias Homes, for example, sent grain to Portugal, Spain, Ireland, Holland and Gascony and imported large quantities of wine in return.[17]

At the heart of the city's economic prosperity in the later Middle Ages lay its role as a major cloth-manufacturing centre, examined more fully in a later chapter.[18] This prominence as a manufacturing and marketing centre for woollen cloth had already begun by the 1350s. By the 1390s, when Wiltshire was the second-largest producer in England, Salisbury marketed over 89 per cent of the county's cloth, most of which would have been produced in the city and immediate hinterland. Major households such as Winchester College and Netley Abbey regularly purchased their cloth in the city, while purchases were also made, with less frequency, by more distant households such as King's College, Cambridge, as in 1466/7.[19]

---

14. Dale, 'New Salisbury', 124, who also provides other examples; D.L. Farmer, 'Two Wiltshire manors and their markets', *AHR*, 37 (1989), 10.
15. W. St Clair Baddeley, 'Early deeds relating to St Peter's Gloucester', *Transactions of Bristol and Gloucester Archaeological Society*, 38 (1915), 34.
16. C. Platt, *Medieval Southampton: the port and the trading community* (London, 1973), 72. See also A.A. Ruddock, *Italian merchants and shipping in Southampton, 1270–1600* (Southampton, 1951).
17. Dale,'New Salisbury', 126.
18. The economy of the city is discussed more fully in J.N. Hare, 'Salisbury: the economy of a fifteenth-century provincial capital', *Southern History*, 31 (2009), 1–26.
19. WRO 192/32; J.N. Hare, 'Netley Abbey: monastery, mansion and ruin', *Proceedings of the Hampshire Field Club and Archaeological Society*, 49 (1993), 215; e.g. WCM 4651 (1421); 5386 (1408); 5406 (1413); 5413 (1420); 5429 (1427); J.S. Lee, *Cambridge and its economic region, 1450–1560* (Hatfield, 2005); C. Dyer, *Standards of living in the later Middle Ages* (Cambridge, 1989), 260; *The first general entry book of the city of Salisbury, 1387–1452*, ed. D.R. Carr, Wiltshire Record Society 54 (Trowbridge, 2001), 103.

As the capital of the west country cloth industry the city became a major focus of imports and exports and a vital centre of marketing for a wide area around. We can see something of this trading role from the remarkable brokage books of Southampton, which record the carts and their contents and destinations as they left Southampton. This town was a major port whose links with Salisbury were vitally important to both towns. Southampton in the fifteenth century was the most important cloth-exporting port outside London, an important exporter of wool and a crucial base for Italian merchants, who brought Mediterranean luxuries and dyestuffs and in return purchased English cloth. Southampton became a virtual outport of Salisbury.[20]

In the 1440s, about a third of all the journeys recorded in the brokage books led to Salisbury.[21] Only Winchester and London compare as major destinations, although these were much less important (15–24 per cent and 15–22 per cent respectively).[22] In Wiltshire, only Wilton and Marlborough seem to have received more than occasional carts (Wilton: 25–44 carts in three published accounts; Marlborough: 2–17), suggesting that the city had become the centre for distribution to other places beyond.[23] Moreover, the locations to which goods were sent seem to be genuine. There seems no reason to falsely claim that they were being sent to the city: it was not at the edge of an area of a particular level of payment. Moreover, merchants from other towns who brought goods to the city seem to have been making a genuine choice. Nicholas Lange of Bristol, for example, took away large quantities of material from Southampton in October 1443: he sent carts to Salisbury with dyestuffs and wine but he also sent wagons to Bristol with a wider range of goods.[24] There was a real choice. James Touker of Bradford exported cloth and evidently had woad to dispose of, which he sold in Salisbury in 1444, but he took it to Bradford itself in 1448.[25]

The wide range of goods imported through Southampton included some items needed by the cloth industry, such as dyestuffs, as noted above. Salisbury received the largest quantity or second-largest quantity of woad for any place in all but 2 of the 18 documented years between 1439 and 1493. Much alum and madder was also imported. The dyes were distributed from Salisbury to smaller, more distant centres. Essentially, merchants took their cloth to the Italian boats and returned with Mediterranean products that these foreign merchants had to sell. But much depended on the policy of the Italian merchants and in the 1460s to 1480s they moved away from Southampton to London, thus restricting Salisbury's trade. These changes may

---

20. On Southampton see Platt, *Medieval Southampton*; O. Coleman, 'Trade and prosperity in the fifteenth century: some aspects of the trade of Southampton', *EcHR*, 2nd series 16 (1963–4), 9–22; Ruddock, *Italian merchants and shipping in Southampton*.
21. 1443–4 over a third (*The brokage book of Southampton, 1443–1444*, ed. O. Coleman, Southampton Record Series 4 and 6 (Southampton, 1960–61), xxvii); 1448–9, 30.5% calculated from W.A. Harwood, 'The trade of Southampton, 1448–9', *PHFCAS*, 55 (2000), 145.
22. The figures have been collected in Hare, 'Salisbury', 10; see also *Brokage book 1439–40*; *Brokage book 1443–4*; *Brokage book 1447–8*; *Brokage book 1448–9* and Harwood, 'The trade of Southampton', 145.
23. *Brokage book 1443–4*, xxix; Harwood, 'The trade of Southampton', 145; *Brokage book 1447–8*.
24. *Brokage book 1443–4*, 97–101. He was also very active in 1447–8.
25. *Brokage book 1443–4*, 303–5, *Brokage book 1447–8*; on Touker, or Terumber, see below (chapter 11).

have lain behind a decline in the city's control over the woad trade, and the growth of the woad trade directly between Southampton and the smaller places in Wiltshire and Somerset later in the century. Clothiers from these centres were now bringing back the woad rather than using Salisbury as a market.

Wine and fish were imported on a large scale before being distributed to the area around. In the 18 documented years Salisbury was the largest recipient of wine from Southampton in 14 years and the second largest in the remaining 4.[26] In the 1440s, 29 per cent of the imported wine went to Salisbury, but, from the evidence of the published texts, very little wine went directly from Southampton to anywhere else in the county, suggesting that Salisbury was serving as a market for the area beyond. She served a similar role for fish, distributing the fish to other places beyond. In 1448 54 per cent of the barrels of herring that were dispatched from Southampton were sent to Salisbury and of the fish sent to Wiltshire only 7.5 per cent went directly to any other centre.

Salisbury's merchants were part of an international trade but their contact with the continent took a variety of forms. Some merchants possessed their own ships or traded in exports and imports themselves. John a Port imported goods from Portugal and the Netherlands, William Barlow dealt in a wide range of miscellaneous goods and John Halle had his own ship at Poole.[27] Others traded on a large scale with the Italian merchants who came to Southampton, exchanging English cloth for the luxuries and dyestuffs that the Italians brought. In 1443–4 William Swayne was responsible for a quarter of the woad imported into the city from Southampton, reflecting his large-scale involvement in the cloth trade.[28] Countless lesser men were also involved in the trade.

The great international traders may be particularly well illustrated by the example of John Halle. We have seen him as a member of a villein family in Amesbury, although his father may have been a member of the corporation and minor office holder in Salisbury. Halle seems to have emerged to economic importance in the 1440s. He does not appear in the brokage book of 1439, but by 1443–4 he had become involved in the international trade, importing from Southampton tar, garlic, soap, oil, herring, salmon and iron, and presumably exporting cloth. By 1448–9 he imported a wider range of products, including wine, spices and woad, and he was even more active in the previous year, when he was responsible for almost 10 per cent of the city's trading journeys from Southampton (89). Later in 1450–51 he supplied Winchester College with about three-quarters of its requirements of wax. The contents of his shop reflect the range of his trade: a variety of cloth, flax, hats, caps, bonnets and other mercery; spices, such as pepper, cloves, mace and ginger; pitch, tar, woad, madder and several sorts of wine. He was also involved in the wool trade and is described in 1467 as alderman and wool merchant, while his reputation as a great wool merchant lived on into the seventeenth century, when it was commented on by Aubrey. He traded

---

26. *Brokage book 1443–4*, xxvi–xxix, 322–7.
27. *Port books 1427–30*, 102–3; *Port book 1439–40*, 22; S. Thrupp, 'The grocers of London: a study of distributative trade', in Power and Postan (eds), *Studies in English trade in the fifteenth century*, 291.
28. Calculated from *Brokage Book 1443–4*; on his large-scale involvement in cloth production see the aulnage account for 1467, TNA: PRO E101/345/9.

beyond England, exporting cloth to Gascony and bringing back wine, and in 1463 possessed at least one ship, the *James of Poole*.[29]

Halle's growing economic activities led to greater political influence in the city and beyond. He rose to prominence in the city in the 1440s, becoming a member of the common council in 1445, and of its governing 'twenty-four' by 1447, mayor in 1450–51 and MP in 1453. He was a dominant force in the politics of the next two decades, holding both the latter offices on four occasions and being a key leader in the city's struggle for independence from the bishop. In the late 1450s and 1460s he was increasingly involved in royal government outside the city. He was the third-largest property owner in the city in 1455 and attempted to show his pre-eminence in his great new stone-built hall, which still survives as a cinema foyer. In the late 1450s and 1460s he was increasingly involved in royal government outside the city. The interests of his family's next generation were to be outside the city, in the world and activities of the county gentry: his son was involved in Buckingham's revolt in 1483 and his daughter was married to Sir Thomas Hungerford, the local head of what remained of that important family.[30]

The relationship between the city and its hinterland is also reflected in the patterns of debt between city merchants and outsiders examined in a sample of records of the Court of Common Pleas by A.R. Bridbury.[31] The locations of the debts ranged from Yorkshire to Sussex and Devon, but most related to Wiltshire, its adjacent counties and to London. Most, in fact, came from the immediate vicinity of the city, but beyond its boundaries was a series of places with a distinctly high number of cases. In Wiltshire these represented the main regional satellites – Devizes, Warminster, Marlborough and Mere, together with neighbouring Wilton. Outside Wiltshire, the main contacts would seem to have been the ports of Southampton, Bristol and Poole, along with Winchester (Hants), Sherborne, Cranborne and Shaftesbury (Dorset), Frome, Wells, Taunton and Croscombe (Somerset), and some of the other cloth-making centres of these counties.

The city attracted visitors through trade, government and justice, or just travel.[32] The high reputation of the cathedral chapter in the early fifteenth century and the growing cult of St Osmund may have added to the attractions, although economic interests were probably most important. Outsiders visited and stayed, and some settled. A tax on aliens in 1440 suggested that there were at least 96 foreigners in

---

29. See above, Chapter 7; D.R. Carr, 'John Halle', in *ODNB* <http://www.oxforddnb.com/view/article/12007> (accessed 20 January 2010); J. Wedgwood, *A history of parliament, I: biographies* (London, 1936), 407–8; E. Nevill, 'Salisbury in 1455 (*Liber Niger*)', *WAM*, 37 (1911), 88–9; *Brokage book 1439–40; 1443–4; 1447–8, 1448–9*; VCH *Wilts* 6, 125–6, W.A. Harwood, 'The pattern of consumption of Winchester College, c.1390–1560', PhD thesis (Southampton, 2003), 309; C. Haskins, *The ancient guilds and companies of Salisbury* (Salisbury, 1912), 264; J. Aubrey, *Aubrey's natural history of Wiltshire: a reprint of 'the natural history of Wiltshire'*, ed. K.G. Ponting (Newton Abbot, 1969), 113, *Cal. Pat. Rl.* 1476–85 (1905), 145.
30. Carr, 'John Halle'; F. Street, 'The relations of the bishops and citizens of Salisbury (New Sarum) between 1225 and 1612', *WAM*, 39 (1916), 185–257, 319–67.
31. A.R. Bridbury, *Medieval English clothmaking: an economic survey* (London, 1982), 71; he also kindly allowed me to look at his analysis of the material, from which I have drawn. I am very grateful for this help.
32. R.B. Pugh, 'The king's government in the Middle Ages', in VCH *Wilts* 5, 38.

Salisbury, whether temporary or permanent, giving it a sizeable element of overseas residents.[33] The influx of visitors who often came for more than a night led to a growth of inn accommodation and services; there were at least 17 inns, which generated further spending within the city. Salisbury had far more inns than other centres in the county, where the larger towns offered no more than 3 or 4.[34] The George, in the prestigious High Street, belonged to the city and probably represented the upper end of the hotel trade, paying the high annual rent of £20 in 1418 and possessing 13 guest rooms, each with between 1 and 3 beds and other furniture in 1474.[35] It could accommodate a small retinue, as probably occurred one evening in 1449, when Lord Moleyns was attacked there by the citizens.[36] The George should not be regarded as typical; the 3 known purpose-built medieval inn ranges in Salisbury all seem to have been added to existing merchants' houses.[37] Here, as elsewhere, inns were now expected to provide a range of private accommodation such as was increasingly found in aristocratic households.[38] They also played a role in marketing, despite the city's regulations.[39] The innkeepers were often substantial figures in the community: Clement Furbour, for example, represented the hostillers' craft in 1441, brought his wine direct from Southampton and probably traded in it as well, contributed substantially to royal loans, and acted as a member of the city's Convocation, as a collector of taxes and as steward of the main merchant guild, or brotherhood, of St George.

The city acted as a major market for food and drink: it imported fish and wine for consumption and distribution, ate and drank the agricultural produce of the neighbouring area and influenced the agriculture of its immediate hinterland. Over 10 per cent of the population were probably occupied in the food industries.[40] The city's role as consumer was reflected in its legislation, which attempted to control the time and place where outsiders could sell their foodstuffs. It sought to ensure that sales were open, were done at specified places and distinguished between the citizens and outsider sellers. Particular attention was given to the butchery trade, while the importance of market gardening and perishable produce is reflected in the demand that 'victuallers coming into the city with cheese, milk, grapes, plums, apples, pears, and other fruits, should in future be made to keep to a place facing Richard Oword's tenement, ... where the new cross is being built'.[41] Consumer demand was also reflected in the growing stimulus to barley production for malt in the vicinity.[42]

---

33. TNA: PRO E179/196/100.
34. The figure is probably a minimum and is calculated from a variety of sources. See especially, Haskins, *Ancient guilds*; for evidence from elsewhere in Wiltshire see below section 10-V.
35. Haskins, *Ancient guilds*, 293–4.
36. Ibid., 291–2.
37. RCHM, *City of Salisbury*, vol. 1 (London, 1980), xlvi.
38. J.N. Hare, 'Bishop's Waltham Palace, Hampshire: William of Wykeham, Henry Beaufort and the transformation of a medieval episcopal palace', *Archaeological Journal*, 148 (1988), 236–7, 246–51; C. Woolgar, *The great household in late medieval England* (New Haven and London, 1999), 59–62.
39. *The first general entry book*, ed. Carr, 218.
40. J. Chandler, *Endless Street: a history of Salisbury and its people* (Salisbury, 1983), 68.
41. *The first general entry book*, ed. Carr, 216–19; quote at 217.
42. See above, Chapter 5.

Plate 10.2 Salisbury, St Thomas's Church: a symbol of civic pride. Notice the grandeur of the rebuilt nave (the responsibility of the parishioners) compared with the choir (the responsibility of the cathedral chapter).

A list of the guilds in 1441 reflects the diversity of occupations within the city, with 39 distinct crafts. On other occasions other lists show that the crafts were arranged in different groups, so that there was evidently some flexibility.[43] Those listed in 1441 varied: there were the rich (such as the mercers, drapers and grocers), growing and important groups such as the tailors, large groups such as the weavers, and the small crafts, such as the grouping made up of the carpenters, bowmakers, coopers, masons, tilers, painters and arrowmakers.[44] In addition to the food and cloth

---

43. A.D. Brown, *Popular piety in late medieval England. The diocese of Salisbury, 1200–1550* (Oxford, 1995), 146–8, and WRO G23/1/2.
44. Haskins, *Ancient guilds*, 60–61.

industries, two broad groups should be singled out. The leather industry was very important and included almost a fifth of the individuals with known occupations in 1399–1400.[45] Building trades were similarly significant, as the prosperity of the town generated demands for construction.[46] Many of the fine timber-framed buildings, some of which still survive, were probably constructed by carpenters based in the city, although they might also operate beyond the city, as at Coombe Bisset.[47] There was fine-quality building in stone, although many of the masons may well have been outsiders, resident merely as long as there was work. Although there was relatively little building work at the cathedral in the fifteenth century, the bishop's palace was largely rebuilt in the latter part of the century. A more significant indicator of civic prosperity was the rebuilding and transformations of the city's churches, of which the largest, St Thomas, was almost completely rebuilt. The aisles were enlarged and a new tower was built at the beginning of the century; later the east end was enlarged and rebuilt after a collapse in 1448, and finally, a new nave, arcades and clerestory were built in the later fifteenth or early sixteenth centuries (Plate 10.2). There was also extensive work at the other parish churches of St Edmund's and St Martin's, but we know nothing of the buildings of the two friaries that once existed and received frequent benefactions, or whether there was any rebuilding there.[48] A few merchants also lavished wealth on stone buildings, of which the hall of John Halle and parts of the building of William Lightfoot still survive.[49]

Although in law the city continued to be the private possession of the bishop, in practice it achieved a growing degree of self-government. The organisation for this lay in the Convocation (which at its greatest included all citizens), but in general comprised an upper council or 'twenty-four', and a wider group of 'forty-eight', together with the municipal officers. In reality, much day-to-day work was done by small unofficial groups. Occasionally the conflict between city and bishop broke out into open conflict, as in the 1460s,[50] but more usually the city silently and gradually accumulated more *de facto* powers. The bishop's court regulated the city and his bailiff presided over it, but the city began to elect its own mayors in the fourteenth century, and these gradually became a source of independent authority. The mayor now attended the fortnightly city court and it became accepted that the latter could not make decisions without the mayor and municipal officers. Later the bishop's bailiff and the city's mayor began to preside jointly over the court. By the fifteenth century the Convocation began to develop self-government, acting as an independent court and making rules for its citizens. It could purchase concessions to self-government, as in 1444 when it bought from the bishop the rights to control the bridges and assizes of ale. The Convocation wrestled with the problems of maintaining the fabric of a great

---

45. Chandler, *Endless Street*, 68, 70.
46. RCHM, *City of Salisbury*.
47. Ibid. lists 21 fourteenth-century houses and 55 fifteenth-century ones, of which the vast majority were timber-framed (lxi–ii); WCM 4630, 4684.
48. Brown, *Popular Piety*, 29.
49. T. Tatton-Brown, 'The church of St Thomas of Canterbury, Salisbury', *WAM*, 90 (1997), 101–9; RCHM, *City of Salisbury*, 24–39, 103–4, 73–6.
50. Street, 'Bishops and citizens of Salisbury', 237–57.

city: it regulated the ditches that ran along the centre of many the town's streets and provided both essential drainage and the water needed for fulling.[51] Other varied regulations concerned the sale of food,[52] buildings and the replacement of thatch by tiles in order to reduce the fire risk, and pollution by butchers. There were attempts to control urban morality, with regulations that restricted prostitution to certain streets, some outside the town, and possibly allowed a municipal brothel.[53]

The self-confident leaders of this great city were not a restricted oligarchy, but emerged from a broad group with a regularly changing membership. The mayors themselves generally came from the highest or second highest levels of that group and most, but significantly not all, belonged to the greater guilds. In the 1390s, 16 of the top 30 in wealth reached this top office, of whom 4 at least were grocers, traders in spices and luxuries. Interestingly, the cloth traders were less likely to obtain this position and, of the top 30 cloth traders in the same period, some of whom worked on an enormous scale, only 4 were to become mayors. By contrast, the officers of the corporation drew on a considerable range of city wealth, and aldermen also came from a wide spectrum of occupations.[54] The events of 1450, when Salisbury was heavily involved in the conflict at the time of Cade's revolt, showed the tensions that lay below the surface of the city's government. Those involved included a significant number of substantial citizens, representatives of the minor crafts and occasional members of the city council, who owned property or worked on their own account, but there were few representatives from the wealthy merchant classes: these were to have their day in the conflicts with the bishop in the 1460s.[55]

The lesser towns of Wiltshire: an urban hierarchy

Something of the relative importance of the towns may be seen in the tax returns. Salisbury dominated the towns of Wiltshire, but below it lay a hierarchy of smaller towns sharing certain common characteristics. The 1377 poll tax figures provide, a useful starting point which can then be supplemented with a wide range of other material.[56] Salisbury's nearest rival by population was its neighbour, the old county town of Wilton, but the latter was clearly in decline and its taxable population in 1377 was less than a fifth of its rival. But population provides only one element in the urban hierarchy, and the 12 next largest communities after Salisbury, those with more than 300 taxpayers, were not exclusively urban. Many were to be found in the areas of

---

51. *The first general entry book*, ed. Carr, 75.
52. Ibid.
53. D.R. Carr, 'From pollution to prostitution: supervising the citizens of fifteenth-century Salisbury', *Southern History*, 19 (1997), 24–41.
54. D.R. Carr, 'The problem of the urban patriciates: office holders in fifteenth-century Salisbury', *WAM*, 83 (1990), 118–35.
55. See below, Chapter 12. J.N. Hare, 'The Wiltshire risings of 1450: political and economic discontent in mid-fifteenth century England', *Southern History*, 4 (1982), 23; Street, 'Bishops and citizens of Salisbury', 185.
56. Beresford, 'Poll tax payers of 1377'. For listings of markets and fairs see S. Letters (ed.), *Gazetteer of markets and fairs in England and Wales to 1516*, List and Index Society Special Series 33 (Kew, 2003).

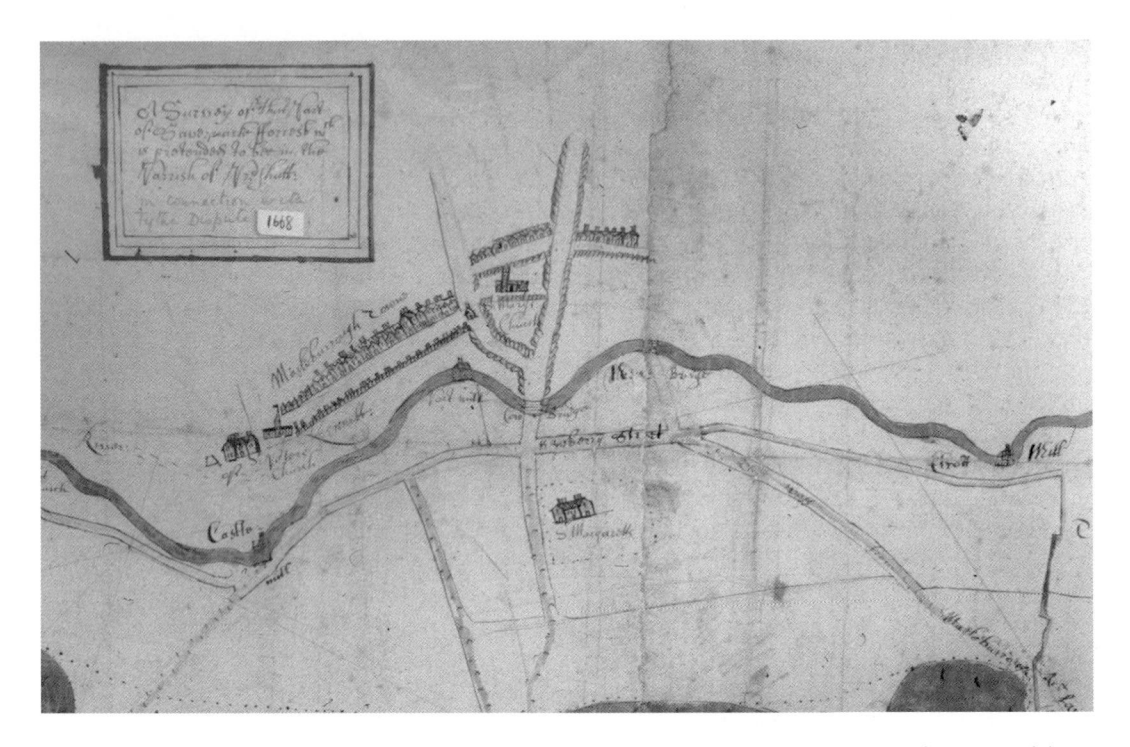

Plate 10.3 Marlborough in 1668, showing the earlier urban expansion between the two parish churches (WRO 1300/46).

dense population in the clay vale, where settlement had expanded late and where the parish and the tax unit consisted of many distinct settlements and farmsteads. Thus this group of 12 most populous places included rural communities such as Donhead and Purton; an area with extensive rural industry in Longbridge Deverill; a parish with a small but clear urban element at Lacock;[57] and a parish with quarries and other occupations at Corsham. Melksham paid tax in 1334 at the rate of a tenth, like other towns. It soon emerged as a centre of the cloth industry, but it is not clear how far its high figure resulted from colonisation of the woodland.[58] All these parishes, except Longbridge Deverill, lay in the main clay vale or the vale of Wardour where opportunities for expansion into the woodland area were easiest and which generally possessed some of the highest rural populations in the county.[59]

Excluding these rural parishes, six towns possessed taxpaying populations of over 300, and thus a population of about 600 or more. Four of these seem to have constituted the main regional centres and showed a number of common characteristics: Wilton (639 taxpayers), Marlborough (462), Malmesbury (402) and

---

57. *Lacock Abbey charters*, ed. K.H. Rogers, Wiltshire Record Society 34 (Devizes, 1979).
58. M.W.Beresford, 'Fifteenths and tenths: quotas of 1334'; 'Poll tax payers of 1377'; 'Poor parishes of 1428', in VCH *Wilts* 4, 294–314; E.M. Thompson, 'Offenders against the statute of labourers in Wiltshire,1349', *WAM*, 33 (1904), 384–409.
59. Beresford, 'Poll tax payers of 1377'; VCH *Wilts* 4. The figures have been mapped in Hare, 'Lord and tenant', 17 and in Lewis, 'Patterns and processes', 180.

Plate 10.4 Malmesbury: the market cross built 'to shelter the poor market traders when it rains', a reminder of the market role of towns (Leland's Itinerary, 488).

Devizes (302) (Plates 10.3 and 10.4). They had all been assessed as boroughs in the tenth of 1334 and contributed heavily in the 1525 returns (with £31 7s, £85 1s 11d, £11 16s 4d and £49 11s).[60] All except Devizes had begun their urban life in the Anglo-Saxon period. They all had a complex of several religious institutions and more than a single parish church: Malmesbury had an abbey and two hospitals; Wilton had an abbey, a friary and three hospitals; and Marlborough had a friary, a small Gilbertine priory and two hospitals. Devizes, the smallest and newest of the four, was also the

---

60. VCH *Wilts* 4, and J. Sheail, *The regional distribution of wealth in England as indicated in the 1524/5 lay subsidy returns*, ed. R.W. Hoyle, List and index society, special series 28 (Richmond, 1998).

least well provided for, with a single hospital and a further one in its suburbs. All possessed guild merchants, a mayor and an element of self-government,[61] and all except Devizes had been selected for the smaller 1275 parliament, all sent MPs to parliament from 1295, all sent MPs more frequently than the other centres in the county, and all were more likely to send one of their own number and not an outsider (although Marlborough was increasingly dominated by outsiders in the fifteenth century). Such representation showed both their importance, as others perceived them, and the readiness of the civic leadership to operate together. All except Malmesbury held meetings of the quarter sessions and could be seen as part of the regular pattern of county government.[62] These towns, apart from Malmesbury, were among the most important centres of debt activity with Salisbury merchants as seen in the records of the Common Pleas, although Malmesbury's absence might reflect links of greater importance with Bristol rather than Salisbury.[63] Of the four, Wilton was a long-established marketing and industrial centre, with baking, brewing, cloth-making and fish and wine distribution, while the others showed a wide range of occupations in the 1379 taxation. Wilton was evidently in severe decline, with a decaying cloth industry and competition from neighbouring Salisbury, and fell from second to sixth in the county population ranking between 1377 and 1525.[64] Malmesbury showed the smallest industrial base in 1379, but it had an abbey to serve, possessed at least three inns and became an important cloth manufacturer by the end of the period, with a high population of taxpayers in 1525. Already in 1379 it seems to have been a centre of the wool trade and there were three woolmongers present. Its sense of corporate identity was reflected in its own myths about bequests from King Athelstan.[65] Both Marlborough and Devizes were major manufacturing centres, especially for textiles, and both were given rights to hold land for charitable purposes.[66] Apart from Salisbury, these were the wealthiest towns in the subsidy assessments of 1524–5.[67]

The remaining towns with more than 300 taxpayers were Mere and Warminster. Both showed much less of a traditional urban pattern. They had been taxed with the rest of the countryside at a fifteenth in 1334, but emerged in the fourteenth century as major centres of the cloth industry, first at Mere (489 taxpayers) and then at Warminster (340). Neither possessed a monastery, friary or hospital. Mere had grown enough by the early fourteenth century to send MPs to parliament, even though this was only a temporary development. They traded extensively with Salisbury, according to the debts recorded in the Common Pleas, although Warminster seemed to replace

---

61. R.R. Darlington, 'Anglo-Saxon Wiltshire', in VCH *Wilts* 2, 18; VCH *Wilts* 6, 9–11; 7, 212; 14, 149; 10, 268; Brown, *Popular piety*, 159; *Wilts Notes & Queries*, 6 (1908–10), 537; TNA: PRO Prob 11/1/10 f78v.
62. VCH *Wilts* 5, 35,78; Roskell et al., *The House of Commons, 1386–1421* (Stroud, 1992), 695–8, 702–8, 716–19; VCH *Wilts* 14, 155.
63. Bridbury, *Medieval English clothmaking*, 71.
64. VCH *Wilts* 6, 9–10.
65. TNA: PRO E179/239/193 xv; VCH *Wilts* 14, 149; *John Leland's itinerary*, ed. J. Chandler (Stroud, 1993); Bridbury, *Medieval English clothmaking*, 71; Brown, *Popular piety*, 159.
66. VCH *Wilts* 12, 212; 10, 253–5, 264–9.
67. Marlborough £85, and forty-third in the country; Devizes £50 and seventy-fourth in the country. Marlborough then had a tax-paying population of 237, making it sixty-sixth in the country. Dyer, 'Ranking lists', 766 and 722.

Mere in importance. The tolls of market and fair at Warminster rose from £5 in 1327 to over £20 in 1380s, and it figured more highly than Mere in the 1525 taxation.[68] Although we lack a poll tax figure for Trowbridge, it should probably be included in this group: it was already a town with a substantial market area by 1383, one tenant inhabiting a manor 28 miles away.[69] It continued to grow in the fifteenth century, when it was a leading centre of the west Wiltshire cloth industry, and in the 1525 lay subsidy returns it had the fourth-highest urban assessment in the county, after Salisbury, Marlborough and Devizes.[70]

Below these large centres lay various small places which lay on the boundary between town and village. As Maitland remarked, for the twelfth century 'we are in the classical land of small boroughs'.[71] Those centres which possessed between 150 and 300 taxpayers, and thus a population of 300–600, in 1377 may usefully be subdivided into four types. Some, like Chippenham, Bradford and Cricklade, were traditional boroughs. Chippenham and Bradford had already become important cloth-producing centres. Cricklade, after a period as an Anglo-Saxon town and mint, was an important centre of the butchering and agricultural trades.[72] Three more centres were smaller but clearly showed urban features. Calne had been an Anglo-Saxon borough, shows evidence of urban expansion in its plan, possessed a hospital, and accommodated a wide range of specified non-agricultural occupations in 1379. It sent MPs to parliament, generally returning MPs who lived in the town or had local connections, and was hardly a rotten borough. In 1377, however, it had only 156 taxpayers. Amesbury was similar: a market centre with two inns and a very rich abbey. Westbury, with 184 taxpayers, also had long traditions, contained burgage tenants[73] and was to become a major cloth-producing town in the fifteenth century. A second group comprised a small group of new towns, established by lords in the twelfth or thirteenth centuries, and part of a wider and familiar development. Vastern (Wootton Basset), Market Lavington and Great Sherston were small in area but had a largely non-agricultural population. Market Lavington was already a wealthy centre in 1334 and possessed merchants, an alehouse keeper and other workers upon whose profits tithes had to be paid. It acquired a fulling mill in the fifteenth century and had a group of 5 alien taxpayers in 1440.[74] At Downton, the earlier settlement was massively enlarged by the bishops of Winchester early in the thirteenth century, and Winchester College made substantial investments on its properties here in the fifteenth century.[75]

---

68. VCH *Wilts* 8, 115; £20 14s 4 ½d in 1380, £22 17s 2 ½d in 1386; WRO 845, manorial papers (4 R II).
69. TNA: PRO DL29/682/11042.
70. Sheail, *Regional distribution of wealth*; see also K. Rogers, *The book of Trowbridge* (Buckingham, 1984).
71. F.W. Maitland, *Domesday Book and beyond* (1897; repr. London, 1960), 215.
72. Thompson, 'Offenders against the statute of labourers'; Table 10.1.
73. *Wilts IPM* ii, 387; see below, Chapter 11.
74. Eighteenth in the county: Beresford, 'Fifteenths and tenths: quotas of 1334', 303; VCH *Wilts* 10, 94–5; E.M. Carus-Wilson, 'The woollen industry before 1550', in VCH *Wilts* 4, 137; TNA: PRO E179/196/100.
75. M.W. Beresford, 'The six new towns of the bishops of Winchester, 1200–55', *Medieval Archaeology*, 3 (1959), 193–5; e.g. WCM 5446, 5441.

A third group comprised manorial centres where trading and a limited range of non-agricultural occupations were found, as at Pewsey, Tisbury, Aldbourne and Swindon. Ramsbury and Corsham should probably be added to this group. Swindon lacks a surviving poll tax list of occupations, but the others all show a substantial body of well-off traders and craftsmen. The final group contains those centres generated by the expansion of the cloth industry that functionally became towns, with a high proportion of their populations dependent on manufacturing and trading. Steeple Ashton in the early fifteenth century had shops, stalls and tolls, although in the mid-fifteenth century these were leased for only 8d. Leland described it as 'a pleasant little market town, which depends largely on its cloth trade', and its great church provides a reminder of its success as a centre of cloth production (Plate 11.1).[76] Other manorial centres, such as Castle Combe and Heytesbury, were transformed by the cloth industry.

Even smaller places, with fewer than 150 taxpayers, could have a distinct urban element. Bedwyn and Ludgershall were long-standing boroughs. The former had once been one of the county's four Anglo-Saxon mints, but Leland contrasted the town's right to send MPs to parliament, which it had resumed in the late fourteenth century, and its appearance in the 1540s ('it is only a poor thing to look at').[77] With 87 and 117 taxpayers these places might seem insignificant, but they were small boroughs in areas of the county (the east) where there was little other urban life. But perhaps Hindon, one of the new towns founded by the bishop of Winchester, offers the most obvious caution in dismissing the importance of the very small town. Although it possessed only 77 taxpayers in 1377, it was certainly not a town in decay. It had been created on a small fragment of a much larger rural manor belonging to the bishop and its inhabitants were exclusively or largely non-agricultural in their employment. It appears comparatively frequently in examples of local manorial sales and purchases. The incomplete poll tax assessment in 1379 shows a varied range of occupations: there were three weavers, one tailor, two butchers, four bakers, seven brewers and one victualler. These, particularly the seven brewers, suggest production for a much wider market than the 77 taxpayers of the borough. It continued to grow in the early fifteenth century, when the accounts show tenants moving in to rent the vacant spaces in the market. The community was sufficiently well-off to refound its church or chapel.[78] Hindon reminds us of the close and vital links between the small towns and the life of the countryside. But how far were these lesser Wiltshire towns in decline? Our fragmentary evidence suggests that the small towns, like the rural communities, experienced early-fifteenth-century growth and continuity, a mid-century recession and then gradual recovery in those areas subject to the impact of the cloth industry, as at Trowbridge, Warminster and Castle Combe (see Chapters 11 and 12).

---

76. VCH *Wilts* 8, 210; *Leland's itinerary*, ed. Chandler, 502. P. Everson has argued for late medieval replanning at Ludgershall, but the complexities of the plan seem open to a variety of interpretations. P. Ellis, *Ludgershall Castle excavations by P. Addyman, 1964–72*, Wiltshire Archaeological Society 2 (Devizes, 2000), 106–14.
77. Roskell et al., *The House of Commons*; *Leland's itinerary*, ed. Chandler, 499.
78. M.W. Beresford, *New towns of the Middle Ages* (London, 1967), 505–6; idem, 'Poll tax payers of 1377', 309; Farmer, 'Two Wiltshire manors', 5, 7; WRO 192/32; TNA: PRO E179/239/193/I; HRO 11 M59 B1/143, 152, 154, 156, 182; *Calendar of Papal Letters*, vi, 51.

Industry and trade

Industry both generated wealth to spend and responded to the needs of consumers. The cloth-making industry became so important that it requires a chapter to itself, but other occupations also helped to generate prosperity. The 1379 poll tax figures provide the opportunity to look at a cross-section of occupations for a few towns and rural centres, and emphasise both the wide range of activities in the main towns and the growing specialisation in the later Middle Ages (Table 10.1). Individual towns might have a particular specialism, but they also needed to offer a wide range of manufacturing and service industries in order to provide for the needs both of the townspeople themselves and those who came from outside. The urban economy provided cloth and clothing, leather goods, processed food from ale to bread, building craftsmen, and other consumer goods and services.

Some towns were dominated by the cloth industry, while others depended on a wider range of occupations, as can be seen by comparing the situation in two of the larger towns: Marlborough and Bradford. Although Marlborough showed a substantial number of cloth and clothing workers (five weavers, a fuller and two shearers) this was small by comparison with the number of leather workers and food workers, and should probably be seen as catering for more than a largely local market. The smaller town of Bradford, with a taxpaying population of 237 in 1377, was less than half the size of Marlborough, but had a wide range of occupations, and was certainly not a single industry town. Here, however, the cloth industry was evidently much more important than leather and, despite its much smaller size, it possessed 42 per cent more cloth-worker taxpayers than Marlborough. Bradford was a cloth town and Marlborough in 1379 was not, although this probably changed in the course of the fifteenth century.

The leather industry has been neglected. As has been remarked for the following period, 'Contemporaries usually took the leather industry for granted, with the results that historians have largely ignored it.'[79] Although its importance has been recognised: Clarkson described it as 'second or third only to the manufacture of woollen cloth as an industrial occupation' and Kowaleski as 'second only to the cloth industry in medieval England', this has not been followed up sufficiently in subsequent research.[80] The importance of the leather industry varied considerably from town to town, but occupational analyses both in Wiltshire and elsewhere show that it was among the most important industries of the period.[81] In Wiltshire, leather workers, mainly tanners, skinners and cobblers, were found dispersed throughout the county in the poll tax returns, but there were concentrations in the towns, particularly in Bradford, Chippenham, Cricklade, Devizes and Marlborough (see Table 10.1). With the

---

79. L.A. Clarkson, 'The leather crafts in Tudor and Stuart England', *AHR*, 14 (1966), 25.
80. Clarkson, 'The leather crafts', 25; M. Kowaleski, 'Town and country in late medieval England: the hide and leather trade', in P.J. Corfield and D. Keene (eds), *Work in towns, 850–1800* (Leicester, 1990), 57.
81. Summed up in the tables in P.J.B. Goldberg, *Women, work and life cycle in a medieval economy* (Oxford, 1992), 46, 48, 60–2. In Winchester, it constituted the third largest group of identifiable traders after the victuallers and the cloth industry (D. Keene, *A survey of medieval Winchester* (Oxford, 1985), 285).

A Prospering Society

Table 10.1
Occupations in some of the main manufacturing and market centres, 1377.

	Cloth and clothing	Leather	Building	Food	Others	Total	1377 taxpayers
Marlborough	12	24	9	19	12	76	543#
Malmesbury	3	2	5	4	9	23	402
Devizes	14	15	8	11	10	58	302
Bradford	17	14	9	8	4	52	237
Calne	10	5	3	8	11	37	156
Cricklade	10	9	3	23	3	48	200
Hindon (incomplete)	3	1		14	2	20	77
Pewsey	7	4	4	2	13	30	267
Tisbury	6	3	1	4	1	15	281
Aldbourne	5		2	4	9	16	253
Ramsbury	8	4	2	4	6	24	161
Heytesbury	6	2	3	3	1	15	164
Christian Malford	20		5		1	26	
Corsham	3		5	2	5	15	341
Chippenham (incomplete)	3	4	2	10	7	26	

Notes: # = 81 in Marlborough barton, 462 in Marlborough borough.
Sources: TNA: PRO E179/239/193; 194/42; 196/42a, 52; 196/44, 52a; M.M. Beresford, 'Poll tax payers of 1377', in VCH Wilts 4. All places are listed where there were at least 15 occupational descriptions.

exception of that in Marlborough, the industry was comparable in size to the cloth industry, and was probably also the second largest manufacturing industry in Salisbury.[82] The poll tax evidence also suggests that the industry was on a larger scale than in most other parts of England. At Devizes, Bradford and Marlborough between 26 and 32 per cent of those whose occupations are known were engaged in the leather trade, but elsewhere in England it seems to have been between 10 and 20 per cent:[83] thus it occupied about 15 per cent of householders in late-fourteenth-century Exeter.[84] Large quantities of hides were exported through Southampton, although these may have come from nearby Hampshire rather than from Wiltshire.[85] The leather industry was thus another rarely considered generator of employment, and a market for agricultural products.

In Wiltshire, as elsewhere, the food industry accounted for about a fifth of specified occupations.[86] The poll tax returns showed the presence in most towns of specific food occupations: Bradford had 4 butchers, 1 baker, 2 brewers, 3 victuallers

---

82. Chandler, *Endless Street*, 68, 70 calculated at 19% compared with 35% for cloth workers in 1399/1400.
83. Goldberg, *Women, work and life cycle*, table 2.2, 46; there may be slight differences resulting from the grouping of occupations, but it is the broad situation rather than precise differences that concern us here.
84. Ibid.; Kowaleski, 'Town and country', 57.
85. See the port books, e.g. *Port book 1439–40*, 52, 56, 72, 84, 56, 65, 67, 97 & 73 (for 1000 lambs pelts); *Port books Ed. IV, passim*, e.g. 182–6 (3 ships in 1480–81 included in their cargoes: 62 dozen calf skins and 160 tanned cow hides; 476 dozen calf skins and 212 lamb skins; 168 cow hides, 133 dozen calf skins and 41 hides).
86. Goldberg, *Women, work and life cycle*, table 2.2, 46.

and 1 fishmonger, and Devizes had a butcher, a baker, 4 brewers and 5 victuallers. But the returns also suggest that, in a few centres, specialisation and specific marketing or industrial roles probably went beyond the immediate hinterland of the town itself. Marlborough had 9 fishmongers but this, at least, was a large town; Cricklade had 10 butchers and 11 brewers, and the incomplete return for Hindon show that this small town had at least 7 brewers.

Towns also needed a building industry, although its nature varied with the availability of raw materials. Marlborough, which lay in the chalk area, had only one mason in 1379, while smaller towns with good-quality relatively cheap local stone, as in the Cotswolds, had more. Of the main towns Marlborough had four carpenters to the one mason, Devizes three of each, Malmesbury three carpenters and two wallers, and Bradford, near the Cotswolds, five masons and four carpenters. In general, most houses were probably timber-framed with wattle and daub panelling, although built on stone footings. Stone buildings were more common in the Cotswolds.

There were two main areas for specialist quarrying during this period, around Hazlebury in the west and Chilmark in the south. Hazelbury provided Cotswold limestone, as used for the monastic buildings of Stanley, Bradenstoke and Lacock (all of which possessed quarries here) and Monkton Farleigh, as well as for Devizes castle and further afield, to Winchester, for example.[87] It continued in use in the later Middle Ages, with 1000 stones being bought for Urchfont from 'next to Hazelbury' in 1461, and this was followed in 1478 by the purchase of 2,000 slates from Hazelbury quarry.[88] Nearby Corsham supplied stone slates to Devizes castle in 1309–10 and 1384–5, 1,000 slates for All Cannings in 1471 and 2,000 for Ludgershall in 1429–34.[89] The quarries here would have accounted for the three masons and a tiler recorded in the poll tax returns of 1379, and the carriage of slates to the opposite end of the county reminds us of the potential scale of the marketing area. There were also quarries nearby at Westwood and Rudloe. The quarries at Chilmark, with neighbouring Teffont and Tisbury, were the source of stone for Salisbury cathedral and much else.[90] The use of Chilmark's stone was widespread in the fifteenth century, as at Durrington, where eight carts of freestone were bought from Chilmark in 1412, at Downton in 1436 and Andover (Hants) in 1451.[91] We know little about the organisation of such quarrying, but the account rolls suggest that most was initially on a small scale with rents usually of less than 5s.[92]

Transport costs in general discouraged wider use and only prestige building could support distant consumption. The transporting of slates from Corsham to All Cannings

---

87. VCH *Wilts* 4, 247; VCH *Wilts* 10, 244; *Building accounts of King Henry III*, ed. H.M. Colvin (Oxford, 1971), 124–8.
88. BL Add Rl 19717; WRO 192/36.
89. VCH *Wilts* 10, 244; WRO 192/28; TNA: PRO SC6/1054/25.
90. VCH *Wilts* 4, 248.
91. WCM 5967, 5991, 5450 (Chilmark); 5390 (from Fonthill); 2685 (36 carts).
92. Rudloe 3s 4d, 2s and 4s – previously 3s; at Westwood in 1413 a quarry was in the lord's hands but previously had produced 5s rent, and new leases for quarries in 1424 were at 1s 8d, 4s, and in 1437 at 1s 8d; Teffont £1, 4s, 3s 4d, 10s (DRO D10/M255; WCL Westwood 1413, 1424, 1437; TNA: PRO SC6/1060/16).

cost 80 per cent of the original purchase price, while the Cotswold slates taken to Ludgershall, noted above, which was on the other side of the county, were for an important addition to the royal house and for the re-roofing of the main hall there.[93] Poorer-quality but more local stone was thus used where available, whether the flint of the downlands or the greensand or corralian limestone of the clay vale. Thus 100 cartloads of stone were brought from nearby Swindon to Wroughton in 1311, while Stanley Abbey had a quarry in Chippenham Forest as well as permission to use the king's quarry at nearby Pewsham.[94] Pewsey stone was also used at Andover (Hants).[95]

Timber was relatively easily accessible throughout the county, but there were areas of regional woodland specialisation. In the thirteenth century, the royal palaces were roofed by shingles from those areas of the county still under royal forest, such as Chippenham. Floor tiles were manufactured in the forest of Chippenham at Naish, and in the south-east at Clarendon. Most roofs would have been covered with thatch, but for more permanent materials stone slates from the Cotswolds or the Chilmark area were used over much of the county. The manufacture of clay tiles developed from the fourteenth century in the south-east of the county at Alderbury. By 1341, this place was supplying the palace at Ludgershall, 16 miles away, and by 1354 and 1365–7 that at nearby Clarendon. In the fifteenth century Alderbury tiles were used at Ludgershall (1436), Winterbourne Stoke (1437), Salisbury (1446), Downton (1410, 1417, 1442, 1466), Bishopstone (1481) and extensively at Clarendon. Salisbury was largely, but not exclusively, a town of tile-covered buildings, and the city agreed in 1431 that all thatched roofs should be replaced by tiles. The 1379 poll tax figures show a large-scale concentration of tile production at Alderbury, with at least 17 tilers.[96] Although other manufacturing centres may still be located the documents emphasise the dominance of these kilns and make a contrast with the much more widely distributed tile production of neighbouring Hampshire.[97]

Other specialist crafts can also occasionally be located. Iron smelting occurred in the forest of Chippenham from the thirteenth century.[98] Pottery was made at Crockerton in Longbridge Deverill in the south-west, Naish and Minety in the vale,

---

93. TNA: PRO E101/593/17.
94. WCL Composite 1311; VCH *Wilts* 4, 411.
95. WCM 2685.
96. TNA: PRO E101/593/17; R.A. Brown, H.M. Colvin and A.J. Taylor, *The history of the king's works: The Middle Ages* (London, 1963), vol. 2, 916; T.B. James and A.M. Robinson, *Clarendon Palace* (London, 1988), 38; BL Add Rl 26594; TNA: PRO E179/239/193 vi, SC6/1054/25/2, 1062/7; A. Richardson, *The forest, park and palace of Clarendon, c.1200–c.1650* (Oxford, 2005), 70, 73; HRO Eccl 2.155832 & 42; WCM 5388, 5410, 5443; *The first general entry book*, ed. Carr, 137. A John Spencer of Alderbury may have been a tile maker but he also took up tiling contracts in Salisbury (ibid., 153).
97. J.N. Hare, 'The growth of the roof-tile industry in later medieval Wessex', *Medieval Archaeology*, 35 (1991), 88–99.
98. VCH *Wilts* 4, 411, 250; see also *Wilts IPM* i, 202.

Laverstock in the south-east, and probably Mildenhall in the north-east.[99] Charcoal was produced locally, in the woodlands of Wiltshire and Hampshire.[100]

Altogether, this extensive network of urban craftsmen and rural industries both helped to generate demands for food and agricultural produce and provided the goods on which farmers could use part of their surpluses. They were both part of the complex inter-relationship between cultivator and artisan, and of the growth of specialisation in this period.

The pattern of marketing

It is difficult to establish the realities of marketing. We can locate the 37 medieval markets and the fairs, and produce theoretical patterns of their trading areas, but it is all too rare for us to gain evidence of specific deals. The manorial account rolls rarely record where the produce was sold. In addition, there were different overlying and competing patterns of trade. Most trade in food and manufactures occurred within distances of about 10 miles. Overlying these local patterns were those of more distant trade within England or abroad, in wool, cloth and sometimes grain.

The scale of the market varied according to both the type of goods being traded and the wealth and status of the purchaser. Some goods, such as building stones or more particularly mill stones, had to travel a considerable distance if they were to be used at all.[101] Major merchants would have travelled widely: the Celys each year left London for their round of wool purchases in the Cotswolds, while Thomas Kitson purchased cloth for export through London.[102] The rich, too, tended to use more distant markets. When Richard Mitford, bishop of Salisbury, stayed at his Wiltshire manors of Potterne and Woodford in 1406–7 he purchased on a national as well as a local scale. As much as 41 per cent of his expenditure was in London, and included preserved fish, wax, jewellery and spices. The next two major purchasing centres were the great ports of Bristol and Southampton, for wine, spices and other goods: the three towns of Bristol, Southampton and Salisbury provided in total 39 per cent of Mitford's purchases. For specific items, Mitford might go further away as with the

---

99. J. Musty, 'The medieval and post-medieval pottery from Budbury', in G.J. Wainwright, 'An iron age promontory fort at Budbury, Bradford-on-Avon, Wiltshire, *WAM*, 65 (1970), 161–2; M.R. McCarthy, 'The medieval kilns at Nash Hill, Lacock', *WAM*, 69 (1974), 97–160; H.E.J. Le Patorel, 'Documentary evidence and the medieval pottery industry', *Medieval Archaeology*, 12 (1968); J. Musty, 'A preliminary account of a medieval pottery industry at Minety', *WAM*, 68 (1973), 86–7; J. Musty, D. Algar and P. Ewence, 'The medieval pottery kilns at Laverstock', *Archaeologia*, 102 (1969), 83–150; Crockerthrop in Mildenhall: J.E.B. Gover, A. Mawer and F.M. Stenton, *Place names of Wiltshire* (Cambridge, 1939). (I am grateful to Professor Dyer for drawing this last reference to my attention.)
100. For Chute, Potterne and Woodford see *Household accounts from medieval England*, ed. C.M. Woolgar (Oxford, 1992), 411–2; for elsewhere see e.g. *Pipe Roll 1301–2*, 232, 319, 407; *Pipe Roll 1409–10*, 82, 214, 255, 273, 306–7.
101. D.L. Farmer, 'Marketing the produce of the countryside, 1200–1500' in Miller, *Agrarian history*, 351–2.
102. E. Power, 'The wool trade in the fifteenth century', in Power and Postan (eds), *Studies in English trade in the fifteenth century*, 48–58; see below, Chapter 11.

medicine bought from Oxford.[103] Mitford's demesnes provided grain and meat, and there were various local purchases. Interestingly, Woodford, near Salisbury, was supplied with wine from Southampton, but Potterne, in the centre of the county, received its wine from Bristol. Salisbury also supplied fresh fish and horseshoes. Mitford's accounts provide a neat reminder of the different trading influences within the county – of a southern Wiltshire that looked south while the west and north-west looked to Bristol; and everywhere was affected by yet more distant London. In contrast, lesser men would have bought and sold in a more localised area.[104]

Mitford's purchases also remind us of patterns of sale and distribution that led from and to the ports. London was far distant, but its growing domination of cloth exports at the end of the fifteenth century made it increasingly important in Wiltshire. The role of Southampton as the outport of Salisbury is also a familiar theme, thanks to the brokage books recording the passage of goods from the port to its hinterland, as discussed above. Southampton, rather than the Salisbury market, was also being used directly by some of the leading figures of the west Wiltshire cloth industry to export their cloths. But the role of Bristol as a centre of trade and industry is much less clear. Fragmentary evidence suggests its importance in the north-west part of the county; we have seen, above, that Mitford's wine for Potterne came from there, and there seem to be some personal links. James Terumber, one of the leading clothiers of the Bradford–Trowbridge area in the second half of the century, seems to have come from Bristol and returned there to the weavers' part of the city. John Long of Devizes traded cloth through Bristol. It has been suggested that the origin of one of the greatest merchants of fifteenth-century Bristol, William Canynges, may have been in Cannings, near Devizes, in the fourteenth century.[105] The Bristol bell founders can be found to dominate the surviving bells of the north of the county, just as those of Salisbury did in the south.[106] Moreover, Bristol merchants crossed the region in trading with both Salisbury and London. As so often, our evidence hints at connections about which we would like to know much more.

Some people traded in agricultural products on a large scale. This was particularly the case with wool and livestock. John Broun of Maiden Bradley, a small undistinguished town, figured prominently in the Hungerford accounts as a regular purchaser of their stock: in 1448 he bought 103 sheep from Winterborne Stoke and in 1450 another 80 from the same manor and 201 from Upton Scudamore. He also purchased wool and, in 1453, the Hungerford's steward paid him £38 10s 5½d for grain and livestock.[107] He was looking after Bishop Ayscough's column of carts at Maiden Bradley when it was attacked and plundered in 1450.

Most large estates collected and sold wool on a regional or estate basis. The total

---

103. C. Dyer, *Everyday life in medieval England* (London, 1994), 259, 260.
104. Ibid., 258–74.
105. Carus-Wilson, 'Woollen industry before 1550', 125–6; J. Sherborne, *William Canynges (1402–74), mayor of Bristol and dean of Westbury College* (Bristol, 1985), 2.
106. Carus-Wilson, 'Woollen industry before 1550', 133; H.B. Walters, *The church bells of Wiltshire: their inscriptions & history* (Devizes, 1927–9), 255–69.
107. R. Payne, 'Agrarian conditions on the Wiltshire estates of the duchy of Lancaster, the lords Hungerford and the bishopric of Winchester', PhD thesis (London, 1940), 217.

produce could be sold to a single merchant, as on the Wiltshire lands of the duchy of Lancaster, where William Tanner bought the wool in 1406–9 and Henry Barton, citizen of London, in 1414.[108] By the fourteenth century the wool of the great estates was increasingly sold to English merchants rather than to Italians.[109] Occasionally, and unusually, a leading landowner such as Cardinal Henry Beaufort became active in exporting wool himself.[110] Wool tended to be marketed on a wider scale; thus the wool of Longbridge and Monkton Deverill in the early fourteenth century was sold to purchasers from Salisbury, Bristol, Winchester, Marlborough and Wells, although more often to purchasers within a 10-mile radius.[111] Isolated manors tended to sell more locally, as with the wool of Kingston Deverill and Bromham.

Most sales and purchases were sold locally within approximately a 10-mile radius: selling at a greater distance increased the transport costs, and the Glastonbury Abbey auditor warned the officials at the Deverills against using more distant markets unless it achieved a 'better sale'.[112] But agricultural products could be carried further. At Ogbourne St Andrews, the bailiff took grain to Newbury, nearly 20 miles away, rather than to the large town of Marlborough, less than 4 miles away. Presumably he felt that the increased distance would be outweighed by the greater price.[113] The importance of the London food market is becoming much better known,[114] but the growth of Salisbury had a considerable impact in developing a concentration on barley production in its immediate hinterland.[115] Larger towns could develop a wider market than a smaller one, as shown by the important town of Andover, in Hampshire: its market area was truncated to the south by the pressure of the city of Winchester, with villagers to the south of Andover looking to the more distant but larger town.[116] The Wiltshire manors produced much grain and livestock for Winchester nunnery and the Cathedral Priory. Relative ease of transport meant that livestock might be purchased at a greater distance than grain, as with the purchases of cattle for St Cross, Winchester, from Ramsbury, Amesbury, Andover and Newbury (Berks.).[117] Particular foodstuffs, such as fish, acquired a large market area. Fish were bought for Warminster, Malmesbury and Salisbury in Exeter, and was able to be sent from a south Devon manor to Erlestoke (Wilts.), although there would have been fishstocks closer at hand.[118] Large quantities of fish were brought from Southampton to Salisbury, including 1,844 barrels of herring in 1447–8, when 54.2 per cent of herring distributed

---

108. TNA: PRO DL29/737/12073; 710/11432; 737/12074.
109. R. Scott, 'Medieval agriculture', in VCH *Wilts* 4, 20.
110. G.L. Harriss, *Cardinal Beaufort* (Oxford, 1988), 413.
111. Farmer, 'Two Wiltshire manors', 10.
112. Ibid., 7.
113. M. Morgan, *The English lands of the abbey of Bec* (Oxford, 1946), 49.
114. Especially through the work of the 'feeding the city' project, e.g. J.A. Galloway, 'London's grain supply: changes in production, distribution and consumption during the fourteenth century', *Franco-British Studies*, 20 (1995), 31–2.
115. See above, Chapter 5.
116. Dyer, 'Small towns', 518, 520; Keene, *Survey of Winchester*, 270.
117. HRO 111 M94 W D1/13.
118. H. Fox, *The evolution of the fishing village: landscape and society along the south Devon coast, 1086–1550* (Oxford, 2001), 99–100.

from Southampton went to Salisbury. Some of the fish were consumed in the city and the rest sold to the towns and villages beyond.

Salisbury itself showed both an international role and a prevalence of local activity within a 10-mile range, the pattern of debt analysed by A.R. Bridbury, suggesting that most of the transactions lay in the immediate neighbourhood. Durrington, almost 10 miles away, was in its orbit, and its lord sold his grain in the city in the mid-fourteenth century. Later, at the end of the following century, the will of Richard Martyn, a Durrington butcher, showed his area of activity. He made bequests to Durrington church and that of Amesbury the nearest town, but also to the Grey Friars at Salisbury and to Upavon in the north of the Avon valley, together with a gift to every church between the two places.

At the growing cloth centre of Castle Combe food sellers also came constantly from an area within a 10-mile radius, and particularly from the nearby towns of Malmesbury and Chippenham. Bakers came from such places as Tetbury (Gloucestershire) and Chippenham; fishmongers from Malmesbury; and butchers from Chippenham and Malmesbury as well as smaller places such as Corsham, Tormarton (Glos.) and Chipping Sodbury (Glos.).[119] Significantly, many of these places were towns themselves. A glimpse at the market area for Trowbridge is provided by the list of those who rented shambles in 1383, although such men were not just involved in the food trade, and cloth may have already become a factor. They mainly came from about 5 miles away, both in Somerset and Wiltshire, but they also came from further afield, from, for example, Frome, Chippenham and Aldbourne. This last case, involving someone who farmed 28 miles away, provides an interesting example of how far a trader's interests could stretch.[120]

In south Wiltshire, the early-fourteenth-century accounts for the Glastonbury Abbey manors of the Deverills reinforce this pattern of short-distance marketing, but with overlying more distant trade. Of the recorded grain sales, 72 per cent of those where the place of sale can be established were within a range of 10.5 miles. As befitted an abbey whose main interests and land lay further west, the manors tended to trade westwards towards Frome, Trudoxhill and Nunney in Somerset, and – the most distant of the regular sale places – to Shaftesbury in Dorset. The small town of Hindon was the only Wiltshire market that it commonly used, with Mere, Maiden Bradley, Warminster and West Knoyle used more infrequently and Tisbury once: all were in south-west Wiltshire. Sometimes the manors traded to the Salisbury area: to Salisbury itself, Combe-by-Salisbury (Coombe Bisset), Wishford or Wilton.[121] Sheep

---

119. E.M. Carus-Wilson, 'Evidences of industrial growth on some fifteenth century manors', in Carus-Wilson, *Essays in economic history*, 166.
120. The tenants came from Frome (Somerset) (2), 7½ miles; Chippenham (4), 11 miles; and Aldbourne (1) 28 miles; and, nearer at hand: from Southwick (1), Bradley (1), Bradford (1), Seend Row (1), Beckington (2), Norton (1). Richard Iremonger the tenant from Aldbourne employed at least a shepherd and a swineherd and was described as an artificer: TNA: PRO E179/239/193/IIa. The other tenants of these holdings who can be identified in the poll tax returns were a butcher, a tanner and an undefined person, all from Chippenham, a woolmonger from Southwyk and a woolmonger from Bradley.
121. Farmer, 'Two Wiltshire manors', 3–8.

from the Deverills were both bought and sold at Hindon Fair, and sometimes pigs were bought, as was tar.[122] Sheep from neighbouring Kingston Deverill in the fifteenth century were also sold at Hindon as well as at Heytesbury. Hindon itself was also heavily involved in the food industry, mainly in baking, brewing and butchering. This was evidently on a much greater scale than that needed to feed a small community of 77 taxpayers, so that its inhabitants must have sold their produce much more widely around the neighbouring industrial and agricultural villages, just as was happening around Castle Combe.

The smooth running of trade required an infrastructure of roads, bridges and inns. Most transport was probably by pack horse and light carts, but roads still needed upkeep. People left money in their wills to this purpose, with 11–12 per cent of fifteenth-century wills in the Salisbury diocese making bequests to roads and bridges.[123] The regular demands made on the transport infrastructure by trade to a market town can be seen in the need for road improvements, particularly on the damp claylands. At Kellaways, Maud Heath's causeway was the product of a late-fifteenth-century bequest to improve the route to the market town of Chippenham across the low-lying wet clays and river valley that lay between. Other examples, linking village and town, are known from documentary sources and from surviving structures, both in Wiltshire and elsewhere.[124] In some cases it is clear that the investment was for the upkeep of main trunk roads. In 1390 a burgess of Bristol gave money to maintain a bridge between Calne and Cherhill on the main Bristol to London route.[125] Most bridges had already been built, but one of the late fourteenth and early fifteenth centuries survives and spans the Bourne at Milford, next to Salisbury.[126]

Inns provided centres of hospitality, service provision and informal trading.[127] They were essential for long-distance trade, providing shelter and food for men and horses alike. In this period they became increasingly complex, with the construction of specialist wings for private accommodation.[128] Their presence can be established from a variety of sources: from the 1379 poll tax, from fines for infringement of various assizes, and from references to rents and seigneurial expenditure in the

---

122. Ibid., 9–10.
123. Brown, *Popular Piety*, 198.
124. J.E. Jackson, 'Maud Heath's causey', *WAM*, 1 (1854), 254–61; and, for other examples of charitable bequests for road improvement for Trowbridge in the will of John Wyckes see Rogers, *Book of Trowbridge*, 29; and between Beckington and Warminster by Lord Hungerford see Jackson, 'Maud Heath's causey', 254. For bequests to bridges and roads in the diocese as a whole see Brown, *Popular piety*, 198. For an example from Suffolk see Betterton and Dymond, *Lavenham*, 16, 113–15.
125. *Wiltshire Notes & Queries* (1908–10), 6, 236.
126. RCHM, *City of Salisbury*, 52; On the national picture see D. Harrison, *The bridges of medieval England* (Oxford, 2004).
127. Dyer, *Everyday life*, 297–8.
128. On inn buildings see W.A. Pantin, 'Medieval inns', in E.M. Jope (ed.), *Studies in building history: essays in recognition of the work of B.H. St J. O'Neil* (London, 1961), 166–91; E. Roberts, 'A fifteenth century inn at Andover', *PHFCAS*, 47 (1991), 153–70. E. Roberts, *Hampshire houses, 1200–1700: their dating and development* (Winchester, 2003), 179–82; idem, 'A fifteenth-century inn at Andover', 153–70; RCHM, *City of Salisbury*, 97–9, 109, 133–4.

account rolls.[129] But figures of inn numbers must be treated with caution, and represent a minimum figure. Salisbury was exceptional in the number of its inns, as noted above, but most towns probably possessed between two and four inns. Warminster, Chippenham, Bradford and Malmesbury had three or four (comparable to large towns like Alton and Basingstoke (Hants)) and Marlborough, Trowbridge, Amesbury and Maiden Bradley had at least two. Some small towns, such as Calne, Hindon, Ramsbury and Downton, or villages, such as Sutton, Charleton, Hill Deverill and Stockton, had a single inn.[130] Their distribution was affected by a variety of factors: by the presence of trade routes, the size of the towns and the presence of institutions such as monasteries that encouraged people to make more than overnight stays. As yet, there is no documentary evidence in Wiltshire for the large scale of investment found elsewhere in southern England, as at Andover (Hants), where Winchester College spent about £400 and Magdalen College about £200 on new inns. These sums reflect the high income that could be generated, and which was probably also applicable to Wiltshire centres. Winchester College expected to receive a rent of £10 per year, although the mid-century recession meant that this was over-optimistic from the beginning.[131] It has not yet been possible to build up a picture of the wealth and importance of our innkeepers. At Salisbury they came from among the important and substantial, but second rank of the mercantile community, while at Andover and Basingstoke in Hampshire they included some of the richest and influential members of the community. There seems little reason why this should not be the same in Wiltshire, as reflected in the situation at Marlborough. The two innkeepers recorded in the 1379 poll tax figures were both among the second most highly assessed men of the town. Robert Wariner had already been a lieutenant and assistant lieutenant of Marlborough castle, submitting accounts for repairs to the royal quarters. Subsequently he acknowledged a debt of £40, was to be mayor and MP for the town and was a frequent surety for other chosen MPs, who included John Polton, the second innkeeper in 1379.[132]

Agricultural producers were part of both short-distance trade between countryside and town and wider patterns of trade that saw wool, cloth and grain being transferred abroad or to other parts of the country. The prosperity of farmers depended on their interaction through the market with others beyond the village, town and countryside thus being inextricably linked. Despite the very real evidence of demographic urban shrinkage in England as a whole, there was also evidence of prosperity.[133] Even

---

129. I hope to discuss the role of inns more fully in a forthcoming paper.
130. *List of the lands of dissolved religious houses*, Public Record Office, Lists and indexes supplementary series 3, vol. 4 (New York, 1964), 90–91, 94; Rogers, *Book of Trowbridge*, 29; BL Add Rl 24330–57; WRO 906/SC5; WCM 4396.
131. Hare, 'Regional prosperity', 113; and Winchester College and the Angel Inn, Andover: a fifteenth-century landlord and its investments', *PHFCAS*, 60 (2005), 187–90; WCM 2678–91, 2694, 2704–10, 2726–35, 2739, 2742; Roberts, 'A fifteenth-century inn at Andover', 153–70.
132. TNA: PRO E179/194/42a; Roskell et al., *House of Commons*, 775–6; *Wiltshire extents for debts, Edward I to Elizabeth I*, ed. A. Conyers, Wiltshire Record Society 29 (Devizes, 1974), 36.
133. Dyer, *Decline and growth*; D.M. Palliser, 'Urban decay revisited', in J.A.F. Thomson (ed), *Towns and townspeople in the fifteenth century* (Gloucester, 1988).

Winchester (Hants), a classic case of obvious urban decline and shrinkage, as shown through contemporary documentation, through extensive archaeological excavation and particularly thorough topographical studies, saw substantial redevelopment along its High Street, with dendrochronology now showing the large scale of fifteenth-century urban rebuilding.[134]

---

134. Keene, *Survey of medieval Winchester*, 86–105; Roberts, *Hampshire houses*; T.B. James and E. Roberts, 'Winchester and later medieval development: from palace to pentice', *Medieval Archaeology*, 44 (2000), 182–6; C. Dyer, 'The archaeology of medieval small towns', *Medieval Archaeology*, 47 (2003), 111–12.

Chapter 11

The growth of the cloth industry

Wiltshire and its neighbours lay at the heart of one of the great economic transformations of the later Middle Ages: 'By the late fifteenth century ... the revolution had been accomplished that turned England from an exporter of raw wool into an exporter primarily of manufactured woollens ....'[1] On a national level, the breakthrough had occurred by the 1390s. Exports had risen from an average of 6,413 cloths in the 1350s to 40,291 in the 1390s.[2] Wiltshire and Somerset had been pre-eminent in this expansion: Somerset manufactured 12,000 cloths each year, making it by far the most productive county, and Wiltshire, with 7,000 cloths, was well ahead of any other rivals. The west country region, including Wiltshire, Somerset, Dorset, Hampshire and Bristol, generated over half of England's cloth manufacturing in 1394–8.[3] In few parts of the country was the impact of such industrialisation as obvious as in Wiltshire.[4]

The impact of the cloth industry went far beyond its own workers. The industry needed inputs of wool and labour, and its workers and employers required food, consumer goods and services. In Wiltshire, the growth of this industry provided one of the key forces for rural change. But its impact varied within the county. Some parts became dominated by cloth production while others saw little change, promoting a further set of regional variations that overlay the agrarian ones. In industry, as in agriculture, county boundaries were of little significance, and the cloth industry will be viewed within a wider regional context. It needs to be examined both spatially and chronologically, and in terms of both short-term and long-term changes.

The manorial sources that dominate this study show the growing demand for land that accompanied industrial growth (see Chapter 12), and occasionally, as at Castle Combe, they show the transformation of the community into a cloth-producing centre.[5] This chapter is dependent on sources more specific to this particular industry. The aulnage accounts, which record the tax imposed on the sale of cloth, must be used with care. Long ago E.M. Carus-Wilson showed that the accounts from 1468 and after for Somerset, Bristol and Wiltshire were an imaginative fabrication of the

---

1. E.M. Carus-Wilson, 'The woollen industry', in M.M. Postan and E. Miller (eds), *The Cambridge economic history of Europe II: trade and industry in the Middle Ages*, 2nd edn (Cambridge, 1987), 678.
2. A.R. Bridbury, *Medieval English clothmaking: an economic survey* (London, 1982), 116.
3. Calculated from H.L. Gray, 'The production and exportation of English woollens in the fourteenth century', *EHR*, 29 (1924), app. ii. Berkshire is linked with Oxfordshire in Gray's figures and has therefore been excluded.
4. For a recent study of another growth area see R.H. Britnell, 'The woollen textile industry in Suffolk in the later Middle Ages', *The Ricardian*, 13 (2003), 86–99.
5. L.C. Latham, 'The decay of the manorial system', MA thesis (London, 1928); E.M. Carus-Wilson, 'Evidences of industrial growth on some fifteenth century manors', in Carus-Wilson, *Essays in economic history*, 159–67.

aulnager, Richard More,[6] that the tax was being leased for a fixed sum, and that many of the names were works of fiction. Despite this, work elsewhere and for earlier times suggests that the aulnage accounts remain a very important and reasonably reliable source for the reconstruction of the industry.[7] Their reliability seems reinforced by the evidence of Salisbury and Somerset. In Salisbury the names recorded on the aulnage accounts compare well with those of other contemporary records, and clearly fluctuate in totals and for individuals from year to year;[8] while, in Somerset, the large number of specified marketing centres (53 in all, with some producing as few as 2 cloths) suggests a considerable degree of accuracy.[9] For some parts of the county the poll tax records of 1379 also provide a useful source for the development of the industry (on the use of this material see Chapter 10). Even the isolated account for 1467, the last one before More became aulnager and the accounts became a fiction, should not be disregarded.[10] It shows the familiar names of many clothiers whose activities can be established from other sources, with a wide range of amounts of production, both in Salisbury and elsewhere in the county, and the lists are ten times as large as that which More later deemed adequate. The aulnage accounts have been used with caution to see something of the distribution of the industry and the scale of some of the production.[11] The figures for cloth exports also help to establish long-term trends for the industry, although they deal with the ports through which cloth was sent (the three major ones being Bristol, Southampton and London) rather than the areas where it was made.

The chronology and distribution of the industry

The growth of the industry occurred in a series of waves: in the later fourteenth century, the early fifteenth, and finally in the later fifteenth and early sixteenth centuries. Within the county there were three main areas of production, each with its own pattern of development (Figure 11.1). Salisbury and its immediately surrounding valleys, particularly those of the Ebble and Wylye, had acquired a major industry by the fourteenth century, concentrating on the production of the lighter rays, or medleys, manufactured from dyed wool. The second area lay in the west of Wiltshire and was already established by 1379, but continued to expand in the fifteenth century. It

---

6. E.M. Carus-Wilson, *Medieval merchant venturers* (London, 1954), 279–91.
7. A.R. Bridbury, *Economic growth: England in the later Middle Ages*, 2nd edn (London, 1975), 33–5; D. Keene, *A survey of medieval Winchester* (Oxford, 1985), 311, 315; D.G. Shaw, *The creation of a community: the city of Wells in the Middle Ages* (Oxford, 1993), 70–71; R.H. Britnell, *Growth and decline in Colchester, 1300–1525* (Cambridge, 1986), 187–8.
8. Bridbury, *Economic growth*, 34, and *Medieval English cloth-making*, 67, 75; J. Chandler, *Endless Street: a history of Salisbury and its people* (Salisbury, 1983), 257–272.
9. TNA: PRO E101/343/28.
10. TNA: PRO E101/345/9; E.M. Carus-Wilson, 'The aulnage accounts: a criticism', in her *Medieval merchant venturers*, 282–88.
11. We should be cautious at seeing the figures as exact. The figures for Bradford Hundred show the overwhelming importance of William Stowford and James [Terumber] of Bradford, as other evidence would suggest, but the exactness of the comparison (236 cloths and a dozen for one, and 236 cloths for the other) must raise suspicions.

A Prospering Society

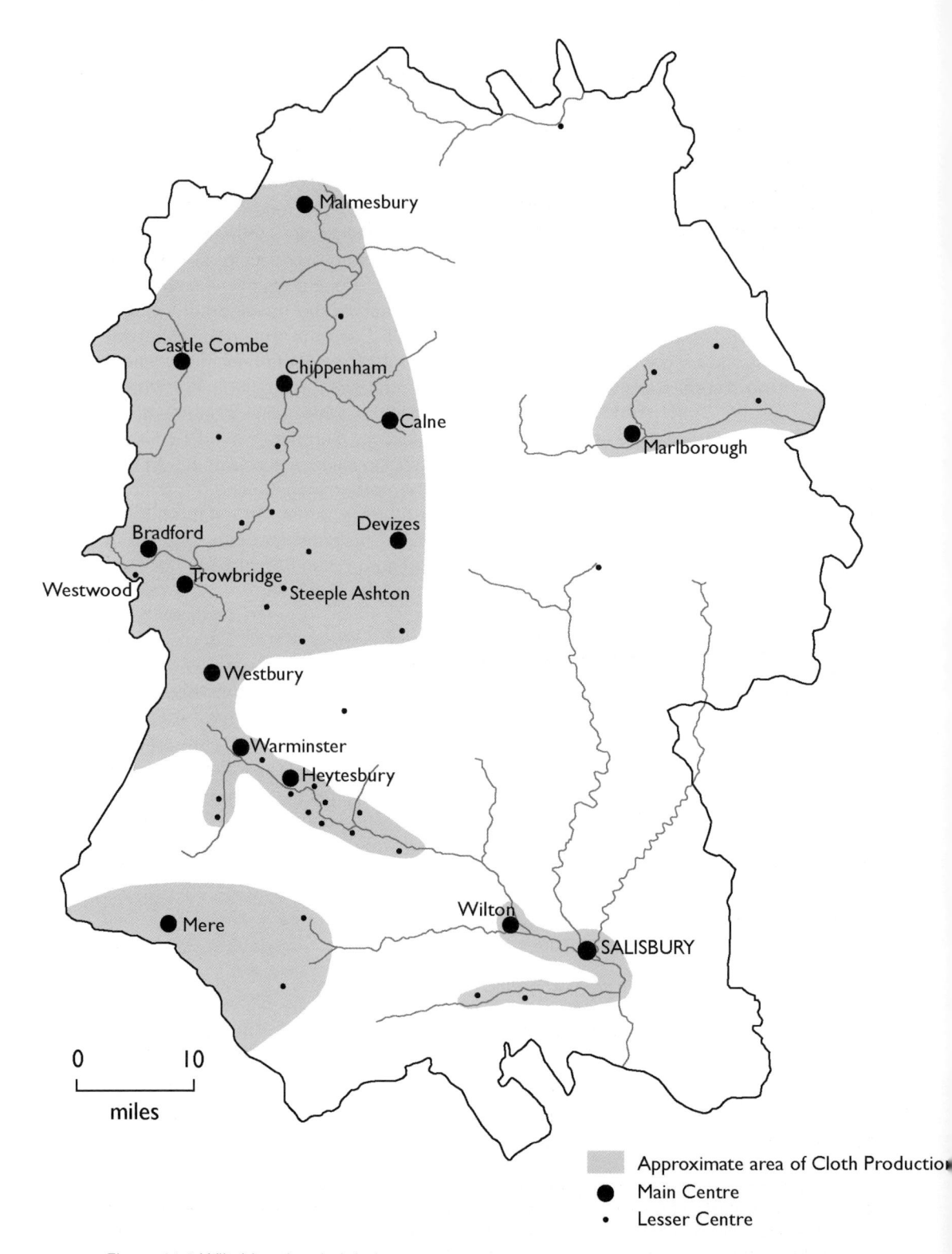

Figure 11.1 Wiltshire: the cloth industry

extended to include new centres and produced an increasing proportion of Wiltshire's cloth. Although it manufactured dyed cloth, this area increasingly concentrated on undyed and heavily fulled broadcloth. Its core lay in the area between Bradford, Trowbridge, Steeple Ashton and Westbury, but it stretched beyond to Devizes and Calne to the east and north-east, to Castle Combe to the north-west, to Chippenham and Malmesbury to the north, to Warminster, Hindon and Heytesbury in the south-east and to Mere in the south-west. Production increasingly expanded from its urban origins into the villages beyond. Finally, a substantial industry had existed in the east of the county in the Marlborough area from the twelfth century. It remained active in the late fourteenth century, and probably grew in the fifteenth century as part of the Berkshire/Thames valley area of kersey production.

Since the twelfth and thirteenth centuries, cloth had been manufactured in Wiltshire for use beyond its area of production. Although the building of fulling mills in the thirteenth century should not be taken as a guide to the distribution of the industry, their existence points to continued industrial activity.[12] By 1356–8 the aulnage accounts show that Wiltshire was part of the most important cloth-manufacturing area of the country: the west country was already responsible for over half the woollens sold in England. Salisbury was not listed separately, but, together with Southampton, Winchester, Shaftesbury and some neighbouring places, it produced 4,412 cloths, suggesting that the city was already important for this industry.[13] Meanwhile, there were also signs of growing industrial production in the west of the county, where a record of offences against the Statute of Labourers in 1349 shows a concentration of spinners in Chippenham Hundred and a smaller concentration of cloth-workers in Melksham.[14]

The next surviving national range of aulnage accounts comes from the 1390s and shows that large-scale growth had taken place in the second half of the fourteenth century. Although Wiltshire was over-shadowed by neighbouring Somerset it was the second largest producer in the country, and now accounted for almost as much as Hampshire, Wiltshire, Somerset, Dorset and Bristol together in the mid-fourteenth century. In the 1390s Bristol, the city of York and Warwickshire were the only other centres manufacturing more than 3,000 cloths, but they remained far behind Wiltshire.[15] The leases of the Wiltshire aulnage also point to further industrial growth in the later fourteenth century, rising steadily from £60 in 1362 to £100 in 1403. Shortly afterwards this was reduced to £80, probably as the export trade went into short-term recession.[16] The yield continued to grow but by 1467, after the collapse of

---

12. E.M. Carus-Wilson, 'The woollen industry before 1550', in VCH *Wilts* 4, 119; for some of the difficulties in interpreting the fulling mills see E. Miller, 'The fortunes of the English textile industry during the thirteenth century', *EcHR*, 2nd series 18 (1965), 71–2 and Bridbury, *Medieval English clothmaking*, 16–25.
13. Gray, 'Production and exportation of English woollens', 21–2.
14. E.M. Thompson, 'Offenders against the statute of labourers in Wiltshire, 1349', *WAM*, 33 (1904), 384–409.
15. Gray, 'Production and exportation of English woollens', 34.
16. £66 14s 4d (1375), £70 (1388), £86 13s 4d (1390): Carus-Wilson, 'Woollen industry before 1550', 124, Bridbury, *Medieval English clothmaking*, 67; J.N. Hare, 'Growth and recession in the fifteenth-century economy: the Wiltshire textile industry and the countryside', *EcHR*, 2nd series 52 (1999), 10.

A Prospering Society

the industry in the 1450s, the tax only yielded £63 in a short period of direct administration.[17]

At the end of the fourteenth century, this west-country industry was still substantially urban.[18] Salisbury dominated Wiltshire's production and sealed over 89 per cent of the county's cloth. While much of this may have been produced in the immediately surrounding area and then brought into the city for sale or finishing, there was evidently an extremely large-scale urban or suburban component. This was seen in the tenter yards of the city and the suburb of Fisherton, in the council records and in the aulnage accounts.[19] Almost 90 per cent of cloths aulnaged in Salisbury in 1396–7 were attributed to names that also occur on a ward list of the citizens in 1399/1400.[20] In 1421 a total of 108 master weavers, 208 journeymen, 53 master fullers, 27 journeymen and some others attended a mass protest meeting of the Salisbury cloth industry. There were thus almost 400 present from a city whose taxed population in 1377 (those aged over 14 years) was 3,226, suggesting that about a quarter of the adult male population of Salisbury was then directly engaged in cloth production.[21] But this excludes dyers and other occupations that were involved in cloth production, as well as apprentices, many of whom would be over 14 years of age. The figure of cloth-workers was thus probably nearer a third than a quarter of the male population. Occupational descriptions in incomplete lists of citizens or guild members for 1399/1400 and 1474/5 suggest that the textile industry may have employed about a third (32 per cent and 42 per cent respectively) of independent traders.[22]

Some of the cloth listed in Salisbury's aulnage accounts would have been made in the nearby countryside. Few 1379 poll tax assessments survive for the city's immediate hinterland, although they show production in the Ebble valley.[23] Salisbury citizens are also found further afield, using fulling mills at Barford St Martin or Leigh near Westbury (25 miles away).[24] The aulnage figures probably represent the production of the city and the immediately surrounding river valleys, with the aulnagers subsequently opening up new sub-divisions as other centres grew. Moreover, beyond Wiltshire, there were other centres whose figures would be dramatically underestimated if their cloth was taxed in Salisbury, and any reduction in Salisbury's assessment must involve boosting those of other important urban centres, such as Winchester, Sherborne or some of the towns of Somerset. Winchester was responsible for 76 or 80 per cent of Hampshire's sealed cloth in 1394–5, and Sherborne for 87 per cent of Dorset's cloth in 1399–1402.[25] In 1395/6 Bath, Wells,

---

17. Calculated from TNA: PRO E101/345/9.
18. Bridbury, *Medieval English clothmaking*, 65–82.
19. Bridbury, *Economic growth*, 48.
20. Chandler, *Endless Street*, 259.
21. *The first general entry book of the city of Salisbury, 1387–1452*, ed. D.R. Carr, Wiltshire Record Society 54 (Trowbridge, 2001); there are discrepancies between these figures and those given in Bridbury, *Medieval English clothmaking*, 69.
22. Chandler, *Endless Street*, 68.
23. TNA: PRO E179/239/193/I and VI (Bishopstone, Croucheston, Faulston and Flamston); there are also references to weavers in Coombe Bisset court rolls (WCM 4396, 4403d).
24. Bridbury, *Medieval English clothmaking*, 80.
25. Calculated from TNA: PRO E101/344/1; Keene, *Survey of medieval Winchester*, 316–17.

Table 11.1
The aulnage accounts: the distribution of Wiltshire's cloth production.

	Wiltshire: total annual production	Salisbury as % of total	Salisbury: annual total	West Wiltshire as % of total	West Wiltshire: annual total
1394–5	4719	89.4	4217	10.6	493
1414–15	3742	73.6	2754	26.4	988
1466–7	3491	22.7		77.3	

Notes: The aulnage accounts are not designed to facilitate comparison. They divide production into the following centres: 1394–5 Salisbury or the rest of the county; 1414–15 Salisbury, Wilton, Devizes, Mere, Castle Combe, Hundred of Warminster, Hundred of Melksham; 1466–7 Salisbury and Wilton, Hundred of Heytesbury, Castle Combe and Malmesbury, Hundred of Westbury, Hundred of Bradford, Devizes and Marlborough.

Wilton has been included with Salisbury, although it is not clear how this would have been accounted for in 1394–5. We may therefore be underestimating the dominance of the Salisbury area. All other centres have been included in West Wiltshire. Marlborough appears only in 1467, when, together with Devizes, it accounted for 7.4% of production. Geographically, it is clearly not part of the West Wiltshire industry, but it cannot be extracted.

1394–5: The Wiltshire account is for 75 weeks, the Salisbury one for 62. Each has been converted into a figure representing a whole year's production. The other two accounts are for half a year (1415: Michaelmas to 1 April); and eighteen months (1466–7: 6 April to Michaelmas), and these have also been converted into an annual figure.

Sources: TNA: PRO E101/345/2 ms 9 & 12; 4 m.8; and 345/9.

Frome and Taunton constituted four out of the five main aulnage units, were all well-established towns and were responsible for 45.5 per cent of Somerset's cloth manufactures.[26] Bristol was also a major industrial centre of cloth production.

But Somerset had already shown an early major breakthrough in rural cloth production, and this trend became increasingly important in neighbouring Wiltshire. The most obvious example of Somerset's rural industrial expansion was Pensford, where a new settlement had grown up at the ford at the edge of two adjoining parishes and become the marketing and fulling centre for the area around. In 1334 it had not even constituted a parish or a tax unit, but by 1395/6 it marketed more than 5,000 dozens, or over one-fifth of Somerset's cloth production.[27] There were also other, less extreme examples of such rural industrial growth. In Wiltshire, the aulnage accounts do not initially distinguish between the cloth marketed in individual centres, apart from Salisbury, and this makes it more difficult to separate rural and urban production. But a good if incomplete set of poll tax returns for 1379 helps fill the gap, even though only the better-off, those who were assessed above the standard 4d, were assigned an occupation. The returns show both the development of a rural industry and the continuation of urban production.[28] Rural expansion probably developed earliest in the west Wiltshire area, between the existing industrial areas of

---

26. TNA: PRO E101/343/28.
27. J.N. Hare, 'Pensford and the growth of the cloth industry in late medieval Somerset', *Somerset Archaeology and Natural History*, 147 (2003), 174–5. For a similar later example, at Stroudwater (Glos.), see Carus-Wilson, 'Evidences of industrial growth', 154–8.
28. Mapped on p. 78 of J.N. Hare, 'Lord and tenant in Wiltshire, *c.*1380–1520, with particular reference to regional and seigneurial variations', PhD thesis (London, 1976).

Somerset and Salisbury, but here the industry retained a large urban core: the tax returns suggest that Bradford and Devizes, and to a lesser extent Calne, Mere and Hindon, were important centres, while the returns do not survive for Trowbridge, Westbury and Warminster, which would all soon become important clothing towns. In the case of Trowbridge there was already evidence of rents being paid for the tenter-racks by 1371.[29] These and other towns should probably be included in any list of major cloth-producing centres, and there are a few other candidates. The importance of the industry varied from town to town. As noted in the previous chapter, Marlborough had twice the number of taxpayers listed at Bradford, but the latter had substantially more who were engaged in cloth production. In Marlborough it was the leather and food industries that were more important (Table 10.1). But Marlborough had a cloth industry and, together with a group of textile workers in Ramsbury, it may have provided a core for later expansion.[30]

The cloth-making industry also grew among the villages of west Wiltshire: Christian Malford had 18 weavers and 2 shearers among the 25 named occupants, Seende had 6 weavers and 1 shearer, and Bulkington 4 weavers.[31] Perhaps the most striking area of concentrated rural textile development lay in Heytesbury Hundred in the upper Wylye valley, where in such villages as Bathampton, Brixton, Boyton and Heytesbury there were 16 weavers and 17 fullers among the 651 adults listed.[32] The similarity of distribution between weavers and fullers probably reflects a situation in which many part-time weavers may not have been given an occupational description and a higher tax assessment. All of these were on the edge of what was subsequently to become the important west Wiltshire cloth industry. Here, as in Somerset and around Salisbury, the rural cloth industry was developing alongside urban production, not as an alternative to it. In the future much of the expansion would occur in rural areas.

The development of water-powered mechanical fulling by utilising the power of swift-flowing streams or rivers offered opportunities for rural growth. But not all types of cloth needed heavy fulling, and towns such as Salisbury and Winchester continued to use traditional methods. The citizens of Salisbury might take cloth to mills in the countryside, but at Salisbury itself the mills were for grinding corn, not for fulling cloths. Here, the traditional light cleaning and fulling was adequate for much of its cloth, as well as those of some other centres.[33] By contrast, the broad cloth of west Wiltshire required heavy and long-drawn-out fulling in order to thicken and felt the fabric. The mechanical water-powered process was essential to produce the expensive heavily fulled but undyed broadcloth that became increasingly characteristic of this area's production.[34] In the early fifteenth century lords continued to invest in

---

29. K.H. Rogers, *The book of Trowbridge* (Buckingham, 1984), 9.
30. TNA: PRO E179/239/193.
31. TNA: PRO E179/239/193/viii, ix.
32. TNA: PRO E179/239/194/42a; Carus-Wilson, 'Woollen industry before 1550', 122–3.
33. Bridbury, *Medieval English clothmaking*, 80–81. The fulling mill referred to at Downton was evidently in difficulties much earlier as its rent had fallen 10s by 1302 (*Pipe Roll 1301–2*, 62); it was eventually replaced by a corn mill (*Pipe Roll 1409–10*, 53) although during its repair it was still referred to as a fulling mill (ibid., p. 63).
34. A.R. Hall and N.C. Russell, 'What about the fulling-mill?', *History of Technology*, 6 (1981), 115–16.

new mills, as at Heytesbury, Warminster and Boynton, but so too did the tenants of Castle Combe, where between 1409 and 1454 one mill was rebuilt and at least four new mills appeared.[35] These new west Wiltshire mills were being built at a time when seigneurial monopolies could not be enforced and by men some of whom could not even claim to possess such rights. They depended on growing demand from local clothmakers for their cloth to be finished and a growing demand for heavy water-powered fulling.

Although the aulnage figures need to be used with caution, they suggest both that Salisbury fell into relative decline compared with the rest of the county, and that it continued to produce cloth on a very large scale. In 1394/5 Salisbury had sealed 89.4 per cent of Wiltshire's cloth, but in 1414/15 this fell to 70 per cent (73.5 per cent including Wilton) and in 1467 (together with Wilton) to a mere 22.7 per cent.[36] But in terms of the city's absolute production, the main fall probably occurred between 1395 and 1415, followed by a period of relative stability. The early fifteenth century was a difficult time for Salisbury's rays,[37] and the problems for the cloth industry in its immediate hinterland, as in the Ebble valley, may have been reflected in the area's agricultural difficulties in the early fifteenth century. Moreover, the fall could have been accentuated by administrative changes if some of the production of the Wylye valley became being aulnaged elsewhere, as at Heytesbury in 1467.

By contrast, growth was greatest in west Wiltshire. The industry had already established itself here by the 1390s, although on a relatively small scale compared with its neighbours in east Somerset and Salisbury. But in 1414/15 the aulnagers divided up the county's growing production outside Salisbury among specific places. The west Wiltshire area now produced 493 cloths, or 26.4 per cent of the county's production. Some centres were urban: Devizes (140) and Mere (80), and the formerly rural Castle Combe (71). Others were in areas described as 'hundreds' where cloth production was spreading beyond individual settlements into the countryside, as in the hundreds of Warminster (129) and Melksham (73).[38] Both these hundreds incorporated areas where a rural industry had already been developing by 1379. In the fifteenth century the names of the west Wiltshire centres of Castle Combe and Devizes became sufficiently well established in London to be used as the names of particular types of cloth.[39]

The first half of the fifteenth century continued to be a period of industrial expansion, despite some difficulties and cut-backs in the early decades. Growth was predominately found in west Wiltshire, and Salisbury declined in relative terms. The national customs figures suggest that the first half of the century began with a fall in trade from 1403 and a prolonged period of low cloth exports until the early 1420s, associated with the general European bullion shortage. This is also seen in Bristol, Southampton and London, the major ports for Wiltshire cloth. Each port exported from a number of other areas, but Wiltshire and Somerset were big enough producers to

---

35. Carus-Wilson, 'Woollen industry before 1550', 129; and 'Evidences of industrial growth', 164.
36. TNA: PRO E101/345/2 ms 9 and 12; 345/4, m 8; 345/9.
37. Bridbury, *Medieval English cloth-making*, 69.
38. TNA: PRO E101/345/4 m. 8. The Melksham figure printed in Carus-Wilson, 'Woollen industry before 1550', 128, is a misprint. The totals are for a winter half-year.
39. Carus-Wilson, 'Woollen industry before 1550', 130, 139.

have affected the trends. In the 1420s and 1430s, exports again reached the level of the 1390s, and a new and higher level was reached in the 1440s. The 1450s and 60s saw a prolonged slump, followed by steady and spectacular growth from the 1480s. At Bristol, the early-fifteenth-century downturn was more prolonged, and the city did not return to the levels of the 1390s until the 1440s. The Southampton figures fluctuated more substantially but had more than recovered by 1422 and reached unprecedented peaks in the 1440s, when it was the second largest exporter of cloth in England. Subsequently deep recession and then recovery and expansion followed.[40] The total received from the aulnage of the county had risen until 1408, but was then cut back, and its subsequent rather static character suggests that the king was failing to keep the farm of the aulnage in line with industrial expansion. The figures for the directly collected aulnage also suggest a fall in production in the opening decades of the century.[41]

These areas of growing production suffered severely from the collapse of the export market in the mid-century recession, when English cloth exports fell by 30 per cent in the 1450s and fell again thereafter.[42] Wiltshire had become more dependent for its livelihood on the cloth industry than at any previous time, a situation that reached an unprecedented level in the 1440s; but its growth was not a unique development, however, and production in some other parts of the country also grew: the aulnage accounts suggest that industrial growth in Suffolk was even more remarkable.[43]

The great size and importance of the west Wiltshire industry in the mid-century is apparent in the number of large-scale producers and traders shown in the 1467 aulnage account, where the average individual's payment was much greater in the hundreds of Bradford and Westbury than elsewhere,[44] and by chance documentation for individual deals. Thus William Athelam of Westbury sold 26 cloths worth £99 to German merchants in London in 1459, and in 1467 was listed as having sealed 62 cloths, while John Wyke of Trowbridge sold 20 cloths worth £100 to Italian merchants in London and, in 1459, suffered the arrest of 102 of his cloths at Trowbridge for alleged failure to pay aulnage. At his death in 1460 he owned a great furnace and dyehouse by the west mill and contributed £10 to rebuilding the parish church.[45] James Terumber, Touker or just James of Bradford, had probably come to Bradford and Trowbridge from Bristol and rose to great wealth. He was able to build an almshouse at Trowbridge and to buy an estate's clip of wool at £40, and in 1463 he was involved in a dispute with a Venetian merchant at Bridport (Dorset) over 29 cloths (which were evidently a small part of his total production). In 1467, he dominated the

---

40. E.M. Carus-Wilson and O. Coleman, *England's export trade, 1275–1547* (Oxford, 1963).
41. Bridbury, *Medieval English cloth-making*, 67.
42. Carus-Wilson and Coleman, *England's export trade*; J. Hatcher, 'The great slump of the mid-fifteenth century', in R.H. Britnell and J. Hatcher (eds), *Progress and problems in medieval England: essays in honour of Edward Miller*, Cambridge 1996, 236–72.
43. Gray, 'Production and exportation of English woollens', 34; H. Heaton, *The Yorkshire woollen and worsted industries* (Oxford, 1920), 85.
44. TNA: PRO E101/345/9. Bradford averaged 159 and Westbury 47; the next largest was Heytesbury Hundred with 34, and then Salisbury and Wilton with 20. Several Bradford traders brought back woad from Southampton in 1465–6 (SCA SC5/5/16).

production of Bradford Hundred and his exports to Southampton produced woad which he sold in Salisbury in 1444 and took back to Bradford in 1448. He leased the market and fair of Trowbridge from the crown, and was also one of the creditors to the Hungerford family when they needed to raise money for the ransom of Lord Moleyns.[46] His friend William Stowford was another of the Hungerford creditors who was engaged in the cloth industry. He exported cloth to Southampton, so that in 1466 he was able to buy 13 ballets of woad and a pipe of wine there, which he took back to Trowbridge, and in 1477–8, together with another merchant, he sent 40 cloths to Southampton. In 1467, he and Terumber dominated the production of Bradford Hundred.[47] Thomas Barkesdale of Keevil sold cloths worth 400 marks on one occasion, while William Page of Devizes disposed of £100 worth of cloth in a single deal[48] and John Horton from Lullington, in the east Somerset cloth district, moved to Wiltshire and exported over 200 cloths through Southampton in 1477–8. His will described him as of Iford, but it is clear that he had close connections with Bradford. He left the business side of his inheritance to his second son who took the family to new heights of wealth.[49] These examples also show that the area and its traders operated within an international system: Terumber dealt with Italian merchants in Bridport and others in Southampton while Athelam and Wyke dealt with German and Italian merchants in London.

The industry in west Wiltshire was partly urban but increasingly rural, and located in villages some of which were being transformed into semi-urban centres. Nowhere has this latter development been better documented than at Castle Combe. This had been a mainly agricultural village in the fourteenth century, although some cloth was already being made there and it possessed a market, but in the early fifteenth century it became a major industrial centre. It was given a separate listing in the aulnage account of 1415 and by the 1430s, if not earlier, its clothiers were selling their cloth at Blackwell Hall, the main cloth market in London. It produced cloth and finished cloth for producers from further afield, as for those at Cirencester.[50] The local cloth industry may have been helped by the military spending of its lord, Sir John Fastolf (1409–59), who purchased cloth to the annual value of £100 in order to supply his troops in the French wars,[51] but the industry was already expanding before this. The number of landless men who now worked in the village and paid chevage rose from 19 in 1394 to 45 in 1418 and to 70 in 1450 (Table 11.2). There were 8 aliens in the village, both Irish

---

45. Carus-Wilson, 'Woollen industry before 1550', 135.
46. Ibid., 134–7; W.H. Jones, 'Terumber's chantry at Trowbridge with a copy of the original deed of endowment, A.D. 1483', *WAM*, 10 (1867), 240–52; TNA: PRO E101/345/9; *Brokage book 1443–4*, 303–5; *Brokage book 1447–8*; M.A. Hicks, 'Counting the cost of war: the Moleyns ransome', *Southern History*, 8 (1986), 25–6.
47. Carus-Wilson, 'Woollen industry before 1550', 135–6; Hicks, 'Counting the cost of war', 25–6; SCA SC5/5/16; *Brokage book 1477–8 and 1527–8*; TNA: PRO E101/345/9.
48. Carus-Wilson, 'Woollen industry before 1550', 136–7.
49. TNA: PRO Prob 11/11/17; *Brokage book 1477–8 and 1527–8*, 5, 24, 101; On Thomas Horton, see below.
50. TNA: PRO E101/345/4 m8; Carus-Wilson, 'Evidences of industrial growth', 162.
51. G.P. Scrope, *History of the manor and ancient barony of Castle Combe* (privately printed, 1852), 201–2.

Table 11.2
Court receipts and chevage: Castle Combe.

Castle Combe	Court receipts	Chevage
1394		19
1414		37
1415		33
1417		45
1418		40
1419	£31 13s 0d	
1420	-	
1421	-	
1422	-	
1423	-	
1424	£33 8s 6d	
1425	£29 14s 4d	
1426	-	
1427	-	
1428	£29 19s 6d	
1429	£19 19s 4d	
1430	£6 13s 4d	
1431	£13 4s 0d	
1432	£6 0s 0d	
1433	£6 11s 9d	
1434	£9 17s 8d	
1435	£28 7s 6d	54
1436	£8 13s 11d	54
1437	£106 6s 8d	47
1438	£20 9s 0d	62
1439	£89 1s 9d	
1440	£3 1s 0d	
1441	£31 2s 1d	
1442	£3 8s 0d	
1443	£20 5s 0d	70
1444	£7 6s 0d	
1445	£6 13s 4d	
1446	£48 10s 0d	
1449		56
1450		70
1451		69
1452		62
1457		44
1458		46
1459		30
1472		33
1473		27+4
1475		29
1476		27
1481		32 [47]

Sources: Figures of court receipts taken from the notebook of William of Worcester (BL Add Mss 28208). A few years show no recorded receipts. Elsewhere profits are listed from courts held in these years. Chevage: BL Add Mss 18250, 18272, 18475, 18478, 18481, 18482, 18486, 18488, 28208.

and French, in 1440. A total of 50 houses and 2 mills were rebuilt during Fastolf's lordship, a sign of the prosperity of the tenants and the demand for housing. The influx of craftsmen led to a need for regulation: opening hours for the taverns were limited, gambling prohibited and craft organisations and their wardens were created for the dyers, fullers and weavers respectively.[52] The industry helped create the considerable fortunes of men such as William Haynes. He was a serf by origin, thus allowing his lord to claim his property after his death; Fastolf received payments of £140 from Hayne's widow for obtaining the possession of his lands and property and £40 from her new husband, reflecting the large scale of Hayne's business enterprises. His brother-in-law, Richard Halwey, held property inside and outside the manor, leased 2 fulling mills, rebuilt his house and built 9 new houses, had 6 or 7 servants by 1450, and was warden of the fullers and dyers in 1444.[53] The household goods held by these affluent clothiers and the evidence of the rebuilding of houses reflected both the expansion of the cloth-making industry and the generation of new jobs outside it.[54] This industrial growth affected the lord's revenues. His rent totals rose slightly, but Fastolf would have benefited most from the rising court profits. Court receipts reached over £20 on 11 occasions, including annual figures of £106 (in 1437) and £89 (1439) (Table 11.2). The lord enjoyed the revenues from an increasingly active court and the servile dues of a few villeins, of whom Haynes was an extreme case. Above all, the lord benefited from the rising entry fines that a growing demand for land enabled him to collect.

William Worcester, Fastolf's tireless steward, looked at the village and its settlements and sought to explain the scene. He commented on the two vills within the lordship: 'one of them is called Overcombe, where dwell the yeomen who are occupied in cultivation and working the soil, which lies upon the hill: and the rest is called Nethercombe, where dwell the men who make cloth, as weavers, fullers and dyers and other craftsmen.'[55] But, unlike Pensford, this village in the valley was not a new industrial creation. The church, parts of which go back to the thirteenth century, was here in the valley, and both it and Overcombe possessed agricultural virgate holdings. But it was in Nethercombe that the industrial expansion of the fifteenth century had occurred. Here the Bye brook was tapped to power the fulling mills and a gig mill (for raising the nap of the cloth). In 1454, one tenant held a triple mill (a wheat mill, a fulling mill and a gig mill) and there were at least another three fulling mills. The settlement of Nethercombe seems to have consisted of West Street and South Street, each with a succession of cottage properties, as well as a group of properties in the area of the old manor court and some which were without identification; there was also a market place. Worcester's distinction between the industrial and rural settlements had evident value for his own day, but did not accurately reflect the origins of the parish's settlement pattern.

Although the west of Wiltshire provided the area of greatest growth, the

---

52. Carus-Wilson, 'Evidences of industrial growth', 165.
53. Ibid., 163–5; a Nicholas Halway was among those on the aulnage account for 1467: TNA: PRO E101/345/9; see also above, Chapter 8.
54. Carus-Wilson, 'Evidences of industrial growth', 161–7; Scrope, *Castle Combe*, 249–50.
55. Scrope, *Castle Combe*, 207.

Marlborough area in the east of the county also seems to have possessed a flourishing industry, based on that already seen in the 1377 poll tax figures. In 1391 one of its clothiers sent cloth to Bristol for export to Ireland.[56] Because of the paucity of the evidence it seems sensible to treat the fifteenth and early sixteenth century together. The town prospered, and by 1524 had risen to be the second-richest and most populous town in Wiltshire. Its trading prosperity is reflected in the wealth of John Goddard (see Chapter 7).[57] The expanding role of cloth is suggested by the aulnage account of 1467, which includes Marlborough with Devizes as one of the specified centres of cloth marketing. There is also evidence of dyeing there and of the substantial import of £30 of Toulouse woad.[58] Marlborough was part of the growing kersey-producing cloth industry that lay to the east in the Kennet and Thames valleys, from Marlborough to Newbury and Reading, and in the towns of north Hampshire. It was an expansion that was already visible in 1466–7 and subsequently became even more important.[59]

Previous prosperity and growth was transformed by the great mid-century depression, which hit Wiltshire as elsewhere.[60] It was particularly noticeable in the cloth industry, where national exports had reached a peak in the 1440s and fell to almost half this by the 1460s.[61] The drop was sudden: between 1446–8 and 1448–50 cloth exports fell by 35 per cent.[62] The trend was clearly shown in the ports that served the Wiltshire industry: Bristol, Southampton and London.[63] This recession was part of a wider European development generated in part by monetary factors and shortage of coin,[64] and its consequences were immense in areas like Wiltshire that had become increasingly dependent on international trade. At the same time, export difficulties damaged domestic consumption and trade. The impact of this recession is examined more fully in the next chapter, but it has already been seen in the dramatic fall in the chevage payments made by the landless workers at Castle Combe. This suggests that in the 1450s the number of these workers more than halved. Castle Combe may have been particularly vulnerable because its growth had been so fast,

---

56. VCH *Wilts* 12, 208.
57. On Goddard see above, Chapter 7.
58. Carus-Wilson, 'Woollen industry before 1550', 140; on Goddard see Chapter 7.
59. Carus-Wilson, 'The woollen industry before 1550', 679; G.D. Ramsay, *The Wiltshire woollen industry in the sixteenth and seventeenth centuries* (Oxford, 1943), 19; J.N. Hare, 'Regional prosperity in fifteenth-century England: some evidence from Wessex', in M. Hicks (ed.), *Revolution and consumption in late medieval England* (Woodbridge, 2001), 111–15; F.J. Baigent and J.E. Millard, *A history of the ancient town and manor of Basingstoke* (Basingstoke, 1889), 290, 319–20; J.N. Hare, 'Church-building and urban prosperity on the eve of the reformation: Basingstoke and its parish church', *PHFCAS*, 62 (2007), 185–9; Kitson purchased from Hungerford, just over the Berkshire border: Carus-Wilson, 'The woollen industry before 1550', 141. On Newbury now see M. Yates, *Town and countryside in western Berkshire, c.1327–c.1600* (Woodbridge, 2007).
60. Hatcher, 'Great slump', 240–45.
61. Britnell, *Colchester*, 44.
62. H.L. Gray, 'English foreign trade from 1446 to 1482', in Power and Postan, *Studies in English trade*, 23.
63. Carus-Wilson and Coleman, *England's export trade*.
64. J. Day, *The medieval market economy* (Oxford, 1987).

but it provides a reminder of the influence of international trade on individual localities.

The recovery from recession seems to have begun in the 1470s, spearheaded by London exports, but it became general only towards the end of the 1480s. The peak levels of national cloth exports in the 1440s were not regained until the 1480s, although initially not consistently. The loss of the Italian fleets and the dislocation of the French trade with the loss of France would have particularly damaged Southampton, such an important outlet for Wiltshire production. Subsequently national exports rose by about 70 per cent between the early 1470s and the late 1520s.[65] These cloth exports were increasingly funnelled through London; in the 1350s it had dealt with 10 per cent of exports, but by the 1530s this had risen to 80 per cent.[66] London's growing dominance in national cloth exports meant that Bristol, despite a full recovery in the last two decades of the fifteenth century, subsequently declined in importance, as, later, did Southampton. Wiltshire cloth was ever more likely to be heading abroad through London, rather than through ports that were nearer.[67]

Just as elsewhere in England, recovery led to some changes in location for the industry. In southern England it expanded westward into west and south Somerset and Devon (looking towards Exeter), and eastward in the Kennet and Thames valley.[68] In Wiltshire the end of the fifteenth century and the early sixteenth century saw continued growth in the west of the county. By the end of the century the clothing centres of the west rivalled, if they did not yet surpass, Salisbury.[69] The importance of this area is reflected in two very different sources. Leland, in his tour in 1542, described and highlighted the pre-eminent clothing activities of Bradford, Trowbridge, Devizes, Steeple Ashton, Westbury and Malmesbury. On Bradford, for example, he remarked that 'the town's entire economy depends on clothmaking'. At Malmesbury, he described how parts of the buildings of the monastery had been converted into rooms full of weaving looms by the new owner, William Stumpe, an 'exceptionally rich clothier'.[70] He also noted some of the other great clothiers: Hall and Lucas of Bradford; Horton of Bradford, Trowbridge and Westwood; Terumber, Alexander and Bailey of Trowbridge; Long and Lucas of Steeple Ashton, each of whom paid for the construction of an aisle of the magnificent new church there (Plate 11.1), and Stokes of Seende. He singled out Thomas Horton, described elsewhere as of Iford and Bradford and of London, as one of three pre-eminent clothiers, and the large scale of his activities is supported by other evidence. He bought wool worth £30 on a single occasion, and was assessed for the 1524 subsidy at the remarkable sum of £450. He personally paid £22 10s in the village of Westwood, but the whole of Bradford town together paid only £6 15s. He used his wealth to found a chantry and almshouse, to

---

65. Calculated from R.H. Britnell, *The closing of the Middle Ages?* (Oxford, 1999), 229.
66. C.M. Barron, 'London, 1300–1540', in Palliser (ed.), *The Cambridge urban history of Britain*, 412.
67. Carus-Wilson and Coleman, *England's export trade*; Carus-Wilson, 'Woollen industry before 1550', 138; on earlier contacts between west Wiltshire and Bristol see John Draper of Trowbridge, John Long of Devizes and James Touker of Bradford (Carus-Wilson, 'Woollen industry before 1550', 133–7).
68. E.M. Carus-Wilson, *The expansion of Exeter* (Exeter, 1961), 20, 29.
69. Carus-Wilson, 'Woollen industry before 1550', 128.
70. *John Leland's itinerary*, ed. J. Chandler (Stroud, 1993), 491, 501, 502, 488–9.

Plate 11.1 Steeple Ashton church: a symbol of the wealth generated by the cloth industry.

build houses at Bradford and Trowbridge, to expand the manor house and to rebuild the church at Westwood (Plate 11.2).[71] The area's importance in the early sixteenth century also emerges clearly from the cloth purchases of Thomas Kitson, the London mercer and merchant adventurer, in the 1530s. Kitson bought from Somerset and Gloucestershire as well as from Wiltshire, and actually bought more cloth from Somerset than from Wiltshire. But over half the suppliers of white broadcloth whose place of business is mentioned came from west Wiltshire. They came from the towns already highlighted by Leland (except for Bradford) and from other known centres such as Keevil, Warminster, Heytesbury, Melksham, Broughton Gifford, Lacock, Chippenham, Calne, Edington (or Hedington) and Longbridge [Deverill]. We must be cautious in drawing conclusions from one man's purchases and his personal contacts during a 10-year period, and not all the names from whom he bought provide the seller's place of residence. But these purchases reinforce the importance of a few major manufacturing centres: above all Westbury, but to a lesser extent also Trowbridge, Warminster and Devizes, and the upper Wylye valley.[72]

---

71. Ramsay, *Wiltshire woollen industry*, 6; TNA: PRO E179/197/155.
72. Carus-Wilson, 'Woollen industry before 1550', 139; C.J. Brett, 'Thomas Kytson and Somerset clothmen, 1529–1539', *Somerset Archaeology and Natural History*, 143 (1999), 31; and C.J. Brett, 'Thomas Kytson and Wiltshire clothmen', *WAM*, 97 (2004), 39–40.

Plate 11.2 Westwood church, with a new tower built by the wealthy clothier and lessee, Thomas Horton.

The industry changed in more than just its location. Increasingly, in the late fifteenth century, Wiltshire produced the heavy undyed, heavily fulled cloth rather than the dyed cloths or rays of Salisbury or the scarlets of Castle Combe. The west of Wiltshire and the Frome valley had already become noted for their white broadcloths in the early and mid-fifteenth century, although they had also produced coloured cloth. It was from these areas that Thomas Kitson bought his supplies of undyed cloth early in the sixteenth century.[73] But this was merely one part of the county's industry. Elsewhere, Salisbury's production remained extensive, albeit declining in relative terms, and that of Marlborough probably grew: both focused on the lighter dyed and lightly fulled cloths.

The impact of the cloth industry

The cloth industry was both urban and increasingly rural. Towns were places of production and marketing. Neighbouring Somerset had led the way in developing rural manufactures, and nowhere was this more obvious than at Pensford, where by 1395/6, a new settlement sealed more cloths than anywhere else in the county. This rural centre showed a larger individual scale of operations than the traditional towns of

---

73. Carus-Wilson, 'Woollen industry before 1550', 138, 134.

A Prospering Society

Table 12.4
Rents: Bromham, Coombe Bisset, Durrington.

	Bromham		Coombe Bisset		Durrington
1345	£15 6s 2¾d				
1377	£18 6s 10d				
1381	£19 0s 0¼d	(84)	£23 0s 2d		
1391	(92) £18 2s 3¾d		£22 19s 2d	(90)	£40 0s 0d
1401	£18 2s 8¼d		£20 14s 2d	(02)	£36 0s 0d
1411	£24 2s 3¾d		£23 0s 0d		£36 0s 0d
1421	£24 9s 1½d		£19 16s 8d		£37 6s 8d
1431	£23 17s 7¼d		£19 9s 0d		£37 6s 8d
1441	£22 5s 1¼d		£15 7s 0d		£37 6s 8d
1451	£30 6s 1¼d		£14 10s 0d	(47)	£38 2s 8d
1461	(59) £29 13s 4¼d		£14 0s 10¾d		£29 8s 7d
1471	(70) £29 12s 4d		£15 0s 0d		£31 19s 11d
1481	£29 3s 7d		£14 4s 3d		£30 2s 9d
1491	(93) £31 1s 11d		£14 13s 0d		£30 2s 9d
1501	£31 16s 6d		£14 4s 6d		£29 2s 11d
1511	(10) £30 6s 2d		£14 11s 6d		£28 17s 10d
1521	£30 13s 4d		£29 8s 10d		

Notes: The figures for Coombe Bisset and Durrington include all the manorial rents including the lease of the demesne. The Bromham figures include two major changes resulting from administrative and not necessarily economic developments. The rise by 1411 was probably the result of some piecemeal leasing of parts of the demesne from 1403, and commuting the ploughing works by 1411. That in 1451, resulted from the final leasing of the demesnes in 1443 and the addition of a rent of £8 per year. Where the relevant account is missing and that from a nearby year has been used, this has been indicated by placing the year in brackets.
Sources: TNA: PRO SC6/1045/14–1049/5; Hen VII/892–903; Hen VIII/3939–43; WCM 4620–4752, 5929–6079.

Aldbourne, Collingbourne and Everleigh, by contrast to the situation at Trowbridge, in the heart of the cloth-producing area.[14] Elsewhere, at Bromham, in west Wiltshire, rents fluctuated more from year to year than on most manors and reached a peak in the 1430s, partly as a result of leasing extra land and the remaining works. There was no evidence of a rise or of a fall in entry fines here, although the high level of fines for three holdings in the last surviving court rolls (1433–6) may represent an increased demand for land. This possibility is reinforced by the totals for the court profits (Table 12.3). As on other manors, these had shrunk earlier in the century but now recovered to the levels of the late fourteenth century.

Some manors showed signs of slackening demand through declining rent totals. Two groups are of particular interest. In the south, the small chalkland manors of Stockton, Coombe Bisset and Kingston Deverill showed evidence of difficulty (Table 12.4). The first two might have been affected by any shrinkage of the cloth industry in the immediate area of Salisbury during the second and third decades of the century.[15] Stockton saw a fall in the profits of the court, with these almost halving between 1399–1410 and 1411–21, and the downward trend continued thereafter (Table 12.5). ntry fines were reduced after about 1400. But at Stockton and to a substantial degree at Coombe Bisset the main fall in rent occurred in the demesne lease, especially in the

---

14. Tabulated in J.N. Hare, 'Lord and tenant in Wiltshire, c.1380–1520, with particular reference to regional and seigneurial variations', PhD thesis (London, 1976), 151.
15. A.R. Bridbury, *Medieval English clothmaking: an economic survey* (London, 1982), 68–70.

The growth of the cloth industry

Plate 11.2 Westwood church, with a new tower built by the wealthy clothier and lessee, Thomas Horton.

The industry changed in more than just its location. Increasingly, in the late fifteenth century, Wiltshire produced the heavy undyed, heavily fulled cloth rather than the dyed cloths or rays of Salisbury or the scarlets of Castle Combe. The west of Wiltshire and the Frome valley had already become noted for their white broadcloths in the early and mid-fifteenth century, although they had also produced coloured cloth. It was from these areas that Thomas Kitson bought his supplies of undyed cloth early in the sixteenth century.[73] But this was merely one part of the county's industry. Elsewhere, Salisbury's production remained extensive, albeit declining in relative terms, and that of Marlborough probably grew: both focused on the lighter dyed and lightly fulled cloths.

The impact of the cloth industry

The cloth industry was both urban and increasingly rural. Towns were places of production and marketing. Neighbouring Somerset had led the way in developing rural manufactures, and nowhere was this more obvious than at Pensford, where by 1395/6, a new settlement sealed more cloths than anywhere else in the county. This rural centre showed a larger individual scale of operations than the traditional towns of

---

73. Carus-Wilson, 'Woollen industry before 1550', 138, 134.

the industry, averaging 83 dozens by comparison with Bath (57) and Wells (22).[74] This smaller individual scale of activity in these older centres was probably also a feature of towns elsewhere. At Salisbury average production was at the equivalent of 43 dozens per year, although this included some very substantial traders. John Coscoumbe, the largest producer in 1396/7, had 304 cloths sealed (or twice that, if converted to dozens). At Winchester average production was at the equivalent of 20 dozens per year.[75] Variations in the scale of production between different areas are also suggested by the 1467 aulnage accounts. Most areas were assessed at an average of 20 or fewer, but the main west Wiltshire area was substantially higher, with 47 at Westbury Hundred and 159 in Bradford Hundred.[76] Elsewhere, a similar contrast between rural and urban industry can be seen in the Essex and Suffolk area, as between Lavenham and Colchester in the 1470s.[77]

In west Wiltshire, cases where these clothiers were making individual bargains of about £100 in the fifteenth century have already been examined. Such major deals must have been based largely on merchants purchasing cloth rather than making it themselves. Some large-scale clothiers were active in both production and trade. In the early sixteenth century many of the west Wiltshire clothiers also engaged in agriculture, as with John Flower of Potterne, Robert Whitaker alias Bathe of Bishopstrowe, Henry Long of Whaddon and Henry Goldney alias Farnewell of Chippenham.[78] Some, such as Thomas Lovell of Trowbridge, a clothier and master mason, were active in other crafts.[79]

With the exception of William Stumpe's boom-time production in the monastic buildings at Malmesbury in the 1540s, cloth was made in workshops and homes. Even Leland's comments about Stumpe having filled every corner of the abbey buildings with looms should not create the idea of some sort of proto-factory. At his death he left his looms to his younger sons: the elder of the two received 10 and the younger received the rest, presumably fewer, suggesting a total of less than 20 looms. The importance of heavy fulling in the west Wiltshire area is also suggested by the fact that many of the great clothiers, such as Stowford, Adlam, Horton, Bailey and Langford, possessed their own fulling mills. Such large capital investment probably affected the structure of the industry in this part of the county.[80]

Most wealthy clothiers employed labour, and this could be on a significant scale. Richard Halwey of Castle Combe had seven servants. John Briggs of Salisbury, who died in 1491, described himself as a clothier and his will shows that he had at least two broad looms and a kersey loom, and employed three journeyman weavers and five household servants (including three women). In Salisbury in 1524 half the

---

74. TNA: PRO E101/343/28.
75. Calculated from TNA: PRO E101/343/28; Chandler, *Endless Street*, 259; Keene, *Survey of medieval Winchester*, 316.
76. TNA: PRO E101/345/9; Heytesbury Hundred, with an average of 34, occupied an intermediate position.
77. Britnell, *Colchester*, 184.
78. Ramsay, *Wiltshire woollen industry*, 12–13.
79. J. Harvey, *English medieval architects*, 2nd edn (Gloucester, 1984), 190.
80. Carus-Wilson. 'Woollen industry before 1550', 136, 142–4.

population were assessed on wages.[81] William Salter of Devizes operated on a smaller scale but bequeathed two looms, one of them to his apprentice.[82] Below such men lay a tier of independent producers who made the cloth and then took it to the nearest market to sell to one of the clothiers. Some of these may have operated at a small scale or on a part-time basis, mixing agriculture with part-time weaving. Others worked as weaving labourers for individual clothiers, and may be recorded in wills when a grateful clothier made bequests. In some cases clothiers probably provided the raw materials for those who wove and spun, and paid for what was done, but the evidence is very elusive.[83]

But how much impact did the industry have on the surrounding areas? Postan was cautious in his assessment of its impact on a national level, suggesting that it might have occupied 0.65 per cent of the population, at the most, to produce the cloths that were exported.[84] But the potential variables are immense. What were the cost of the various labour inputs into cloth production?[85] How did trends in production compare with those of exports? What was happening to demand in the domestic market, at a time when, in per capita terms, people were better off and had more money to spend? Dyer has suggested that, in 1500, domestic demand may have been twice that of exports.[86] Cloth manufacturing also generated further jobs in processing the product. In Heytesbury Hundred in 1379 16 weavers and 17 fullers were recorded, but there were also 24 tailors and 4 drapers.[87] Clothiers and clothworkers increased the demand for food, for food products and for consumer goods: in the well-documented manor of Castle Combe butchers, bakers and fishmongers came in from neighbouring towns to sell their wares. Above all, the clothworkers were not thinly spread throughout the country but were concentrated in particular places, and this greatly increased the economic impact of the industry. On a regional level, the west country produced 54 per cent of the country's cloth in the 1390s, but a few years before, in 1377, it had possessed only 14 per cent of the population. For Wiltshire, the figures were 14.8 per cent of cloth and only 3.4 per cent of population.[88] National figures that ignore this regional specialisation and impact are potentially misleading. But such industrial growth also left these areas vulnerable to industrial recession.

Why did the cloth industry develop so spectacularly in west Wiltshire? The area possessed the natural benefits of local supplies of wool and fuller's earth (in the

---

81. Bridbury, *Medieval English clothmaking*, 78–9; W.G. Hoskins, 'English provincial towns in the early sixteenth century', in P. Clark (ed.), *The early modern town: a reader* (London, 1976), 101.
82. J. Waylen, *Chronicles of the Devizes, being a history of the castle, parks and borough of that name* (London, 1839), 284.
83. Ramsay, *Wiltshire woollen industry*, 14–16; Carus-Wilson, 'Woollen industry before 1550', 145–6.
84. M.M. Postan, 'The fifteenth century', in M.M. Postan (ed.), *The Cambridge economic history of Europe*, i, *The agrarian life of the Middle Ages*, 2nd edn (Cambridge, 1966), 45; and 'Some agrarian evidence of declining population in the later Middle Ages', in his *Essays on medieval agriculture*, 198.
85. A point emphasised by Carus-Wilson, *Medieval Merchant Venturers*, 261.
86. C. Dyer, *An age of transition? Economy and society in the later Middle Ages* (Oxford, 2005), 150.
87. TNA: PRO E179/194/42a.
88. Figures calculated from Gray, 'Production and exportation of English woollens'; R.B. Dobson, *The peasants' revolt of 1381* (London, 1970), 55–7. The figures exclude Berkshire.

Cotswolds and outcropping under the chalk), but both of these could have been brought from outside. Joan Thirsk has explained its location in terms of the different farming regions and practices within the county, the cloth industry growing in the non-manorialised 'cheese' region of the county.[89] Such a correlation may have helped to sustain the industry in the sixteenth and seventeenth centuries, but it seems less convincing as an explanation of the origins of the industry. In the 1390s it was in the chalklands, as around Salisbury, where the manor was still most firmly entrenched and cloth production was dominant. The west Wiltshire production area grew in the late fourteenth and fifteenth centuries, but it included the chalkland area of the upper Wylye valley, where the manorial structures remained intact. As late as 1467 Heytesbury Hundred was responsible for 19 per cent of Wiltshire's production.[90] Yet the west Wiltshire area remained ripe for development, if cloth production were to expand further in the west of England. It was located between two existing industrial areas, Salisbury and east Somerset, that had both already gone through rapid industrial expansion and might have difficulty in growing further. It already had cloth-producing centres that could provide a basis for the future development of the industry here. Its streams and its fuller's earth were needed for the heavily fulled cloth that was in high demand, and on which west Wiltshire was increasingly to focus. The nature of the contrasting farming regions and the availability of labour may therefore have had a greater impact on the longevity of the industry here than on its initial location. This was a period when the decline of the manorial structures within the Cotswolds and claylands saw the break-up of demesnes and customary holdings. These changes would have helped to provide opportunities for cottagers and part-time employment and would have sustained the industry in later centuries.

---

89. J. Thirsk, 'Industries in the countryside', in F.J. Fisher (ed.), *Essays in the economic and social history of Tudor and Stuart England* (Cambridge, 1961), 70–76.
90. TNA: PRO E101/345/9.

Chapter 12

Growth and recession: a chronology

A number of general themes have emerged in previous chapters. Wiltshire had inherited regional patterns of rural society that were reinforced in this period, and became key elements in its history during the next few centuries. The contrasts between the chalk and cheese, between large-scale capitalist farming and the world of the family farm, were already apparent and growing. As in other places, the later Middle Ages saw a general demographic decline, but here other developments ran counter to this trend. Above all, the growth of the cloth industry generated increased local demand for work and increased the incentive for people to migrate between areas. Labour was needed to make cloth and to provide the food, consumer goods and services needed by an increasing industrial population. Finally, within the period of study, there were chronological divisions that need to be explained, such as those between phases of growth and recession.

These developments were not unique to Wiltshire and reflect historians' recent concerns about the regional nature of agriculture, of agrarian society, and of regional economies.[1] A clearer view of society in the later Middle Ages has been emerging which combines a decline in the overall population with a growing commercialisation of the economy;[2] it is both more complex and more interesting than that hitherto available. As John Hatcher has remarked, 'The more that is discovered about the experience of the later Middle Ages, the more difficult it becomes to squeeze the emergent facts into a single descriptive or explanatory model.'[3] This chapter seeks to integrate the details discussed in earlier parts of the book into a coherent economic chronology.[4]

Manorial accounts may help to establish economic trends and the fluctuating demand for land. The study of individual well-documented manors in Wiltshire

---

1. J. Thirsk, 'The farming regions of England', in Thirsk (ed.), *The agrarian history of England and Wales: vol. 4, 1500–1640* (Cambridge, 1967) E. Miller (ed.), *The agrarian history of England and Wales: vol. 3, 1348–1500* (Cambridge, 1991); J. Hatcher, *Plague, population and the English economy, 1348–1530* (Basingstoke, 1977); and *Rural economy and society in the duchy of Cornwall, 1300–1500* (Cambridge, 1970), 148–73. More recently, and for neighbouring areas, M. Yates, 'Change and continuities in rural society from the later Middle Ages to the sixteenth century: the contribution of west Berkshire', *EcHR*, 52 (1999), 617–37, and now her *Town and countryside in western Berkshire, c.1327–c.1600* (Woodbridge, 2007); J.N. Hare, 'Regional prosperity in fifteenth-century England: some evidence from Wessex', in M. Hicks (ed.), *Revolution and consumption in late medieval England* (Woodbridge, 2001), 105–26.
2. R.H. Britnell, *The commercialisation of English society, 1000–1500*, 2nd edn (Manchester, 1990); J. Day, *The medieval market economy* (Oxford, 1987).
3. Hatcher, 'Great slump', 239.
4. R.H. Britnell, 'The economic context', in A.J. Pollard (ed.), *The Wars of the Roses* (Basingstoke, 1995); J. Hatcher, 'The great slump of the mid-fifteenth century', in R.H. Britnell and J. Hatcher (eds), *Progress and problems in medieval England: essays in honour of Edward Miller* (Cambridge, 1996), 236–72.

A Prospering Society

Table 12.1
Movement of rent income (in %).

		1405–45	1445–65	1465–1500
Northern clay vale	Poole	-27.4	+2.0	+6.3
	Oaksey	-23.7	+0.8	+0.5
	Stratton	-17		
	Wroughton			+3.7
Central clay vale	Bromham		-1.3	+5.7
West Wiltshire textile area (core production areas)	Trowbridge	+3	-1.3	+9.0
	Castle Combe	+2.4		
	Heytesbury	+23.7	-12.9	+6.8
	Sutton Veny	+9.3	-9.6	+4.0
Vale of Wardour	Teffont		-23.7	
Salisbury area	Coombe Bisset	-27.0	-4.3	+3.6
	Homington		-1.7	
Salisbury Plain and Marlborough Downs	Winterbourne Stoke		-15	+1.8
	Stockton	-4.2		
	Durrington	+3.6	-16	+7.5
	Upavon	-0.6		
	Collingbourne Ducis	+1.4	-1.8	+8
	Everleigh	-1.0	+0.8	+4.0
	Aldbourne			+1.5
	Willsford	+9.7		+2.6
	All Cannings		-0.8	+1.2
	Urchfont			+1.7

Notes: The comparison between the rents at the beginning of a period and its end are based on the same items. Where there is doubt about the strict compatability of the two figures the comparison has been left out. The rent items may, however, be changed between one period and another. Figures are taken from up to + or – 5 years beyond the official start and finish dates of the various periods.
The figures are mapped in J.N. Hare, 'Growth and recession in the fifteenth-century economy: the Wiltshire textile industry and the countryside', EcHR, 2nd series 52 (1999), 7–8.

suggested that the century should be divided into three phases: a period of growth in the first half of the fifteenth century continuing late-fourteenth-century developments; the period of mid-century recession from about 1450 to the 1480s; and, finally, the period of late-fifteenth-century growth. These phases coincided with the changing fortunes of the cloth industry. On the basis of this earlier work, it seems valid to compare an account for the decade 1400–1410 with one from the end of the first period, 1440–50, or to compare the latter with one from the 1460s or 1470s (Table 12.1). This chronology forms the basic structure of the rest of this chapter. Such comparisons are possible only where we are comparing rents rather than items that fluctuate dramatically from year to year, such as totals from the sale of produce. Once the demesnes were leased, they too counted as a rent, although the annual fluctuations generated by harvest and market conditions were now much reduced. Rents now generally remained constant from year to year, although the amount actually collected might vary from year to year. Leasehold rents have therefore been included but only where the items incorporated in the lease have not changed during the intervening period: thus the inclusion of demesne arable in a lease from which it was formerly excluded would render valid comparison impossible.

Growth

The later fourteenth century saw the dramatic growth of the Wiltshire cloth industry, which, by 1400, became of national importance. The industry was dominated by Salisbury and its neighbouring valleys, but a substantial and more rural industry was emerging in the west of Wiltshire. Such growth helped to maintain a flourishing agricultural sector. The last two decades of the century saw demesne agriculture on some of the chalkland estates reach a high point of activity, as on the estates of Winchester Cathedral Priory or those of the bishopric of Winchester. The pastoral sector, including sheep, pigs and rabbits, saw particular expansion. The arable demesne of the bishopric had seen substantial shrinkage before the Black Death, as the bishops had sought to make the most of the high demand for land. But there is no evidence of any parallel development on the priory estates, where arable farming was as extensive as ever. At Durrington, in a long list of 87 land transactions from 1377 to 1509, 4 out of only 5 purchases of reversions came from the period 1383–91, suggesting this was a period of high demand for land in the rural hinterland. It was also a time of rapid turnover of peasant names in this period, here and at Coombe Bisset, together suggesting considerable activity on the land market. At Stockton the growth in demand was reflected in the state of entry fines, with all 5 half-virgates recorded between 1388 and 1403 producing fines of £1 or more. At Downton the revenues of the rectory were at their peak in the decades either side of 1400, while at Bromham, away from the chalklands, agricultural revenue also reached new heights.

The cloth industry continued to expand in the first half of the fifteenth century, despite some difficulties and cut-backs in the early decades. These were reflected in a temporary fall in exports from 1403, but subsequently the situation recovered and expansion continued. The earlier export levels of the 1390s were again reached in the 1420s and 30s, and achieved a new and higher level in the 1440s. Such trends had implications for those parts of England that were dependent for their livelihood on cloth-making. Salisbury remained an affluent and important manufacturing centre, but showed signs of difficulty at the start of the century before recovery set in, and its cloth production declined in relative terms compared with the rest of the county. By 1467 the west Wiltshire area produced about 70 per cent of the county's cloth (see Table 11.1). Salisbury's production had fallen sharply, as had that of Devizes, and the rural districts had grown. Here, as elsewhere, cloth-making in the fifteenth century both developed in existing areas and expanded beyond these. In some counties, as in Somerset, production was geographically relatively static, but in Hampshire the industry opened up in new areas in the north of the county.[5]

The expansion of the west Wiltshire textile area increased the demand for land. Trowbridge was one of its most important centres and showed slightly rising rent totals (Table 12.2), with rents rising in the 1440s, and signs of growth in court profits.

---

5. J.N. Hare, 'Pensford and the growth of the cloth industry in late medieval Somerset', *Proceedings of the Somerset Archaeology and Natural History Soc*, 147 (2003), 173–80, and 'Regional prosperity', 114–15, and 'Church-building and urban prosperity on the eve of the reformation: Basingstoke and its parish church', *PHFCAS*, 62 (2007), 185–7.

Table 12.2
Rents: the duchy of Lancaster.

Date	Collingbourne	Everleigh	Trowbridge
1373	£75 16s 2½d		
1393	£72 13s 9½d		
1400	£30 19s 2d	£27 19s 1d	£74 8s 5½d
1406	£30 18s 11½d	£74 4s 2¾d	
1412	£31 16s 11½d	£27 15s 2¾d	£73 10s 5d
1417	£31 14s 11¾d	£28 0s 3¾d	£76 19s 9¾d
1431	£30 12s 7¾d	£27 5s 7d	£76 12s 11½d
1444	£31 9s 3½d*	£27 13s 5½d*	£76 8s 10½d
1451	£30 18s 11¾d*	£27 10s 10½d*	£77 11s 5½d
1456	£76 12s 7d		
1462	£30 15s 9½d*	£27 17s 7¾d*	£75 8s 1½d
1481	£28 6s 1½d*	£76 18s 10¾d	
1505	£33 19s 3½d*	£29 3s 4d*	£82 3s 0d

Notes: In order to allow for the effects of leasing the demesne pastures at Everleigh and Collingbourne, the starred totals have been adjusted. The value of the leased pastures has been extracted by assuming that these are represented by the increase in the value of the lease immediately after the inclusion of the pastures. The amount deducted was £8 13s 4d in the case of Collingbourne and £3 13s 4d for Everleigh.
Sources: TNA: PRO DL29/682/11039; 686/11123; 687/11134; 690/11185; 728/11981; 728/11991; 730/12007; 731/12016; 731/12023; 732/12034; 733/12043; 734/12044; DL28/23/12A.

Rent totals also rose in the 1440s at Warminster, another major urban cloth centre.[6] Production expanded into the countryside, as around Heytesbury and Warminster, in areas where it had already developed by 1379. Rent rolls showed significant growth on the manors belonging to the Hungerfords, as at Heytesbury, and here they also invested heavily in a new fulling mill. Other mills appeared at Warminster and Boyton,[7] while Hindon, a market centre for the neighbouring manors, showed evidence of prosperity and expansion.[8] Further north, Castle Combe provides a classic example of rapid rural industrial growth.[9]

In general, we lack sources that enable us to track the movement of people on a statistical basis. The alien subsidy of 1440 provides lists of foreigners who were resident or held land[10] and the Wiltshire returns seem substantial, but are less full than for many other counties, particularly coastal ones. Fortunately, they do seem to provide the place of origin with some consistency: of the total of 369, 30 were 'Duche', 214 were various types of Frenchmen and 125 were Irish.[11] These figures provide a minimal indication of the scale of immigration, but, more importantly, if the Irish and the French were being drawn into this area, would not those nearer at hand (the Welsh or other English) also come? To provide a crude indicator of the scale of

---

6. TNA: PRO DL29/733/12041 & 12043; WRO 845/manorial papers/14.
7. Carus-Wilson, 'Woollen industry before 1550', 129.
8. See above, Chapter 10.
9. See above, Chapter 11.
10. S.L. Thrupp, 'A survey of the alien population of England in 1440', *Speculum*, 32 (1957), 262–72, provides an introduction to this source.
11. Ibid., 270–72.

Table 12.3
Court receipts: Bromham.

	No. of years	Decennial average
1381–90	(8)	£4 17s 4½d
1391–1400	(4)	£3 5s 0d
1401–1410	(4)	£2 17s 7d
1411–20	(8)	£2 15s 11d
1421–30	(5)	£1 19s 9½d
1431–40	(7)	£3 8s 8d
1441–50	(7)	£3 13s 8d
1451–60	(8)	£1 5s 9d
1461–70	(4)	£1 10s 7d
1471–80	(4)	17s 11d
1481–90	(7)	£1 10s 8d
1491–1500	(7)	£2 9s 2½d
1501–10	(5)	£2 13s 9d
1511–20	(5)	£3 6s 0d
1521–26	(3)	£1 11s 0d

Sources: TNA: PRO SC6/1045/23–1049/5; Hen VII/892–903; Hen VIII/3939–43.

such immigration, these figures will also be expressed as a percentage of the town or area's taxable population in 1377. This ignores the impact of any urban growth since that date, the slight variation between the starting age for the two taxes (14 in 1377 and 12 in 1440) and the virtual absence of women from the alien returns, although not from the poll tax returns.[12]

Alien immigration seems to have been a particular feature of the towns, two of which lay outside the west Wiltshire area: Salisbury (96 aliens, or the equivalent of 3% of taxpayers in the 1377 total) and Marlborough (27, or 3%). The west Wiltshire cloth towns also figure prominently in the returns: Devizes (24: 4%), Chippenham (16: 6%), Bradford (16: 7%), Warminster (14: 4%) and Malmesbury (15: 4%). But aliens also migrated to the countryside. Chippenham Hundred (excluding the town itself) included the area around the Castle Combe industry and had the largest number of aliens (33, of whom 8 were at Castle Combe itself). There were 8 in Whorwellsdown Hundred, with 3 Frenchmen in the noted cloth-producing centre of Steeple Ashton. Near Devizes, there were 15 in Swanborough Hundred, including 5 at Lavington.[13] There was also notable growth in the Bradford area. Immigration from France may also reflect the impact of the growing trade between England and northern France during the Lancastrian occupation, and demographic movement in the aftermath of war and occupation. Two-thirds of the aliens in Salisbury were French or Breton.

Beyond this cloth-producing region lay its agricultural hinterland. This was an area of continuity. Here rent totals were approximately stable or rising, underpinned by the prosperity and demands of industry. This was the situation in the chalklands at Durrington, Everleigh and Collingbourne (see Table 12.2). But, below the surface, there were hints of difficulties. On the duchy of Lancaster estate, court receipts fell at

---

12. The Wiltshire account is TNA: PRO E179/196/100. The 1377 figures are printed in Beresford, 'Poll tax payers of 1377', in VCH *Wilts* 4.
13. Lavington seems to have acquired a fulling mill in the fifteenth century (Carus-Wilson, 'Woollen industry before 1550', 131).

A Prospering Society

Table 12.4
Rents: Bromham, Coombe Bisset, Durrington.

		Bromham		Coombe Bisset		Durrington
1345		£15 6s 2¾d				
1377		£18 6s 10d				
1381		£19 0s 0¼d	(84)	£23 0s 2d		
1391	(92)	£18 2s 3¾d		£22 19s 2d	(90)	£40 0s 0d
1401		£18 2s 8¼d		£20 14s 2d	(02)	£36 0s 0d
1411		£24 2s 3¾d		£23 0s 0d		£36 0s 0d
1421		£24 9s 1½d		£19 16s 8d		£37 6s 8d
1431		£23 17s 7¼d		£19 9s 0d		£37 6s 8d
1441		£22 5s 1¼d		£15 7s 0d		£37 6s 8d
1451		£30 6s 1¼d		£14 10s 0d	(47)	£38 2s 8d
1461	(59)	£29 13s 4¼d		£14 0s 10¾d		£29 8s 7d
1471	(70)	£29 12s 4d		£15 0s 0d		£31 19s 11d
1481		£29 3s 7d		£14 4s 3d		£30 2s 9d
1491	(93)	£31 1s 11d		£14 13s 0d		£30 2s 9d
1501		£31 16s 6d		£14 4s 6d		£29 2s 11d
1511	(10)	£30 6s 2d		£14 11s 6d		£28 17s 10d
1521		£30 13s 4d		£29 8s 10d		

Notes: The figures for Coombe Bisset and Durrington include all the manorial rents including the lease of the demesne. The Bromham figures include two major changes resulting from administrative and not necessarily economic developments. The rise by 1411 was probably the result of some piecemeal leasing of parts of the demesne from 1403, and commuting the ploughing works by 1411. That in 1451, resulted from the final leasing of the demesnes in 1443 and the addition of a rent of £8 per year. Where the relevant account is missing and that from a nearby year has been used, this has been indicated by placing the year in brackets.
Sources: TNA: PRO SC6/1045/14–1049/5; Hen VII/892–903; Hen VIII/3939–43; WCM 4620–4752, 5929–6079.

Aldbourne, Collingbourne and Everleigh, by contrast to the situation at Trowbridge, in the heart of the cloth-producing area.[14] Elsewhere, at Bromham, in west Wiltshire, rents fluctuated more from year to year than on most manors and reached a peak in the 1430s, partly as a result of leasing extra land and the remaining works. There was no evidence of a rise or of a fall in entry fines here, although the high level of fines for three holdings in the last surviving court rolls (1433–6) may represent an increased demand for land. This possibility is reinforced by the totals for the court profits (Table 12.3). As on other manors, these had shrunk earlier in the century but now recovered to the levels of the late fourteenth century.

Some manors showed signs of slackening demand through declining rent totals. Two groups are of particular interest. In the south, the small chalkland manors of Stockton, Coombe Bisset and Kingston Deverill showed evidence of difficulty (Table 12.4). The first two might have been affected by any shrinkage of the cloth industry in the immediate area of Salisbury during the second and third decades of the century.[15] Stockton saw a fall in the profits of the court, with these almost halving between 1399–1410 and 1411–21, and the downward trend continued thereafter (Table 12.5). ntry fines were reduced after about 1400. But at Stockton and to a substantial degree at Coombe Bisset the main fall in rent occurred in the demesne lease, especially in the

---

14. Tabulated in J.N. Hare, 'Lord and tenant in Wiltshire, *c.*1380–1520, with particular reference to regional and seigneurial variations', PhD thesis (London, 1976), 151.
15. A.R. Bridbury, *Medieval English clothmaking: an economic survey* (London, 1982), 68–70.

Table 12.5
Court receipts: Stockton.

	No. of years	Decennial average
1399–1400	(11)	£4 3s 4d
1411–22	(7)	£2 7s 4d
1427–47	(11)	£1 2s 8d
1451–6	(2)	£2 17s 4d
1472–87	(4)	£1 4s 0d
1490–9	(5)	17s 5½d
1506–27	(5)	19s 8d

Sources: BL Add Rl 24395–9, 24713, 24400–16; 24875; 24417–24; 24429, 24426, 24430, 24432–33; WRO 906/SC7–10, 906/SC17.

1430s,[16] pointing to difficulties either with agriculture, in marketing agricultural surpluses, or perhaps in the local cloth industry. At Downton the cash generated by the rectory reached a peak in the 1390s and first decade of the following century, reaching over £100 in some years, and then fell in the next two decades, particularly in the 1420s. There was some recovery, although this was not consistent, and Winchester College generally received a figure approaching nearly £60.[17] The financial problems of the 1420s were partly driven by a failure in the barley harvests, as shown in the Downton tithes.[18] The difficulties of this crop were also seen on the bishopric demesne here, and yields seem to have been low in 1423, 1426 and 1429. Such difficulties with barley were also more widespread, as at Urchfont in 1421, 1423, 1426 and 1429,[19] and can be seen in southern England more widely. The bishopric of Winchester's accounts suggest that there were some very dry periods during the growing seasons of the 1420s, as in 1420, 1423, 1424 and possibly 1425, and wet harvests. Further east, on the Battle Abbey lands in west Sussex, the decade was characterised by excessive rain and poor spring crops. The precise weather conditions must, of course, remain a matter for speculation,[20] but such difficulties penalised those areas that had shifted to greater dependence on malt production. In Wiltshire the south probably suffered both from such overdependence and from the relative lack of subsequent growth: while by 1450 the rest of the county had recovered from

---

16. BL Add Rl 24396–24417 & WRO 906/SC7–10, the drop was a single one from £24 to £23 in the value of the lease between 1417/8 and 1419/20; the fall at Coombe Bisset was mainly the result of a succession of reductions in the lease of the manor (rents and demesne), initially at £22 and with a reduction in turn by £2 in 1421, £4 in 1437, to £6 in 1438, and £7 in 1451 (WCM 4630, 4651, 4667, 4668, 4680; there were also some individual reductions in customary rents); WRO 192/28.
17. Calculated from WCM 5362–5519.
18. See above, Chapter 5.
19. WRO 192/20. An assessment of the grain produced was included on the court rolls of the period. Normally the demesne produced more wheat than barley, but in four of the twelve years this was reversed, showing a concentration in the 1420s.
20. J.Z. Titow,'Le climat à travers les rôles de comptabilité de l'évêché de Winchester (1350–1458)', Annales Économies Sociétés, Civilisations, 25 (1970), 337–40, 342; P.F. Brandon, 'Late-medieval weather in Sussex and its agricultural significance', Transactions of Institutte of British Geographers, 54 (1971), 4, 7, 12.

the problems of the 1420s, such an upturn was much less evident in the south.

There was also evidence of decline in the manors in the north of the county, with falling rents in the first part of the century at Oaksey, Poole and Stratton.[21] Here the cloth industry had much less influence and the declining demand reflected the situation found elsewhere in England. Moreover, in these areas the more general demographic fall would have been accentuated by the movement of people to the more prosperous cloth-producing areas nearby. At Wroughton entry fines fell from about 1420. Coleshill, immediately over the county border in Berkshire, showed all the signs of declining population: land was surrendered, became vacant and fell into the lord's hand, the departures of serfs grew and enclosed fields emerged.[22]

Recession

The cloth industry and the countryside were transformed by the deep depression in international trade that hit the economy in the middle of the century.[23] National exports had reached a peak in the 1440s and fell to almost half this by the 1460s.[24] The collapse was sudden – between 1446–8 and 1448–50 cloth exports fell by 35 per cent – and would have struck particularly heavily those areas that had become so dependent on the cloth industry during the preceding period of growth.[25] A European trade recession[26] now created difficulties for the cloth export trade and thus for particular parts of Wiltshire. Such a recession did not merely reduce employment in the cloth industry itself but would also have hit the wool producers (for export and import markets) and those who produced the consumer goods and services that had depended on a prosperous cloth industry. The fortunes of the cloth industry, of other manufactures and of agriculture had become intertwined.

The slump in cloth exports in about 1450 was sudden and exacerbated by government actions in three major market areas. The capture of the Bay fleet had been backed by the government and had led to the towns of the Hanseatic league launching an embargo on English exports which, had it been fully effective, would have ruined the important markets of Germany and the Baltic. The resumption of the French war, the loss of France and the continued conflict between the two countries led to disruption of the French market which continued until the treaty of Picquigny in 1475. Finally, conflict with Burgundy had led to a loss of the Flemish market.[27] The dramatic fall in exports threw people out of work and led to a drop in the price of cloth

---

21. Tabulated in J.N. Hare, 'Growth and recession in the fifteenth-century economy: the Wiltshire textile industry and the countryside', *Economic History Review*, 2nd series 52 (1999), 16, table 4; Stratton in MCM 4321b.
22. R. Faith, 'Berkshire: fourteenth and fifteenth centuries', in Harvey, *The peasant land market*, 154–7.
23. Hatcher, 'Great slump'.
24. R.H. Britnell, *Growth and decline in Colchester, 1300–1525* (Cambridge, 1986), 44.
25. E.M. Carus-Wilson and O. Coleman, *England's export trade, 1275–1547* (Oxford, 1963).
26. Day, *The medieval market economy*.
27. M.M. Postan, 'The economic and political relations of England and the Hanse from 1400 to 1475', in Power and Postan (eds), *Studies in English trade in the fifteenth century*, 127–9, appendix C, 407; H.L. Gray, 'The production and exportation of English woollens in the fourteenth century', *EcHR*, 29 (1924), 23; E.M. Carus-Wilson, *Medieval merchant venturers* (London, 1954), 42, 272; Carus-Wilson and Coleman, *England's export trade*, 8–9; Britnell, 'The economic context', 44–6.

and, with it, the demand for wool (although this was also affected by falling wool exports). In areas in which all aspects of the economy had become dependent on the prosperity of the cloth industry, the sudden collapse would have generated unemployment, under-employment and widespread social discontent, as seen in the Wiltshire risings of 1450.

In 1450 William Ayscough, the bishop of Salisbury and a leading member of Henry VI's unpopular government, was murdered at Edington Priory church. In addition, his property (moveables and residential) was attacked at Potterne, Ramsbury, Woodford and Salisbury. It has been traditional to view this murder as the product of political discontent focused on the unpopular ministers of Henry VI at a time of very obvious political failure, with the loss of France: it thus appeared as a pale reflection of Cade's revolt.[28] Political protest was certainly an important aspect of what happened in 1450; the government was unpopular on both a national and a local scale, while the defeat of royal forces at Sevenoaks and the king's retreat to Leicester had demonstrated its weakness. The rebels had a political programme which highlighted Ayscough as a minister who should be punished, targeting him and his possessions just as elsewhere they had already killed other ministers: the Duke of Suffolk, Bishop Moleyns, Lord Saye and Sele and William Crowmer. They attacked Ayscough's property just as elsewhere others attacked that of other royal ministers: the bishops of Norwich and of Lichfield, the abbot of Gloucester, and later the duke of Somerset. Ayscough probably knew the danger and was heading for what he hoped would be a safe, and perhaps defensible, base well away from London, at Sherborne in Dorset.[29]

But what happened in 1450 was more than just a political protest, and economic discontent probably lay at its heart. Here, as elsewhere in England, the cloth areas seem to have been particularly prone to discontent at this time, and Wiltshire seems to have been generally troubled in the summer of that year. There had been some attacks on the bishop's property before matters peaked on 28–29 June, when the bishop's baggage train was attacked at Maiden Bradley and he himself was attacked and killed in Edington; both places were in the area of the west Wiltshire textile industry. Most of those indicted for the attacks at Edington came from within six miles of the village. Two different indictments give figures of 40 and 600 for the number of those involved, while 74 were individually indicted. On the same day over 300 men were said to have congregated in Salisbury, 25 men being specifically indicted. For several days the city and its surrounding areas seem to have been very disturbed, with the property of the bishop and the canons apparently the focus of conflict. At Salisbury, a crowd estimated at 500 or more broke into the palace and destroyed the muniments and probably damaged the buildings,[30] and the bishop's residence at Woodford was also attacked. His other major houses in Wiltshire, Potterne and

---

28. The risings are discussed in more detail in J.N. Hare,'The Wiltshire risings of 1450: political and economic discontent in mid-fifteenth century England', *Southern History*, 4 (1982), 13–31. E.F. Jacob described them as 'local cases of indiscipline': *The fifteenth century* (Oxford, 1961), 332. The most recent study of Cade's revolt from a political standpoint is I.M.W. Harvey, *Jack Cade's rebellion of 1450* (Oxford, 1991). See also R. Griffiths, *The reign of Henry VI* (London, 1981), 610–65.
29. Hare,'Wiltshire risings', 20, 24.

A Prospering Society

Table 12.6
The Wiltshire risings of 1450: occupational groups of those indicted (percentages).

	Edington	Salisbury 29 June	All episodes 29 June–4 July
Gentlemen and yeomen	15	24	13
Labourers	15	3	12
Agricultural producers	22	0	17
Food trade	10	24	11
Leather trade	0	10	5
Miscellaneous manufactures	0	14	6
Building industry	7	7	7
Cloth industry	23	17	22
Others (double descriptions)	9	0	6
Total number of indictments	68	29	139

Notes: 6 men have double descriptions and have been included as 'others'. The figures are expressed as a percentage of the total number of indictments. Gentleman, yeomen and labourers do not provide an occupational description but have been included here for completeness.
Source: TNA: PRO KB 9/133 and 134/1.

Ramsbury, were attacked in July. Other risings or gatherings occurred during the summer at Tilshead (2 July), Devizes (12 July), when 300 men were said to have been involved, Wilton (20 July), when about 40 were mentioned, at Devizes again (29 July), when an attempt was made to ambush the sheriff of Wiltshire, and finally at Biddeston (31 July). The county remained disturbed in August, with a reference to a further rising in Wiltshire in late July or early August and a report from East Anglia that the Wiltshire area was still heavily disturbed. There was an assembly and intended attack on the parish church of Bradenstoke (20 August) and a large-scale rising at Edington (28 August), followed by a smaller rising at Malmesbury (1 September) and a renewal of trouble at Sherborne (Dorset) (11 September), when a crowd broke into the abbey church. On 20 September the government felt it necessary to commission a powerful group of local lords and gentry to restore order in Wiltshire and the neighbouring counties.[31] Disturbances seem to have been concentrated on Salisbury itself and the west Wiltshire cloth-producing area.

Much of our evidence comes from the indictments brought before a commission of *oyer et terminer* in the following year. The heavy involvement of the cloth industry is also shown by an occupational analysis of those who were indicted. At least 30 per cent of those with occupational descriptions and 22 per cent of all those indicted were engaged in the cloth trade. Moreover, these figures probably underestimate the involvement of this industry because they exclude those with status rather than occupational descriptions or those whose involvement was important but part-time. James Touker of Bradford, yeoman, for instance, was probably James Terumber or

---

30. The extensive rebuilding of the bishop's palace at Salisbury under his successor Bishop Beauchamp may suggest that the buildings there had been severely damaged (RCHM, *Salisbury: the houses of the Close* (London, 1993), 53–72).
31. Hare, 'Wiltshire risings', 15.

Touker of Bradford, one of the great clothiers of the third quarter of the century.[32]

At Salisbury and Sherborne the struggle between civic and ecclesiastical authorities provided a long-running sore. Salisbury, the prosperity of which was heavily dependent on the cloth industry, had its own long-standing quarrels with the bishop; here, relations had soured under Ayscough and the quarrel would break to the surface under his successor, Bishop Beauchamp. A shadowy picture can be built up of some of those involved at Salisbury, but it is not clear how far we should see the unfolding events as part of a conflict between bishop and citizens or between a ruling oligarchy and its inferiors.[33] The indictments generally exclude the greater city landowners, the leading city political figures, or those involved in the long-distance trades, although they include two families involved in such trade and two men described as gentlemen. (The ruling elite and its members, men like John Halle and John Aport, were subsequently to lead the city in the very different and bitter conflict with the bishop for independence.) Nor do the risings seem to have been the work of the poorest sectors of the community, with only one labourer indicted. Instead they probably involved the mainstream of civic life: those in the food, cloth and leather trades (Table 12.6) or men who worked on their own account, such as John Gayne, a carpenter. There were men of substance in their crafts who were on the fringes of civic power, such as Randulph Pakker, William Swyngell and John Cathero, who represented their crafts at a meeting in 1440 and were occasional members of the city council, while Thomas Felde also fell into the latter category. Like the city itself, such men suffered in the economic recession, and local grievances added to national ones. At Sherborne (Dorset) a long-standing conflict between the citizens and their lord, the abbot, focused on the citizens' aspirations for independence expressed in their recent rebuilding of the parish church and the abbey's insistence that it should have a monopoly over baptism. In 1437, tensions had lead to a riot and to the burning of some of the new building works in the abbey. Now, in 1450, changing circumstances led to an armed crowd entering the abbey church and forcing concessions.[34] Sherborne, like Salisbury, was a major cloth-producing centre.

The recession in textile manufacture that fed the Wiltshire risings occurred beyond Wiltshire, as is reflected in events elsewhere. There is much evidence for the heartland of Cade's revolt in Kent, but elsewhere scattered fragments show the wider dispersal of the conflict and general correlation between disorder and cloth production. The risings involved the main commercial centres of Kent; Colchester, Hadleigh and Norwich in East Anglia; Newbury and Hungerford in the Thames valley; somewhere near Gloucester in the Cotswolds; Sherborne in Dorset; and probably Winchester and Coventry.[35]

---

32. Ibid., 17. The figures are calculated from TNA: PRO KB 9/133 and 134/1. The next largest group was the agricultural producers (e.g. husbandmen) with 17%. On Terumber see above pp. 184–5. Of those involved at Edington on 29 June 23% were in the cloth industry, and of those involved in Salisbury there were 17%.
33. For further details of personnel, Hare, 'Wiltshire risings', 22–3; now supplemented by *The first general entry book of the city of Salisbury, 1387–1452*, ed. D.R. Carr, Wiltshire Record Society 54 (Trowbridge, 2001).
34. Hare, 'Wiltshire risings', 23–4.
35. Ibid., 25–7.

The suddenness of the fall in exports in 1450 inaugurated a 20-year period of economic difficulties evidenced wherever English overseas trade can be measured.[36] Here it was probably made worse by Southampton's loss of much of the Italian trade.[37] Such problems would also have created difficulties in those domestic industries that had become dependent on the prosperity of the exporting industries. Falling cloth exports and prices meant that unemployment would be likely to rise and many in work would have less spending power, thus accentuating the domestic depression. At Castle Combe, where growth had been so spectacular, the number of the male wage-earners paying chevage, having risen throughout the first half of the century, dropped sharply in the 1450s and halved from 1450 to 1481 (see Table 11.2). Recession was as dramatic as the earlier growth. Trowbridge, one of the main towns, showed falling rents, generally lower receipts from the manorial courts and growing arrears from 1456.[38] In the west of the county rent falls occurred particularly in cottage tenements at Warminster, Upton Scudamore, Sutton Veny and Heytesbury, reflecting the difficulties among the wage-earners and less well-off during a recession.[39] At Hindon, a textile and marketing centre that had been growing in the early fifteenth century, the court profits fell substantially by 1460 to about half their previous level, and this reduction persisted.[40]

In Salisbury, the mid-century recession were reflected in the concern of the city fathers about vagabondage in the 1450s. This was followed by further dislocation of trading patterns as the Italian trade moved from Southampton to London. The rent of the George Inn fell and the city was unable to raise the full expected rent from land given to it in order to finance obits or prayers for the dead; in the 1470s some ceased to be celebrated. Rent defects from this fund rose dramatically from £2 4s 6d in 1449–50 to £16 14s 8d in 1453–4 and again in the 1470s.[41] The city also showed a decline in its proportion of the woad brought in from Southampton: about 34 per cent of Southampton's woad went to Salisbury in the 1440s, but this fell to only 21 per cent in the 1460s, although it suffered less than its older rival Winchester.[42] Nevertheless, it retained its high standing in taxation and population throughout the later Middle Ages, and kept its position as a major cloth-producing centre. Its temporary difficulties in the early and middle part of the century do not suggest that it was anything other than a busy, bustling and prosperous city, subject to the short-term recessions and tensions that went with urban and industrial life.

The problems of the mid-century were not merely industrial, but also agricultural, with major problems in two related parts of chalkland farming. Wool prices slumped

---

36. Hatcher, 'Great slump', 240–44.
37. Carus-Wilson and Coleman, *England's export trade*.
38. Hare, 'Lord and tenant', table i, 151; TNA: PRO DL29/734/12044, 685/11101, 686/11110, 11113, 11123, 11125.
39. WRO 845/manorial papers/14; TNA: PRO SC6/1061/20, 1059/18, 1054/8.
40. HRO 11 M59 B1/198, 199, 200, 211.
41. WRO B23/1/44/2–8.
42. HMC, *Report on manuscripts in various collections, vol. iv, The Corporation of Salisbury*, London 1907, 201; C. Haskins, *The ancient guilds and companies of Salisbury* (Salisbury, 1912), 291–3; A.D. Brown, *Popular piety in late medieval England: the diocese of Salisbury, 1200–1550* (Oxford, 1995), 167–8; D. Keene, *A survey of medieval Winchester* (Oxford, 1985).

and the villagers suffered whether they produced wool or food for the market or were engaged part-time in industrial activities. Durrington provides a particularly clear and well-documented example of the range of agricultural problems. Here, the rents of the standard virgate tenements were reduced. For several years Winchester College, the lord of the manor, had failed to extract the full rental and part of it had been pardoned. Then, in 1461, it reduced all the rents – a virgate from 20s to 16s and a half virgate from 9s to 7s; as well as the lease of the demesne, some demesne acres and three cottages. The lessee, too, had his rent reduced.[43] Despite this, the lord's revenue continued to fall in the 1460s and 1470s, and there were continued difficulties in collecting the rents. In addition, the lord felt it necessary to spend heavily on his tenant properties, with the 1460s seeing the peak of this expenditure. Arrears rose from £24 in 1470 to £58 in 1479. A year later, John Langford, who had leased until 1478, was pardoned £58 because he had nothing in goods from which it could be raised, and thereafter arrears remained low. Finally, the period 1441–7 saw the rate of family disappearance reach its low point, suggesting a stagnant landmarket in which there was little desire to come into the village or to go elsewhere.[44]

Such difficulties were also found on other chalkland manors. At Winterbourne Stoke, on the Hungerford estate, the entry for decayed rents rose from £2 3s 11d in 1448 to £8 7s 1d in 1465. Rent reductions occurred here on 21 virgates, 2 half-virgates, a parcel of land and only 3 cottages. As at Durrington, it was the main agricultural tenements that saw the greatest rent reductions. At Heytesbury there was a substantial fall in the rent paid for the leased demesne after 1468. Several manors also show evidence of increased difficulty in collecting rents from the 1450s to the 1480s, as at All Cannings, Wroughton and Bromham, the latter two away from the chalk.[45] And these problems continued at Coombe Bisset and Enford in the 1480s.[46] At the former the expected rent income from the manors had fallen substantially in the 1460s and 1470s, and did not recover until the 1490s (see Table 12.4). The wholesale character of the rent cuts at Durrington and Winterbourne Stoke must also raise the question of whether tenants brought collective pressure to bear in order to force rent reductions.[47] Cash liveries fell substantially at Downton rectory in the 1450s (Table 12.7).

Our price data for this area and time are exceedingly limited, but a crucial factor in farmers' problems seems to have been the collapse in wool prices after an earlier period of difficulty.[48] In previous decades the price of wool had averaged 3.9s and 3.7s per stone respectively. In the 1450s it was 2.7s, only 73 per cent of that of the previous decade. While the average price recovered in the 1460s it remained low in the early years of the decade.[49] The difficulties here reflected those found elsewhere.

---

43. WCM 6016. In 1441 there were ten cottages recorded.
44. WCM 6025, 6033–35; above Table 8.1.
45. TNA: PRO SC6/1062/9, 13; Hare, 'Lord and tenant', tables v–vii, 162–4.
46. WCM 4710–20; WCM 6035; Hare, 'Lord and tenant', table vi, 163.
47. C. Dyer, 'A redistribution of incomes in fifteenth century England', in R.H. Hilton (ed.), *Peasants, knights and heretics* (Cambridge, 1976), 206–13.
48. T.H. Lloyd, *The movement of wool prices in medieval England* (Cambridge, 1973), 25–6; Hare, 'Lord and tenant', table vii, 69.
49. Calculated from Lloyd, *Wool prices*, table 1.

The 1450s, 1470s and 1480s were times when the price of wool relative to wheat reached its lowest levels since the thirteenth century.[50] Wool prices in the second half of the century have been calculated at a quarter below that of the first half,[51] although this drop may have been exaggerated by the predominance in the later figures of regions who tended to produce poorer, cheaper wool. In the middle of the century some lords found it impossible to dispose of their wool at acceptable prices and kept it in store for several years, despite the loss that this entailed.[52] Peasant farmers, however, could not afford to wait. In the south of England the difficulties of wool sales encouraged lords to give up their sheep flocks, despite frequently continuing sheep farming long after the arable land had been leased. In 1440 many of the great estates still maintained a demesne flock, but by 1480 most of these manors had now leased out their flocks (see Chapter 6). A few estates only continued to maintain large sheep flocks. This seems to have been the case in Dorset and south Wiltshire, as on the lands of Wilton and Shaftesbury Abbeys, but does not seem to have been typical of Wiltshire as a whole.[53]

The farming economy had become increasingly based on large-scale capitalist agriculture (employing labour and high investment) and the sale of agricultural surpluses (wool, wheat, barley and meat) to the markets of the textile-producing areas. The slump in demand and in the prices of such an important part of the farm's cash crop would have had disastrous effect on lords and on the substantial peasants who were equally geared up to the market. By contrast, those Wiltshire manors that had already suffered in the early part of the century seem to have escaped. Rents remained stable in the north of the county, and they even rose at Poole.[54] Rent levels here had not been dependent on the earlier expansion or the foreign markets and thus the area escaped the recession lightly, its earlier decline inoculating it against the slump.

Recovery

The recovery from the mid-century slump was piecemeal and ragged. This may reflect the reality of the situation or the insensitivity of the manorial records, which responded more obviously to an inability to collect rent than to possible increases as the demand for land grew. In cloth exports, the disasters of the 1450s and 1460s were followed by the beginnings of recovery in the 1470s and afterwards, particularly through London and Bristol, two key ports for Wiltshire.[55] A period of steady and dramatic expansion continued into the early sixteenth century, and exports were

---

50. Ibid., table 4.
51. D.L. Farmer, 'Prices and wages, 1350–1500', in Miller (ed.), *Agrarian History of England and Wales*, 467; Hatcher, 'Great slump', 250.
52. Farmer, 'Prices and wages', 462–3; Lloyd, *Wool prices*, 26.
53. J.N. Hare, 'Regional prosperity in fifteenth-century England: some evidence from Wessex', in M. Hicks (ed.), *Revolution and consumption in late medieval England* (Woodbridge, 2001), 118–19.
54. Hare, 'Growth and recession', 16, table 4.
55. Hatcher, 'Great slump', 270–72; Carus-Wilson and Coleman, *England's export trade*.

Table 12.7
Cash liveries to the lord: Bromham, Coombe Bisset and Durrington (decennial average).

	Bromham: cash liveries and payments of taxation	Bromham excluding taxation		Coombe Bisset		Durrington	
1326–43						£46 16s 0d	(4)
1344–45	£47 3s 3½d		(1)				
1350–56						£39 19s 0½d	(4)
1352–77		£39 16s 1½d	(4)				
1380–90	£40 14s 7d		(8)	£21 13s 4d	(3)		
1390–1400	£25 10s 5d	£24 2s 4d	(4)	£21 10s 1d	(9)	£35 19s 11d	(10)
1400–1410	£30 11s 5d	£29 0s 7d	(4)	£20 3s 5½d	(10)	£35 11s 6d	(10)
1410–20	£29 19s 10d	£27 16s 4½d	(7)	£22 0s 8d	(10)	£32 18s 9d	(10)
1420–30	£29 13s 0½d		(4)	£17 13s 5d	(10)	£36 17s 2d	(10)
1430–40	£35 1s 2d	£33 14s 11d	(5)	£15 13s 7d	(10)	£31 8s 10d	(10)
1440–50	£31 9s 1½d		(7)	£13 5s 9d	(9)	£41 18s 4d	(10)
1450–60	£30 3s 3½d		(7)	£13 7s 8d	(10)	£33 9s 5d	(10)
1460–70	£29 1s 2½d		(4)	£12 4s 11d	(10)	£27 13s 1½d	(10)
1470–80	£29 14s 7d		(4)	£11 5s 3½d	(10)	£29 11s 5d	(10)
1480–90	£30 14s 4½d		(7)	£11 1s 11½d	(10)	£31 14s 4d	(10)
1490–1500	£32 10s 8d		(7)	£14 3s 2d	(10)	£30 11s 1d	(10)
1500–1526	£33 15s 2½d		(7)				
1501–10				£13 5s 4½d	(10)		
1511–20				£13 11s 11d	(10)		

Notes: Bromham – (a) Three of the figures for the period 1352–77 came from the central accounts of Battle Abbey. The payment for 1375 was exceptionally high (£70 1s 6½d). (b) The taxation entries are mainly of ecclesiastical taxation; they have been included with the cash payments so that the figures may give a clearer idea of economic trends. (c) The receipts for 1421 included £11 6s 8d from the arrears of Walter Beauchamp for the rent of a sub-manor. (d) In 1443, 1444 and 1445 the demesne was leased but its value was not accounted for. It is presumed that the farmer either accounted separately on his own account, or accounted directly to central officials. The value of the lease three years later (£8 per year) has been added to the figures for these years. (e) From 1476–7 the sacrist's farm is included in the account. To provide comparability the value of this lease has been deducted. This assumes that all the lease was paid in the appropriate year. The lease rendered £2 10s 0d from 1476–7 and £2 from 1480.
Durrington – (f) The average for the 1390s is for the period 1389–1400. (g) The decade 1431–40 saw expenditure of £53 14s 0d on the mill with £48 19s 8d spent in the two years 1438–9. Decennial averages for expenditure on the mill and demesne buildings are given in J.N. Hare, 'Durrington, a chalkland manor in the later Middle Ages', WAM, 74–5 (1979/80), table IV, 143.
Sources: see Hare, 'Durrington', Table IV. The central accounts of Battle Abbey are in the Henry Huntington Library, San Marino, CA (BA 80–82). I have used the photostats of these documents held in the Beveridge collection of the University of Durham's Department of Palaeography.

increasingly dominated by London. The sixteenth-century decline of Bristol and Southampton suggests that exports of Wiltshire cloth were ever more likely to be heading abroad through the most distant port of London.[56] Cloth prices recovered well in the late 1470s and had reached their pre-slump level by the beginning of the following decade. Wool prices recovered in the mid-1460s, and again in the 1480s, but

---

56. Carus-Wilson, 'Woollen industry before 1550', 138.

otherwise failed to reach their pre-slump level with any consistency.[57] The flourishing state of the west Wiltshire cloth industry in the early sixteenth century is shown by Leland's tours in the 1540s and the purchases of Thomas Kitson, the London mercer and merchant adventurer. Meanwhile Salisbury remained important, and its rental revived. Marlborough and its environs seem to have seen economic growth as part of the kersey production of the Thames and Kennet valleys.[58]

Rural recovery took various forms. Industrial expansion led to a growth of rents in the cloth town of Trowbridge in the last decades of the century, as decayed rents were again collected (see Table 12.2). At the end of the century the prosperity of the industry led to large-scale rebuilding works at parish churches. But there were also signs of this recovery extending to the countryside beyond as wool prices recovered.[59] On some manors the value of the demesne lease rose, as at Wroughton, where it increased by £1 from £9 13s 4d between 1461 and 1488. Elsewhere, some of the decayed rents could be collected again. At Wexcombe, such decayed rents fell from £3 10s 3d to £2 0s 10d between 1448 and 1485, while at Durrington some of the vacant holdings were retaken in the 1460s and the annual total of decayed rents was reduced from £8 14s 1d in 1461 to £6 18s 2d in 1463 and further to £6 10s 9d in 1468. At Durrington arrears had risen in the 1470s but were low thereafter. Finally, new rent items might be introduced, as at Wexcombe and Wilsford, which, although not great in money terms, indicate a distinct improvement in the position of the landlord.[60] Moreover, the lords were now collecting the bulk of their anticipated revenue and there seemed no great problem of rent collection at such manors as Wexcombe, Wilsford and Stratton, and on the manors of the duchy of Lancaster, or at Kingston Deverill, Wroughton or Bromham (belonging to three different ecclesiastical estates). Even apparently large debts were cleared, as at Urchfont or All Cannings.[61] Occasional difficulties were recorded still in the 1480s, as at Enford and Coombe Bisset. Insufficient entry fines survive to establish clear trends, but at Bromham the court profits rose to a substantially higher level in the 1490s, and this probably reflected higher yields (Table 12.3). In the 1480s and 1490s the lords' cash income recovered at places such as Bromham, Coombe Bisset and Durrington (see Table 12.7). At Downton rectory the cash livery had fallen in mid-century but thereafter remained steady at this new level throughout the rest of the century. In general, a picture of modest recovery may be seen, although agricultural producers were still heavily dependent on the vagaries of wool prices, which nationally remained low.[62] Once again agriculture seemed to be prospering.

---

57. J.H. Munro, 'Monetary contraction and industrial change in the late medieval Low Countries 1335–1500', in N.J. Mayhew (ed.), *Coinage in the Low Countries* (Oxford, 1979), 155; Farmer, 'Prices and wages', 514–15; Lloyd, *Wool prices*, 42–4; Munro shows a full recovery from the 1480s onwards.
58. See above, Chapter 11.
59. TNA: PRO DL29/687/11134, 690/11185; Lloyd, *Wool prices*.
60. Hare, 'Lord and tenant', 174–7, tables x–xiii.
61. J.N. Hare, 'The lords and their tenants: conflict and stability in fifteenth century Wiltshire', in B. Stapleton, *Conflict and community in southern England* (Stroud, 1992), 26, and 'Lord and tenant', table vii, 164.
62. Farmer, 'Prices and wages', 515–16.

The Wiltshire evidence reinforces the idea of a great slump in the mid-fifteenth century, but suggests an important qualification. Although many areas elsewhere suffered a longer-term recession from about the 1420s,[63] in Wiltshire the growth of the cloth industry generated high prosperity until about 1450. The collapse of foreign markets for cloth, and of wool prices, produced a more general economic crisis: a short-term interruption to a longer-term pattern of growth that was subsequently to be resumed in the latter decades of the fifteenth century and continued into the sixteenth.

63. Britnell, 'The economic context'; Hatcher, 'Great slump'.

Conclusion

This study has, it is hoped, shed light both on the long-term regional developments in a small part of England and on the wider world of later medieval England. It has reinforced the understanding of the period that has emerged from other regions and yet also requires us to qualify such conclusions. It has, moreover, emphasised elements of both continuity and change within the county itself. The period inherited much, but it left a legacy which would characterise the social and economic world of Wiltshire in the early modern centuries. It saw an increasing divergence between the rural economies of the chalklands and the claylands and the growing dominance of the west Wiltshire cloth industry. In a real sense, this was a period of transformation.

The contrasts between the large-scale agriculture of the chalkland and the claylands were nothing new, but they grew in this period and we may see emerging the contrasting worlds of the large-scale capitalist farmer of the chalklands and the family farm of the claylands that were to be so familiar to Thomas Davis in the eighteenth century.[1] In the chalklands the large demesnes had been leased as a whole to individuals who now engaged in very large-scale agriculture, often with massive expenditure on the large sheep flocks the manure of which ensured the prosperity of arable farming. There was also a growing accumulation of large-scale agricultural holdings, so that the holder of a single virgate tenement no longer counted among the village aristocracy. Together these developments generated the world of gentry farming that would later produce the high capital investment of floated water meadows.[2] Elsewhere, away from the chalk, demesnes and agricultural tenancies were often broken up and stratification was much less: here the family farm remained characteristic and there was a growing concentration on pastoral farming.

Industry and towns were not new, but their growth and above all that for cloth had transformed the county's economy, giving parts of it the industrial base that it was to retain until the nineteenth century. There was a wide range of specialisms, but above all this was an area where the economy was transformed in the later Middle Ages by the growth of the cloth industry. Areas like western Wiltshire (with its growing emphasis on heavily fulled and undyed cloth) or the areas around Salisbury and Marlborough became part of a wider international pattern of European trade; Wiltshire's cloth merchants traded with foreigners in the great ports and with the Londoners in the capital. Behind the large-scale operations of a few known clothiers lay the countless weavers and spinners who largely depended on the market for their

---

1. T. Davis, *General view of the agriculture of Wiltshire* (London, 1794), and E. Kerridge, 'Agriculture 1500–1793', in VCH *Wilts* 4, 43–64.
2. A familiar development and a breakthrough in agriculture in the seventeenth century which allowed the cost of considerable investment in the maintenance of larger flocks, more manure and higher grain yields. See e.g. E. Kerridge, 'The floating of the Wiltshire water meadows', *WAM*, 55 (1953), 105–18, and J. Bettey, *Wiltshire farming in the seventeenth century*, Wiltshire Record Society 57 (Trowbridge, 2005), 236–75.

A Prospering Society

food, raw materials and consumer goods. Here, as in parts of East Anglia, cloth-making was transforming the local agrarian economy, generating increased prosperity and greater specialisation. It sucked in labour from outside and rents were buoyant. But growth generated its own problems, as an increasing part of the population became dependent on industrial prosperity and the export trade, and was thus vulnerable to economic recession. When the cloth industry suffered, the whole population did too, as seen in the social discontent and falling rents that accompanied the economic downturn of the mid-century.

Agricultural producers provided the industrial areas with wool, grain, ale and meat, and the demand maintained rent levels for most of the period. This demand may have encouraged many lords to continue their traditional direct management of agriculture much longer than elsewhere in England, above all in the chalklands. In general the tenants were able to pay their rents except in the mid-century recession, although there were clear regional variations. They lived in well-constructed timber-framed buildings with private chambers decorated with painted cloths and furnished with bedding and other consumer goods. They shifted the balance of their agricultural activities in order to fit in with the demands of the market. The contraction of the arable acreage opened up new opportunities for wider pastoral farming in which the rearing of sheep, pigs and rabbits met the demands of those in specialist employment or industry. The tenants' decisions regarding arable farming were also dominated by the market, as shown by the shift to barley in the Salisbury area, where tenants' specialisation was even more notable than that on the great demesnes. In this world, the position of the peasantry was being transformed. Old burdens were lost: serfdom and labour services had all virtually disappeared. At the same time there were new opportunities to acquire land: the rough and ready equality between the holders of the greater customary tenements had now vanished in a world of increased rural stratification. But there were also elements of continuity. The manor and its agriculture remained intact, particularly in the chalkland. The apparently revolutionary transformation in land ownership that came with the Reformation and the Dissolution of the monasteries was a change in legal ownership that did not change the basic pattern of agriculture. The leasing of the demesnes had opened up dramatic opportunities for tenant classes, but it also continued the basic pattern of land-holding. Stripped of any links with serfdom, the old customary tenure became the copyhold tenure of the succeeding centuries.

Urban and rural life was underpinned by growing specialisation. The 1379 poll tax returns show rural specialisation both in the cloth and tailoring industries which catered for distant markets,[3] and in other occupations individuals provided a more local service for neighbouring villages. Towns were also occupied in the production of cloth and its finishing and processing, and serviced many of the villages in their hinterland; for example, small towns such as Hindon brewed for a wider area than the town itself.

The developments of the period also left their marks on the present landscape. Uncultivated strip lynchets and shrunken and deserted villages are a reminder of the demographic decline that hit all parts of the country. Although much of the wealth of the area was spent on what, in the long term, has become lost ephemera, some has survived. Above all, much wealth was lavished on the building of the parish churches, and particularly of those parts that were the community's responsibility (generally excluding the chancel). The surviving buildings underplay the importance of this fifteenth-century rebuilding, since Victorian restoration has often replaced perpendicular windows and details by more 'correct' earlier features, as at Durrington. Large-scale new building is seen in the town churches of Salisbury, Trowbridge and Devizes or in the 'cloth' churches of Keevil and Steeple Ashton. Beyond the relatively small number of complete rebuilds, much of the county during this period saw a wide range of examples of new towers, extensions or heightening of aisles and naves and extensive refenestration. It is a rebuilding that extended beyond the cloth-producing areas to the wider agrarian hinterland. While Wiltshire may lack the spectacular perpendicular churches of Somerset and East Anglia, the evidence nevertheless points to substantial expenditure on church rebuilding.[4] Manor houses such as Great Chalfield and monastic rebuilding, as at Lacock, reinforce this impression of prosperity.

Wiltshire provides a good example of the growing complexity of late medieval society: while some areas and social groups prospered, others declined. It was a world of growing opportunities, mobility and choices and of an increasingly important market. But economic expansion also generated potential vulnerability. This study emphasises the need for more local studies if we are to be able to understand the diversity of this period; developments here have a significance that goes far beyond this single county, and beyond southern England. Behind the continuities – the patterns of fields and settlement, the different regional patterns of agriculture, the interactions between the villager and the world beyond – lay changes that were of long-term significance. They emerged from long-standing patterns of agrarian life and short-term industrial transformation and demographic change, but they were to lay down the shape of agrarian society for the succeeding centuries.

Bibliography

Primary sources, unprinted

The materials belonging to several estates have become scattered among various archives. To help future users, these have been cross-referenced.

Badminton, Gloucestershire: Badminton House Muniments (now in Gloucestershire Archives)

Hilmarton 110/5/3 & 4 (12 accounts, 38 courts)

Cambridge, King's College Muniments

Accounts for Brixton and the Ogbournes: WB2/1–7, CC148
Register Ledger Book I

Chippenham (formerly Trowbridge), Wiltshire Record Office (now Wiltshire and Swindon Archives)

1422 Alvediston: Box 6 nos 86–109 (was in Wilton House Muniments)
Bishopric of Salisbury records: *Liber Niger*; register of bishop Ayscough.
Salisbury City Records: Ledger Books A & B (G23/1/1; 1/2); chamberlain's accounts (G23/B23/1/44/1–8)
Stockton: Accounts 906/SC7–10, SC17; Court 906/SC2; 16; 18. Westwood 906/SC14
Urchfont accounts: 192/36, 283/18, 24/2, 2/8 (1453–1522) (see also BL and John Rylands); Court rolls 192/20 (1423–43) (see also BL). All Cannings: 192/28 (1450–1527). Kingston Deverill: accounts 192/32 (1397–1502). Warminster: 845/manorial papers/14 [uncatalogued when used, now returned to Longleat]
Miscellaneous manors: accounts 192/29; 34; 35; 468/19; 492/8; 492/13–15, 17, 19, 23; 795/1; 1728/70, 1742/6786; Savernake collection (Crofton and composite account of Esturmy manors, then unnumbered); courts 192/16; miscellaneous 212B/2290–2; 214/8

Devizes Library of Wiltshire Archaeological Society

Sir Thomas Philipps, Miscellanea A; Wiltshire Archaeological Society MSS vol 241, 61

Dorchester, Dorset Record Office

Rudlowe and Westbury: D10/M251, M252/1–8. M253; D16/M60, 6, 71, 80

Huntingdon Library, San Marino, California

Photostats of Battle Abbey accounts in the Department of Palaeography, University of Durham

London, British Library

Add Mss 2165 (Transcript extents of Malmesbury Abbey; Harl Mss 28208 (Terrier of Glastonbury). Miscellaneous account rolls: Eg Rl 8633, 5, 6, 9, 42, 43; Add Rl 6277; Add Ch 66520; 26594, 26873, 27679, 28005, 28008; Add Rl 17478–514; Add Rl 28067, 92, 96, 98, 99, 28016, 28122; 15142. L 66602 (Urchfont)

Castle Combe: Add Mss 28208 (notebook of William of Worcester). Add Mss 28211/f4, 2b, 18250, 18272, 18475, 18477, 18478, 18481, 18482, 18483, 18484, 18485, 18486, 18490, 13/488, 28208, 18250, 18272, 18555

Enford: Harl Rl X7–17; W8–30; V20–29 (see also WCL)

Stockton: Accounts Add Rl 24395–24433; Court Add Rl 24330–57; 24376–82; 24713; 24716; Rental: BL Add Rl 24394 (see also WCL)

Urchfont: accounts Add Rl 19717–22, 26, 28–30, 66602–3 (1461–1519); courts Add Rl 66602 (see also WRO)

Westwood: Add Rl 24371, 2 (see also WCL)

London, London School of Economics

Beveridge prices and wages collection Box B2 (grain prices from Bishopric of Winchester Pipe Rolls)

London, The National Archives: Public Record Office, Kew

Account rolls (SC6): Bromham: 1045/14–1049/5; Hen VII/892–904; Hen VIII/3939–49; 1107/10; miscellaneous manors: 978/14; 1045/7, 9, 10; 1049/9, 11, 13, 14, 16; 1051/16, 17, 21; 1052/1, 2, 15; 1053/1, 12; 1054/4–11, 14, 16, 17, 24–5; 1055/10; 1056/6, 7, 10–14; 18, 21, 22; 1057/1, 2, 4, 22; 1057/3; 1058/1, 7, 8, 15, 21; 1059/1, 13, 14, 16–22, 24; 1060/16, 18, 20–22; 1061/10, 13, 20, 22, 30–2; 1062/6, 7, 9, 13, 25/2, 3; 1092/16; 1093/4, 2; 1117/3, 4, 8, 9, 10; 1141/6, 5. Hen VII/939, 942, 950, 970; Hen VIII/3956, 3958

Court rolls (SC2): Bromham: 208/16–26; miscellaneous manors: 1048/45, 46

Duchy of Lancaster account rolls (DL29): 1/1; 1/3; 641/11193; 652/10553, 10555; 653/10564, 10565, 10569; 654/10577, 10581, 10587, 10590; 657/10623, 10628; 658/10635, 10640; 659/10647, 10653, 10657; 660/10663; 682/11039, 11042, 11044, 11058; 683/11061, 11068, 11069, 11070, 11072, 11134; 684/11074; 685/11074, 11087; 686/11110, 11113, 11123, 11125; 687/11129, 11134, 11135, 11137; 688/11153, 11156; 690/11185; 691/111202, 11209; 692/11218; 693/11226, 11227, 11229; 694/11235, 11246, 710/11432, 11433, 11436, 11445, 11446, 11450, 11456; 728/11981, 11991; 729/11993–4, 11997, 11999, 12002, 12005; 730/12007; 12009; 12013, 731/12015, 12016, 12023; 732/12034, 733/12037, 12039, 12040, 12041, 12042, 12043; 734/12044; 737/12071, 12073, 12074, 12075, 12076, 12078, 12082, 12085, 12086, 12087, 12089 (for Trowbridge see also WRO); also DL28/23/12A; DL37/53–8; DL42/15–18; DL43 9/34; 15; 14/4; IND 17593 & 4

Miscellaneous surveys: E315/56; Wards 2/94c/9. 101/593/17; E106/2/2 & 3; E357/ 4, 5, 7, 39, 42; KB9/133 & 134/1; SC11/816; Card index: Itinerary of Henry III

Tax records E179/239/193; 194/42; /196/42a, 52; /196/44, 52a, 100; /197/155, 156, 161; /242/47; E101/344/1 & 7 (1379 Poll tax); E179/155–61. Extents of alien monasteries E106/2/2 & 3

Aulnage accounts E101/342/2; 343/28; 344/3–4, 17; 345/2, 4, 5, 7, 9, 10; 346/7, 22a, 25; 347/17. Ancient indictments KB 9/133 & 134/1. Memoranda repertory rolls IND 7037–9. Escheator's accounts. E357/4, 5, 7, 39, 42. Wills Prob 11 (those wills belonging to families of demesne lessees)

Longleat House Manuscripts (used on microfilm)

9599–9605, 9643, 9760, 9815, 10696, 10699, 10762, 11216

Manchester, John Ryland's Library

Rylands Charter 170, 171, 173 (Urchfont)

Oxford, Bodleian Library

Ewelme: A35 40, 46, 47

Oxford, Magdalen College Muniments

Otterbourne (Hants): accs 55/11/ 56/4, 42/35, 42/37; courts 63/17
Oxford, Merton College Muniments, Oxford
Stratton: (acc) 4306, 7, 4321c, 4324b, 4322c, 4322 h, i; (court) 4323 a–c; 4324 c

Oxford, New College Archives

Alton Barnes: (acc) 5810, 5819, 5822–24, 5826–31, 5838, 5842, 5859, 5960 m1–8. Colerne 5963 mm1–39, 5964; Court 2734

Salisbury, Dean and chapter

Chapter Act books: Reg Burgh; Reg Machon; Reg Newton; Reg Hutchins
Communars' accounts: 1–4, 7, 9, 12, 15, 19, 29, 41, 45–8a, 54, 75, 83, 89 (1361–1407)
Press I H–L/1–7 (Lavington); Press S/10 (Sherborne) (see also TNA: PRO SC6/1141/6, 5); Press II Miscellaneous manorial accounts/Potterne; Press III Potterne Box A–C/52; Press I Ramsbury

Winchester, Hampshire Record Office

5M50 2691, 2 (Michelmersh); 111 M94 W N2/1 & 2/2 (Alton Priors); 6M56/5; 93M47/C1; 83M85 W/1; J.Z. Titow, 'Field Crops and their cultivation in Hampshire 1200–1350 in the light of documentary evidence', unpublished paper
Bishopric of Winchester. These have been renumbered. The new is 11 M59 B1/1– and the old Eccl 2 159270– (for a correlation of the two sets of references up to 1454–5 see 'appendix' in R.H. Britnell (ed.), *The Winchester pipe rolls and medieval English society* (Woodbridge, 2003), 183–8). This list does not include the later account books. No attempt has been made to survey this vast archive. In tackling particular problems I have looked at the accounts for individual manors and particular years. Eccl 2 15900; 11M59 B1/136, 154, 157, 158, 168–72, 192, 193

Winchester, Cathedral Library

The estate records of the cathedral priory (including the manorial records and stockbook of the cathedral priory, but not the registers of the Common Seal) have now been moved from the cathedral library to HRO. They were already being re-catalogued and have therefore been referred to by the date of the account. I have used three main series: composite accounts from the whole estate from 1248 to 1318, (given a reference specifying composite and the date), and the accounts and court rolls of single manors (given the place and date). Enquiries concerning the medieval cathedral archives should be sent to HRO (see also BL, WRO, HRO for additional documentation for this estate).

Composite accounts for all the priory manors 1311 and 1318, for Wiltshire manors together with additional account and court rolls. Alton Priors accounts 1373 and 1395; Overton accounts for 1248, 1280, 1282, 1283, 1309, 1312, 1316, 1318. Westwood accounts 1365–1500; courts 1359–1518 (see also BL and WRO); Wroughton accounts 1419–1529, court rolls 1372–1507

Hampshire manors: Hannyton 1338, 1367, 1378; Chilbolton WCL Box 12/29, 34; Crondal 1383; Wootton 1346, 1361, 1373; Sutton 1330, 1387; Littleton 1400

Obedientary manors: Bishopstone 1371–2, 92; Ham 1363, 1470; Hinton 1445, 7, 63, 1514, 29

Register of Dean and Chapter (formerly of the Cathedral Priory) vols I and II

Stockbook of the priory (1390–92) (Charter cupboard)

Winchester, Winchester College Muniments

Coombe Bisset: account rolls 4620–4752; courts rolls 4389a–g; 4396a–h; 4397a–r; 4400f–k, r–ee; 4396a–h; 4397a–r; 4398a–j; 4400ee–a; 4402; 4403; 4404 (not a complete coverage of the surviving rolls); rentals etc. 4350; 4351b; 4353; 4354; 4359; 4362; 5596; 13373

Downton Rectory: accounts 5362–5519

Durrington: accounts 5929, 5930, 5939, 5940–44, 48, 5950–6079; courts 5650a–r; 5651a–b; 5652a–d; 5653d–f; 5655u–a; 5656a–m; rentals etc. 5596; 5601Aa; 5601Ca, Cc; 13373; 5603A; 5603d; 5603e; 5604; 5606Aa; 4349

General: 22992; 22125; 29, 33; 86/35, 87/35; 20007–17

Miscellaneous: (Andover, Hants) 2655–2742. (Hyde Abbey) 12188, 89, 92

Primary sources, printed

Abstracts of feet of fines relating to Wiltshire for the reign of Edward III, ed. C.R. Elrington, Wiltshire Record Society 29 (Devizes, 1974).

Abstracts of Wiltshire inquisitiones post mortem: returned into the Court of Chancery in the reigns of Henry III, Edward I, and Edward II A.D. 1242–1326, ed. E.A. Fry, Wiltshire Archaeological and Natural History Society (London, 1908).

Abstracts of Wiltshire inquisitiones post mortem returned into the Court of Chancery in the reign of King Edward III A.D. 1327–1377, ed. E. Stokes, Wiltshire Archaeological and Natural History Society (London, 1914).

The account book of Beaulieu Abbey, ed. S.F. Hockey, Camden Society, 4th series 16 (London, 1975).

Accounts of the cellarers of Battle Abbey, 1275–1513, ed. E. Searle and B. Ross (Sydney, 1967, and Sussex Record Society).

Accounts and surveys of the Wiltshire lands of Adam de Stratton, ed. M.W. Farr, Wiltshire Archaeological and Natural History Society Records Branch 14 (Devizes, 1959).

Andrew's and Dury's map of Wiltshire, 1773, a reduced facsimile, ed. E. Crittall, Wiltshire Archaeological and Natural History Society Records Branch 8 (Devizes, 1952).

The book of Bartholomew Bolney, ed. M. Clough, Sussex Record Society 63 (Lewes, 1964).

The brokage book of Southampton, 1439–1440, ed. B.D.M. Bunyard, Southampton Record Society 40 (Southampton, 1941).

The brokage book of Southampton, 1443–1444, ed. O. Coleman, Southampton Record Series 4 and 6 (Southampton, 1960–61).

The Southampton brokage book 1447–8, ed. W.A. Harwood, Southampton Record Series 42 (Winchester, 2006).

The brokage books of Southampton for 1477–8 and 1527–8, ed. K.F. Stevens and T.E. Olding, Southampton Record Series 28 (Southampton, 1985).

Building accounts of King Henry III, ed. H.M. Colvin (Oxford, 1971).
Calendar of Close Rolls, Henry VI: volume 3: 1435–1441, ed. A.E. Stamp (London, 1937).
Calendar of entries in the papal registers relating to Great Britain and Ireland, 6, 1404–15, eds W.H. Bliss and J.A. Twemlow (London, 1904).
Calendar of the Patent Rolls, 1476–85 (London, 1905).
The cartulary of Bradenstoke Priory, ed. V.C.M. London, Wiltshire Record Society 35 (Devizes, 1980).
Compotus rolls of the obedientiaries of St. Swithun's Priory, Winchester, ed. G.W. Kitchen, Hampshire Record Society 7 (Winchester, 1892).
Custumals of Battle Abbey, in the reigns of Edward I and Edward II (1283–1312), ed. S.R. Scargill-Bird, Camden Society 2nd series 41 (London, 1887).
The first general entry book of the city of Salisbury, 1387–1452, ed. D.R. Carr, Wiltshire Record Society 54 (Trowbridge, 2001).
The great chartulary of Glastonbury Abbey, ed. A. Watkin (Somerset Record Society, 1947).
The great roll of the pipe for the twenty-seventh year of the reign of King Henry the Second, A.D. 1180–1181, Pipe Roll Society 30 (London, 1909).
The great roll of the pipe for the thirty-second year of the reign of King Henry the Second, A.D. 1185–1186, Pipe Roll Society 36 (London, 1914).
Household accounts from medieval England, ed. C.M. Woolgar (Oxford, 1992).
Inquisitions and assessments relating to feudal aids. Vol. 5, Stafford to Worcester and *vol. 6, York and additions* (London, 1908; 1920).
Interdict documents, ed. P.M. Barnes and W.R. Powell, Pipe Roll Society 72 n.s. 34 (London, 1960).
John of Gaunt's register, 1379–83, ed. E.C. Lodge and R. Somerville, Camden Society 3rd series 56, 57 (London, 1937).
John Leland's itinerary, ed. J. Chandler (Stroud, 1993).
Kirby's quest for Somerset: Nomina villarum for Somerset of 16th of Edward III, Exchequer lay subsidies which is a tax roll for Somerset of the first year of Edward III, County rate of 1742, hundreds and parishes etc of, as given in the Census of 1841, ed. F.H. Dickenson, Somerset Record Society 3 (London, 1889).
Lacock Abbey charters, ed. K.H. Rogers, Wiltshire Record Society 34 (Devizes, 1979).
The lay subsidy of 1334, ed. R.E. Glasscock (London, 1975).
List of the lands of dissolved religious houses, Public Record Office, Lists and indexes supplementary series 3, vol. 4 (New York, 1964).
The local port book of Southampton, 1439–40, ed. H.S. Cobb, Southampton Record Series 5 (Southampton, 1961).
'The manor of Chilbolton', ed. J.S. Drew (unpublished typescript, 1945).
'The manor of Houghton', ed. J.S. Drew (unpublished typescript, 1943).
'The manor of Michelmersh', ed. J.S. Drew (unpublished typescript, 1943).
'The manor of Silkstead', ed. J.S. Drew (unpublished typescript, 1947).
Ministers' accounts of the earldom of Cornwall, 1296–1297, ed. L.M. Midgley, Camden Society 3rd series 66, 68 (London, 1942).
Nomina villarum in *Inquisitions and assessments relating to feudal aids*, vols 5 and 6, (1998, 1920).
The pipe roll of the bishopric of Winchester, 1210–1211, ed. N.H. Holt (Manchester, 1964).
The pipe roll of the bishopric of Winchester, 1301–2, ed. M. Page, Hampshire Record Series 14 (Winchester, 1996).
The pipe roll of the bishopric of Winchester, 1409–10, ed. M. Page, Hampshire Record Series 16 (Winchester, 1999).
The port books or local customs account of Southampton for the reign of Edward IV, ed. D.B. Quinn and A.A. Ruddock, Southampton Record Society 37, 38 (Southampton, 1937–8).
The register of the common seal of the Priory of St. Swithun, Winchester, 1345–1497, ed. J. Greatrex, Hampshire Record Series 2 (Winchester, 1978).

The register of John Chandler, Dean of Salisbury 1407–17, ed. T.C.B. Timmins, Wiltshire Record Society 39 (Devizes, 1984).
Registrum Malmesburiense: the register of Malmesbury Abbey, ed. J.S. Brewer and C.T. Martin, Rolls Series 72 (London, 1879–80).
Rolls of the fifteenth of the ninth year of the reign of Henry III for Cambridgeshire, Lincolnshire and Wiltshire; and, Rolls of the fortieth of the seventeenth year of the reign of Henry III for Kent, ed. F.A. and A.P. Cazel, Pipe Roll Society 83, n.s. 45 (London, 1983).
Select documents of the English lands of the Abbey of Bec, ed. M. Chibnall, Camden Society 3rd series 73 (London, 1951).
Somerset medieval wills (1383–1500), ed. F.W. Weaver, Somerset Record Society 16 (London, 1901).
Somerset medieval wills (1501–1530), ed. F.W. Weaver, Somerset Record Society 19 (London, 1903).
The Southampton port and brokage books, 1448–9, ed. E. Lewis, Southampton Record Series 36 (Southampton, 1993).
Survey of the lands of William, 1st earl of Pembroke, ed. C.R. Stratton, Roxburghe Club (Oxford, 1909).
Tropenell cartulary, ed. J.S. Davies, Wiltshire Archaeological and Natural History Society (Devizes, 1908).
Two sixteenth century taxation lists, 1545 and 1576, ed. G.D. Ramsay, Wiltshire Record Society 10 (Devizes, 1954).
Valor Ecclesiasticus temp. Henr. VIII, ed. J. Caley and J. Hunter (London, 1810).
Wiltshire extents for debts, Edward I–Elizabeth I, ed. A. Conyers, Wiltshire Record Society 28 (Devizes, 1974).
Wiltshire farming in the seventeenth century, ed. J.H. Bettey, Wiltshire Record Society 57 (Trowbridge, 2005).
The Wiltshire tax list of 1332, ed. D.A. Crowley, Wiltshire Record Society 45 (Trowbridge, 1989).

Secondary sources

Astill, G. and Grant, A. (eds), *The countryside of medieval England* (Oxford, 1988).
Aston, M., *Medieval Village Research Group Report* 30 (1982), 11.
—, *Medieval Village Research Group Report* 31 (1983), 11–2.
—, 'A regional study of deserted villages in the west of England' in M. Aston, D. Austin and C. Dyer (eds), *The rural settlements of medieval England* (Oxford, 1989), 105–28.
— and Lewis, C. (eds) *The medieval landscape of Wessex* (Oxford, 1994).
Aston, T.H. (ed.), *The Brenner debate* (Cambridge, 1985).
Aubrey, J., *Aubrey's natural history of Wiltshire: a reprint of 'the natural history of Wiltshire'*, ed. K.G. Ponting (Newton Abbot, 1969).
Baigent, F.J. and Millard, J.E., *A history of the ancient town and manor of Basingstoke* (Basingstoke, 1889).
Bailey, M., 'The rabbit and the medieval East Anglian economy', *Agricultural History Review*, 36 (1988), 1–20.
Ballard, A., 'The manors of Witney, Brightwell and Downton', in A.E. Levett, *The Black Death on the estates of the see of Winchester* (Oxford, 1916).
Barron, C.M., 'London, 1300–1540' in Palliser (ed.), *The Cambridge urban history of Britain*, 395–440.
— and Harper-Bill, C. (eds), *The church in pre-reformation society: essays in honour of F.R.H. Du Boulay* (Woodbridge, 1985).
Barron, R.S., *The geology of Wiltshire: a field guide* (Bradford-on-Avon, 1976).
Bean, J.M.B., 'Landlords', in Miller (ed.), *Agrarian history of England and Wales*, 526–86.
Beastall, T.W., 'Landlords and tenants', in G.W. Mingay (ed.), *The Victorian countryside* (London, 1981), 428–38.

Bennett, J.M., *Ale, beer and brewsters in England: women's work in a changing world, 1300–1600* (New York and Oxford, 1996).

—, 'The ties that bind: peasant marriages and families in late medieval England', *Journal of Interdisciplinary History*, 15 (1984–5), 111–29.

Benson, R. and Hatcher, H., *Old and New Sarum or Salisbury*, being vol. VI of Sir R.C. Hoare, *A history of modern Wiltshire* (London, 1843).

Beresford, M.W., 'Fifteenths and tenths: quotas of 1334'; 'Poll tax payers of 1377'; 'Poor parishes of 142', in VCH *Wilts* 4, 294–314.

—, *The lost villages of England* (London, 1965).

—, *New towns of the Middle Ages* (London, 1967).

—, 'A review of historical research (to 1968)', in M.W. Beresford and J.G. Hurst, *Deserted medieval villages* (London, 1971), 3–75.

—, 'The six new towns of the bishops of Winchester, 1200–55', *Medieval Archaeology*, 3 (1959), 187–215.

Betterton, A. and Dymond, D., *Lavenham: industrial town* (Lavenham, 1989).

Bettey, J.H., *The suppression of the monasteries in the west country* (Gloucester, 1989).

—, *Wessex from AD 1000* (London, 1986).

Biddick, K., *The other economy: pastoral husbandry on a medieval estate* (Berkeley/Los Angeles, CA, 1989).

Birrell, J., 'Deer and deer farming in medieval England', *Agricultural History Review*, 40 (1992), 112–26.

—, 'Personal craftsmen in the medieval forest', *Agricultural History Review*, 16 (1968), 91–107.

Bolton, J.L., *The medieval English economy* (London, 1980).

—, '"The world turned upside down": plague as an agent of economic and social change', in M. Ormrod and P. Lindley (eds), *The Black Death in England* (Stamford, 1996), 17–78.

Bond, J., 'Forests, chases, warrens and parks in medieval Wessex', in Aston and Lewis (eds), *The medieval landscape of Wessex*, 115–58.

Bowen, H.C. and Fowler, P.J., 'The archaeology of Fyfield and Overton Down', *Wiltshire Archaeological and Natural History Magazine*, 58 (1962), 98–115.

Brandon, P.F., 'Cereal yields on the Sussex estates of Battle Abbey during the later Middle Ages', *Economic History Review*, 2nd series 25 (1972), 403–20.

—, 'Late-medieval weather in Sussex and its agricultural significance', *Transactions of the Institute of British Geographers*, 54 (1971), 1–17.

Brent, J.A., 'Alciston manor in the later Middle Ages', *Sussex Archaeological Collections*, 106 (1968), 89–102.

Brett, C.J., 'Thomas Kytson and Somerset clothmen, 1529–1539', *Somerset Archaeology and Natural History*, 143 (1999), 29–56.

—, 'Thomas Kytson and Wiltshire clothmen', *Wiltshire Archaeological and Natural History Magazine*, 97 (2004), 35–62.

Bridbury, A.R., *Economic growth: England in the later Middle Ages*, 2nd edn (London, 1975).

—, 'English provincial towns in the later Middle Ages', *Economic History Review*, 2nd series 34 (1981), 1–24.

—, *Medieval English clothmaking: an economic survey* (London, 1982).

Britnell, R.H., *The closing of the Middle Ages?* (Oxford, 1999).

—, *The commercialisation of English society, 1000–1500*, 2nd edn (Manchester, 1990).

—, 'The economic context', in A.J. Pollard (ed.), *The Wars of the Roses* (Basingstoke, 1995), 41–64.

—, *Growth and decline in Colchester, 1300–1525* (Cambridge, 1986).

—, 'The Winchester pipe rolls and their historians', in Britnell (ed.), *The Winchester pipe rolls*, 1–19.

— (ed.), *The Winchester pipe rolls and medieval English society* (Woodbridge, 2003).

—, 'The woollen textile industry in Suffolk in the later Middle Ages', *The Ricardian*, 13 (2003), 86–99

Brown, A.D., *Popular piety in late medieval England: the diocese of Salisbury, 1200–1550* (Oxford, 1995).
Brown, R.A., Colvin, H.M. and Taylor, A.J., *The history of the king's works*, vols 1 and 2, *The Middle Ages* (London, 1963).
Campbell, B.M.S., *Before the Black Death: studies in the 'crisis' of the early fourteenth century* (Manchester, 1991).
—, *English seigniorial agriculture, 1250–1450* (Cambridge, 2000).
—, 'A unique estate and a unique source: the Winchester pipe rolls in perspective', in Britnell (ed.), *The Winchester pipe rolls*, 21–43.
—, Bartley, K.C. and Power, J.P., 'The demesne-farming systems of post-Black Death England: a classification', *Agricultural History Review*, 44 (1996), 131–79.
Cardigan, earl of (Brudnell-Bruce), *The wardens of Savernake forest* (London, 1949).
Carpenter, C., 'The fifteenth century gentry and their estates', in M. Jones (ed.), *Gentry and lesser nobility in late medieval Europe* (Gloucester, 1986), 36–60.
Carr, D.R., 'From pollution to prostitution: supervising the citizens of fifteenth-century Salisbury', *Southern History*, 19 (1997), 24–41.
—, 'John Halle', in *ODNB* <http://www.oxforddnb.com/view/article/12007>.
—, 'The problem of the urban patriciates: office holders in fifteenth-century Salisbury', *Wiltshire Archaeological and Natural History Magazine*, 83 (1990), 118–35.
Carus-Wilson, E.M., 'The aulnage accounts: a criticism', in her *Medieval merchant venturers*, 279–91.
—, (ed.) *Essays in economic history*, vol. 2 (London, 1962).
—, 'Evidences of industrial growth on some fifteenth century manors', in Carus-Wilson (ed.), *Essays in economic history*, vol. 2, 151–67.
—, *The expansion of Exeter* (Exeter, 1961).
—, *Medieval merchant venturers* (London, 1954).
—, 'The woollen industry', in M.M. Postan and E. Miller (eds), *The Cambridge economic history of Europe II: trade and industry in the Middle Ages*, 2nd edn (Cambridge, 1987), 614–90.
—, 'The woollen industry before 1550', in VCH *Wilts* 4, 115–47.
— and Coleman, O., *England's export trade, 1275–1547* (Oxford, 1963).
Chandler, J., *Endless Street: a history of Salisbury and its people* (Salisbury, 1983).
Clarkson, L.A., 'The leather crafts in Tudor and Stuart England', *Agricultural History Review*, 14 (1966), 25–39.
—, *Proto-industrialization: the first phase of industrialization?* (Basingstoke, 1995).
Cobbett, C., *Rural rides* (Harmondsworth, 1967).
Coleman, O., 'Trade and prosperity in the fifteenth century: some aspects of the trade of Southampton', *Economic History Review*, 2nd series 16 (1963–4), 9–22.
Collinson, J., *The history and antiquities of the county of Somerset* (Bath, 1741).
Crawford, O.G.S., *The Andover region* (Oxford, 1922).
Cunnington, M.E., 'A medieval earthwork near Morgan's Hill', *Wiltshire Archaeological and Natural History Magazine*, 36 (1910), 590–98.
Dale, M.K., 'The city of New Salisbury', in VCH *Wilts* 6, 69–90.
Darlington, R.R., 'Anglo-Saxon Wiltshire', in VCH *Wilts* 2, 1–34.
—, 'Introduction to the Wiltshire Domesday', in VCH *Wilts* 2, 42–112.
Davenport, F.G., *The economic development of a Norfolk manor, 1086–1565* (1906; repr. London, 1967).
Davies, R.R. 'Baronial accounts, incomes and arrears in the later Middle Ages', *Economic History Review*, 2nd series 21 (1968), 211–29.
Davis, T., *General view of the agriculture of Wiltshire* (London, 1794).
Day, J., *The medieval market economy* (Oxford, 1987).
Dewindt, E.B., *Land and people in Hollywell-cum-Needingworth* (Toronto, 1972).
Dobson, R.B., *The peasants' revolt of 1381* (London, 1970).

Dodds, B., 'Estimating arable output using Durham Priory tithe receipts, 1341–1450', *Economic History Review*, 57 (2004), 245–85.

—, 'Managing tithes in the late Middle Ages', *Agricultural History Review*, 53 (2005), 125–40.

Donkin, R.A., *The Cistercians: studies in the geography of medieval England and Wales* (Toronto, 1978).

Doubleday, H.A. and Page, W. (eds), *A history of Hampshire and the Isle of Wight*, The Victoria History of the Counties of England, vols 1–5 (London, 1900–1912).

Drew, J.S., 'Manorial accounts of St Swithun's Priory Winchester', repr. in Carus-Wilson, *Essays in economic history*, vol. 2, 12–31.

Driver, J.T., 'The career of John Whittockesmede, a fifteenth century Wiltshire lawyer and parliamentary carpet bagger', *Wiltshire Archaeological and Natural History Magazine*, 92 (1999), 92–9.

—, 'A "perillous covetous man": the career of Thomas Tropenell Esq. (c.1405–88), a Wiltshire lawyer, parliamentary burgess and builder of Great Chalfield', *Wiltshire Archaeological and Natural History Magazine*, 93 (2000), 82–9.

Du Boulay, F.R.H., *An age of ambition* (London, 1970).

—, *The lordship of Canterbury* (London, 1966).

—, 'A rentier economy in the later Middle Ages: the archbishopric of Canterbury', *Economic History Review*, 2nd series 16 (1964), 426–38.

—, 'Who were farming the English demesnes at the end of the Middle Ages?' *Economic History Review*, 2nd series 17 (1965), 443–55.

Dyer, A., *Decline and growth in English towns, 1400–1640* (Basingstoke, 1991).

—, 'Ranking lists of English medieval towns', in Palliser (ed.), *The Cambridge urban history of Britain*, 755–70.

Dyer, C., *An age of transition? Economy and society in the later Middle Ages* (Oxford, 2005).

—, 'The archaeology of medieval small towns', *Medieval Archaeology*, 47 (2003), 85–114.

—, 'Changes in the link between families and land in the west midlands in the fourteenth and fifteenth centuries', in Smith (ed.), *Land, kinship and lifecycle*, 305–11.

—, 'Changes in the size of peasant holdings in some west midland villages' in Smith (ed.), *Land, kinship and lifecycle*, 277–94.

—, *Everyday life in medieval England* (London, 1994).

—, 'Farming practice and techniques. E: the west midlands', in Miller (ed.), *The agrarian history of England and Wales*, 222–37.

—, 'How urbanized was medieval England?' in J.M. Duvosquel and E. Thoen (eds), *Peasants and townsmen in medieval Europe* (Gent, 1995), 169–83.

—, *Lords and peasants in a changing society: the estates of the bishopric of Worcester, 680–1540* (Cambridge, 1980).

—, *Making a living in the Middle Ages: the people of Britain, 850–1520* (New Haven, CT, and London, 2002).

—, 'A redistribution of incomes in fifteenth century England', in R.H. Hilton (ed.), *Peasants, knights and heretics* (Cambridge, 1976), 192–215.

—, 'Sheepcotes: evidence for medieval sheep farming', *Medieval Archaeology*, 39 (1995), 136–64.

—, 'Small towns, 1270–1540', in Palliser (ed.), *The Cambridge urban history of Britain*, 505–37.

—, *Standards of living in the later Middle Ages* (Cambridge, 1989).

—, 'Tenant farming and tenants farmers. E: the west midlands', in Miller (ed.), *Agrarian History of England and Wales*, 636–47.

—, *Warwickshire farming, 1349–c.1520: preparations for agricultural revolution*, Dugdale Society Occasional Papers (Oxford, 1981).

—, 'Were late medieval English villages "self-contained"?' in C. Dyer (ed.), *The self contained village* (Hertford, 2007), 6–27.

Ellis, P., *Ludgershall Castle: excavations by Peter Addyman, 1964–72*, Wiltshire Archaeological

Society 2 (Devizes, 2000).

English Heritage, *Farleigh Hungerford castle* (London, 1970).

Evans, T.A.R. and Faith, R. (eds), 'College estates and university finances, 1350–1500' in J. Catto and R. Evans (eds), *The history of the university of Oxford, ii: late medieval Oxford* (Oxford, 1992), 635–707.

Everitt, A., 'The marketing of agricultural produce', in Thirsk (ed.), *Agrarian history of England and Wales*, 466–592.

Faith, R., 'Berkshire: fourteenth and fifteenth centuries', in Harvey, *The peasant land market*, 106–77.

—, 'Peasant inheritance customs in medieval England', *Agricultural History Review*, 14 (1966), 77–95.

—, 'The peasant land market in Berkshire in the later Middle Ages', PhD thesis (Leicester, 1962).

Farmer, D.L., 'The famuli in the later Middle Ages', in R.H. Britnell and J. Hatcher (eds), *Progress and problems in medieval England: essays in honour of Edward Miller* (Cambridge, 1996).

—, 'Grain yields on the Winchester manors in the later Middle Ages', *Economic History Review*, 2nd series 30 (1977), 555–66.

—, 'Marketing the produce of the countryside, 1200–1500' in Miller (ed.), *Agrarian History of England and Wales*, vol. 3, 324–430.

—, 'Prices and wages, 1350–1500', in Miller (ed.), *Agrarian History of England and Wales*, vol. 3, 431–525.

—, 'Two Wiltshire manors and their markets', *Agricultural History Review*, 37 (1989), 1–11.

Fenwick, C.C., *The poll taxes of 1377, 1379 and 1381*, Records of Social and Economic History, new series, 27, 29 (London, 1998–).

Finberg, H.P.R. (ed.), *Gloucestershire studies* (Leicester, 1957).

— *Tavistock Abbey* (Cambridge, 1951).

Fowler, P.J., *Landscape plotted and pieced: landscape history and local archaeology in Fyfield and Overton, Wiltshire* (London, 2000).

— and Bidwell, I., *The land of Lettice Sweetapple: an English countryside explored* (Stroud, 1998).

—, Musty, J.W.G. and Taylor, C.C., 'Some earthwork enclosures in Wiltshire', *Wiltshire Archaeological and Natural History Magazine*, 60 (1965), 1–23.

Fox, H., *The evolution of the fishing village: landscape and society along the south Devon coast, 1086–1550* (Oxford, 2001).

Fritze, R.H., 'Faith and faction: religious changes, national politics and the development of local factionalism in Hampshire, 1485–1570', PhD thesis (Cambridge, 1981).

Fry, A.H., *The land of Britain, part 87, Wiltshire* (London, 1940).

Fry, C.B., *Hannington: the records of a Wiltshire village* (Gloucester, 1935).

Fryde, E.M., *Peasants and landlords in later medieval England, c.1380–1525* (Stroud, 1996).

Galloway, J.A., 'London's grain supply: changes in production, distribution and consumption during the fourteenth century', *Franco-British Studies*, 20 (1995), 31–2.

Genet, J.P., 'Economie et société rurale en Angleterre au XVè siècle d'après les comptes de l'hôpital d'Ewelme', *Annales Économies Sociétés, Civilisations*, 27 (1972), 1449–71.

Goldberg, P.J.B. (ed.), *Women in medieval English society c.1200–1500* (Stroud, 1997) (previously published as *Women is a worthy wight: women in English medieval society*).

—, *Women, work and life cycle in a medieval economy* (Oxford, 1992).

Goodman, F.R., *Winchester: valley and downland* (Winchester, 1934).

Gover, J.E.B., Mawyer, A. and Stenton, F.M., *The place names of Wiltshire* (Cambridge, 1939).

Graham, H., '"A woman's work…": labour and gender in the late medieval countryside', in Goldberg, *Women in medieval English society*, 126–48.

Grant, R., 'Forests', in VCH *Wilts* 4, 391–460.

Gras, N.S.B. and Gras, E.C., *The economic and social history of an English village* (Cambridge,

MA, 1930).

Gray, H.L., 'English foreign trade from 1446 to 1482', in Power and Postan (eds), *Studies in English trade in the fifteenth century*, 1–38.

—, 'The production and exportation of English woollens in the fourteenth century', *English History Review*, 29 (1924), 13–35.

Greatrex, J., 'The administration of Winchester Cathedral Priory in the time of Cardinal Beaufort', PhD thesis (Ottawa, 1972).

—, 'The reconciliation of spiritual and temporal responsibilities: some aspects of St Swithun's as landowners and estate managers (c.1380–1450)', *Proceedings of the Hampshire Field Club and Archaeological Society*, 51 (1996), 77–87.

—, 'St Swithun's Priory in the later Middle Ages', in J. Crook (ed.), *Winchester cathedral: nine hundred years, 1093–1993* (Chichester, 1993), 139–66.

Griffiths, R., *The reign of Henry VI* (London, 1981).

Hall, A.R., and Russell, N.C., 'What about the fulling-mill?' *History of Technology*, 6 (1981), 113–19.

Hallam, H.E. (ed.), *The agrarian history of England and Wales, ii: 1042–1350* (Cambridge, 1988).

Hanna, K.A. (ed.), 'An edition with introduction of the Winchester cathedral custumal', MA thesis (London, 1954).

Hare, J.N., 'Agriculture and land use on the manor', in Fowler, *Landscape plotted and pieced*, 156–7.

—, 'Agriculture and rural settlement in the chalklands of Wiltshire and Hampshire from c.1200 to c.1500', in Aston and Lewis (eds), *The medieval landscape of Wessex*, 159–69.

—, 'The bishop and the prior: demesne agriculture in medieval Hampshire', *Agricultural History Review*, 54 (2006), 187–212.

—, 'Bishop's Waltham Palace, Hampshire: William of Wykeham, Henry Beaufort and the transformation of a medieval episcopal palace', *Archaeological Journal*, 148 (1988), 222–54.

—, 'Change and continuity in Wiltshire agriculture: the later Middle Ages', in W.E. Minchinton (ed.), *Agricultural improvement: medieval and modern*, Exeter Papers in Economic History 14 (Exeter, 1981), 1–18.

—, 'Church-building and urban prosperity on the eve of the reformation: Basingstoke and its parish church', *Proceedings of the Hampshire Field Club and Archaeological Society*, 62 (2007), 181–92.

—, 'The demesne lessees of fifteenth century Wiltshire', *Agricultural History Review*, 29 (1981), 1–15.

—, *The dissolution of the monasteries in Hampshire* (Winchester, 1999).

—, 'Durrington, a chalkland manor in the later Middle Ages', *Wiltshire Archaeological and Natural History Magazine*, 74–5 (1979/80), 137–47.

—, 'Growth and recession in the fifteenth-century economy: the Wiltshire textile industry and the countryside', *Economic History Review*, 2nd series 52 (1999), 1–26.

—, 'The growth of the roof-tile industry in later medieval Wessex', *Medieval Archaeology*, 35 (1991), 86–103.

—, 'Lord and tenant in Wiltshire, c.1380–1520, with particular reference to regional and seigneurial variations', PhD thesis (London, 1976).

—, 'The lords and their tenants: conflict and stability in fifteenth century Wiltshire', in B. Stapleton, *Conflict and community in southern England* (Stroud, 1992), 16–34.

—, 'Lord, tenant and the market: some tithe evidence from the Wessex region', in B. Dodds and R.H. Britnell, *Agriculture and rural society after the Black Death: common themes and regional variations* (Hertford, 2008), 132–46.

—, 'The monks as landlords: the leasing of the demesnes in southern England', in Barron and Harper-Bill (eds), *Church in pre-reformation society*, 82–94.

—, 'Netley Abbey: monastery, mansion and ruin', *Proceedings of the Hampshire Field Club and Archaeological Society*, 49 (1993), 207–27.

—, 'Pensford and the growth of the cloth industry in late medieval Somerset', *Proceedings of*

the *Somerset Archaeology and Natural History Soc*, 147 (2003), 173–80.
—, 'Regional prosperity in fifteenth-century England: some evidence from Wessex', in M. Hicks (ed.), *Revolution and consumption in late medieval England* (Woodbridge, 2001), 105–26.
—, 'Salisbury: the economy of a fifteenth century provincial capital', *Southern History*, 31 (2009), 1–26.
—, 'The Wiltshire risings of 1450: political and economic discontent in mid-fifteenth century England', *Southern History*, 4 (1982), 13–31.
—, 'Winchester College and the Angel Inn, Andover: a fifteenth-century landlord and its investments', *Proceedings of the Hampshire Field Club and Archaeological Society*, 60 (2005), 187–97.
Harper-Bill, C., 'The piety of the Anglo-Norman knightly class', in *Proceedings of the Battle conference on Anglo-Norman studies*, 2 (Woodbridge, 1979), 63–77.
Harrison, B., 'Demesne husbandry and field systems on the north Hampshire estates of Saint Swithun's Priory, Winchester, 1248–1340', forthcoming.
—, 'Field systems and demesne farming on the Wiltshire estates of St Swithun's Priory, Winchester', *Agricultural History Review*, 43 (1995), 1–18.
Harrison, D., *The bridges of medieval England* (Oxford, 2004).
Harriss, G.L., *Cardinal Beaufort* (Oxford, 1988).
Harvey, B., 'The leasing of the abbot of Westminster's demesnes in the later Middle Ages', *Economic History Review*, 2nd series 22 (1969), 17–27.
—, *Living and dying in England 1100–1540: the monastic experience* (Oxford, 1993).
—, *Westminster Abbey and its estates* (Oxford, 1977).
Harvey, I.M.W., *Jack Cade's rebellion of 1450* (Oxford, 1991).
Harvey, J., *English medieval architects*, 2nd edn (Gloucester, 1984).
Harvey, P.D.A., *Manorial records*, Archives and the User 5 (London, 1999).
—, *A medieval Oxfordshire village: Cuxham, 1240–1400* (Oxford, 1965).
— (ed.), *The peasant land market in medieval England* (Oxford, 1984).
—, 'The peasant land market in medieval England', in Razi and Smith (eds), *Medieval society and the manor court*, 392–407.
—, 'The pipe rolls and the adoption of demesne farming in England', *Economic History Review*, 2nd ser 27 (1974), 345–59.
Harvey, R.B. and Harvey, B.K., 'Bradford-on-Avon in the fourteenth century', *Wiltshire Archaeological and Natural History Magazine*, 86 (1993), 118–29.
Harwood, W.A., 'The household of Winchester College in the later Middle Ages', *Proceedings of the Hampshire Field Club and Archaeological Society*, 59 (2004), 163–79.
—, 'The pattern of consumption of Winchester College, *c*.1390–1560', PhD thesis (Southampton, 2003).
—, 'The trade of Southampton, 1448–9', *Proceedings of the Hampshire Field Club and Archaeological Society*, 55 (2000), 142–68.
Haskins, C., *The ancient guilds and companies of Salisbury* (Salisbury, 1912).
Hatcher, J., 'England in the aftermath of the Black Death', *Past and Present*, 144 (1994), 3–35.
—, 'English serfdom and villeinage: towards a reassessment', *Past and Present*, 90 (1981), 3–39.
—, 'The great slump of the mid-fifteenth century', in R.H. Britnell and J. Hatcher (eds), *Progress and problems in medieval England: essays in honour of Edward Miller* (Cambridge, 1996), 236–72.
—, *Plague, population and the English economy, 1348–1530* (Basingstoke, 1977).
—, *Rural economy and society in the duchy of Cornwall, 1300–1500* (Cambridge, 1970).
Heaton, H., *The Yorkshire woollen and worsted industries* (Oxford, 1920).
Hicks, M.A., 'Chantries, obits and almshouses: the Hungerford foundations, 1325–1478', in Barron and Harper-Bill, *Church in pre-reformation society*, 123–42.
—, 'Counting the cost of war: the Moleyns ransom', *Southern History*, 8 (1986), 11–31.
—, 'The piety of Margaret Lady Hungerford', *Journal of Ecclesiastical History*, 38 (1987), 19–38.
—, 'Restraint, mediation and private justice: George, duke of Clarence as "good lord"', *Journal*

of Legal History, 4 (1983), 56–71.
—, 'St Katherine's Hospital, Heytesbury: prehistory, foundation and refoundation, 1408–72', *Wiltshire Archaeological and Natural History Magazine*, 78 (1984), 62–9.
Hilton, R.H., *Bond men made free: medieval peasant movements and the English rising of 1381* (London, 1973).
—, *The decline of serfdom in medieval England* (Basingstoke, 1969).
—, *The economic development of some Leicestershire estates in the fourteenth and fifteenth centuries* (Oxford, 1947).
—, *The English peasantry in the later Middle Ages* (Oxford, 1975).
—, *A medieval society: the west midlands at the end of the thirteenth century* (London, 1966).
— (ed.), *Peasants, knights and heretics* (Cambridge, 1976).
—, 'Towns in English medieval society', in Holt and Rosser, *The medieval town*, 19–28.
—, 'Winchcombe Abbey and the manor of Sherborne', in H.P.R. Finberg (ed.), *Gloucestershire studies* (Leicester, 1957).
Himsworth, S., *Winchester College Muniments*, 3 vols. (Chichester, 1976–84).
HMC (Historical Manuscripts Commission), *Report on manuscripts in various collections vol iv, The corporation of Salisbury* (London, 1907).
Hoare, Sir R.C. (et al.), *The history of modern Wiltshire*, 5 vols (London, 1822–52).
Holmes, G.A., *The estates of the higher nobility in fourteenth-century England* (Cambridge, 1957).
Holt, R. and Rosser, G. (eds), *The medieval town* (London, 1990).
Hooke, D., 'The administrative and settlement framework of early medieval Wessex', in Aston and Lewis (eds), *The medieval landscape of Wessex*, 83–95.
Hoskins, W.G., 'English provincial towns in the early sixteenth century', in his *Provincial England* (London, 1963), and in P. Clark (ed.), *The early modern town: a reader* (London, 1976).
Howell, C., *Land, family and inheritance in transition: Kibworth Harcourt, 1280–1700* (Cambridge, 1983).
—, 'Peasant inheritance customs in the Midlands, 1280–1700', in J. Goody, J. Thirsk and E.P. Thompson (eds), *Family and inheritance* (Cambridge, 1976), 112–55.
Hughes, M., 'Settlement and landscape in medieval Hampshire', in S.J. Shennan and R.T. Schadla-Hall, *The archaeology of Hampshire: from the Palaeolithic to the Industrial Revolution*, Hampshire Field Club and Archaeological Society 1 (Winchester, 1981), 66–77.
Hutchins, J., *The history and antiquities of the county of Dorset*, vol. 3 (1868; repr. Wakefield, 1973).
Jackson, J.E., 'Maud Heath's Causey', *Wiltshire Archaeological and Natural History Magazine*, 1 (1854), 251–64.
Jacob, E.F., *The fifteenth century* (Oxford, 1961).
James, M.K., 'The borough of Wilton', in VCH *Wilts* 6, 1–37.
James, T.B. and Roberts, E., 'Winchester and later medieval development: from palace to pentice', *Medieval Archaeology*, 44 (2000), 181–200.
James, T.B. and Robinson, A.M., *Clarendon Palace* (London, 1988).
Jones, W.H., 'Terumber's chantry at Trowbridge with a copy of the original deed of endowment, A.D. 1483', *Wiltshire Archaeological and Natural History Magazine*, 10 (1867), 240–52.
Keene, D., *A survey of medieval Winchester* (Oxford, 1985).
Keil, I.J.E., 'The estates of Glastonbury Abbey in the later Middle Ages', PhD thesis (Bristol, 1964).
—, 'Impropriator and benefice in the later Middle Ages', *Wiltshire Archaeological and Natural History Magazine*, 58 (1963), 351–61.
Kempson, E.G.H., 'Wroughton Copse: a note on the documentary evidence', in H.C. Bowen and P.J. Fowler, 'The archaeology of Fyfield and Overton Down', *Wiltshire Archaeological and Natural History Magazine*, 58 (1962), 113–15.
Kerridge, E., 'The agrarian development of Wiltshire, 1540–1640', PhD thesis (London, 1951).

—, *Agrarian problems in the sixteenth century and after* (London, 1969).
—, *The agricultural revolution* (London, 1967).
—, 'Agriculture 1500–1793', in VCH *Wilts* 4, 43–64.
—, 'The floating of the Wiltshire water meadows', *Wiltshire Archaeological and Natural History Magazine*, 55 (1953), 105–18.
—, 'The sheep fold in Wiltshire and the floating of the water meadows', *Economic History Review*, 2nd series 6 (1954), 282–9.
Kershaw, I., 'The great famine and agrarian crisis in England, 1315–1322', in Hilton (ed.), *Peasants, knights and heretics*, 85–132.
Kirby, J.L., *The estates of Edington Priory* (Edington, 1966).
—, 'The Hungerford family in the later Middle Ages', MA thesis (London, 1939).
Kirby, T.F., 'Records of the manor of Durrington', *Archaeologia*, 59 (1904), 75–82.
Kite, E., *The monumental brasses of Wiltshire* (1860; facsimile edn Bath, 1969).
Kite, E.A., 'Some notes on the death of Humphrey, duke of Gloucester AD1447 and the subsequent murder of William Ayscough, bishop of Salisbury', *Wiltshire notes and queries*, 7 (1911), 84–9.
Kowelski, M., 'Town and country in late medieval England: the hide and leather trade', in P.J. Corfield and D. Keene (eds), *Work in towns, 850–1800* (Leicester, 1990), 55–73.
Latham, L.C., 'The decay of the manorial system', MA thesis (London, 1928).
Lee, J.S., *Cambridge and its economic region, 1450–1560* (Hatfield, 2005).
Leech, R., *Small medieval towns in Avon* (Bristol, 1975).
Le Patorel, H.E.J., 'Documentary evidence and the medieval pottery industry', *Medieval Archaeology*, 12 (1968), 101–26.
Letters, S. (ed.), *Gazetteer of markets and fairs in England and Wales to 1516*, List and Index Society Special Series 33 (Kew, 2003).
Levett, A.E., *The Black Death on the estates of the see of Winchester* (Oxford, 1916).
Lewis, C., 'Patterns and processes in the medieval settlement of Wiltshire', in Aston and Lewis (eds), *The medieval landscape of Wessex*, 171–93.
Liveing, H.G.D., *Records of Romsey Abbey* (Winchester, 1912).
Lloyd, T.H., *The movement of wool prices in medieval England* (Cambridge, 1973).
Lomas, R.A., 'The priory of Durham and its demesnes in the fourteenth and fifteenth centuries', *Economic History Review*, 2nd series 31 (1978), 339–53.
Luckett, D.A., 'Crown patronage in local administration in Berkshire, Dorset, Hampshire, Oxfordshire, Somerset and Wiltshire, 1485–1509', DPhil thesis (Oxford, 1992).
McCarthy, M.R., 'The medieval kilns at Nash Hill, Lacock', *Wiltshire Archaeological and Natural History Magazine*, 69 (1974), 97–160.
MacCulloch, D., 'Bondmen under the Tudors', in C. Cross, D. Loades and J.J. Scarisbrick (eds), *Law and government under the Tudors* (Cambridge, 1988), 91–110.
Macfarlane, A., *The origins of English individualism: the farming, property and social transition* (Oxford, 1978).
McFarlane, K.B., *England in the fifteenth century* (Oxford, 1981).
—, *The nobility of later medieval England* (Oxford, 1973).
McOmish, D., Field, D. and Brown, G., *The field archaeology of the Salisbury Plain training area* (Swindon, 2002).
Maitland, F.W., *Domesday Book and beyond* (1897; repr. London, 1960).
Mate, M., 'The East Sussex land market and the agrarian class structure in the late Middle Ages', *Past and Present*, 139 (1993), 46–65.
—, 'The farming out of manors: a new look at the evidence from Canterbury Cathedral Priory', *Journal of Medieval History*, 9 (1983), 331–43.
—, 'Pastoral farming in south-east England in the fifteenth century', *Economic History Review*, 2nd series 40 (1987), 523–36.
Mathew, D., *The Norman monasteries and their English possessions* (Oxford, 1962).

Meekings, C.A.F., 'The early years of Netley Abbey', in his *Studies in thirteenth century justice and administration* (London, 1981), XVII, 1–37.

Miles, T.J. and Saunders, A.D., 'The chantry priests house of Farleigh Hungerford Castle', *Medieval Archaeology*, 19 (1975), 165–94.

Miller, E. (ed.), *The agrarian history of England and Wales: vol. 3, 1348–1500* (Cambridge, 1991).

—, 'England in the twelfth and thirteenth century: an economic contrast', *Economic History Review*, 2nd series 24 (1971), 1–14.

—, 'Farming practice and techniques. I: the southern counties', in *The agrarian history of England and Wales*, 285–303.

—, 'The farming of manors and direct management', *Economic History Review*, 2nd series 26 (1973), 138–40.

— 'The fortunes of the English textile industry during the thirteenth century', *Economic History Review*, 2nd series 18 (1965), 64–82.

—, 'Tenant farming and tenants farmers. I: the southern counties', in Miller (ed.), *Agrarian History of England and Wales*, 703–21.

— and Hatcher, J., *Medieval England: rural society and economic change, 1086–1348* (London, 1978).

— and Hatcher, J., *Medieval England: towns, commerce and crafts* (London, 1995).

Morgan, M., *The English lands of the abbey of Bec* (Oxford, 1946).

Mullan, J., 'The transfer of customary land on the estates of the bishop of Winchester between the Black Death and the plague of 1361', in Britnell, *Winchester pipe rolls*, 81–107.

— and Britnell, R., *Land and family: trends and local variations in the peasant land market on the Winchester bishopric estates, 1263–1415* (Hatfield, 2010).

Munro, J.H., 'Monetary contraction and industrial change in the late medieval Low Countries, 1335–1500', in N.J. Mayhew (ed.), *Coinage in the Low Countries* (Oxford, 1979), 95–165.

Musty, J., 'The medieval and post-medieval pottery from Budbury', in G.J. Wainwright, 'An iron age promontory fort at Budbury, Bradford-on-Avon, Wiltshire, *Wiltshire Archaeological and Natural History Magazine*, 65 (1970), 161–2.

—, 'A preliminary account of a medieval pottery industry at Minety', *Wiltshire Archaeological and Natural History Magazine*, 68 (1973), 79–88.

— and Algar, D., 'Excavations at the deserted medieval village of Gomeldon near Salisbury', *Wiltshire Archaeological and Natural History Magazine*, 80 (1986), 127–69.

—, Algar, D. and Ewence, P., 'The medieval pottery kilns at Laverstock, near Salisbury', *Archaeologia*, 102 (1969), 83–150.

Nevill, E., 'Salisbury in 1455 (*Liber Niger*)', *Wiltshire Archaeological and Natural History Magazine*, 37 (1911), 66–92.

Newman, E., 'Medieval sheep-corn farming: how much grain yield could each sheep support?' *Agricultural History Review*, 50 (2002), 164–80.

Page, F.M., '"Bidentes Hoylanndie": a medieval sheep farm', *Economic History*, 1 (1929), 603–13.

Page, M., 'The peasant land market in southern England: the estate of the bishops of Winchester', in L. Feller and C. Wickham (eds), *Le marché de la terre au Moyen Age* (Rome, 2005).

—, 'The transfer of customary land on the estates of the bishopric of Winchester before the Black Death', in Britnell, *Winchester pipe rolls*, 61–80.

—, 'William Wykeham and the management of the Winchester estate, 1366–1404', in W.M. Ormrod (ed.), *Fourteenth century England*, vol. 3 (Woodbridge, 2004), 99–119.

Palliser, D.M. (ed.), *The Cambridge urban history of Britain: Vol. 1, c.600–c.1540* (Cambridge, 2000).

— 'Urban decay revisited', in J.A.F. Thomson (ed.), *Towns and townspeople in the fifteenth century* (Gloucester, 1988).

Pantin, W.A., 'Medieval inns', in E.M. Jope (ed.), *Studies in building history: essays in*

recognition of the work of B.H. St J. O'Neil (London, 1961).
Passmore, A.D., 'Medieval enclosures at Barbury and Blunsdon', *Wiltshire Archaeological and Natural History Magazine*, 50 (1943), 194–5.
Payne, R., 'Agrarian conditions on the Wiltshire estates of the duchy of Lancaster, the lords Hungerford and the bishopric of Winchester', PhD thesis (London, 1940).
Pelham, R.A., 'The distribution of sheep in Sussex in the early fourteenth century', *Sussex Archaeological Collections*, 75 (1934), 128–35.
Pevsner, N., *The buildings of England: Wiltshire* (Harmondsworth, 1963).
— and Cherry, B., *The buildings of England: Wiltshire*, 2nd edn (Harmondsworth, 1975).
Phillipps, T., *Institutiones Clericorum in Comitatu Wiltoniae, 1297–1810* (privately printed, 1825).
Platt, C., *Medieval Southampton: the port and the trading community* (London, 1973).
Postan, M.M., 'The economic and political relations of England and the Hanse from 1400 to 1475', in Power and Postan (eds), *Studies in English trade in the fifteenth century*, 91–153.
—, *Essays on medieval agriculture and general problems of the medieval economy* (Cambridge, 1973).
—, 'The fifteenth century', in M.M. Postan, *Essays on medieval agriculture*, 41–8.
—, 'Medieval agrarian society in its prime: England', in M.M. Postan (ed.), *The Cambridge economic history of Europe*, i, *The agrarian life of the Middle Ages*, 2nd edn (Cambridge, 1966), 549–632.
—, *The medieval economy and society* (Harmondsworth, 1975).
—, 'Some agrarian evidence of declining population in the later Middle Ages', in M.M. Postan, *Essays on medieval agriculture*, 186–213.
Postles, D., 'Brewing and the peasant economy: some manors in late medieval Devon', *Rural History*, 2 (1992), 133–44.
Power, E., *The wool trade in English medieval history* (Oxford, 1941).
—, 'The wool trade in the fifteenth century', in Power and Postan, (eds), *Studies in English trade in the fifteenth century*, 48–58.
— and Postan, M.M. (eds), *Studies in English trade in the fifteenth century* (London, 1933).
Power, J.P. and Campbell, B.M.S., 'Cluster analysis and the classification of medieval demesne systems', *Transactions of Institute of British Geographers*, new series 17 (1992), 227–45.
Pugh, R.B., 'The commons of Wiltshire in medieval parliaments', in VCH *Wilts* 5, 72–9.
—, 'The early history of the manors in Amesbury', *Wiltshire Archaeological and Natural History Magazine*, 52 (1947), 70–110.
— (gen. ed.), *A history of Wiltshire*, The Victoria History of the Counties of England, vols 1–17 (Oxford, 1953–2002).
—, 'The king's government in the Middle Ages', in VCH *Wilts* 5, 1–43.
Purser, T.S., 'The county community of Hampshire, c.1300–c.1530, with special reference to the knights and esquires', PhD thesis (Southampton, 2001).
Rackham, O., *The history of the countryside* (London, 1987).
Raftis, J.A., 'The concentration of responsibility in five villages', in *Medieval Studies*, 28 (1966), 92–118.
—, *The estates of Ramsey Abbey* (Toronto, 1957).
—, *Tenure and mobility* (Toronto, 1964).
Ramsay, G.D., *The English woollen industry, 1500–1750* (Basingstoke, 1982).
—, *The Wiltshire woollen industry in the sixteenth and seventeenth centuries* (Oxford, 1943).
Razi, Z., 'The erosion of the family-land bond in the late fourteenth and fifteenth centuries: a methodological note', in Smith (ed.), *Land, kinship and lifecycle*, 295–305.
—, 'The myth of the immutable English family', *Past and Present*, 140 (1993), 3–44.
— and Smith, R.M., 'The historiography of the manorial court rolls', in Razi and Smith, *Medieval society and the manor court*, 1–35.

— and Smith, R.M. (eds), *Medieval society and the manor court* (Oxford, 1996).
RCHM (Royal Commission on Historical Monuments), *Churches of south-east Wiltshire* (London, 1987).
—, *City of Salisbury*, vol. 1 (London, 1980).
—, *Salisbury: the houses of the Close* (London, 1993).
—, *Stonehenge and its environs* (Edinburgh, 1979).
Richardson, A., *The forest, park and palace of Clarendon, c.1200–c.1650* (Oxford, 2005).
Rigby, S.H., *English society in the later Middle Ages: class, status and gender* (Basingstoke, 1995).
Roberts, E., 'The bishop of Winchester's deer parks in Hampshire', *Proceedings of the Hampshire Field Club and Archaeological Society*, 44 (1988), 67–86.
—, 'A fifteenth century inn at Andover', *Proceedings of the Hampshire Field Club and Archaeological Society*, 47 (1991), 153–70.
—, *Hampshire houses, 1200–1700: their dating and development* (Winchester, 2003).
—, 'Overton Court Farm and late-medieval farmhouses of demesne lessees in Hampshire', *Proceedings of the Hampshire Field Club and Archaeological Society*, 51 (1996), 89–106.
Rogers, J.E.T., *A history of agriculture and prices*, vols 1–4 (Oxford, 1866–82).
—, *Six centuries of work and wages: the history of English labour* (London, 1906).
Rogers, K.H., *The book of Trowbridge* (Buckingham, 1984).
—, 'Salisbury', in M.D. Lobel (ed.), *Historic towns*, vol. 1 (London, 1969).
—, *Warp and weft* (Buckingham, 1986).
Roskell, J.S., 'Three Wiltshire Speakers', *Wiltshire Archaeological and Natural History Magazine*, 56 (1956), 272–358.
—, Clark, L. and Rawcliffe, C., *The House of Commons, 1386–1421* (Stroud, 1992).
Ruddle, C.S., 'Notes on Durrington', *Wiltshire Archaeological and Natural History Magazine*, 31 (1901), 331–42.
Ruddock, A.A., *Italian merchants and shipping in Southampton, 1270–1600* (Southampton, 1951).
St Clair Baddeley, W., 'Early deeds relating to St Peter's Gloucester', *Transactions of Bristol and Gloucester Archaeological Society*, 38 (1915), 19–46.
Savine, A., 'Bondmen under the Tudors', *Transactions of the Royal Historical Society*, 17 (1903), 235–89.
—, *English monasteries on the eve of the dissolution* (Oxford, 1909).
Schofield, R.S., 'The geographical distribution of wealth in England, 1334–1649', *Economic History Review*, 2nd series 18 (1965), 483–510.
Scott, R., 'Medieval agriculture', in VCH *Wilts* 4, 7–42.
Scrope, G.P., *History of the manor and ancient barony of Castle Combe* (privately printed, 1852).
Searle, E., *Lordship and community: Battle Abbey and its banlieu* (Toronto, 1974).
Shaw, D.G., *The creation of a community: the city of Wells in the Middle Ages* (Oxford, 1993).
Sheail, J., 'The distribution of taxable population and wealth in England during the early sixteenth century', *Transactions of the Institute of British Geographers*, 55 (1972), 111–26.
—, *Rabbits and their history* (Newton Abbot, 1971).
—, *The regional distribution of wealth in England as indicated in the 1524/5 lay subsidy returns*, ed. R.W. Hoyle, List and index society, special series 28 (Richmond, 1998).
—, 'The regional distribution of wealth in England as indicated by the 1524/5 lay subsidy returns', PhD thesis (London, 1968).
Sherborne, J., *William Canynges (1402–1474), mayor of Bristol and dean of Westbury College* (Bristol, 1985).
Shillington, V., 'Social and economic history', in VCH *Hants* 5.
Slocombe, P.M., 'Two medieval roofs in west Wiltshire', *Wiltshire Archaeological and Natural History Magazine*, 80 (1986), 170–75.
Smith, M.W., 'Snap: a modern example of depopulation', *Wiltshire Archaeological and Natural History Magazine*, 57 (1960), 386–90.

Smith, R.A., *Canterbury Cathedral Priory* (Cambridge, 1943).

Smith, R.M., 'Coping with uncertainty: women's tenure of customary land in England c.1370–1430', in J. Kermode (ed.), *Enterprise and individuals in fifteenth century England* (Stroud, 1991), 43–67.

—, 'Human resources', in Astill and Grant, *Countryside of medieval England*, 188–212.

— (ed.), *Land, kinship and lifecycle* (Cambridge, 1984).

Somerville, R., *History of the duchy of Lancaster*, vol. 1 (London, 1953).

Stephenson, M.J., 'Wool yields in the medieval economy', *Economic History Review*, 2nd series 41 (1988), 368–89.

Storey, R.L., 'The foundation and medieval college, 1379–1530', in J. Buxton and P. Williams (eds), *New College Oxford, 1379–1979* (Oxford, 1979), 3–43.

Street, F., 'The relations of the bishops and citizens of Salisbury (New Sarum) between 1225 and 1612', *Wiltshire Archaeological and Natural History Magazine*, 39 (1916), 185–257, 319–67.

Sutton, D., *Westwood Manor* (London, 1962).

Tatton-Brown, T., 'The church of St Thomas of Canterbury, Salisbury', *Wiltshire Archaeological and Natural History Magazine*, 90 (1997), 101–9.

Taylor, C.C., *Dorset* (London, 1970).

—, 'Strip lynchets', *Antiquity*, 40 (1966) 277–83.

—, 'Three deserted medieval settlements in Whiteparish', *Wiltshire Archaeological and Natural History Magazine*, 63 (1968), 39–45.

—, 'Whiteparish: a study of the development of a forest-edge parish', *Wiltshire Archaeological and Natural History Magazine*, 62 (1967), 79–102.

Thirsk, J. (ed.), *The agrarian history of England and Wales, IV: 1500–1640* (Cambridge, 1967).

—, 'The farming regions of England', in Thirsk (ed.), *The agrarian history of England and Wales*, 1–112.

—, 'Industries in the countryside', in F.J. Fisher (ed.), *Essays in the economic and social history of Tudor and Stuart England* (Cambridge, 1961), 70–88.

Thompson, E.M., 'Offenders against the statute of labourers in Wiltshire, 1349', *Wiltshire Archaeological and Natural History Magazine*, 33 (1904), 384–409.

—, 'Wiltshire parishes: records of Erchfont with Stert', *Wiltshire Notes and Queries*, 4 (1902–7), 295–304, 356–65, 393–403, 441–51, 494–9, 544–51; and 5, 9–16, 60–67, 104–17, 153–68, 199–211, 248–61, 295–301.

Thomson, J.A.F., *The later Lollards, 1414–1520* (Oxford, 1965).

Thrupp, S.L., 'The grocers of London: a study of distributative trade', in Power and Postan (eds), *Studies in English trade in the fifteenth century*, 247–92.

—, 'A survey of the alien population of England in 1440', *Speculum*, 32 (1957), 262–73.

Titow, J.Z., 'Le climat à travers les rôles de comptabilité de l'évêché de Winchester (1350–1458)', *Annales Économies Sociétés, Civilisations*, 25 (1970), 312–50.

—, *English rural society, 1200–1350* (London, 1969).

—, 'Evidence of weather in the account rolls of the bishop of Winchester, 1209–1350', *Economic History Review*, 2nd series 12 (1959), 360–407.

—, 'Field crops and their cultivation in Hampshire, 1200–1350 in the light of documentary evidence', unpublished paper, HRO 97/M97/C1.

—, 'Land and population on the bishop of Winchester's estates', PhD thesis (Cambridge, 1962).

—, 'Lost rents, vacant holdings and the contraction of peasant cultivation', *Agricultural History Review*, 42 (1994), 97–114.

—, 'Some difference between manors and their effects on the condition of the peasants in the thirteenth century', *Agricultural History Review*, 10 (1962), 1–13, repr. in W.E. Minchinton (ed.), *Essays in agrarian history*, vol. 1 (Newton Abbot, 1968), 39–51.

—, *Winchester yields: a study in medieval agricultural productivity* (Cambridge, 1972).

Trow-Smith, R., *A history of British livestock husbandry to 1700* (London, 1957).

Underdown, D., *Revel, riot and rebellion: popular politics and culture in England 1603–1660*

(Oxford, 1985).
Vincent, N., *Peter des Roches: an alien in English politics, 1205–38* (Cambridge, 1996).
Waites, B., *Monasteries and landscape in north-east England* (Oakham, 1997).
Walters, H.B., *The church bells of Wiltshire: their inscriptions & history* (Devizes, 1927–9).
Watkins, A., 'Cattle grazing in the forest of Arden in the later Middle Ages', *Agricultural History Review*, 37 (1989), 12–25.
Watts, K., 'Wiltshire deer parks: an introductory survey', *Wiltshire Archaeological and Natural History Magazine*, 89 (1996), 88–98.
Waylen, J., *Chronicles of the Devizes, being a history of the castle, parks and borough of that name* (London, 1839).
Webb, E.D., 'Notes on Aldbourne church', *Wiltshire Archaeological and Natural History Magazine*, 28 (1895), 159.
Wedgwood, J., *A history of parliament, I: biographies* (London, 1936).
Whittle, J. 'Individualism and the family-land bond: a reassessment of land transfer patterns among the English peasantry c.1270–1580', *Past and Present*, 160 (1998), 25–63.
— and Yates, M., '"Pays réel or pays légal": contrasting patterns of land tenure and social structure in eastern Norfolk and western Berkshire, 1450–1600', *Agricultural History Review*, 48 (2000), 12–26.
Wood, P. and Whittington, G., 'Further examination of strip lynchets north of the vale of Pewsey in 1958', *Wiltshire Archaeological and Natural History Magazine*, 28 (1960), 332–8.
Woolgar, C., *The great household in late medieval England* (New Haven, CT, and London, 1999).
Yates, M., 'Change and continuities in rural society from the later Middle Ages to the sixteenth century: the contribution of west Berkshire', *Economic History Review*, 2nd series 52 (1999), 617–37.
—, *Town and countryside in western Berkshire, c.1327–c.1600* (Woodbridge, 2007).
Youings, J., *The dissolution of the monasteries* (London, 1971).

Index

Places are in Wiltshire unless stated otherwise stated

Adlam (Athelham) 184, 192
Administration of estates 37–42, 83, 89–98, 106, 125,
Alciston (Suss) 47, 86
Aldbourne: leasing 87; lessees 100–11; manor and estate 34; rabbits 72–4; revenues and debts 196, 200; 80, 164, 166, 172; settlement and fields 13; sheep 46, 67–70
All Cannings: arable 89; buildings 91, 167; leasing and lessees 100, 102, 112, 114; rents and debts 196, 207, 210; sheep 66, 87, 88
Alton (Hants) 149–50, 174
Alton (S. Avon) 30, 128
Alton Barnes 33, 66, 86, 96–7, 100–1, 113
Alton Priors: agriculture 41–7, 51–6, 60–1, 64–6; contribution to estate 42–3, 71, 89; labour services 119
Alweys (of Colerne) 103, 127, 136
Amesbury 104, 154: agriculture 44, 46, 73, 145; town 163, 171–2, 174
Amesbury Priory 32, 122, 126–7
Andover (Hants) 167–8, 171, 174
Andrew, R. 38
Arable farming: by lord 43–45, 60–63, 92–5; by tenant 53–7, 74–8; *see also* wheat, rye, bere, barley, dredge, oats, vetch, peas and beans
Ashton 67, 80, 143: Steeple Ashton 146, 164, 179, 189–90, 199, 215
Ashton Gifford 13
Assarts 13, 15, 18–19, 22–3, 118
Aubrey, J. 28–9
Aulnage 176–7, 179–81, 188, 192

Bailey, T. 189, 192
Barbury 49
Barkesdale, T. 185
Barley: consumption 41, 51, 60, 62, 89, 112, 140–2, 156, 171; difficulties 76–7, 201; demesne production 21, 42–5, 60–3, 94–5; tenant production 54–7, 74–9, 139, 201, 208, 214
Barlow, W. 154
Barton, H. (of London) 171
Basingstoke (Hants) 150, 174
Bath (Som) 37, 180, 192
Battle Abbey (Sussex): agriculture 80, 93, 95–6; estate and administration 33, 37–8; leasing 83–4, 86–7, 89, 91; revenues 209; settlements 23, 25; wool sales 67
Bec Abbey (Normandy) 33, 47, 56
Bedwyn 164
Benger family of Alton Barnes 37–8, 100–1, 113
Bere 42, 44, 51, 54, 56
Berwick St James 34, 57, 69, 86–7, 106

Bishopstone (S. Wilts): agriculture 25, 44, 60–2; Black Death 26; building 168; leasing 91; livestock 50–2, 72; settlement 19, 21–2, 28–9; sheep 45, 79
Bohun estate 34, 86
Box 85
Boynton 183
Bradenstoke 204
Bradenstoke Abbey, 25, 33, 52, 167
Bradford: agriculture 23–4, 32, 47, 50–1, 61–2, 67, 80; brewing 62–63; brewers, 75–6, 103, 140–3; bridges 152, 158, 173; cloth production 177, 182, 184–5, 189–90, 192; growth 199, 204–5; industry 165–7, 169, 170, 172, 174; location 162–4, 166–7, 173, 214; named individuals 112, 139, 145, 158; town 107, 153, 163
Briggs, J. 192
Bristol: cloth production and exports 176–9, 183–4, 208–9; named merchants 153, 170, 184; trade with Salisbury 153, 155, 162; trade elsewhere with Wiltshire 169–73, 188–9,
Brixton Deverill 46, 105, 109
Brokage Books (of Southampton) 153–5, 170
Bromham: demesne agriculture 44–5, 50–1, 61–2, 66–7, 71, 80, 92–6, 171; demesne leased 83–6; demesne lessees 100; labour services 119–20; land market 118, 132–4, 140; manor and administration 33, 37–8, 40; occupations 141–3; revenues and debts 196–7, 199–200, 207, 209–10; settlement 15, 23, 25; tenant agriculture 80
Broun, J. 170
Buildings: building industry 141, 143–4, 158–9, 166–9, 204; decay of 120; lords 203–4, 215; manorial and farm buildings 21, 23–4, 32, 41, 48–9, 91; tenants 21, 144, 187, 214
Bulford 123, 144
Bulkington 182
Butchers: county figures 141, 143; location 51, 80, 109, 143, 145–6, 159, 163–4, 166–7, 172–3, 193; named individuals 109, 143, 145–6, 172

Calne 80, 163, 166, 173–4, 179, 182, 190
Castle Coombe (*see also* Haynes): agriculture and leasing 84–5; cloth industry 164, 176, 179, 181, 183, 185–8, 191–2, 206; manor 36, 38; market 172, 173, 193; serfdom 126–9; settlement 15, 19; rents 196, 198–9; tenantry 117–9, 135
Cattle (*see also* cows and oxen) 50–3, 70–2, 80–2
Chalklands (region of county) 7–22, 26–30, 41–58, 60–79, 83–92, 118–19, 125, 140, 206–7

Index

Charleton 174
Cheese 50, 68, 80, 89, 156
Cheese and clay vale (region of county) *see* vales
Chilbolton (Hants) 42, 51
Chilmark 167–8
Chippenham: agriculture 51, 80; cloth production 179, 190, 192; immigration 199; leasing 85, 89; settlement 17; town 163, 165–6, 168, 172–4
Chitterne 88
Christian Malford 27, 44, 51, 166, 182
Church buildings 175–6, 182, 202, 205, 207–9, 222–3, 228, 233
Cirencester (Glos) 185
Clarendon 17, 34, 73, 152, 168
Cloth industry: expansion 182–8, 208–10; impact 191–4, 196–200; international trade 153, 155; production and distribution 177–91; recession 179, 184, 188–9, 202, 205–8; *see also* fulling mills
Cloth, types of: broadcloth 179, 182, 190–1; kerseys 179, 188, 210; rays 177, 183
Colerne 15, 33, 85, 127, 142
Colerne, William of (abbot of Malmesbury) 23, 42
Common pasture 13, 16, 145
Coscoumbe, J. 192
Cows 52, 72, 80–2, 112, 127, 139
Colchester (Essex) 192, 205
Colerne 15, 33, 85,127, 142
Colerne, William of (abbot of Malmesbury) 23, 42
Coleshill (Berks): agriculture 80–1; peasant housing 144; serfdom and mobility 117, 122–3, 125–6, 202
Collingbourne (Ducis) 13, 34: agriculture 44, 46, 67, 69, 70, 87; leasing 91, 100, 102–3, 106, 113; revenue and debt 196–200
Colonisation 3, 15–20, 33, 55, 160
Coombe Bisset: agriculture 78, 79; buildings 91, 144, 158; land market 132, 134, 138–9; leased 85; lessees 100, 102, 104; manor 33; occupations 140–3; rents 196–7, 200–1, 207, 209–10; serfdom 124; tenantry 118–19, 120, 122–3
Corsham: agriculture 51, 84; land market 118, 131; town and occupations, 160, 164, 166–7, 172
Cotswolds (region of county) 7–10, 15, 41, 50, 84–5, 140, 167–9
Coventry (Warwick) 86, 205
Cricklade 80, 105, 163, 165–7
Croscombe (Som) 155

Damerham 27, 44, 46, 51–2, 57, 125
Danyell family of Kingston Deverill 113–14
Davis, T. 7
Devizes 80: cloth industry 182–3, 185, 188, 189–90, 193; growth and recession 197, 199, 204, 215; town 149, 155, 161–3
Domesday Book, 32
Downton 26, 33, 163, 174, 182: buildings 78, 145, 167–8; demesne agriculture 25, 43–5, 50–2, 60–1, 68, 72, 78–9, 142; leasing 84, 91; rectory 33; revenues and debts 197, 201, 207, 210; settlement 19, 21–2, 27, 29; tenant agriculture 62, 74–9
Dredge 44, 54, 56, 61, 63, 94–5
Durham (Durham) 86
Durrington 26, 33, 86: agriculture 13, 43–4, 46, 61, 66, 68; buildings 91, 144–5, 167; land market 118–19, 132, 134–9; leasing and lessees 85, 100–4, 112–14, 118; occupations 142–3; revenue and debt 196–7, 199–200, 207, 209–10; serfdom 124–5, 128–30; tenantry 29, 79, 120, 122–3, 145, 172; *see also* Hickes, Martyns, Weylot

Eastrop 81, 117–18, 125
Ebbesbourne Wake 61–2, 85
Edington 44, 46, 60–2, 66–7, 71, 190, 204–5
Edington Priory, 33, 126, 203
Edington (William of) 33
Enclosure 16–18, 22, 25, 27
Enford: agriculture 41–4, 46, 48, 50–1, 53–5, 60–2, 64–7, 71–2, 87–9; leasing 89–90, 100, 102–3, 106, 113; occupations 143; revenues and debts 40, 207, 210; settlement 13, 40; tenantry 125, 132–4, 139, 143
Esturmy family 37
Everleigh 13, 34: agriculture 44, 67, 69–70, 73, 87; leasing 100, 105–6; revenue and debt 196–200
Exeter (Devon) 166, 171, 189

Faccombe (Hants) 129
Fastolf, J. 36, 38, 125–8, 185, 187
Faulston 28, 180
Fish 143, 154, 156, 162, 167, 169, 170–2, 193
Fisherton 150–1, 180
Flamston 28, 180
Flower, J. 192
Forest and woodland 3, 7, 15–8, 23, 25, 52–3, 75, 118; occupations 140, 168–9
Frome (Som) 153, 172, 181
Froste, W. 39
Fulling mills 163, 179, 180, 182–3, 187, 192, 198, 199

Gentry 33, 35–40, 55, 99, 106, 113–14, 116, 155, 204, 214
George, The (Salisbury) 156
Glastonbury Abbey: agriculture 46, 50–2, 57, 66, 67, 71; estate 32; leasing 91; marketing, 171–2; settlement 17, 19, 27; tenure 119, 125–6
Gloucester Abbey 43–5, 47, 50, 152, 203
Goddard family 102–3; 107–114, 127, 129, 188
Goldney, H. 192
Greenfield, J. 39
Grimstead, East 37
Grittleton 17, 27, 44, 50–2

Hadleigh (Suffolk) 149, 205
Halle, J. (of Salisbury) 126–7, 154–6, 158, 205
Halwey family (of Castle Combe) 187, 192
Harvests 20, 76–8, 196, 201
Harvest family (of Urchfont), 101, 112–14
Haynes family (of Castle Combe) 36, 126–8, 135–7, 187

Heytesbury 119: agriculture 13, 61–3, 66, 73, 93; industry 143, 164, 166, 181–4, 190–4; leasing 84–6; market 173, 179; revenue and debts 196, 198, 206–7
Hickes family (of Durrington) 103, 121, 135
Highworth 81
Hill Deverill, 174
Hilmarton: agriculture 51, 66; estate 37; leasing 85–6, 89–91, 100, 105, 107, 115, 119; serfdom 124
Hindon: cloth industry 182; market 172–4, 179; occupations 80, 85, 164, 166–7, 214; revenues and debts 198, 206, 214
Hinton 41, 47, 170
Horses 51–3, 65, 70, 72, 81, 94, 139, 170, 173
Horton, family (of Westwood) 149, 185, 189, 191–2, 105, 107, 112, 115
Housing, peasant 144–5, 157
Hungerford (Berks) 188, 205
Hungerford family 155: agriculture 62–3, 66–7, 84, 87, 170; estate 34–39; leasing 97, 105–6; revenues and debt 185, 198, 207

Idmiston 30, 44, 46, 52, 120, 125
Industry see cloth, leather, building, quarries, tiles, pottery
Inglesham 53–4, 56, 81
Inns 156, 162, 163, 173–4, 206
Ivychurch Priory 33

Jurisdiction, profits of 186–7, 199, 201

Keevil 185, 190, 215
Kings College, Cambridge 170
Kings Somborne (Hants) 69, 73, 87
Kingsmill family (of Basingstoke) 39
Kingston Deverill: leasing 97, 100, 102, 106, 113–14; manor 33; marketing 173; revenues and debts 200, 210; sheep 48, 66–9, 85, 88
Kington St Michael, 44, 50, 61
Kington St Michael Priory 33
Kitson, T. 169, 188, 190, 191, 210
Knoyle 19, 23, 25, 43–5, 50–2, 57, 60–3, 172
Knoyle, Robert of 152

Labour services 118–20, 214
Lackham 37
Lacock 160, 190
Lacock Abbey 33, 83, 87–9, 91, 167, 215
Lancaster, duchy of estate 4, 34–5, 38: agriculture 47, 67, 69, 72–3, 79, 86–7, 97, 171; leasing 106, 114; revenue and debts 198–9, 210
Land market 119, 123, 131–9: differentiation 137–9; inheritance 129, 132–6; influences on land market 134–6; land-holding at death 130–4; mobility 121–3; widows 103, 119–21, 123, 126, 132–7; women 133–5
Lange, N. (of Bristol) 153
Langford family of Durrington 102, 207
Lavenham (Suffolk) 149, 192
Laverstock 85, 169
Lavington 67, 199
Lavington Market 67

Leasing of demesnes 83–9: breaking up of demesnes 85; variations and regional characteristics 84–6, 90–2, 96–8; causes of 92–8
Leather trade 141, 158, 165–6, 182, 204–5
Lightfoot, W. 158
London merchants with links to Wiltshire 107–9, 112, 171, 190: trade 153–5, 169–71, 173, 177, 181, 183–5, 206–10
Long, H. 192
Long Melford (Suffolk) 149
Longbridge Deverill: demesne agriculture 61, 66, 71–2, 119; tenant agriculture 76, 79, 119, marketing 142, 152, 171–3, 190; industry 160, 168
Lovell, T. 192
Ludgershall 17, 34, 91, 164, 166–8

Magdalen College, Oxford 174
Maiden Bradley 170, 172, 174, 203
Maiden Bradley Priory 33
Malmesbury 128: cloth industry 181, 189, 192, 199, 204; town 160–2, 166–7, 171–2, 174; trade 80
Malmesbury Abbey 15, 17–18, 25, 32, 42, 81, 127
Manorial records: account rolls 4–5, 31, 38, 96, 102, 169; court rolls 4, 74, 79, 117, 120, 135, 140
Manufacturing (see also cloth, leather, buildings, pottery) 157–8, 165–9
Marketing patterns 169–73
Markets and fairs 163, 169, 172, 185
Marlborough: agriculture 73, 80; cloth 179, 181–2, 188, 191; industry 165–7, 171, 174; population 199, 210, 213; royal residence 34; settlement 17–8; town 107, 109–10, 112, 149–50, 153, 155, 160–3
Martyn (of Durrington) 113, 130, 143, 145, 172
Mascalls (of Strockton) 101, 103
Mere: agriculture 13, 44, 46, 52; cloth 179, 181–3; town 155, 162–3, 172
Melksham 37, 38, 160, 179, 181, 183, 190
Merton College, Oxford 53
Migration and mobility 26, 121–3, 124–9, 190–9
Mildenhall 73, 107, 110, 169
Mills and millers 20, 83, 141, 143–4, 169, 209 see also fulling mills
Minety 168
Mitford, R. (bishop of Salisbury) 169–70
Moleyns 35, 156, 185, 203 see also Hungerford
Monkton Deverill: agriculture 66–8, 72, 79, 119, 152; marketing 171–3
Monkton Farleigh Priory 33, 80, 89,167

Netley Abbey (Hants) 33, 39, 67, 84, 87–9, 152
New College, Oxford 33, 86, 96, 116, 127
Newbury (Berks) 109, 126, 171, 188, 205
Noble, N. 109

Oaksey 19, 85, 100, 105, 118, 196, 202
Oats (see also arable farming): consumption 42–3, 63; demesne 43–5, 60–3, 94–5; tenant farming 53–7, 74–8, 139

Index

Ogbournes (St George and St Andrew): agriculture 44, 46, 47, 50–2, 57, 68, 80; leasing 110–12, 114, 119, 127; marketing, 171
Open and common fields 13, 15–16, 19, 23, 26–7, 45, 119
Overton: agriculture 41–2, 44, 46–57; 64–6, 71, 73; leasing 89, 91, 111; settlement 19, 20–1
Overton (Hants) 73, 91
Oxen 21, 51–2, 65, 72, 81, 94

Page, W. 109, 185
Parks 53, 72, 81
Pastoral farming: by lords 45–52, 63–74; by tenants 57–8, 77–9, 81
Peas and beans, 44, 54, 61, 75, 77, 94, 96 see also arable farming
Pensford (Somerset) 181, 187, 191, 197
Pewsey 46, 164, 166, 168
Pigs: in clay vale 80, 94; demesne 42, 50–3, 65, 70–2, 79, 89; growth of sector 197; marketing 51, 173; tenant pigs 139
Poll tax: 1377 18, 147–50, 159; 1379 occupations 149, 51, 80, 85, 140–3, 159, 164–8, 173–4, 180–1
Poole 25, 85, 196, 202, 208
Poole (Dorset) 154–5
Population: decline 6, 26–30, 59; growth 12–25, 67–8; movement 121–3, 195, 198–9, 202; urban 147–50
Port, John a 154
Pottery 168–9
Profits of demesnes and manors 196–211
Purton 125, 160

Quarries 167–8

Rabbits 72–4, 87, 99, 214
Raddon 20–1, 48–9
Ramsbury 32, 127, 174, 182, 203–4: agriculture 41; marketing 171; town 164, 166
Regions 7–18; 43–5, 61, 80–2, 117–19
Risings of 1450 203–6
Roads 173
Romsey Abbey 46, 60, 66–7, 71, 86
Rushall 104, 106
Rye see also arable farming 44–5, 54, 56, 61, 62, 94–5

Salisbury 149–59: buildings 144, 167, 168; cloth industry 177, 179, 180–94; market for agriculture 43, 60, 67, 71, 78, 138–9, 142, 145–6, 152; market for wider trade 152–4, 156, 162, 169–70; merchants 109, 126–7, 154–6; risings of 1450 203–5; see also Halle
Salisbury, bishops of 32, 37, 41, 67, 87
Salisbury, earls of 34
Serfs and serfdom 36, 81, 101–2, 117–18, 123–30, 136, 139, 145, 187
Services: labour 118–20, 129; servants 143
Settlements 12–13: expansion 15–18, 19–25; shrinkage 27–30
Sevenhampton 44, 50, 54, 56, 81, 84
Seymour family 37

Shaftesbury (Dors) 155, 172, 179
Shaftesbury Abbey 24, 32, 39, 47, 70, 88, 98, 208
Sheep: labour services 119; leasing 87–8, 90, 97–8, 170, 172–3; management 47–8, 66; manure 13, 23, 25, 45, 50, 58, 63, 66, 68; milking 68; parish and tenant flocks 57–8, 78–9, 106–7, 112, 114, 127, 129, 139, 145, 170, 172–3; post Black Death 63–70; profitability 69–70; scale before Black Death 40–2, 45–50; settlement 20–5; sheep houses 48–9; wool sales 67, 172–3; in vale 80–1, 93–4, 96
Sherborne (Dorset) 155, 180, 203–6
Slaughterford 51–2, 128
Southampton (Hants) (see also Brokage books): cloth exports 177, 179, 183–5, 189; Salisbury–Southampton trade 152–4, 156, 171–2; spices 154, 159, 169; trade 166, 169–170, 172, 188–9, 206, 209
Stanley Abbey 25, 33, 61, 80, 85, 92, 167–8
Stannford, J. 38, 70, 103, 106–9, 114–15
Stert 33, 86, 96
Stockton 26: agriculture 41–4, 46, 51, 60, 64–6, 71, 85–6, 88–9; land market 131–2, 134, 139; leasing 90–1, 100, 102–3; occupations 141–4, 174; revenue and debt 196–7, 200–1; serfdom 124–5; tenantry 119, 120
Stourton family 37
Stowford, W. 177, 185, 192
Stratton St Margaret: agriculture 50, 53–4, 56; land market 131–2, 134, 139; leasing 84, 105; revenue and debts 40, 196, 202, 210; tenants 117
Stumpe, W. 189, 192
Sutton 174
Sutton Veny 106, 196, 206
Swans 42, 89
Swayne, W. 126, 154
Swindon 18, 164, 168

Tailors 141, 143, 157, 164, 193
Tanner, W. 171
Taxation: 1412 31, 34–7; 1524/5 subsidy 48, 115, 149, 162; see also poll tax
Teffont 61–2, 73, 84–5, 167, 196
Tenure: copyhold 117, 120, 214; customary 117–19; subleasing 114, 120
Terumber, J. alias Touker 153, 170, 177, 184–5, 189, 204
Thatch 21, 48, 141, 144, 159, 168
Tiles and tilers 48, 53, 140–1, 157, 159, 167–8
Tilshead 146, 222
Tisbury 32, 67, 164, 166–7, 172
Tithes 53–63, 74–9, 99, 110, 163, 201
Towns 147–94: urban hierarchy 159–64
Trade: international 152–4, 184–5, 188, 202–3
Tropenell 37
Trowbridge 25, 34, 38, 128: agriculture 50, 66; leasing 84, 85; revenue and debts 196–8, 200, 206, 210; town and cloth 107, 163, 172–4, 179, 182, 184–5, 189–90, 192
Twynho family 39

239

Upavon 86, 104, 106, 107, 137, 145, 196
Urchfont 32, 167: agriculture 46, 50, 52, 60, 66–8, 70, 87–9; land market 136; leasing 100–1, 112; revenues and debts 40, 196, 201, 210; tenantry 125

Vales (regions of county) 7–18, 23–5, 33, 160, 168, 196: agriculture 43–5, 51–3, 55, 57, 59, 61, 80–2; landholding and market 118, 131, 143; leasing 84–5
Valor Ecclesiasticus 31–3, 88–9
Vetch 54, 56, 75–7
Village occupations 140–4

Warminster 37, 109: agriculture 44, 61, 68, 71, 79; cloth and town 155, 162–4, 171–4, 181–90, 199; revenues and debts 198, 206
Welles, J. 109
Wells 155, 171, 180, 192
Westbury family 38, 106
Westminster Abbey 84, 86–7, 90–1
Westwood: agriculture 44; cloth industry 189, 191; estate 42; leasing 84–6, 89–91, 100, 105, 107, 115, 149; quarries 167
Weylot family (of Durrington and Coombe Bisset) 100, 104–5, 120–1, 128–9, 135, 139, 143, 145
Wheat: consumption 42–3, 112; demesne production 43–5, 54, 56–8, 60, 63, 94–5; tenant production 53–9, 74–8, 139, 201
Whitsbury 46, 57
Whittocksmede, J. 37–9, 125
Wilton 150, 152–3, 155, 159–62, 172, 181, 183–4, 204, 208
Wilton (E. Wilts) 85
Wilton Abbey 32, 67, 70, 87–9, 98
Winchester: buildings 167; cloth industry 179–80, 182, 192; decline and recession 175, 205–6; Hyde abbey 37, 46, 67; industries 165; as a market 66, 153, 155, 171; St Cross 171; St Mary's abbey 62, 66, 87–9, 96, 98

Winchester, bishops of: administration and estate 5, 32; agriculture, 41, 43, 45–7, 50–3, 56, 59–63, 67, 70–8; land market 133–5; 163–4, 197, 201; leasing 81, 84, 86–8, 91–3, 96–8; sales of produce 43; settlement, 19, 21–2, 25–6, 163–5; tenantry 118
Winchester Cathedral Priory: administration and estate 5, 32, 38–9, 171, 197; agriculture 42, 46–7, 50–3, 63–5, 67, 70; leasing 84, 86–7, 89, 91, 96, 98, 111; serfdom 125–6; settlement and fields 13, 23, 26; tenant agriculture 56
Winchester College: buildings 144–5, 152, 163, 174; as consumer 152–4, 174; estate 33, 104, 116, 122; revenue and debts 201, 207; serfs 126, 128–9; tithes 74–8
Wine 152–6, 162, 169–70, 172, 185
Winterbourne Earls 4
Winterbourne Monkton 44, 51, 119
Winterbourne Stoke 61–3, 73, 86, 168, 196, 207
Wishford 123, 135, 172
Woad 153, 154, 184–5, 188, 206
Woodland 3, 7, 13, 15–17, 19–20, 23, 25, 50–1, 75, 118, 140, 147, 160, 168, 169
Wool 45, 112, 139: organisation of estate sales 47–67, 69, 106; prices 70, 87, 202–3, 206–8, 209–11; profitability 69–70, 73, 87–8, 97–8; trade 152–4, 162, 170–2, 184, 189
Wootton Basset 25, 81, 163
Worcester, bishopric of 47, 64, 70, 86–7, 90, 99, 106, 114–15
Worcester, William 36, 38, 47, 64, 186–7
Wroughton: agriculture 15, 23, 40–4, 46–7, 49, 51–2, 60, 64–5, 81; buildings 168; land market 131–2, 134, 139; leasing 85, 86, 89; revenue and debts 196, 202, 207, 210; tenantry 117, 124–6
Wykeham, William of (bishop of Winchester) 33

Yields 58, 70, 92–7, 201, 210